TURNING THE PAGE

JEFFREY R. DI LEO

Texas Review Press
Huntsville, Texas

FIRST EDITION

Requests for permission to acknowledge material from this work should be sent to:

Permissions
Texas Review Press
English Department
Sam Houston State University
Huntsville, TX 77341-2146

Cover Design: Nancy Parsons
Author Photograph: Nina Di Leo

Library of Congress Cataloging-in-Publication Data

Di Leo, Jeffrey R., author.
   Turning the page : book culture in the digital age — essays,
reflections, interventions / Jeffrey R. Di Leo. -- First edition.
      pages cm
   Contains selected articles first published between 2002 and 2013 in
the journal American book review.
   Includes bibliographical references.
   ISBN 978-1-937875-51-0 (pbk. : alk. paper)
   1. Books and reading--Technological innovations. 2. Book industries
and trade--History--20th century. 3. Book industries and trade--
History--21st century. 4. Literature, Modern--History and criticism. 5.
Education, Humanistic. 6. Learning and scholarship.
I. American book review. II. Title.
   Z1003.D516 2014
   070.509'04--dc23
                                                      2013044819

The millennium about to end has . . . also been the millennium of the book, in that it has seen the object we call a book take on the form now familiar to us. Perhaps it is a sign of our millenium's end that we frequently wonder what will happen to literature and books in the so-called postindustrial era of technology.

—Italo Calvino, *Six Memos for the Next Millenium* (1988)

CONTENTS

PREFACE

To read Jeffrey Di Leo's *Turning the Page* is to experience literary history since 2006 as an interpolated narrative in reverse. "Interpolated" is Gérard Genette's term for the mode of narration famously exemplified by Richardson's *Clarissa*, in which the action of representing occurs between the actions represented, situating the narrator in their midst. Lovelace storms off in high dudgeon, following yet another rebuff, and no sooner has the door locked than Clarissa is penning her epistle, heart pounding, unable to withhold the words pouring onto our page. It is the normal mode of sportscasting.

Although Di Leo's narrating is hardly so breathless, it is, in fact, no less immersed. As the introduction explains, from late 2006 through early 2013, Di Leo wrote a column on the state of book culture, "Page 2," for *American Book Review*. In each new issue, he discussed recent press closings, digital print innovations, book burnings, data on reading practices, the passing of influential novelists, political attacks on the liberal arts, the growing popularity of e-books, and tensions between free-market economics and human expression in words. Some of Di Leo's brief essays are rich with facts, documenting the concentration of market influence in a dozen U.S. publishers, reporting the recession's effect on university presses, and recounting the rise and fall of Borders. Others meditate on the future of print editions, public libraries, English departments, or novel reviewing. And several discuss recent books,

Marjorie Perloff's *Unoriginal Genius*, Carlin Romano's *America the Philosophical*, Harold Jaffe's *Jesus Coyote*, or reconsider in present context earlier ground-breaking works, William Gass's *Willie Masters' Lonesome Wife*, Raymond Federman's *Double or Nothing*, Italo Calvino's *If on a winter's night a traveler*. In each of these essays, Di Leo maintains an impressive thoughtfulness and balance, resisting the allure of both neoliberal apocalypse and technological utopia, while, like Clarissa Harlowe and Bob Costas, always seeming close to the action.

And that is because, like other interpolated narrators, he is. In 2007 Jeffrey Di Leo became *ABR*'s sole editor and publisher, accepting responsibility for continuing, in newly challenging circumstances, the review's thirty-year mission. That mission has been to support American literary independence, fostering critical discussion of emergent movements and heterodox authors, especially those affiliated with presses of distinct and often controversial commitments, that are regularly ignored by mainstream media. Founded in 1977 by novelist Ronald Sukenick, *American Book Review* has always conceived of itself, not merely as another site for documenting the literary scene, but as a force for shaping it. For this reason, Di Leo's "March of the Penguins," his column on the 2012 merger of Penguin and Random House, concludes, not with speculations about the meaning of market consolidation for American culture generally or even with predictions for mid-list writers, but with reflections on the new opportunities for independent and digital presses. Strategy and description merge in such commentary, opening events onto the future and adding a dimension of significance not found in retrospective accounts.

In describing Arizona's 2010 law prohibiting courses on Native American and Mexican American literature, Di Leo reminds us: "Two of the writers whose works now sit in an Arizona storeroom are editors of this publication—and all of the writers banned from these Arizona students are ones we champion." There is a concreteness about such passages that we experience as our own ambiguous historical distance. And Di Leo's concluding call to action—"We need to support our colleagues in ethnic studies . . . by assigning their works in our classes and inviting them to speak on our campus" — invests with a potentially disturbing significance the lapsed time. Throughout *Turning the Page* we encounter possibilities never realized, openings ignored. The result is not a history of the book since 2006 any more than *Clarissa* is a history of Clarissa's rape. The aim of narrating in both cases is to alter events, and so, in retrospect, each documents them.

But historical immediacy represents only a part of, or perhaps a partial perspective on, the disarming directness of Di Leo's writings. For a storyteller, interpolated narration differs from retrospection in its more radical questionableness, recounting actions before being able to determine, not just how, but even if they will count. If there's a gain in this uncertainty, it's that the risks are out-matched by the evanescent and otherwise lost opportunities. When Di Leo doesn't sound engaged, he oscillates between aghast and astonished. The question he keeps confronting is: what institutional and economic conditions would foster a U.S. literary culture in which its readers and writers could genuinely believe? And the answer, complicated in even a homogeneous and traditional society, becomes almost unmanageable with the rate of current change and increasing diffuseness of the question itself.

In his 2007 column on the phenomenon of "public book proposals"—described by a sponsor of such proposals as "the ultimate pre-publication, market-based focus group"—Di Leo explains how the publishing giant Touchstone Books/Simon & Schuster plans to collaborate with a web-based marketing game to allow the public to "bid" on previously vetted groups of book proposals. The proposal receiving the highest "investment," that is, the most pre-publication evidence of likely readership, gets published. Although befuddling in its removal of the editor's role as cultural arbiter or judge, this scheme, like publishers' mining of e-book data on readers' preferences, raises the question for Di Leo of how literary value should be determined: "Better books are not necessarily books that better meet the expectations of readers. In fact, one could argue that better books are ones that *do not* meet reader expectations . . . ." Although suspicious of centralized, top-down market-control, Di Leo doubts that polling readers or basing editorial decisions on up-to-the-instant marketing figures represents progress.

After all, if our writers, reviewers, editors, and publishers no longer know what makes a book worth publishing, how is anyone else supposed to?

The paradox is not merely the dull old saw that best-sellers are often bad books, but rather the sharper, more deeply cutting one that it is precisely our collective understanding of literary value, of good and bad, that any genuinely exciting culture should seek to transform. In 2010, Di Leo tells us, *The Chronicle of Higher Education* reported that a New York University law professor was being sued for libel after having written and published a less-than-glowing review of another scholar's book. Like basing university curricula on economic demand, this episode suggests to Di Leo a defensive and reactionary, rather than affirmative and progressive, stance toward value. "The vast majority of book reviews tend to be positive rather than negative not because there are more good books out there than bad ones, but because the possible effects of negative reviewing are much less appealing than the effects of positive reviewing . . . . But do these current practices really help the cause of book reviewing?" The anger someone may face after disappointing one of countless constituencies—readers, authors, publishers, critics, marketing directors, professional peers, friends, politicians, students, a boss, or university administrators—can be, not just intimidating, but costly. Only those convinced that they can see what matters, even when others don't, will be prepared to stand up to it, and where such conviction is either in short supply or without influence, those charged with making judgments, if they're not ego-maniacs, will seek external justifications — i.e., a basis in data, in law, or in established customs and conventions — to make their judgments seem less arbitrary than mere expressions of personal taste.

In these circumstances, it can look as though all of us in America were expecting someone outside of ourselves to tell us what we want, even when nothing seems to be outside ourselves but ourselves. This dependence for self-access on externally mediated feedback, famously extolled by Baudrillard, has in our book culture's digital age begun to look rational. Kobo, a provider of e-readers and e-books, now enables all of us, with unprecedented literalness, to keep up with our reading. Di Leo explains: "Consider, if you will, Kobo's 'Reading Life' feature, one of a number of social reading products currently available. To find out more information about any of the books in your Kobo collection, all you have to do is tap on the cover. The menu then allows you to share what you are reading on Twitter, Facebook or through email. A pulse indicator tells you how much social activity is occurring on that book's page. If you tap the pulse, you can see what others are saying about the book or join in the conversation about it yourself . . . . You can also see how many times the book has been read, how many people liked it, and get a list of who is reading it right now." However, this hyperreality does not stop with those behaviors that merely mirror yours, for Kobo's e-reader also provides you with statistics on yourself, i.e. "hours read, hours per book, total hours reading, times you read, and what you read (books, newspapers, magazines) . . . . It also tells you the percentage of your library that you have read and total number of pages turned." The question is not whether this much information is a good or bad thing. How could more hurt? The real question is its human motivation. Why does someone feel a need to know what those doing what you're doing, including yourself, is doing? There's something odd about this craving to confront our alienated selves, to reunite with our own othered behavior, and perhaps a surprising consequence of the internet will be that, precisely by making its satisfaction virtually unlimited, we will discover our craving's source.

Of course, no economic or technological infrastructure can do more than sustain opportunities, or not unless it's to eliminate them. Prior to any outbreak of new significance, no one's ever sure a change hasn't been disastrous, and as Di Leo repeatedly points out, the consequences of even so dire a development as the disappearance of book-review supplements from the nation's major newspapers, a sign for many literati of our culture's imminent end, remain ambiguous. The topic running throughout *Turning the Page* that, more than any other, reveals Di Leo's position in the midst of his story, is *American Book Review* itself. Whether considering its relation to the academy, the possibilities for digitally archiving past editions, the effect of changes in the practice of book reviewing, or the need to sell more ads, Di Leo's discussions of *ABR* are a continuous reminder that, rather than merely reflecting contemporary book history, *ABR* inhabits the crisis it describes.

Following an account of how Random House's early twentieth-century, risk-taking publications of Joyce and Stein led to its eventual subdivision into sixty mutually competing imprints, none of which displays the adventurousness or clarity of its founders, Di Leo reflects on the relation of *ABR* to the new digital technologies. "Book reviewing is caught between its printed past and its digital future," he remarks. "We know that online publication has its benefits, but are torn by our *customary* ties to print media . . . . [A]s people increasingly turn to Kindles and other electronic devices to read books, the product itself is turning away from paper—shouldn't the product review head the same direction?" And yet he pauses: "Without paper and ink, *ABR* becomes something different—but is it still the same publication?" The question with which he wrestles is whether print is merely a platform, one that in its relative neutrality allows remediation without serious loss or distortion, or whether translation to computer screen more closely resembles, e.g., reformatting movies for TV, reproducing paintings as posters, recording live music on CD, or reinterpreting *Beowulf* as a video game or graphic novel. Beyond the question of whether changes in mediation can enable any project to continue, there lingers the question of the stakes.

In 2009, Quirk Books announced a new book series in which classic works of English and European fiction were "enhanced" by adding to the original text scenes of graphic violence, macabre fantasy, and sensational action. The first titles included *Pride and Prejudice and Zombies* and *Android Karenina*, both of which, Di Leo tells us, were immediate hits. These mash-up fictions seem both zany and bizarre, as though products of competing desires, of deep ambivalence toward the cultural past. Without a continuing and shared ambition to overcome our present, to inherit what is genuinely challenging in our culture, such works—which initially included 85% of the original—might have seemed just stifled, like a wild party our sanctimonious elders had crashed. But given present anxieties and dissatisfactions, they release something widely felt.

Bakhtin famously described how, in Rabelais's fiction, the act of profaning, of iconoclastic bawdry, became the sacred's form of persistence, making vulgarity into eternity's mundane face. The question of remediation's stakes is how culture's material basis can incarnate other than the briefest meaning, and until that meaning's past, no one's ever sure. In saying that we experience Di Leo's interpolated narrative *in reverse,* I don't mean just that history's documentation occurs in time, but that we see the opening page of *Turning the Page* emerge from pages turned before. At the end of 2006, Di Leo wrote his first installment of "Page 2," entitled here "A Formidable Past," in which he assumes responsibility for the continuity of *American Book Review.* He recalls the early works championed by *ABR* and the role of *ABR*'s columns and reviews in shaping Di Leo's own commitments. "The history of *American Book Review* consists of nearly thirty years of continuous engagement .... At its core are writers writing about writers: people who live with words, who allow words to dominate their being." In this beginning there's no hint of the robotic libraries of our present book's opening, no foreshadowing of critical reflection's displacement by data retrieval, or the passing of so many whom in 2006 Di Leo cites as guides. "I have been a frequent contributor to *ABR* and a fervent fan," he remarks. "I believe in the value of its mission, in the maintenance of its practices, and in the promise of its future." Every word in *Turning the Page* is written in the present, and where the present's meaning is staked, nothing will substitute for belief.

—*R. M. Berry*

ACKNOWLEDGEMENTS

Over the course of its history, the *American Book Review* has thrived because of the many wonderful people who have written for it and thanks to the dedicated stewardship of its editors. Its current editorial composition is a mix of new faces and people who have been associated with the publication back to its earliest days.

I have been fortunate to work and learn from many who have been associated with the publication far longer than myself—and for this I am most appreciative. In particular, I would like to express my gratitude to Rudolfo Anaya, Andrei Codrescu, the late Raymond Federman, Charles B. Harris, Larry McCaffery, the late Rochele Ratner, Ishmael Reed, Charles Russell, John Tytell, and Barry Wallenstein, from whose conversation, comments, and guidance I have learned so very much about this publication and its history.

I should like to express my gratitude to all of the individuals who joined the *ABR* editorial team after I assumed the role of editor and publisher. I would especially like to single out R. M. Berry, Michael Bérubé, Dagoberto Gilb, Dinda L. Gorlée, Charles Johnson, Cris Mazza, Christina Milletti, Lance Olsen, and Tom Williams, whose active engagement with this publication has brought aboard a new generation of readers.

Behind the scenes, there is a complex and busy day-to-day life of *ABR* that would not be possible without the support of many individuals. I would especially like to thank Vikki Fitzpatrick, Katie Moody, and Sandra

Wood for the support roles that they have afforded this publication. I would also like to thank the three managing editors with which I have had the distinct pleasure to work: Charles Alcorn, David Felts, and Jeffrey A. Sartain. Each has had a major role in the shaping of the publication in general, and "Page 2" in particular. Finally, without top-level administrative support at the University of Houston-Victoria, *ABR* at UHV would not be possible. To this end, Presidents Tim Hudson and Philip Castille, and Provosts Don Smith, Suzanne LaBrecque, and Jeffrey Cass have proven to be major advocates of the humanities in America through their support of this journal and its associated reading series—and for this, I am most grateful.

I am also most grateful to Eric Miles Williamson for suggesting to me the idea of publishing this book; to Paul Ruffin for supporting its publication; and to Keri Farnsworth for the help she has given me in preparing this manuscript for publication.

Finally, I would like to thank my wife Nina for her unfailing encouragement, support, and patience.

INTRODUCTION

Ralph Berry and I were having dinner at the 2006 American Writing Programs meeting in Austin with a group of authors from our *Fiction's Present* book project when the subject turned to the *American Book Review*. Word was that the publisher, Charles B. Harris, was looking for a new home for the journal.

I loved the publication and wanted to help.

After everyone departed, Berry and I walked down Sixth Street and talked about the important role of the journal in contemporary American literature. Both of us feared for its future—and both were searching for a solution.

Up to that point, I had written a few reviews for *ABR*, but knew very little else about it. Like most readers of and contributors to publications, I had virtually no sense of its internal workings. Though my dealings with the editors regarding my reviews were pleasant, I knew little about the *ABR* staff and operations.

After more conversations with Berry—and later conversations with Harris and his staff—I became increasingly interested in the possibility of bringing *ABR* down to Texas.

I really had no aspiration to take on more editorial work—let alone a large and complex publication like *ABR*—but the opportunity seemed at least worth consideration.

So, I pitched the idea of bringing the journal to Victoria, Texas.

Much to my surprise, there was a lot of support for it both within our university and in the community. Our notoriously frugal provost, Don Smith, said it was the best opportunity to ever come across his desk, and our president, Tim Hudson, enthusiastically supported the idea. Within the community, a number of patrons immediately came forward, including former University of Houston System Regent, Dorothy Alcorn, who later made a major donation that launched the American Book Review Endowment.

The lone star of Texas was soon shining over *ABR*.

On July 7, 2006, a University of Houston-Victoria press release announced that I was to become an *ABR* editor and that our university would have a major role in the production of the journal. Asked what he foresaw for *ABR* as a result of its new affiliation, Harris said, "Professor Di Leo's impressive record as an administrator, scholar and reviewer ensures that *ABR's* quality will be sustained and, as a result of the 'new blood' Professor Di Leo's leadership will bring, rejuvenated for a new generation of readers."

I have done my utmost to live up to Harris' expectations.

Not only have we maintained a high level of quality over the past seven years, we have also greatly expanded the readership of *ABR*. The publication is as strong now or stronger than it has been at any time in its over thirty year history. We also started the *ABR* Reading Series, which has brought over 60 writers to date to Victoria to share their work with students and community members.

My own contribution though can be seen most directly in a feature called "Page 2."

This feature was launched by Harris and other editors in the November/December 2005 issue, which was about a year before I joined the publication. Found on the second page of the issue, "Page 2" was intended as a space for commentary on book and writing culture.

When I assumed the role of sole editor and co-publisher with Harris in the November/December 2006 issue of *ABR*, I contributed my first "Page 2." Its subject was the formidable past of *ABR* and my new role as editor; my second "Page 2" was much the same, though it looked forward to a new beginning for *ABR*.

The next four took on a distinctive topic—and with increasing energy. One was on my desire to provide easy access to critical theory in *ABR*, another was on the disappearance of book reviews in newspapers, and still another on the notion of public book proposals. By the time a year of writing these entries had passed, I had become sole editor and publisher of *ABR*.

Read from back to front, this book is a chronological record of my written contributions to *ABR* over the past ten years. It includes everything from my early reviews to my most recent "Page 2" entries. The common themes are book and publishing culture, and how they intersect with current problems in the humanities and the rise of neoliberalism. I've opted though to organize them in reverse chronological order, beginning with more recent works on "social reading" and book bannings in Arizona and concluding with my early engagements with the work of Raymond Federman and Harold Jaffe.

"Page 2" pieces often take up the themes of *ABR* issues, but sometimes are just investigations of my own areas of interest or concern related to book and writing culture.

They are meant to raise questions more than to provide answers.

Looking over these pages and thinking about them as contributions to the history of this great American publication fills me with a strong sense of pride and satisfaction.

It also reminds me of something Harris said to me when we were discussing the future of the journal; he said that whoever becomes editor of *ABR* will be taking part in literary history.

At the time, I did not know exactly what he meant.

But now, after seven years of editing the journal and over 60,000 words of contribution to it, I am beginning to understand.

ABR is not just a book review — it is also the heart and soul of writerly writing and small press publishing. A publication where breaking the rules of writing is always more valued than following them; and where risking failure in the pursuit of innovation is more admirable than scoring a best seller.

Matters such as these are the stuff of literary history — and matters such as these are the stuff of *ABR*.

Victoria, TX
4/30/13

TURNING THE PAGE

1

ROBOTS IN THE STACKS

What is to become of libraries in the digital age? What does it mean for libraries to be "state of the art" at a time when most users prefer to download their books rather than load them into a book bag? When more books than ever are available digitally?

Libraries are finding it increasingly difficult to justify purchasing and shelving new titles when the demand for e-books is increasing and the use of p-books is decreasing.

At most libraries today, the stacks are getting smaller and the servers are getting larger.

Space formerly used for bookshelves is being converted into computer stations, study space, and coffee bars This repurposing of the stacks is a postcard from the libraries of the future.

Existing p-books are more for decoration than use. They are increasingly merely a nostalgic nod to the library's past, rather than its future. A "service" for the serendipitous luddites who still dream of finding that special book in the stacks that will unlock their imaginations—and send their thought and writing to new heights.

While the undignified use of p-books as set design for libraries of the future is bad news for bibliophiles, it does not portend the demise of the library. Unlike bookstores, many of which had to close in response to changes in technologies of the book, and increasing e-book sales and online p-book sales, libraries do not need to rely on the continuing presence of p-books in order to keep their doors open.

Still, like bookstores, libraries serve particular communities and select their holdings based on the needs of those communities. Unlike bookstores, they can repurpose their physical space to meet the changing informational needs of their communities.

Borders without p-books is not a bookstore; a library without p-books can still be a library — and perhaps an even better one.

In spite of the chorus of dystopian visions of the demise of the library in the digital age, there is an opportunity now for libraries to reimagine themselves at a time where the majority of their physical space need not be occupied by decaying rows of p-books. This should not be difficult as libraries have always been prime fodder for our imaginations.

They are that room in the mansion that is both mysterious and magical — and yet tinged with sadness. That space where the collected wisdom of generations can inspire one day, and be gone the next as was the case in ancient Alexandria when their magnificent library burned leaving future generations to wonder who would commit such a horrific crime — and what irreplaceable knowledge went up in smoke? In fact, it might be argued that some of the best writing that the world has known has come in response to libraries driving our imaginations and pushing our pens.

Think of the library that drove Don Quixote "to become a knight errant, and to travel about the world with his armour and his arms and his horse in search of adventures, and to practice all those activities that he knew from his books were practiced by knights errant." This magical place kept Quixote "so absorbed in these books that his nights were spent reading from dusk till dawn, and his days from dawn till dusk, until the lack of sleep and excess of reading withered his brain, and he went mad." "Everything he read in books," writes Cervantes, "took possession of his imagination: enchantments, fights, battles, challenges, wounds, sweet nothings, love affairs, storms and impossible absurdities."

Unlike Quixote's library, which drove him mad and into the world, Jorge Luis Borges' mysterious library only drove him deeper into the library — which he viewed as the world. "The universe (which others call the Library) is composed of an indefinite, perhaps infinite number of hexagonal galleries," writes Borges in "The Library of Babel." "In the center of each gallery is a ventilation shaft, bounded by a low railing," continues Borges. "From any hexagon one can see the floors above and below — one after another, endlessly."

If Quixote's library was a magical "special collec tion," then Borges' library was the perfect library as it "contained all books." "[T]he librarian deduced that the Library is 'total' — perfect, complete, and whole," writes Borges, " — and that its bookshelves contain all possible combinations of the twenty-two orthographic symbols (a number which, though unimaginably vast, is not infinite) — that is, all that is able to be expressed in every language."

With the magic and mystery of Alexandria and La Mancha and Borgesian ventilation shafts, we arrive today at the opening of a new library whose sheer presence addresses the question of what libraries look like in the digital age.

This month an amazing new library opened up on the campus of North Carolina State University.[1] Here 1.5 million books are housed by size in bins where they are retrieved by robots. Having robots in the stacks allows the library to store these books with one-ninth the space of a traditional library.

The space saved has allowed this library to open about 100 rooms for group study and collaborative projects. Many of these rooms have state of the art technology such as video display walls and 270-degree 3D digital environments.

For those who pine to roam the stacks, the library offers a simulated experience through its computer-generated "virtual shelf." And if the book on the virtual shelf is an e-book, one can even browse through it.

For those who actually want to see and touch books on shelves, they have about 40,000 p-books for human browsing. No robots allowed.

Though the majority of the books in this library are engineering and textiles books, one can easily imagine other special collections housed in this way — with, for example, robots fetching H. G. Wells and Asimov or old tales of chivalry and romance.

The James B. Hunt Jr. Library in Raleigh is truly a library from the future though one may still ask, "Is it pointless?" In a footnote at the end of his Babel story, Borges tells us "Letizia Alvarez de Toledo has observed that the vast Library is pointless; strictly speaking, all that is required is *a single volume*, of the common size, printed in nine- or ten-point type, that would consist of an infinite number of infinitely thin pages."

A similar observation may be made about the Hunt Library: strictly speaking, all that is required is *a single computer*, of the common size, that would provide access to all of the books in the world. Perhaps even an iPad will do. Which presents the question: Why not just scan the p-books rather than create robots to retrieve them?

The answer seems to be that it would take too long. But how long is too long, particularly when perfection is at stake? When the future of libraries *are* e-books?

What is the perfect library of the digital age? One that contains every conceivable e-book — or one that has a robot that gets your p-books for you?

Libraries have long captivated our imagination–and unleashed our fears. The 18,712 metal bins used to store books in the Hunt are either the future of libraries — or the last hurrah for p-books in the digital age of the library. It is eerie the way these bins look and feel like sepulchers — with robots harvesting books from them.

In his 1939 essay, "The Total Library," Jorge Luis Borges speculated that a "half-dozen monkeys provided with typewriters would, in a few eternities, produce all of the books in the British Museum." In the shadows of the Hunt, one might now ask whether it would take robots any less time? For that matter, ask how long would it take them to scan in all the p-books in the Hunt? Or whether the Hunt is merely tilting at digital windmills?

2

MARCH OF THE PENGUINS

How big can a publisher get? Is it possible that the publishing industry will soon mirror the auto and steel industries? Would a Big Three Book-Maker industry be good for authors and readers?

Looks like the wait to find out won't be a long one.

On October 29, 2012, the two largest trade-book publishing corporations in the world—Random House and Penguin—announced that they will be merging. If approved by government regulators, the new Penguin Random House will account for about one in four books sold worldwide.

"Holy paperbacks, Batman! Penguin is trying to take over the publishing world!"

Or so it would seem. Worldwide revenues from this new publishing company will be in the neighborhood of 4 billion dollars. However, the annual revenues of Penguin's parent company are even larger.

Pearson, the UK corporation which owns the Penguin Book Group, is by far the largest publishing corporation in the world with annual revenues of nearly 8.5 billion dollars. It has 41,000 employees in 70 countries, and publishes over 4,000 fiction and non-fiction books per year. Pearson Education is the source of 75% of its revenue, with the remainder divided between Penguin (18%) and the Financial Times (7%).

Though roughly a quarter the size of Penguin, Random House is the eighth largest publishing company in the world. Owned by Germany's Bertelsmann AG, Random House had annual revenues in excess of 2.2 billion dollars in 2011. However, with revenues in excess of 3.8 billion the previous year, one wonders what role this revenue loss played in their merger with Penguin.

To put these revenue and publishing numbers in some context, remember that of the 85,000 publishers in the Bowker database, twelve of them account for almost two-thirds of U.S. trade and mass-market book sales — and now one of them will account for one-quarter alone. Also recall that the annual revenues of Penguin Random House will be more than the combined revenues of 58,795 U.S. trade and mass-market publishers, that is, over 95% of all U.S. publishers.

This enormous financial and market-share advantage has created a lot of concern — and both companies are already working hard to contain it.

Markus Dohle, Random House chairman and CEO, who will assume the position of CEO of the new combined publishing company, wrote to his Random House colleagues that he aims "to retain the distinct identities of both companies' imprints."

Distinct identities? Who is he kidding? That world was lost when Random House went public and started swallowing up publishing houses back in the 1960s.

It bears remembering that both Random House and Penguin have already absorbed much of their competition over the past fifty years. In the United States alone, Random House includes the imprints Alfred A. Knopf, Anchor, Ballantine, Bantam, Broadway, Clarkson Potter, Crown, Delacorte, Dell, Del Rey, Dial, Doubleday, Everyman's Library, Fawcett, Fodor's Travel, Golden Books, Harmony Ivy, Kids@Random, Main Street Books, Nan A. Talese, One World, Pantheon, Random House, Schocken, Shave Areheart Books, Spectra, Spiegel & Grau, Strivers Row Books, The Modern Library, Three Rivers Press, Villiard, Vintage, and Wellspring, and Penguin Book Group includes Ace, Alpha, Avery, Berkley, Current, Dial Books,

Dutton, Firebird, Frederick Warne, Gotham, G. P. Putnam's Sons, Grosset & Dunlap, HP Books, Hudson Street Press, Jeremy P. Tarcher, Jove, New American Library, Penguin, Penguin Press, Perigee, Philomel, Plume, Portfolio, Price Stern Sloan, Puffin, Putnam, Riverhead, Sentinel, Speak, Tarcher, and Viking. Add to this list the UK imprints of both companies, and the combined Penguin Random House company will result in over 100 different imprints in the U.S. and UK alone.

The only distinctive difference that will come out of this new company are its profits — which will be the largest ever by one company in the history of trade publishing.

There is also worry that authors will lose more of their creative autonomy and will be reduced even more to merely equations or numbers by the new mega-corporation. To assuage this fear, Dohle wrote in the same letter that "authors remain the center of everything we do" and that "creative autonomy" "will be a defining hallmark" of Penguin Random House. It is one thing for Dohle to say it, but quite another to realize it in a publishing environment where capital — not creativity — is the prime directive, and where autonomy must be cleared by the accounting office.

Of all the things in Dohle's letter, the least controversial is his claim that the other defining hallmark of Penguin Random House will be "great resources." We know what this will mean for shareholders, but what will this mean for authors, agents . . . and readers?

A major fear of course is that reduced competition between Random House and Penguin will result in lower advances and profits for authors and agents, and fewer publishing options for writers — now that two of the Big Ten are One.

Both Dohle and John Makinson, who is slated to become Chairman of the new company, and who is currently Chairman and CEO of Penguin, try to calm these concerns. In fact, Makinson writes in his letter to the global Penguin Group that "exactly the opposite will happen," namely that the "publishing imprints of the two companies will remain as they are today, competing for the very best authors and the very best books." But again, it is hard to believe that the merger will result in more choices and more competition in the book industry. So are we really to believe that the imprints of this company are going to compete vigorously against each other for titles? For example, in the same way that one imprint of Random House bid against another imprint for the follow-up novel to Charles Frazier's *Cold Mountain*?

Recall the imprint competition: on the basis of what is said to have been a one-page proposal, one of Random House's imprints offered an advance of over five million dollars to the author. Not to be outdone, another of their imprints offered an 8.25 million dollar advance. Frazier's follow-up novel, *Thirteen Moons*, however, did not even cover the initial advance, let alone the actual one. Though the competition benefited Frazier, it did not add to the bottom line of the company. One would assume that Random House now has more safe-guards to protect against events like this occurring again—though this year's 1.6 billion dollar revenue dip might suggest otherwise.

Make no mistake: this merger is not about protecting creative autonomy or bringing about more opportunities for authors and options for readers. Rather, it is about maximizing profit in an industry that is rapidly changing. In fact, it may be more about the digital transformation of the publishing world than anything else. And the competition may not be from within the publishing world, but rather from the distribution and sales world.

Amazon reports that it sells 114 e-books for every 100 printed books. And it has been predicted that it will soon account for 50% of U.S. trade sales *in all formats* as early as this year. Dohle's letter indirectly confirms their worries about the challenges presented by Amazon when he says that the merger "will accelerate our digital transformation, while ensuring a strong future for print." He also says that it will put them in a better position "to provide copyright protection, and to support our authors' intellectual property."

To be sure, the path for the world's largest book publishers will continue to be bigger and bolder mergers. And soon, the publishing industry will probably need to be renamed the "infotainment" industry when suitors like Walt Disney and Time Warner come knocking. This is publishing in the age of neoliberalism. A world, in the words of Pierre Bourdieu, with "no other law than that of maximum profit." It is "unfettered capitalism without any disguise," writes Bourdieu, "a very smart and very modern repackaging of the oldest ideas of the oldest capitalist."

Though Makinson may try to make the case that this extreme concentration of publishing capital is going to benefit "creative and editorial independence," and will allow them "to take risks with new authors," don't believe it. It will be about as much risk as the market analysis of radical capitalism allows — which won't be much. I'm certain that a William Gaddis or Djuna Barnes would not get very far in the world of neoliberal publishing risk.

That being said, the rise of a corporate publishing monopoly opens a huge opportunity for acts of aesthetic resistance by both the small and digital publishing worlds. As the larger presses become more monolithic, homogenized and profit-driven, the smaller presses can thrive as sites of aesthetic and editorial heterogeneity. And direct access to digital distribution systems such as Amazon and recognition networks such as Facebook provide unprecedented support and visibility to publications that might have otherwise gone unseen in warehouses or small press catalogues. Let the Penguins of the world continue their march toward monopoly. In the end, however, it is most likely a march toward extinction — and a boon for small press publishing.

3

SOCIAL MEDIA AND THE REVIEW

Where should you go to find out about the latest novel by your favorite author? Or to learn about the hottest works in your area of interest? Until the end of twentieth century, the clear and unambiguous answer to these questions was "book reviews." Today, though, "book blogs" and "social reading" are competing—and compelling—responses to these questions. So, how do you choose?

In many ways, book reviews are now the throwback choice.

Written by specialists and generalists alike, book reviews populated magazines, journals, newspapers, and other forms of print media up until the rise of the World Wide Web. Some were written by nationally recognized writers for nationally distributed publications like the *New York Times Book Review* and *The Nation*; others by "professional reviewers" who sold their reviews to different publications; and still others by "non-professionals" who gave their efforts to scores of periodicals that put aside valuable print space for reviews.

Reviews have been contested and controversial throughout their history, and there have always been efforts to improve them. In perhaps the best recent study of book reviewing, Gail Pool's *Faint Praise: The Plight of Book*

Reviewing in America (2007), three specific suggestions are made: (1) "we need to devise a better means of choosing books for review"; (2) "we need to find better ways to reward reviewers"; and (3) "we need to better train . . . reviewers and review editors, better preparing them for the technical constraints and demands of the genre and, more broadly, alerting them to critical and ethical issues in the field."

But as the print publication age gives way to the electronic age, concerns like those raised by Pool seem distant—particularly when viewed through the lens of "book blogs" and "social reading."

The issue of a "better means of choosing" books evaporates when the constraints of print publication gives way to the expanses of the electronic dissemination. Book blogs cover and recover every imaginable corner of the book world. The "Book Blogger Directory" (bookbloggerdirectory.com), for example, has links to "Fiction Book Blogs," "Non-Fiction Book Blogs," "Religious Book Blogs," and "Young Adult Book Blogs." The sublinks under "Fiction Book Blogs" alone then list "Children's Under 12," "Comics & Graphic Novel," "Erotica, GBLT & Adult Romance," "Historical, Classic Literature," "General Fiction, Poetry, Everything!," "Action Adventure, Mystery, Horror & Thrillers, Espionage," "Romance," "Science Fiction & Fantasy," and, last, but not least, my favorite of the sublinks, "Paranormal Romance & Urban Fantasy."

In the world according to book blogs, Pool's "better means of choosing" issue translates into "opportunities for coverage." Book blogs as a genre don't have selectivity issues because anything can be covered, or, "selected." Whereas Pool was concerned with lack of selectivity in book reviews because it leads to "overlooking good books, overpraising bad ones," in the case of book blogs, the concern is not "overlooking good books" (How is it possible to miss one when all seem to be included?) but "overpraising bad ones."

To be sure, the most obvious negative potential to be found in the book blog is its capacity to become a bad books paradise. Pool's comment about finding better ways to train reviewers and review editors seems remote from the world of book blogging. While there are bloggers and blog editors that meet the demands Pool is placing on book reviewers, the vast majority of book bloggers and blog editors do not. Nor is it reasonable to expect them to become versed in the "technical constraints and demands of the genre" since server space is their only technical constraint and time is the main requirement of the genre.

Critical and ethical issues involved in book blogging are only beginning to emerge. However, unlike book reviewing for financial compensation, which has its own ethical and critical issues, reviews in book blogs are seldom compensated. Still, opportunities for logrolling—or even blogging on one's own work—are widely available.

Book reviewing can also be hindered by academic career aspirations. In a recent article for *The Chronicle of Higher Education*, Rachel Toor, who spent a dozen years as an acquisitions editor at Oxford and Duke University Presses, wonders if "the time spent reviewing other people's books" is "more important than writing your own stuff?" For her, now an assistant professor, it clearly is not. "It's better to write one good article than to review 20 books," comments Toor, "and even better to write one good book." While the choice between writing and reviewing may be a false dilemma, her point is that book reviewing is not highly compensated or valued within the academy—and here she is right.

Following this academic logic, one can assume that book blogging is worth even less in academe than book reviewing. If book review is only marginally recognized and rewarded by academe, then book blogging will probably be compensated even less. The problem here is not the genre (book reviewing or book blogging), but a system of reward that is based on genre, not impact. I can imagine many scenarios where a book review or a book blog, if judged by its impact on professional discourse, can be shown to have more impact than an article or even a book. Why then would one want to compensate its author less simply based on its genre?

It is at this point that book reviews and book blogs start to converge. Both have the potential to change the way we look at a book or an author. And, given the ubiquity of and ease of access to book blogs, they are arguably even better positioned to do this than book reviews, where the shrinking number of venues and relatively limited accessibility can restrict their impact.

If book reviewing represents the past, and book blogging the present, then social reading clearly points toward the future. Social reading, with shared quotes and annotations embedded in the text, becomes an even more immediate reviewing process, a "review as you read." Reviews will become more like close readings with electronic annotations, and books will come pre-loaded with comments from "expert readers." Alternatively, comments and commentaries could come from multiple sources to form a single review text, a review constantly subject to further shaping and review, collected in the fashion of a "wikireview." E-books have the capacity now to carry their commentary within them, collecting opinions from the experts to the novices. The challenges for reviewers though still remain: to write relevant, high quality reviews and to find reward in reviewing.

4

THANK GOD IT'S FRIDAY

In 1984, at the age of fifty-four, John Barth published his first collection of essays, lectures, and other non-fiction pieces. The book was entitled *The Friday Book* because, at that time, Barth spent his Fridays writing non-fiction — a routine which he continued for the next thirty years. Both Barth and his wife were teachers, and they took advantage of their Monday-through-Thursday teaching schedules to escape from Baltimore for long weekends across the Chesapeake Bay at their eastern shore retreat in Chestertown, Maryland. Barth found that composing non-fiction on Friday was not only a "logistical convenience," as he did not need "to haul the accumulating notes, drafts, and research materials for whatever novel was in the works back and forth across the Bay," but that it was also an important departure from his weekday morning routine of "scratching away at some extended prose fiction."

A second collection of Friday writing, *Further Fridays: Essays, Lectures, and Other Nonfiction, 1984-1994*, followed in 1995. Now in 2012, at the age of 82, he has published *Final Fridays: Essays, Lectures, Tributes & Other Nonfiction, 1995-*, which is indicated as his "final" collection of non-fiction.[2] However, the open-ended date in his subtitle leaves the door open for what would be a most welcome fourth volume of Friday writings.

Final Fridays is divided into two sections, the larger "On Reading, Writing, and the State of the Art," and "Tributes and Memoria." Barth discusses a wide range of writers and writings, but a few appear repeatedly and clearly play an important role in his own literary life. Two that stand large are Jorge Luis Borges and Italo Calvino, and the essay "'The Parallels!': Italo Calvino and Jorge Luis Borges" is one of the liveliest in the book.

Barth presents both Borges and Calvino as writers for whom politics plays only a marginal role in their work: of Borges, Barthes reports that "he said that only once did he break his own rule against political writing"; of Calvino, Barth says that while he "came to describe himself as a 'political agnostic,' he maintained a lively interest in the Italian political scene and wrote scathingly of the assassination of Aldo Moro." His framing of the relationship of politics to the art of Borges and Calvino is representative of his own relationship to politics throughout the collection: Barth by and large avoids it in his discussions of reading, writing, and the state of the art.

The major exception to this is found in a rejected piece, which turns out to be one of the most exciting entries in the collection. "The Relevance of Irrelevance: Writing American" was originally commissioned in 2002 by the State Department as part of a collection to be distributed to U.S. embassies and consulates around the world. The collection was meant to "illustrate American values through having various authors consider what makes them an American writer." Barth's essay, which closes with a scalding indictment of the Bush administration's responses to the attacks on the World Trade Center, was rejected for its "explicit commentary on the events of September 11." The essay, subsequently first published in Italian translation in the anthology *Undici settembre* in 2003, opens its final section as follows: "Now: As a matter of biographical fact, I happen to be no fan of the present administration in Washington, or of U.S. unilateralism in foreign affairs: No anti-ABM or anti-landmine treaties or Kyoto protocols or International Court of Justice for us Yanks, thanks!" Barth's directness here stands out in a collection otherwise bereft of political engagements, and provides an interesting view of another area of his thought.

"The muses," writes Barth, "care not a whit about our personal profiles, and not much more than a whit about our politics; their sole concern is that we achieve the high country of Mounts Helicon and Parnassus, whether despite or because of where we're coming from, and this these two elevated spirits [Borges and Calvino] consistently did." Barth's "elevated spirits" approach to reading, writing, and the arts may rankle those invested in the notion that every form of art has a political dimension. "One cannot make a distinction between political art and non-political art," argues Chantal Mouffe, "because every form of artistic practice either contributes to the reproduction of the given common sense — and in that sense is political — or contributes to the deconstruction or critique of it." But the political clearly is not Barth's preferred approach to artistic practice or critique. In the context of discussing Borges and Calvino, Barth recalls André Codrescu's comment regarding García Marquez's "buddyhood" with Fidel Castro that "one can be simultaneously a great artist and a political idiot."

The journey through the twenty-five essays that make up the front section of this book is one through the origins of Barth's muse:

> I have steered my own writerly course by the various lights of Faulkner, Joyce, Machado, and Borges, not to mention Cervantes, Boccaccio, Rabelais, and Scheherazade; my muse's DNA, like that of most writers, is a *mestizo* smorgasbord of these and many other literary-ethnic input, and while I freely acknowledge my debt to them and to the assorted literary traditions that produced them, it is not the sort of debit that requires payment.

Nevertheless, Barth shows his gratitude in this collection, which contains energetic commentary on works ranging from François Rabelais' *The Life of Gargantua and Pantagruel*, Laurence Sterne's *Tristam Shandy*, and Boccaccio's *Decameron*, to the Sanskrit tale cycles (*Panchatantra* and *The Ocean of the Streams of Story*), the

Bible, and his beloved *Arabian Nights*, which is discussed in numerous essays.

The joy of reading this book stems from the honesty, passion, and energy with which Barth writes about the books and authors that have influenced and inspired him. His are not close readings so much as readings of books that are close to him. The final section is decidedly the most personal, particularly the closing essays. The first six are reflections on contemporary authors: Donald Barthelme, John Hawkes, Leslie Fiedler, William H. Gass, Joseph Heller, and John Updike. Though brief, the pieces provide incredible insights on these writers. Barth comments that he "once considered, half-seriously if only briefly, perpetrating a book to be called *Introductions to Contemporary Literature*," which would collect his insights on Borges, Calvino, Coover, Eco, and Vonnegut, among others. If these introductions were even half as good as the ones included in *Final Fridays*, Barth needs to seriously consider such a project. The final two essays of the book, on his father and twin sister, are touching and not to be missed.

Final Fridays covers many different and interesting topics that are sure to intrigue anyone who cares about contemporary literature. One of the book's virtues is its range: from the future of the book and the role of place in fiction to discussions of writers past and present, *Final Fridays* covers a lot of ground. From these varying reflections, we learn about not only Barth the writer and critic, but also Barth the teacher, colleague, father, husband, brother, and son. *Final Fridays* is an incredible journey with one of the most important writers of the latter half of the twentieth century. You will be energized by Barth's passion for and love of literature — and life. Here's looking forward to another set of Friday writings from the master.

5

DATA MINING FICTION

You are being read by what you read. Google knows where you read; Apple knows what you read; and Amazon knows how you read. How does it feel to have the object of reading transferred from your book to your self?

Print books were a grossly inefficient means of collecting data on your reading behavior. The composition of your bookshelf was mostly a private matter, as was whether the books on your shelf were being utilized or just collecting dust. Your dogeared pages and annotations were only known by those with direct access to your library.

But digital books tell all.

As Alexandra Alter outlines in a recent *Wall Street Journal* article, data mining of your e-books can determine everything from how long it took you to read a page of the novel you just downloaded to how much of it you actually read. When you re-read a page, data is collected; when you highlight a line or make an annotation, data is collected; even when you give up on a book, data is collected. Virtually everything you do with a digital book can be captured by data mining.

We can now acquire more precise information about what books people are buying and who specifically is buying them. But more significantly, we now know much more about how people are using the digital books they acquire.

Kobo, a major provider of e-readers and e-books, keeps a record of how long it takes each of its eight million users to read their e-books and whether they finish them. Kobo knows, for example, that readers of George R. R. Martin's *A Dance with Dragons* read on average about 50 pages per hour — and that most of the readers who started reading this 1,000 page-plus fantasy novel completed it.

With 2.5 million books in their inventory, reading behavior data from Kobo is a treasure trove for publishers hungry for more than just sales information. The capacity to track not just what books people buy, but also whether — and how — they read them, provides an entirely new dimension to the book industry.

Jim Hilt, vice president for e-books at Barnes & Noble, which controls over 25% of the digital book market through its Nook e-reader, says that his company has "more data than we can use."

"The bigger trend we're trying to unearth is where are those drop-offs in certain kinds of books," said Hilt, "and what [we can] do with publishers to prevent that." His company has already used it to produce "Nook Snaps" — short books on non-fiction subjects aimed at responding to data indicating that Nook readers routinely give up on long works of non-fiction.

Scott Turow's books have sold over 25 million copies and have been translated into 20 languages. Still, he claims that he does not know who buys his books. "I once had an argument with one of my publishers," comments Turow, "when I said, 'I've been publishing with you for a long time and you still don't know who buys my books,' and he said, 'Well, nobody in publishing knows that.'"

So what would the president of the Authors Guild do with this information if he had it?

"If you can find out that a book is too long and you've got to be more rigorous in cutting," says Turow, "personally I'd love to get the information."

But should the shaping of written works be decided not by writers and editors, but by the mean of the median of the responses of their e-reading public?

The world doesn't need fifty shades of reading-behavior-data-generated fiction—even though I'm sure that sales-hungry publishers would disagree. "If we can help authors create even better books than they create today," comments Hilt, "it's a win for everybody."

Better books are not necessarily books that better meet the expectations of readers. In fact, one could argue that better books are ones that *do not* meet reader expectations, but rather defy or challenge them. They may not be as "reader-friendly" or sell as many copies, but it is these "writerly" books that are the engine of narrative innovation and aesthetic interest.

To be sure, there is no turning away from the shift from print to digital books. A recent study has indicated that over one-fifth of American adults have read an e-book in the past year. Moreover, the same study reports that e-books are preferable to printed books when it comes to "Reading books in bed," "Having a wide selection of books to choose from," "Reading books while traveling or commuting," and "Being able to get a book quickly." The only areas where printed books are preferable are "Reading with a child" (81% prefer printed books) and "Sharing books with others" (69% prefer printed books).

I guess the next question that should be asked is: Will the rise of e-books bring us "better books," or will it simply amount to "better book *sales?*"

The "social reading" aspect of e-books certainly has the potential to positively transform reading behavior and to create literary community in a way not possible in the age of print.

Consider, if you will, Kobo's "Reading Life" feature, one of a number of social reading products currently available. To find out more information about any of the books in your Kobo e-book collection, all you have to do is tap on the cover. The menu then allows you to share what you are reading on Twitter, Facebook, or through email. A pulse indicator tells you how much social activity is occurring on that book's page. If you tap the pulse, you can see what others are saying about the book or join in the conversation about it yourself. If you want to share a passage you are reading with others, you just swipe it and email or tweet it. You can also see how many times the book has been read, how many people liked it, and get a list of who is reading it right now.

The options for creating literary community through social reading software like Kobo's "Reading Life" are only limited by your time and imagination. Moreover, the level of self-awareness of your individual reading behavior as well as the reading life of others is without precedent. Kobo allows you to view your own statistics regarding pages turned, hours read, hours per book, total hours reading, times you read, and what you read (books, newspapers, magazines). You can also view the reading stats of others. It also tells you the percentage of your library that you have read and total number of pages turned.

According to Kobo, 8 million people read this way. With 1 million free titles available for download, the Kobo "reading experience" is indeed appealing. But one must question how all of the data collected by Kobo and other social reading venues will be utilized by the publishing industry.

In the print age, this was the stuff of dystopic fiction; in the digital age, few seem to be concerned that they are being read through the books that they are reading.

6

ANOTHER ONE BITES THE DUST

American literature is slowly going out of business. The publisher of *The Collected Works of Langston Hughes* and *The Complete Sermons of Ralph Waldo Emerson* is closing up shop.

Starting this July[3], the University of Missouri Press will begin to phase out operations. The press, which was founded in 1958 by University of Missouri English professor William Peden, has published approximately 2,000 titles over the course of its history.

Eclectic in its reach, the press has an impressive catalogue that includes offerings in Women's Studies, African American Studies, Creative Nonfiction, Journalism, and American, British, and Latin American Literary Criticism. It serves its region with series such as the *Missouri Biography Series* and *Missouri Heritage Readers Series*, and American letters in general with series such as the *Mark Twain and His Circle Series* and the *Southern Women Series*.

The press' catalogue is deep and rich, and holds gems for both the serious scholar and general interest reader. In addition to the seminal collections of Emerson and Hughes, my own recent favorites are Gail Pool's *Faint Praise: The Plight of Book Reviewing in America* (2007) and Ned Stuckey-French's *The American Essay in the American Century* (2011).

One of the measures of a great university is the strength of its press. Press strength is determined by its catalogue, and its catalogue by the choices of its editors and the impact of its authors.

University presses are non-profit enterprises. Though these presses may reach a level of financial self-sufficiency in their operation, they are by and large underwritten by their host university. This is part of the investment of higher education.

Most of the monographs produced by scholars have a limited audience — and very few make their publishers any money. However, their publication is still an important aspect of scholarly activity and knowledge dissemination.

The University of Missouri system afforded its press a $400,000 annual subsidy.

To gain a perspective on this figure and the value of the press to the university, one only has to consider that the head basketball coach at Mizzou makes $1.35 million per year — and the head football coach makes $2.5 million per year.

The interim director of the press makes just under $75,000 — less than an assistant baseball coach. The acquisitions editor makes just under $35,000 — less than an athletic trainer.

Closer to the cost of subsidizing the press are the salaries of the assistant head football coach and the linebacker coach/defensive coordinator, who each make just over $340,000 per year.

How does one compare a football season to a publishing season? Is an 8 and 5 season more valuable than 30 books published? Is running a press worth losing an assistant coach or two?

In total, the University of Missouri employs over 17,500 individuals. Currently, the press employs 10 people, though in 2009 it was nearly twice that number. The economic crash of 2008 forced many state universities such as the University of Missouri to reassess their priorities and scale back.

Mizzou made their priorities clear: in 2010, the University of Missouri's head football coach received a $650,000 raise.

Louisiana State University, another football powerhouse, slated its university press for closure in 2009. Somehow, this press survived the state budget crisis. However, given that it is nowhere near as popular as their football team, I'm sure that it sleeps with one eye open, waiting for the day that university officials have to decide between a subsidy for the press—or a pay raise for Coach Saban.

Other presses were not so lucky.

Eastern Washington University, Southern Methodist University, and the University of Scranton all closed their presses.

And even the celebrated University of California Press tightened its belt by discontinuing its poetry series.

University of Missouri administrators are said to be "hashing out ways to create a new and sustainable model to operate a university press."

They also assure us that "any future press won't look like the current operation."

"We believe the publication of scholarly work is important," said the president of University of Missouri. "We're working very diligently on what" the new press "will look like."

While there is no indication where the University of Missouri administration will go with this, the options here are limited. The most obvious, however, is to go digital.

And here there is some precedent.

Though Rice University closed its traditional press in 1996, it re-opened in its wake an all-digital press in 2006. According to Eugene Levy, who helped finance the revived press during his term as provost at Rice, the all-digital press was costing Rice $150,000 to $200,000 per year. "This was intended as an experiment," said Levy.

Coming from the Andrew Hays Buchanan Professor of Astrophysics at Rice, the word "experiment" gains even more gravitas.

Rice hoped to save money by not printing books. Comments Levy, "The hope was that, without the burden of having to maintain a print inventory, the press might sustain itself largely on revenues from print-on-demand sales." What they found out was that there "are base costs that are irreducible"—"and that printing is only one of them."

By 2010, it was determined that there would be

no way to recover even the minimal cost of operations. Combine this with slow sales and a fiscal crisis — and the result is a failed experiment.

Rice shut down its all-digital press in the fall of 2010.

However, the decision was not without its detractors.

One of the board members — who wished to remain anonymous — commented that new models of academic publishing are not going to be derived from a sales model. "We're moving to a different era of scholarly communication where it's more accessible to more people, and where we don't have to worry about commercial viability," said the anonymous board member. Humanities publishing is being killed by placing emphasis on commercial viability — "there is no commercial viability," added the board member.

No matter what the form and how diligent the work, a university press requires resources. Just as it takes resources to run a successful athletic program, so too does it take an investment to run a university press.

And comparatively speaking, the costs are negligible: an editor makes less at Mizzou than an athletic trainer, and even the assistant baseball coaches make more than the press director.

Perhaps the solution is not to compare athletic salaries to press salaries but to treat university presses on the same level as athletic programs. Both are auxiliary operations subsidized by the university, and both play an important role in higher education.

Perhaps we need to measure the scholarly impact of the books published by the press in the same way we measure the impact of the gymnastics or baseball team winning a game or their division. Or think of the cultural capital and prestige generated by the press as akin to the bowl victories or NCAA titles.

And just as we don't scrap athletics if one of our teams loses games or money, we shouldn't scrap university presses if they don't generate enough revenue to cover their operation.

While it may not be the most popular decision for the University of California Press to take one type of book off of their list, if it makes their press more viable in some way, it is akin to downsizing or closing down a sport to make an athletics program stronger.

Think of the $200,000 invested by Rice or the $400,000 at Mizzou as the cost of being a *strong* university—a cost that in the big picture is most likely a fraction of the cost of one athletic coach.

What does it mean when a university press fails? It does not mean that its authors were unsuccessful or that its press was run poorly. Rather it means that its university has abandoned part of its scholarly mission: namely, supporting the publication of books that are the lifeblood of its faculty—and academia itself.

7

JUST THE FACTS, MA'AM

How would you respond to the news that a piece you read in a favorite magazine contained factual inaccuracies? Would you feel any differently if you knew that these inaccuracies were aimed at providing you with a "better and truer experience?"

This was the reasoning of a University of Iowa professor confronted with accusations of factual inaccuracies by his fact-checker.

In 2003, an essay commissioned by *Harper's* from writer John D'Agata was later rejected by the magazine by reason of factual inaccuracy. The piece was later published by *The Believer* after seven years of revisions and arguments over its factual infelicities.

"Aren't you worried about your credibility with the reader?" asked Jim Fingal, the fact-checker for *The Believer*. "Not really, Jim, no," said D'Agata. "I'm not running for public office. I'm trying to write something that is interesting to read."

The battles between *The Believer's* meticulous fact-checker and the author of a lyrical but factually "free" meditation on a Las Vegas teen suicide are presented in *The Lifespan of a Fact.*[4] While there is also reason to question the veracity of the exchange as recorded in the book (it too prioritizes the creation of something "interesting to read" over a strict historic record), this should not be the standard by which it is judged.

The Lifespan of a Fact provides a comprehensive snapshot of a demanding and often unseen aspect of the publishing process. It is valuable in its critical depiction of fact-checking as a contested space, particularly for writing that bridges the scholarly and creative worlds.

Some may label this writing "creative nonfiction" or simply "nonfiction," but D'Agata snarls at these designations. He prefers a more rarified term — one with a well-established canon tracing back to antiquity: the essay.

"And indeed, if we dig down into the history of essays," writes D'Agata, "we will find writers like Natalia Ginzburg and Mary McCarthy and George Orwell and Henry Thoreau and Charles Lamb and Thomas De Quincey and Daniel Defoe and Christine de Pisan and Sei Shōnagon and St. Augustine and Plutarch and Seneca and Cicero and Herodotus and dozens of other masters of this form who regularly altered facts in order to get a closer understanding of what they were experiencing."

Why then does *Harper's* need a fact-checker if Cicero did without?

Because readers expect it. Magazines worth reading place a high value on factual integrity. A great deal of time, effort, and resources are put into verifying the veracity of sources and statements. Without fact-checking, publications run the risk of jeopardizing their intellectual and scholarly integrity — if not opening themselves to accusations of slander and libel.

Harper's is *Harper's* because it takes this care.

Still, as the D'Agata argument illustrates, there exist historically significant and currently vital forms of writing that are irreducible to statements of fact. Nor are they pure products of authorial invention.

The essay is one of these forms. But what is it?

I admire Robert Musil's thoughts on the genre because he incorporates the essay form into a way of life. In *The Man without Qualities* (1930), the Austrian novelist wrote that an essay is rather the unique and unalterable form assumed by a man's inner life in a decisive thought. Nothing is more foreign to it than the irresponsible and half-baked quality of thought known as subjectivity. Terms like true and false, wise and unwise, are equally inapplicable, and yet the essay is subject to laws that are no less strict for appearing to be delicate and ineffable. There have been more than a few such essayists, masters of the inner hovering life, but there would be no point in naming them. Their domain lies between religion and knowledge, between example and doctrine, between *amor intellectualis* and poetry; they are saints with and without religion, and sometimes they are also simply men on an adventure who have gone astray.

Musil's critical question remains vital: "A man who wants the truth becomes a scholar; a man who wants to give free range to his subjectivity may become a writer; but what should a man do who wants something in between?"

The answer for Musil was to write essays, and D'Agata has picked up the call.

The essay has always been not quite scholarship, but not a pure act of imagination. This came to the fore in the work of twentieth-century thinkers like Musil, who grappled with balancing the worlds of science with those of art and utilized the essay as a kind of middle ground. The essay's Janus-faced nature gave it a power and promise to complicate and mediate the disparate discourses of science and art.

Yet the liberties that D'Agata takes in reshaping his depiction of events are problematic for some readers. In an era of strong rhetoric and general distrust of the media, a writer's revisions of time and place can be troubling.

"You feel that it's inappropriate for me to have done this," writes D'Agata to Fingal. "While I feel that it's a necessary part of my job to do this; that what I'm doing by taking these liberties is in fact making a better work of art—and thus a better and truer experience for the reader—than I could have if I'd stuck to the facts."

What is this "better and truer" experience that D'Agata claims as his aim? It rings as an instantiation of political satirist Stephen Colbert's "truthiness"—"the truth that comes from the gut, not books."

Colbert uses the term to mock current political rhetoric and facile claims of opinion as fact, yet "truth that comes from the gut" seems an apt description of D'Agata's aim. The aesthetic "truth" and natural grace, the *universalization* from facts that D'Agata strives to achieve become the motivation for his alteration of key terms and incidents. He is in pursuit of beautiful writing and purity of insight. Beauty becomes truth, truth beauty.

But how far are we then from fiction?

The fact-checker's standard of truth as accuracy is inappropriate in this form of writing. The standards of scholarly approaches are inapplicable; fact-checking is a waste of resources. But what then should readers expect from writing of this kind?

In 1997, in collaboration with Deborah Tall, D'Agata began to write about the "lyric essay," a form that "partakes of the poem in . . . its distillation of ideas and musicality of language" and "partakes of the essay . . . in its overt desire to engage with facts."

Ten years ago, when his piece on teen suicide was commissioned by *Harper's*, he asked, "What happens when an essayist starts imagining things, making things up, filling in blank spaces, or—worse yet—leaving the blanks blank? What happens when statistics, reportage, and observation in an essay are abandoned for image, emotion, expressive transformation?"

Answer: the lyric essay, an essay that "behave[s] less like an essay and more like a poem." "It takes the subjectivity of the personal essay and the objectivity of the public essay, and conflates them into a literary form that relies on both art and fact, on imagination and observation, rumination and argumentation, human faith and human perception."

The D'Agata affair raises significant questions about the relationship between scholarly and creative works—questions that are complicated by a postmodern epistemological climate that contests the boundaries between fact and fiction, objectivity and subjectivity.

In this context, why would an editor assign a meticulous fact-checker like Fingal to the work of an essayist who "starts imagining things, making things up, filling in blank spaces?" Like novelist Raymond Federman, who preferred to quote passages from other writers from memory rather than consult the original text, D'Agata acknowledges that facts in his essays are always subject to poetic license.

In the case of both writers, heavy-handed fact-checking defeats the spirit of their style. Both require acceptance of their particular aesthetic terms as a condition of reading.

But in this climate, where facts are regularly altered by the media to serve militaristic and corporate agendas, altering facts to meet the aims of "art" or to give the reader a "better and truer" experience may seem naïve.

Perhaps the problem is not that D'Agata is slanting his fact. Perhaps it is the aesthetic motivation that gives some readers pause. Or perhaps the problem is that he is *unashamedly* doing what many other figures fail to admit.

The essay is a space for insightful commentary, but insight does not equal truth. Perhaps the resistance to D'Agata's work ultimately stems from its honesty—its aim to achieve a depiction that stretches expectations of both scholarship and fiction for the reading public. If this kind of "truth from the gut" comes at the price of factual *dis*honesty, so be it. As D'Agata himself noted, he's not running for public office. His "truthiness" aims at inspiration without journalistic rigor.

Let's put a fact checker to *Dragnet*'s hero Joe Friday, who never said "Just the facts, ma'am." Though the factual fidelity of "All we want are the facts, ma'am" or "All we know are the facts, ma'am" would please an intrepid fact-checker, its apocryphal version is more memorable and aesthetically satisfying—a "better and truer experience."

8

AMERICA'S AGORA OF IDEAS

Carlin Romano sees an America full of philosophers. Romano's America is not an enclave of anti-intellectual culture that eschews philosophy, but rather is fertile ground for the growth of a highly philosophical community of thinkers. Demonstrating this premise would be a daunting task for any contemporary writer. But add to this the further assertion that twenty-first-century America is the most philosophical culture *in world history,* and you have a thesis that would make even Francis Fukuyama blush.

But such is the project of Carlin Romano's ambitious new book, *America the Philosophical.*[5] Romano, a critic-at-large for *The Chronicle of Higher Education* and long-time book critic for *The Philadelphia Inquirer*, engages a broad subject in this long, though entertaining, and highly accessible book. The result is a kind of treasury of anecdotes and musings from Romano's many years of writing about the books and thinkers that occupy America's agora of ideas.

Scattered throughout the book is material from nearly two hundred interviews with figures, ranging from Susan Sontag and Michel Foucault to Phil Donohue and Hugh Hefner. Romano has had remarkable access to movers and shakers in America's marketplace of ideas, and excerpts from these discussions form the highlights of the book. The author relays scores of offbeat anecdotes from these conversations, which in themselves are reason enough to read the book. Revealing details such as Kenneth Burke's "poorly furnished, dilapidated apartment" with its "indoor thermometer, still sealed in its plastic and cardboard casing, hung from a nail on the wall" and the "bottles of vermouth and vodka" that "dotted the sink top" help the reader form a visual connection to the thinkers Romano is discussing—a connection that is often absent in more serious scholarship.

However, Romano often shares details about philosophers' personal lives at the expense of engaging their work and contributions. For example, we learn of Martha Nussbaum's relationships with Amartya Sen and Cass Sunstein, as well as Romano's opinion that Kwame Anthony Appiah is "like Alain Locke, gay but not politically crusaderish on the subject." Such details give the book more of a gossipy, tabloid feel than a philosophical one, especially when they drag on for pages, as in the case of Martin Heidegger's relationship with Hannah Arendt. Rather than trying to figure out whether Arendt was *the* woman in Heidegger's life, these pages would have been more productively used discussing Arendt's philosophical contribution to America the philosophical.

The author never shies away from sharing his sharp opinions—and he has quite a collection. Romano sums up Robert Nozick's position thus: "Ethics, apparently, had been founded in a classroom with a piece of chalk." Of Noam Chomsky's political philosophy, Romano posits, "He simply lacked supportable truths most of the time."

The philosophical hero of the book is Richard Rorty. Romano's thirty-page chapter on him far outweighs his discussions of any other single thinker aside from Isocrates and John Rawls. In Rorty, Romano sees the contemporary epitome of "philosophy as an ever-expanding practice of persuasion, rather than a cut-and-dried discipline that hunts down eternal verities and comes pushpinned for media (or internal) consumption," and in Isocrates, a figure that supports a way of looking at philosophy that never caught on in the Western intellectual tradition. In contrast to Rorty and Isocrates, Rawls is presented as symptomatic of the failure of analytic philosophy because his widely known theory of justice has not faired well in the twenty-first century.

Romano clearly has an issue with the American Philosophical Association and seemingly almost all of its nearly 11,000 members. For him, the philosophical work of APA members is not the right type of "philosophy," particularly when viewed from the lens of Rorty and Isocrates' respective notions of philosophy. Nevertheless, it is one thing to tout a more expansive view of philosophy as persuasion, and conclude that by this notion, there is more to American philosophy than the APA's analytic philosophers have proposed; it is another thing to reject analytic philosophy and the work of the APA membership *in toto* on the basis of the success of the philosophy of Rawls — and the establishment of a new philosophical standard.

America the Philosophical is a broad-stroke treatise that fails to convince. Through Romano's anecdotes and comments on the American intellectual agora are welcome fuel to discussions of philosophy in America and will surely spark considerable commentary and debate, they do not establish their major claim. There is no doubt that we live in a culture that has many thoughtful and engaged thinkers. The jump from this thought to "America in the early twenty-first century towers as the most philosophical culture in the history of the world" is a stretch.

Moreover, for someone who spends considerable time down-playing the role of truth and argument in philosophy to then say that America is "an unprecedented marketplace of truth and argument that far surpasses ancient Greece, Cartesian France, nineteenth-century Germany, or any other place one can name over the past three millennia" is akin to a failure he attributes to Fukuyama and others. If Fukayama's *The End of History and the Last Man* (1992), which Romano says "failed to convince," in part, because "[h]e tended, like many authors of broad-brush treatises, to exaggerate whenever it served his purpose," a similar criticism could be leveled at *America the Philosophical*.

If America is the apex of philosophical culture in world history, marked by "philosophers" such as Hugh Hefner and Bill Moyers, then perhaps it *is* better that we disassociate it with the philosophical thought of Socrates, Descartes, and Hegel — as Romano suggests — so as not to tarnish the reputation of history's philosophical masters. In the spirit of Hericlitus' river into which no man can step twice, I am willing to agree that philosophy is continuously changing. However, I'm not yet ready to substitute that flowing watercourse for Hefner's "recessed pool" — the one that Romano tells us is "made from granite and Palo Verde rock."

Philosophy in America today is strong, diverse, and changing because organizations like the APA encourage philosophical pluralism and a variety of different conceptions of philosophy. There is also strong philosophical work being conducted within other professional organizations like the American Comparative Literature Association and the Modern Language Association. Each of these organizations is able to support a variety of approaches to philosophy without asking that we embrace Isocrates and reject Socrates — or worse yet, to adopt totalizing, grand narratives about America's place in the history of philosophy. Ultimately, Romano's *America the Philosophical* fails to persuade and is a flawed, though provocative, intervention into American philosophical culture.

9

HIDE IT FROM THE KIDS

Teachers in Arizona are advised to avoid discussion of race, ethnicity, and oppression—and to stop teaching works that deal with these topics.

Boxes of books by Native American and Mexican American writers were taken from classrooms—and the teachers who used them will be monitored to assure that the books do not make a return.

Two of the writers whose works now sit in an Arizona storeroom are editors of this publication—and all of the writers banned from these Arizona students are ones we champion.

Arizona's HB 2281 prohibits any courses or classes that "[a]dvocate ethnic solidarity instead of the treatment of pupils as individuals." This move by Arizona legislators shows how the neoliberal cult of the individual works in the post-9/11 atmosphere of xenophobic fear to deter the public from developing notions of solidarity and community. Proponents of the bill state that the cultural studies classes violate a state law banning classes that "promote resentment toward a race or class of people." This house bill aims to curtail the spread of cultural and area studies throughout the state—and to dismantle the existing programs in schools and universities.

Some opponents of the law see it as a bookend to SB1070, the strict immigration law that was passed in 2010. They believe that this new law is a further attempt to rein in the growing social and political influence of Latinos in Arizona.

The Tucson Unified School District did its part to help the neoliberal cause by recently banning specific books from their curriculum. The banned books were all part of their much-celebrated Mexican American Studies Department Reading List. These works include Sandra Cisneros' *The House on Mango Street* (1984) and Junot Diaz's *Drown* (1996).

They also include *ABR* associate editor Dagoberto Gilb's *The Magic of Blood* (1993) and contributing editor Rudolpho Anaya's *The Anaya Reader* (1995).

Arizona's cultural logic seems to be that if these books are taken out of curricular circulation, and if students are not permitted in school to learn about their cultural and literary heritage, then the students' solidarity with their ethnic group will evaporate.

At this point in our cultural history, it seems ludicrous to have to defend the study of culture and critical thinking. We should not need to defend ethnic literature—especially in places like Tucson where 60% of the student population is from an ethnic group that is invisible in the general curriculum. But reactionary behavior such as that in Arizona shows that there is still a need.

Cultural and critical studies make our educational system stronger. They provide an interdisciplinary framework to discuss issues of race, class, and gender, a place to consider the prejudices that threaten our democratic way of life. Barring students at any level from creatively exploring their culture and critically examining their society is antithetical to democratic values, and destructive and demoralizing to students.

The emergence and institutionalization of cultural and critical studies in the 1990s paved the way for the many area studies that flourish and are still forming today. This list includes gender studies, race studies, sexuality studies, disability studies, as well as many others. The Tucson Unified School District's Mexican American Studies Department is the result of the normalization of cultural studies in America. To see it mangled by myopic and hateful public servants is to view the destructive effective of neoliberal imperialism firsthand.

Area studies allow for critical inquiry into a wide range of aspects of culture. One of their central merits is that they regard the creative explorations of fiction writers as equally valuable to the work of social scientists. Consequently, in area studies, a work of fiction is potentially as capable of exposing social and cultural injustices as the work of historians and philosophers.

This empowerment of creative writers by cultural and critical studies though is a double-edged sword.

On the one hand, it makes the work of writers who deal with issues of race, class, gender, and sexuality an important window for viewing society and culture. Such work is noteworthy in the age of cultural and critical studies not just on aesthetic or literary grounds, but also on social and political ones.

On the other hand, as writing that can challenge or debunk received notions of culture and society, it becomes a threat to those who wish to maintain the status quo or worse. Consequently, it is dismissed as a form of "advocacy" and viewed as a threat to society.

But really, how threatening is Laura Esquivel's *Like Water for Chocolate* (1989)?

It may encourage a student to read Esquivel's *Malinche* (2006), or to learn more about Mexican *cocina* — or to want to cook.

Compared with the abject, aestheticized violence of much film and game culture taken in by youth today, the work of writers such as Anaya, Cisneros, Díaz, and Gilb is life-affirming. But without a classroom and a teacher to guide students towards these meaningful works, they have as much chance of changing lives as a video game without a machine on which to play it.

Perhaps this is why Tuscon also banned the landmark work of critical pedagogy, Paulo Freire's *Pedagogy of the Oppressed* (1968), for a committed teacher is just as dangerous to the neoliberal order as student ethnic solidarity.

Amidst all of this neoliberal madness, what then is to become of ethnic studies? If Arizona's cultural logic prevails, ethnic studies, as well as cultural and critical studies, will gradually disappear from the curriculum. And it won't just be Mexican American and Native American studies that disappear—but all area studies not directly associated with corporate profit and military interests.

We need to support our colleagues in ethnic studies who are still fighting the war for curricular inclusion. We can do this by assigning their works in our classes and inviting them to speak on our campus. If you don't know who these writers are or what books they have written, then just ask the Tucson school board about the books they are hiding from the kids.[6]

10

AIN'T NO SUNSHINE

Advocates for the advancement of the "neoliberal arts" just found a new champion in the Sunshine State.

Speaking to a business group in Tallahassee recently, Florida Governor Rick Scott summed up the crisis facing the humanities by attacking the use of state funds to support liberal arts education.

"How many more jobs do you think there is for anthropology in this state?" asked Governor Scott. "Do you want to use your tax dollars to educate more people who can't get jobs? In anthropology? I don't."

Quibble if you will whether a finance major is more likely to get a job today after graduation than a philosophy major — or whether a young accountant is a better potential employee than a newly minted anthropologist — when the budget gets tight, liberal arts programs are the first to be scapegoated.

When the State University of New York had to cut $640 million from its budget last year, the president of its Albany campus cut its classics, theater, French, Russian, and Italian programs.

And the University of Nevada, Las Vegas and Howard University both proposed eliminating their philosophy programs.

Howard's proposal is particularly disappointing because the American philosopher Alain Leroy Locke, architect of the Harlem Renaissance, was a founder of the department and chaired it from 1921 to 1953.

Though cuts and proposals for program elimination like these are becoming more commonplace within the corporate university — and usually draw opposition from many corners of the academy — it is a particularly disturbing sign of the times when a celebrated Historically Black University that counts Thurgood Marshall and Toni Morrison among its many distinguished graduates considers the elimination of philosophy from its offerings.

But such are the times in which we live: where philosophy, theater, and classics programs — programs that directly link the academy to its formation over two thousand years ago in ancient Greece — have to fight to survive.

Is it possible for anyone who knows or cares anything about Greek drama or philosophy to even suggest their elimination from the academy? Is our educational system so economically bankrupt that we must make it intellectually bankrupt as well by eliminating foundational areas of study?

Governor Scott asked, "Do we need to do all those programs, rather than the first thing is we've got to raise tuition every year?"

By this, he means, in hard economic times, universities should not be asking whether to raise tuition.

Rather, they should be asking whether they should eliminate the philosophy department.

Scott is far from alone in advocating this sentiment. In fact, this seems to be the major way state governments have been responding to budget shortfalls.

And given that the National Governors Association estimates that state governments control nearly two-thirds of all higher education funding, there is major reason for concern within the liberal arts.

All liberal arts departments are fair game for cutbacks, if not closure, in the age of the neoliberal university.

Responding to charges like those of Governor Scott and actions that serve to shut down active liberal arts programs is perhaps the most daunting challenge facing the humanities today. Why?

Without state support for humanities education within the university or advocacy for existing liberal arts programs, we risk diminishing our capacity to produce critically engaged and socially committed citizens.

Liberal arts majors excel at persuasive communication, critical thinking, and cultural awareness. We need to put these skills to use in defense of the disciplines we value.

The humanities are only as relevant to contemporary society as we make them. Yet to assess them solely on their employment potential reduces their value to its most trivial dimension. Once we lose our capacity to understand and ability to demonstrate the value of seminal yet difficult areas of study such as philosophy, much more is at risk than their diminishment as academic disciplines. We risk diminishing our democratic values and associated way of life.

The state legislator or university president who did not major in a liberal arts discipline cannot be expected to champion how they impact lives or their role in society. It is the task of those of us who have dedicated our careers to the liberal arts to educate others, to advocate for the liberal arts, to demonstrate their value and earn other's support.

The governor of Florida is just the latest proponent of the corporate curriculum and the neoliberal arts. There will be many more with even more extreme proposals, particularly if the economy continues to falter. We advocates of the humanities must exercise patience, and wait out the corporatization of the curriculum and the decreases in funding for humanities research and scholarship. At the present moment there ain't no sunshine for the humanities — least of all in Florida.

11

THE POLITICS OF SUBVENTION

Your publisher informs you that your scholarly book won't have an index unless you create it. Permission or copyright fees for works you used in your book will not be covered by the press; you are expected to finance them. If you want your book to be copyedited by someone other than yourself, you'll have to pay his or her fees.

Scenarios like this are not uncommon in the humanities. For years, publishers—and many very good ones—have requested that authors cover certain costs of publication. However, given the dismal state of the economy, particularly in the publishing world, it's not surprising to find publishers making new subvention requests.

Publishers are requesting that authors perform more of the work in preparing books for publication. This does not make these publishers *vanity presses*, nor does it make these works *self-published* works. It is one thing to request increased authorial assistance in the book production process; it is quite another to request that authors pay the cost of book production—and then some.

A request for subvention fees—funds to underwrite the cost of publication—does not in and of itself make a press a vanity press. Nor are requests for subvention fees a sign of lesser quality or integrity on the part of the publisher. After all, many of the most prestigious journals in business and the sciences regularly require subvention fees of their authors. In fact, most colleges and universities who support publication from their faculty have subvention funds — and even policies regarding their allocation. Take, for example, Middlebury College.

Middlebury, like most colleges and universities, has an explicit policy on subvention fees. It states that "The College will assist faculty with production costs and reprint costs for scholarly publications through the Scholarly Publication Subvention Fund (SPSF)." In reference to "Scholarly Books and Artistic Works," Middlebury's subvention policy says that

> Assistance will be provided (as funding permits) for tenured and tenure-track faculty to cover production costs when an academic publisher requires a subvention as a condition for publication. It may also be used for indexing, copyright or permission fees, or copy editing (i.e., copy editing of the final version of a manuscript after it has been accepted for publication). The funds for copy editing will only be paid to an independently-hired editor (not to the publishing press). The maximum grant amount for each book project is $2,000 and repayment is not required.

The presence of such policies in many faculty manuals indicates the normalcy of subvention requests from publishers. And if Middlebury's $2,000 were not generous enough, the college also offers faculty members the opportunity to apply "to the Dean of the Faculty for a loan to cover production costs in excess of $2,000."

Middlebury's policy is typical of academic subvention policies. It is built upon the assumption that faculty will at times *be required* to provide subventions to their publishers for both scholarly books and artistic works.

The only proviso comes in the last line of the policy: "The faculty member may not be the publisher, producer, or agent."

Given the dismal economic state of publishing, authors must expect increasing requests from publishers for subventions, given the dismal state of funding in higher education, faculty should not be surprised to discover more limited subvention funds.

Authors who are surprised by a request for a subvention are advised to acquire a better understanding of the economics of book publishing before they jump to conclusions about the integrity of the publisher or the press.

The recent dustup regarding BlazeVOX [books] publisher Geoffrey Gatza's request for subventions from his authors exposes not the vanity of his press, but rather the vanity of authors who scorn any financial outlay toward the publication of their books.

Gatza requested a recent group of authors pay a $250 subvention fee if they wanted print versions of their books in addition to electronic versions. The fee was not necessary if they agreed to online publication.

This was the first time that subvention fees have been requested of BlazeVOX authors, the request was made to help cover costs due to the loss of a major underwriter of the press.

By Gatza's own estimate, "books by new [BlazeVOX] authors sell around 25-30 copies" — and most of the books published by BlazeVOX will not sell enough copies to recoup even the modest cost of his print-on-demand publishing model.

So why so much anger towards Gatza for asking for a subvention — to save his press?

My assumption is that the anger is not so much about Gatza's request for a subvention but rather that the subvention request is an indicator of the small circulation of the work to be published. Friends and family might snap up 25-30 copies, but in general, the book will not have greater reach.

This is why the offer to publish the book online without subvention seems to be mainly overlooked by the folks who are upset with Gatza for the audacity of requesting a print subvention fee. While the culture is shifting, the anxiety of electronic publication remains. Even though an online version offers a potentially longer and wider reach for their book — and is an arguably much more progressive mode of publication — the subvention fee foregrounds the fact that only their close relatives and diehard fans will buy a print copy of their masterpiece.

And Gatza is no longer in the financial position to foot the bill for their print vanities.

Perhaps the authors complaining about Gatza's subvention fee should consider the advice of one of the authors he published this year.

"If you arrange a raise for your companion/Get some poetry," writes poet Gloria Frym in her new book, *Mind Over Matter: A Tribute to Poetry* (2011).

> Raise money for sick words and kids
> If you like what you hear or read
>
> Say something with your checkbook
> Mr. Trustee of the Big Family Trust
>
> Poetry doesn't mind its own business
> Or anyone else's unless
> They don't pay up.

Or, instead of vilifying a publisher who is appropriately dealing with the financial difficulties facing the humanities and dedicated to keeping the free-flow of innovative new poetry moving against the odds of decreasing readership and sales, go purchase some small-press poetry. Both the poets and the presses will be most grateful.

12

THE RISE OF CORPORATE LITERATURE

How prepared are you to teach a course on "corporate" literature? What would you say to someone who does not recognize the value of a liberal arts education? How would you argue for the value of reading contemporary fiction to someone who aspires to be an accountant? The ongoing challenges facing the humanities are making these questions more common — and responses to them more significant.

Many believe that the future of the humanities hinges in large part on the ability of people who share a passion for the liberal arts to be able to articulate that passion to others. Seeing and hearing people who are fully committed to their art is often believed the best way of supporting the arts. Poets who intensely and emphatically read their poetry reveal their commitment to their art; the philosopher who cleverly turns every statement into a question and undermines beliefs demonstrates the perennial and complex nature of philosophy; the novelist who convinces others to believe in her characters and care for their well-being shows the power of mimesis.

However, if there is a "crisis" in the humanities, it may be because these traditional ways of drawing people into the humanities are no longer working. Students facing the prospect of going into debt to attend college are less interested today in studying things that might be good for the mind, but are potentially hard on their wallets — and career aspirations. A generation or two ago, students were more passionate about things like poetry and history. The current generation though is more committed to pursuing lucrative vocational careers than enjoying the wonders of the liberal arts — to relieving their massive student debt than pursuing majors that they believe will only exacerbate their economic woes.

Pollster Daniel Yankelovich has noted that "75 percent of high school seniors and 85 percent of their parents said college is important because it 'prepares students to get a better job and/or increases their earning potential.'" In itself, the situation would not be so dire for the liberal arts if these students and their parents had some knowledge of — if not appreciation for — the liberal arts. After all, corporate employment aspirations (and success) are not mutually exclusive with an appreciation for the liberal arts. However, according to Yankelovich, "44 percent of students and 19 percent of their parents could not answer the question, What does a liberal arts education mean?" In addition, Yankelovich's polling indicated that "[t]he overall impression of liberal arts education among 68 percent of the students and 59 percent of the parents was negative or neutral."

These beliefs about higher education and its value would be challenges for the humanities even in good economic times. However, since the economic meltdown of 2008, they have made the situation in the humanities even worse. The rising cost of higher education and the shrinking job market coupled with prevailing perceptions about the value of a college education have had a decidedly negative impact on the liberal arts.

Some of the more disturbing numbers associated with this negative impact are the decreasing numbers of humanities majors. For example, 40 years ago, 64,286 students received bachelor's degrees in English. However, in 2007, it was reported that the number of bachelor's degrees awarded in English had shrunk to 53,040. This drop would not be so significant if one did not also consider that during this period, the total number of bachelor's degrees almost doubled. Taking this into account, the 64,286 majors in 1971 equates to approximately 128,500 in 2007, thus bringing the weighted decrease in English majors over this span to around 60%.

Perhaps a better gauge of the state of the liberal arts though is the number of students who attended liberal arts colleges, but did not receive degrees in the liberal arts. In 1987, just over 10% of all students attending the 225 liberal arts colleges in the U.S. received degrees in vocational fields; whereas by 2008, that percentage rose to nearly 30%. At the lowest tier (or ranked) liberal arts colleges, the percentage is well over 50%.

Can the liberal arts get a bigger slap in the face than this? Is there no clearer indicator of the decreasing value of a liberal arts education than students attending liberal arts colleges but in increasing numbers *not* majoring in the liberal arts? In the same way that a drastic increase of business majors at colleges dedicated to the arts would not be a good sign for the arts, so too are increasing numbers of vocational majors at colleges dedicated to the liberal arts. One goes to Juliard to study opera—not operations management; one goes to Williams to study philosophy—not finance.

Vocational aspirations and careerism among students are radically altering liberal arts education in America. The liberal arts curriculum is slowly giving way to vocational— or, if you will, *corporate*—instruction. If something is not done about this soon by critically engaged academics, there is every reason to believe that the move toward more vocational courses and majors will accelerate. The liberal arts curriculum that remains will increasingly be tailored to serve the needs of an increasingly, vocationally, and corporately minded student base. In this climate, it would not be unexpected to see the literature curriculum detached from its aesthetic and critical foundations, and repositioned on a corporate or vocational base—particularly if it wants to survive in the neoliberal university (or universe). How then do we as educators meet the demands of vocationally motivated undergraduate students *and* resist emptying our liberal arts courses from their historical, political, and critical roots? How do we protect the distinctiveness of the liberal arts, while at the same time persuade vocationally minded students of their significance?

It is my belief that we need to heed rather than denigrate the desires of our students, and engage them in a progressive form of dialogue with and through the liberal arts courses that we offer. "Corporatizing" literature courses (or literature in the corporate university) does not mean that we ignore the historical and political dimensions of the works that we are teaching; rather, it means that we need to be careful not to assume that students *prima facie* care about the critical foundations of texts. Teaching corporatized literature courses requires a more complex dialogue between teacher and students in order to respect mutual desires. In the end, however, this respect of different desires may be one of the only ways to prevent the eventual extinction of large swaths of the liberal arts curriculum — especially if our corporate liberal arts courses bring about a greater knowledge of and appreciation for the liberal arts.

Writers and critics need to be concerned with the crisis in the humanities. While some have preferred to react to recent events in the humanities by questioning whether it really is a "crisis" or whether it really is not as bad as it appears, others have written off the crisis as someone else's problem or lowered their expectations about being able to save the humanities. In the end, though, such responses only serve as convenient "red-herrings" for the destructive forces working to bring the humanities down. There will be plenty of time to split philosophical hairs about the "perceived" versus the "real" state of the humanities when the neoliberal arts revert back to being the liberal arts. However, until then, to ignore or write off the problems facing the humanities is to be part of the problem.

13

WHO'S IN? WHO'S OUT?

The passing of time provides clarity and perspective on literary art for which there is no substitute. It removes the distractions of writerly personality, and foregrounds the writerly products. Today's fashion becomes yesterday's failure; yesterday's failure becomes today's fashion. Overlooked or overrated — literary and critical gems are only visible with hindsight.

Consider all the emerging authors prognosticated by critics and writers to become the next James Joyce or Samuel Beckett or Jorge Luis Borges and how few have risen to the accolades. Or remember those who became recognized as masters only in the slow brew of critical time — writers like Franz Kafka, Felipe Alfau, Roberto Bolaño, and Raymond Federman.

One gauge of a literary generation's power is its ability to exhibit critical foresight. To provide sharp prognostications of fiction's future and the trajectory of current writers. To put hype and marketing aside and focus on the impact of writing and criticism.

This highly speculative endeavor is perhaps the most difficult act in contemporary letters. Looking forward to a place where the writing and criticism today may be viewed against the relief of time. Such acts are more than just critical games. Rather, they are important exercises in helping direct our current writing and critical energies.

American Book Review wants to know what the writing and criticism worlds will be like ten years from now. What authors will be in? What type of writing will be out? What poets will have faded, and who will be high up on our radar? What will be the "in" approach to criticism, and what will look like an historical artifact?

14

FROM ÉCRITURE TO RÉCRITURE

Marjorie Perloff's new book, *Unoriginal Genius: Poetry by Other Means in the New Century*,[7] pulls the poetics of citation from the dustbin of twentieth-century comparative literary history and places it on the forefront of contemporary poetic innovation. Perloff begins by reminding us that the primarily negative reception of the most famous twentieth-century poem in English, T.S. Eliot's *The Waste Land* (1922), was in large part based on its extensive use of citation. Critics objected to Eliot's use of lines borrowed from and notes based on other texts, and to the lack of personal emotion in the poem. One early critic even charged that Eliot suffered from "an indolence of the imagination" while still admiring his "sophistication."

Beginning with Eliot, Perloff takes the reader on a journey through key figures and texts ranging from twentieth-century giants such as Ezra Pound, Walter Benjamin, Marcel Duchamp, and Eugen Gomringer through early twenty-first-century literary innovators such as Charles Bernstein, Susan Howe, Kenneth Goldsmith, and Toko Tawada. Through close readings of texts by these authors and others, Perloff elegantly demonstrates how citation "has found a new lease on life in our own information age." Her project not only provides new insight on underappreciated forms such as concrete poetry, and lesser-known theoretical works such as Walter Benjamin's *Archades Project* (1927-1940), but also makes a strong case for "citationality" as a key concept in contemporary literary and critical theory.

"Citationality," writes Perloff, "with its dialectic of removal and graft, disjunction and conjunction, its interpenetration of origin and destruction, is central to twenty-first-century poetics." This concept is exemplified in not only the Latin, Greek, Italian, French, and German foreign-language citations in Eliot's masterpiece, but also in Pound's collagist method and multilingual poetics, which Perloff sees as "his anticipation of digital linkage in the creation of narrative assemblage." Alternately and aptly termed "récriture" by the contemporary French literary historian Antoine Compagnon, citationality is, in Perloff's words, "the logical form of 'writing' in an age of literally mobile or transferable text—text that can be readily moved from one digital site to another or from print to screen, that can be appropriated, transformed, or hidden by all sorts of means and for all sorts of purposes."

The power of Perloff's book, six of the seven chapters of which were delivered as the 2009 Weidenfeld Lectures in European Comparative Literature at Oxford, is not simply its defense of the contemporary significance of the concept of citationality. Rather, its strength is to be found in the way she uses a fluid notion of this concept to open up new dimensions of some of the most complex and difficult texts from twentieth- and early twenty-first-century literary history. For example, her reading of Benjamin's enigmatic *Arcades Project* as an "ur-hypertext" and paradigmatic work of récriture is simply brilliant. Not only does she persuasively argue against the view that Benjamin's "encyclopedic collection of notes the writer made over thirteen years of reflection on the Paris Arcades (Passages)" is merely, in the words of Theodor Adorno, a "wide-eyed presentation of bare facts," but also that it is arguably the key text to understanding the equally complicated work of contemporary poets such as Susan Howe and Kenneth Goldsmith.

For Perloff, works like Kenneth Goldsmith's *Soliloquy* (2001), a poem which transcribes every word he spoke over the course of a week in New York City, and Susan Howe's *The Midnight* (2003), a book-length poem which includes photographs, paintings, maps, catalogs, facsimiles of tissue interleaves, and enigmatic captions, share with Benjamin's masterpiece "intricately appropriated and defamiliarized texts" that serve to "reimagine" their source sites. In Perloff's hands, poetry by other means, such as montage, collage, recycling, appropriation, citation, plagiarism, and cutting and pasting, is the poetry of the age of hyper-information. The unoriginal genius of its "authors" is not the creativity of its language, but rather the way in which its language can be uniquely regarded as, in the words of Compagnon, "simultaneously representing two operations, one of removal, the other of graft." Writes Goldsmith, this conceptual or "uncreative" writing "obstinately makes no claim to originality." "Come to think of it," comments Goldsmith, it is not even "writing" as "no one's really written a word of it." "It's been grabbed, cut, pasted, processed, machined, honed, flattened, repurposed, regurgitated, and reframed," writes Goldsmith, "from the great mass of free-floating language out there just begging to be turned into poetry." Perloff's brilliance in this book is getting us to appreciate both the genius of contemporary uncreative writing and its connections to the work of early twentieth-century masters such as Eliot, Pound, and Benjamin.

15

THE EXECUTOR'S DILEMMA

This month[8] Little, Brown and Company published
David Foster Wallace's unfinished novel, *The Pale King*.
Wallace, who ended his own life in September of 2008,
supposedly left 250 pages from the novel in the center
of his desk. What was missing was instructions for the
executors about what to do with the unfinished manuscript.
According to Michael Pietsch, the editor charged with
creating a publishable book from piles of manuscript pages
and notes, "the fact that he left those pages on his work
table is proof he wanted the book published."

Proof? Proof is a yellow sticky note bearing the lines:
"Please publish posthumously — DFW" or a comment to
his wife or agent about publication. Anything less is only
proof that Hachette Livre UK, the parent company of
Little, Brown and Company, the largest trade publisher
in the United Kingdom, has found yet another way to
cash in on the growing demand for everything Wallace
(even Wallace's undergraduate philosophy dissertation on
Richard Taylor has found its way into print of late courtesy
of Columbia University Press).

Wallace's longtime agent, Bonnie Nadell, also
speculated on the author's intentions, saying "If there had
been a spotlight on those pages, it could not have been more

obvious." "I felt in my heart," continued Nadell, "and so did Karen Green, David's widow, that he wanted people to see it, and ultimately the reasons to publish outweighed the reasons not to."

But there is a big difference between providing access to the manuscript and the many handwritten journals and notebooks associated with the composition of the novel, and publishing it as a posthumous novel.

Posthumous materials such as letters, diaries, drafts, and notebooks are the common — and expected — literary residua of a writer's life tragically interrupted in media res. And these moments of authorial incompleteness and fragments of writerly process reveal a different aspect of the writer than his or her published works. For writers of Wallace's stature, one expects these items to be catalogued and made publically accessible in a library's or center's archives. There they would be preserved for scholarly pursuits and creative engagements — and perpetual nourishment for the literary imagination. Anyone who has spent time in an archive knows the singular joy of discovering new dimensions of writers through unseen and unpublished manuscripts. However, between archival access and publication of unfinished works as finished work, there is great difference.

My general feeling is that if the author does not read the page proofs, then publishers should not publish the work with the author's name on it — especially if the only proof of authorial desire to publish was leaving an incomplete manuscript on his desk. Or, if the unfinished work is published, it should be as close to a reproduction of the original materials left behind by the author as possible. Though a "scholarly" edition or "facsimile" version is much less polished and duller than a creative projection of the final manuscript such as Pietsch's, it still is a more powerful work. Why?

For one, unless the narrative structure is clear, any effort to establish it is merely speculation. In the case of *The Pale King*, the Little, Brown and Company editor really had no idea how to order the manuscript material because the novel has only the palest glimmer of a plot. However, instead of releasing the material in a more fluid form *à la* a "shuffle novel" or allowing aleatoric instincts to disorder it, Pietsch used a spreadsheet to establish a chronology of events, which was then used to order the sections. When things did not fit in chronological order, he then followed his instincts.

Moreover, Pietsch took the liberty of adding 20 percent of the material contained in Little, Brown and Company's version of *The Pale King* from material that was not available in typescript. He also edited out Wallace material that he felt was unnecessarily repetitive or slowed down the novel. While the editor's role in shaping the final volume is always considerable, in this case, the author has no final read-through.

Like the Nabokov family's decision to publish *The Original of Laura* (2009) in spite of the author's directions to destroy any unfinished work upon his death, the publication of Wallace's abandoned manuscript seems like the creation of a "literary event" to squeeze a few more bucks out of a popular author's industry. Thus far, it seems, thankfully, that critics will be kinder to Wallace than they were to Nabokov.

Perhaps publishing the 250 pages as found would have been the most "logical" step. Better yet, give them to us in facsimile form. Let us see a Wallace novel taking shape, and let the Wallace-heads argue how to fill in the gaps. Let the plotlessness and disunity engage our imaginations, rather than projecting this mirage in the desert of postmodern literary history.

I don't doubt that Wallace wanted readers to engage the novel that he was writing and the process he used to build his maximal fictions. But I wonder how a writer who fretted over punctuation would have acquiesced to the Frankenstein released by Little, Brown and Company.

Should unfinished posthumous novels be published or should they be relegated to library archives for study and commentary? My own feeling is that we should use the legacy of writers like Wallace to drive readers back to libraries and archives to see the formative "stuff" of great writers. Let incomplete final efforts such as Wallace's stand as examples of the painstaking process that artistic creation often is.

While I have not yet seen the mountain of materials from which Pietsch created *his* Wallace novel, I look forward to the day when I can spend time with them in the University of Texas' Ransom Center. I may not be able to form as complete a structure for the novel as Pietsch did, but I would rather engage it in its disorganized glory.

In this age of new media and shifting intellectual property rights, creative people are struggling to maintain material rights and creative control. While having more David Foster Wallace on the shelf will be welcomed by many readers, there remains a tinge of exploitation that leaves me with reservations. I understand the executors' dilemma, and the perils of "proof of intent," but I retain strong overriding sympathies for any artist who is unable to reclaim creative rights. Let dead authors live in completeness through their published work — and leave unpublished work in its valuable incompleteness.

16

BYE, BYE BORDERS

One of the more visible signs of neoliberalism in publishing has been the decline of independent booksellers — and the corresponding rise of the book superstore. While corporate publisher mergers, market-based editorial decision making, and multi-million dollar author advances are less visible to the general public, huge book megastores — often near boarded up independent bookstores — are a part of the American landscape. Book superstores are as common now to American strip malls as Walmart and Target, and in some cities are even found among luxury stores such as Louis Vuitton and Tiffany's.

Fifty years ago, three quarters of trade books were purchased at independent bookstores. Thirty years ago, competition from mall bookstores slashed this number in half. The meteoric rise of superstores like Barnes & Noble and Borders cut this number in half again five years ago. What's not to like about cappuccino machines, cozy leather chairs, and a mountain of Tom Clancy novels?

But now it seems even the megastores have overreached their rise. One half of the contemporary book-superstore dynamic duo just filed for bankruptcy. It seems that while everyone did enjoy the cappuccino machines, cozy chairs, and free reading materials, this didn't necessarily translate into the actual *sale* of books. And while Borders' recent filing for Chapter 11 might be sweet revenge to those who ran and loved the independents, don't expect a renaissance of the independent bookstore. Consumers increasingly prefer to shop for books online, where they can find big discounts and take advantage of immediate download.

The demise of Borders only strengthens online bookselling giant Amazon, which is predicted to account for 50 percent of U.S. trade sales *in all formats* by 2012. To get a perspective on this number, consider that just five years ago, all of the superstores and chains in the U.S. combined only accounted for 45 percent of the U.S. book retail market. Soon Amazon *alone* will be responsible for half of all book sales in the U.S. — with and without cappuccino.

If there is a silver lining to this development, at least Amazon makes available many more small-press books than Borders and its corporate companions — and easily fills your order for a title by Raymond Federman or Cris Mazza. Shopping at the chains never did that (I make a habit of looking for my favorite *ABR*-reviewed authors in any bookstore).

Much like Random House, whose transformation from premier literary publishing house to market-fundamentalist megacorporation can be linked to its going public and its corporate takeover by RCA, the metamorphosis of Borders from darling of the independent bookstore world to its pariah can be associated with its purchase by another large corporation — in this case, Kmart.

In 1971, Tom and Louis Borders opened a small bookstore in the college town of Ann Arbor, Michigan. Its success over the years encouraged the owners to open a second store in 1985 in nearby Detroit. When this store did well, they opened others. The stores were known throughout the Midwest and Northeast for their wide selection of new titles, but Borders stores retained their roots as academic booksellers. At any Borders, one could find piles of bestsellers alongside thousands of individual copies of scholarly titles — something unusual at the time for a bookstore chain.

Kmart, renowned for its "blue-light specials" on underwear and soap, acquired Borders in 1992, and merged it with Waldenbooks, the mall bookstore staple that it had acquired in 1984. The merger, called Borders Group (though I think "Kbooks" would have been more appropriate), went public in 1995.

While the acquisition of bookstore chains by a department store might sound strange, it seems fitting given that at one point department stores in the U.S. were among the leading sellers of books. Shortly after they first started selling books in the late nineteenth century, department stores likes Macy's of New York became national leaders in book sales. And by the early 1950s, it has been estimated that between 20 to 40 percent of trade books were sold by department stores. These businesses favored books in their inventory because they were believed to raise the class of the store, and appealed to a more cultured — and wealthy — clientele.

One of the consequences of this corporate merger with Kmart was that Borders Group started closing many of its Waldenbooks, and opening up more Borders superstores. From 1993 to 1994 alone, Borders went from 44 to 85 superstores — whereas Waldenbooks was reduced by nearly 60 stores during the same period. And Borders was not the only bookstore increasing its number of superstores at the time: so too was Barnes & Noble, which had bought the other mall chain bookstore staple, B. Dalton Booksellers, in 1986. By 2006, the number of Borders superstores rose to nearly 500 in the U.S. alone — often in prime locations such as on Chicago's Magnificent Mile or Market Street in San Francisco. But Borders' fall has turned out to be faster than its rise.

To be sure, Borders Group's failings were not just about books. A poor real estate strategy, over-investment in music (another anguished industry), and inefficient inventory management contributed to the decline. When the company filed for bankruptcy on February 16, 2011, Borders hadn't been profitable for five years.

In 1994, Borders Group operated almost twelve hundred bookstores. Today, just before filing for bankruptcy, there remain one half that number — and another 30 percent are set to close. Fittingly, the vacant shells of these large stores in prominent locations like Michigan Avenue are as much a visual reminder to all who pass by them of the shortcomings of market-fundamentalist-based decision making as are the piles of remaindered book-mountain titles. These vacated stores are a highly visible sign of the emptiness of neoliberal practices in publishing.

So what now for the independent booksellers? The difference between the book superstore and an independent bookseller ends with the common trait that they both stock and sell books. Whereas independent bookstores are defined for their eclectic and idiosyncratic inventories, mall bookstores like B. Dalton and Waldenbooks, and superstores like Barnes & Noble and Borders are characterized by the consistency and homogeneity of their inventories. While each independent bookstore makes its own inventory decisions, department stores and corporate chains have a few people making purchasing decisions *for all of their stores.*

The recent rise of chains aimed to *simulate* the appearance of high-end independent bookstores by having rows of beautiful bookcases with ladders alongside plush chairs and gourmet coffee, but in the process destroyed the *aura* of the bookstore. By regulating and standardizing the appearance and stock of the corporate bookstore in the same way that McDonald's regulates and standardizes its appearance and menu, they in effect deconstructed the notion of the bookstore they sought to emulate. Just as independent restaurants don't look alike or have the same menu — let alone food that tastes exactly the same — independent bookstores don't all sell the same books or look alike. That's the beauty of independence.

Browsing an independent bookstore for the first time can be an *unsettling* experience. The unfamiliarity with the layout and organization of titles, and with the stock itself, lends an element of adventure. At their best, independent books are unique assertions of aesthetic tastes.

Mass-market chain stores, however, sacrificed adventure for familiarity. Their over-reliance on bestsellers and reluctance to embrace valuable backlist titles led to a homogenizing of offerings. But now even this strategy is failing.

As the industry undergoes a painful contraction, booksellers and publishers will need to reexamine their relationship in a changing market. It's unfortunate that a number of jobs will be lost, and that there will be fewer places to physically browse for books. But perhaps there is a positive element for small-press authors.

Perhaps with the decline of the mass-market chains, the lure of "big" books for quick bucks will be somewhat lessened. Perhaps booksellers and publishers will reinvest in a long-standing relationship of developing authors and promoting backlist titles, as they did before mass merchandising changed the process. Well-written manuscripts from lesser-known authors might have more of a voice in an environment less dependent on mounds of bestsellers. And writers—and readers—just might benefit.

17

SUPERSIZE THAT NOVEL

What does neoliberalism mean for fiction writing, reading habits, and bookselling? What are the consequences of writing fiction in an age of corporate mega-publishing? How are reading habits affected by narrative aesthetics determined by market-fundamentalism? What does it mean to be a bookseller at a time when a fistful of chains dominate the national landscape?

Nearly three-quarters of active publishers in the U.S. have annual revenues between zero and $50,000; roughly another twenty percent put their annual revenues between $50,000 and one million dollars.

In total, these figures represent the annual revenues of almost 60,000 — or 95 percent — of U.S. publishers.

Considering the large percentage of publishers with annual revenues less than $50,000, it could be argued that small press publishing *populates* the national landscape though corporate publishing *controls* it.

Nonetheless, all still follow the prime directive of publishing: to sell books.

Oh yeah, and I almost forgot: and to get people to read them.

One might argue that what separates a corporate publisher from a small press publisher is that the former want people to *buy* books, whereas the latter want people to *read* them — or even *believe* in them.

In a way, the American political landscape mirrors our publishing landscape. Namely, a case could be made that political power is concentrated among the wealthiest 5 percent of our nation, even as the remaining 95 percent dominate in numbers.

Whereas in American politics, wealth yields a disproportionate amount of political power, in American publishing, capital yields a disproportionate amount of market control.

The great myth of American publishing is that it is controlled by aesthetic values.

This might have been the case years ago when the Random House of Bennett Cerf pushed to publish a novel which opens with the line "Stately, plump Buck Mulligan came from the stairhead, bearing a bowl of lather on which a mirror and a razor lay crossed."

It is not the case when its contemporary neoliberal instantiation outbid itself to publish the next novel of the author whose first novel began with the line "At the first gesture of morning, flies began stirring."

Yes, outbid *itself.*

Which is either like tripping over your own shoelaces — or tripping over the outstretched foot of the editor in the cubicle next to you.

The novel that got Random House tripping over their own feet was a first novel whose hardback sales in the late 1990s had exceeded 1.6 million copies.

Such things capture the attention of market-driven corporate publishers — "At first gesture of a market, calculators began stirring."

Based on what is said to have been a one-page proposal, one of Random House's 60 imprints, divisions, and groups offered an advance of over five million dollars to the author.

However, not to be outdone by one of their co-division rivals (and after McTeague rolled over in his grave), another division of Random House offered over *eight* million dollars.

The name of the novelist and whether the advance paid off for Random House are irrelevant to the conditions which they exemplify: the effects of neoliberal-based decision-making in the publishing world.[9]

A climate of publishing where the advance for a second novel exceeds by eight times the annual publishing revenue of 95 percent of American publishing houses—or roughly 60,000 publishers—presents a sad state for American letters.

If Random House was willing to offer the author of this second novel an eight-million-dollar advance, one can only imagine how much they were willing to invest in marketing the book. For example, in generating mainstream media interest in this author and their work as "essential summer reading" or buying national distribution support to ensure that "the next great American novel" is available for purchase in your local Walmart or Borders.

To say that hearing this book news over and over again in major media outlets, and seeing this book prominently displayed in every big box bookstore chain in America doesn't affect reading habits and impact sales would be naïve.

However, to say that it *fashions* reading/buying behavior would be more accurate.

American publishing in the age of neoliberalism is controlled by markets and calculators—not publisher demographics or aesthetic value. The more that mega-publishers invest in large market fiction and avoid small market fiction, the more the aesthetic innovation and narrative diversity will flourish among small presses.

And, of course, in the era of neoliberalism the big corporations have the ear of policy makers in changing the market to suit their needs. Not to mention the increasing "professionalization" of the industry which values agents over writers.

In the neoliberal climate of corporate publishing, it is not surprising to see a rise in small press publishers devoted to diversity and innovation—and a widening of the financial gap between small presses and corporate publishers.

And even among the big house publishers, one is beginning to see some distance among them.

Of the 4,000 publishers that have annual sales over one million dollars, less than 20 percent have annual sales over $50 million — and only 12 have annual sales over $150 million.

And among the Big 12, the twelfth largest has only one-tenth of the sales of the largest.

This kind of concentration of publishing capital entails a type of power akin to that held by the Bush and Kennedy families in American politics.

Again, that Random House *alone* sells more books than 76,500 U.S. trade and mass-market publishers *combined* is as much a cause for celebration among writers as is the fact that McDonald's serves more hamburgers than any other restaurant in America.

So, would you like to supersize that novel?

18

WRITING FOR RCA

In 1932, when Random House sought to legally publish *Ulysses* in the United States, it was Bennett Cerf, one of the co-owners of the publishing house that contacted James Joyce. After receiving Joyce's consent to publish, Cerf had a copy of the book sent from Paris to New York, and then arranged for customs officials to seize it at the docks so that he could prepare for a court battle over it. Ten minutes after Judge John Woolsey of the New York district court delivered his verdict that the book was not legally obscene, Clef had the typesetters at Random House working on Joyce's masterpiece.

To many, Cerf, who co-founded Random House in 1925 with Donald Klopfer, and whose press also published Sinclair Lewis, William Faulkner, Gertrude Stein, Truman Capote, and John O'Hara, is one of the heroes of American publishing. Though Joyce's book had been published some ten years earlier by Sylvia Beach's Shakespeare & Co. in Paris, because it was banned in the English-speaking world, Joyce did not profit from it until Clef stood up for it in court. The legal publication of *Ulysses* by Random House finally allowed Joyce — rather than the *Ulysses* bootleggers — to reap more of the financial rewards of its publication.

In hindsight — and from a less flattering perspective — moves like Clef's acquisition of *Ulysses* and the building of a top-tier list of authors by his press can be seen as laying the groundwork for the rise of contemporary corporate publishing.

That is to say, it foreshadows a publishing world where Simon & Schuster is a subsidiary of CBS, and HarperCollins is owned by News Corporation, the multimedia conglomerate founded by Rupert Murdoch; where twelve publishers out of approximately 85,000 account for almost two-thirds of U.S. trade and mass-market book sales; where 90 percent of active publishers account for less that 10 percent of total book sales; where Random House alone accounts for over 13 percent of all U.S. book sales and has world-wide sales revenues of almost 2.4 *billion* dollars; and where Random House *alone* sells more books than 76,500 U.S. trade and mass-market publishers *combined*.

How did this happen? How did it come to be that a few publishing corporations now control the majority of book sales in the United States? And what does it mean for the 76,500 "small" presses that reside in the shadows of corporate publishing giants like Random House?

In the case of Random House, by the 1950s, the co-owners began to worry about what would happen to the company if one of them died. Cerf said, "Donald and I knew that the real value of the company had increased each year, but nobody knew by how much." He continued, "If its value was too high, how could the survivor afford to buy the other half, and how could the widow of the one who died raise enough cash to pay the estate tax?"

Worries about the future of their company if one of them died led to Cerf and Klopfer to sell 30 percent of their stock to the public in 1959. "From then on," writes Cerf, "we were publishing with one eye and watching our stock with the other." "Instead of working for yourself and doing what you damn please, willing to risk a loss on something you want to do, if you're any kind of honest man, you feel a responsibility to your stockholders," wrote Cerf.

Going public opened the door to expanding the business, which it did shortly after going public by acquiring both Knopf and Pantheon. Soon Time-Life took an interest in merging with Random House — a deal which eventually fell through when it became clear that the U.S. Department of Justice would most likely oppose the merger on anti-trust grounds. In 1965, however, Random House was sold to RCA for 40 million dollars, at which point Cerf stepped down as president.

Cerf said they accepted RCA's offer because "it was one of the great corporations of the country."

And who would disagree? The sale allowed one of RCA's writers, Truman Capote, to become one of its recording artists, releasing an album of readings from scenes from *In Cold Blood* in 1966.

By the time Random House was acquired by RCA, it was a much different publishing house from the one where Cerf wrote to Joyce about publishing *Ulysses*.

Further acquisitions and mergers followed including its sale in 1980 from RCA to S.I. Newhouse, a wealthy businessman and owner of a range of television stations, newspapers, and magazines, to its sale again in 1998 to Bertelsmann.

Today, "Random House" consists of over 60 imprints, divisions, and groups in the U.S. and UK alone.

Oh yeah, and I almost forgot: one of them is called "Random House."

Random House is a perfect example of the effects of the rise of a ruthless new form of market capitalism that scholars have been warning us about for years. "It reifies and glorifies the reign of what are called the financial markets," comments the French sociologist and philosopher, Pierre Bourdieu, "in other words the return to a kind of radical capitalism, with no other law than that of maximum profit, and unfettered capitalism without any disguise, but rationalized, pushed to the limit of its economic efficacy by the introduction of modern forms of domination, such as 'business administration,' and techniques of manipulation, such as market research and advertising."

This form of unfettered capitalism, says Bourdieu, "sets up as the norm of all practices, and therefore as ideal rules, the real regularities of the economic world abandoned to its own logic, the so-called laws of the market." While it has its roots in the classical liberal economic theories of Adam Smith and David Ricardo, it is more closely associated with the neoliberalism of Friedrich Hayek and Milton Friedman. As a consequence, it has resulted in, among other things, the rise of authoritarianism, the suspension of civil liberties, the privatization of public spaces, and the upward distribution of wealth.

As Henry Giroux succinctly puts it, "neoliberalism is an ideology and politics buoyed by the spirit of a market fundamentalism that subordinates the art of democratic politics to the rapacious laws of a market economy that expands its reach to include all aspects of social life within the dictates and values of market-driven society."

There is no doubt that the publishing industry has been forever changed by the rise of neoliberalism. What though does the rise of neoliberalism and corporate publishing mean for the 76,500 "small" presses that reside in the shadows of corporate publishing giants like Random House? Is their position any different than it was before Random House went public and was purchased by RCA? And what is the effect of the rise of neoliberalism in the publishing of fiction writing, reading habits, and bookselling?

Is writing for Cerf and Klopfer any different than writing for Rupert Murdoch or RCA? Discuss.

19

THE MEDIUM IS THE QUESTION

Would you rather read a book review in print or as a searchable document on a website? How about delivered to you online via email or Facebook? Or tweeted to your mobile device through your Twitter account?

For most readers, these are not difficult questions.

As Herodotus said (quoting Pindar), "Custom is king."

If you're accustomed to receiving the *American Book Review* on paper, then chances are you'll prefer to keep it that way.

If you are more inclined to use new media, then an online or social media option will be more appealing.

In the best of all possible worlds, print access would mirror digital access, and everyone would be satisfied.

But contemporary publishers don't live in the best of all possible worlds—they're just looking to survive.

In an age where publishers feel pressure from new technologies, we witness a radically diminished amount of print coverage devoted to book reviews. Many newspapers have either ceased publishing book reviews or dramatically reduced the number of reviews they print.

Part of the reason for this decline is that readers increasingly prefer to get their reviews (and news) online.

As a consequence, fewer advertising dollars from book publishers are directed to support print media review outlets, giving newspapers little financial incentive to justify continued review publication.

Some papers have made the move to new media with their tongues implanted firmly in cheeks. *Washington Post* reviewer Ron Charles takes on the persona of an outrageously over-the-top host in the spirit of Stephen Colbert in his "Totally Hip Book Review."

In a review of Danielle Evans' latest collection of short stories, Charles wears meat on his head *à la* Lady Gaga as proof of his "hipness" and derides letter writers who "cling to outmoded standards of the past" such as copy editing and fact checking. However fun and funny these clips may be, is sarcasm really the best response to the pressures put on publications to convert to new media formats?

For a publication like *ABR*, founded in the print-only era of the 1970s and forged through more than thirty years of continuous paper and ink production, the question of online-only publication is a more complicated one.

ABR is not about to discontinue book reviews because reviewing books is our primary mission—a mission that remains as relevant today as it was in 1977: to provide a review venue for books that are largely ignored by the mainstream media.

Nevertheless, the truth of the matter is that the reach of our reviews *is* far more extensive online than in print. Moreover, if we were founded today, factors of reach, access, and production cost might have created an online publication from the outset.

Book reviewing is caught between its printed past and its digital future. We know that online publication has its benefits, but are torn by our *customary* ties to print media.

As reviewers of products that are based in print and paper (the books themselves), we are uncomfortable with the thought of giving up print media entirely — though we recognize that for the most part print review coverage is but a nostalgic nod to our past. But as people increasingly turn to Kindles and other electronic devices to read books, the product itself is turning away from paper—shouldn't the product review head the same direction?

Without paper and ink, *ABR* becomes something different—but is it still the same publication?

What separates reviews in *ABR* from reviews in another publication or for a blog is not the medium, but the *affiliation*.

ABR reviews—like those from publications such as *The New York Times Book Review* or the *London Review of Books*—carry critical authority. This affiliation was established not on the basis of its media (print), but rather by years of publication of reviews that have shaped the history of American innovative and small-press literature.

ABR is the same publication online as it is in print.

It is not, as some might contend, legitimated by its materiality; rather, its continuous media evolution is evidence of its relevancy to a new generation of readers and reviewers.

For those who built their careers in the print age, there is still some anxiety about seeing their writing in cyberspace; there exists the feeling that it is not "real" or "legitimate" until it can be read on paper. These readers and reviewers are navigating the same transition in letters and publication that confronts the rest of the publishing industry. Still, print remains a temporary condition for reviewing, and one that will be a past chapter in the history of publishing within a decade or two.

As readers of this publication know, for a little over a year, we offered six to eight reviews in each issue exclusively online. The feature, called "LineOnLine," ran from our January 2008 through March of 2009. However, we discontinued LineOnLine after we reached an agreement with Johns Hopkins University's *Project Muse* to make all of our reviews available online commencing January 2010.

But this still leaves us with a gap—and a bit of a dilemma.

While we plan in the years to come to make the entire thirty-year print run of *American Book Review* available online through Project Muse—including the reviews that have to this point only been available through our website—what do we do, if anything, with the reviews that have never been in "print?"

We thought that with this issue we might turn a bit nostalgic and offer you a selection of the reviews that we published online only. It is called the "Best of LineOnLine," and the reviews that were chosen for the issue foreground and celebrate the quality of all of the excellent reviews that were featured online.

The cult of the printed word is going to take a while before it disappears—particularly for those of my generation and before who have grown accustomed to seeing their writing on paper.

I must confess that I still eagerly wait for the print version of my publications—even if they have already appeared online. And while I know that their online presence far exceeds their print reach, I also know that seeing my article in print produces a different feeling than seeing it digitally.

I'm sure that this is the same for others of my generation as well—the lot of us who came of age producing manuscripts on typewriters and photocopiers, rather than laptops and wireless connections.

To fulfill *ABR*'s mission of championing and reviewing books neglected by other outlets, we will continue to reach audiences who find us online and those who read only the printed publication. It is in this spirit that we offer our print readers the opportunity to see some of the excellent reviews they may have missed in our online offerings.

20

DO ANDROIDS DREAM OF ANNA KARENINA?

In an age where the classic literary masterpieces have lost their cache, who would have thought that a book series based in the classics of Western literature would be a publishing mega-success?

Note: these classics are not your great-grandfather's classics, but no one seems to be complaining.

In 2009, Quirk Books launched Quirk Classics, a series of books which aims — in the words of their mission statement—"To enhance *classic* novels with pop culture phenomena." The books in this series intermingle "the work of classic literary masters with new scenes of horrific creatures and gruesome action."

Fortunately for the publishers, all of the works they blend are already in the public domain. Consequently, Quirk is free to publish them in whatever form they see fit—or perhaps more accurately, whatever form they see sales.

And they do.

The first volume in the series, *Pride and Prejudice and Zombies*, released in April of 2009, has become wildly popular. According to the *Guardian*, in a little over a year, over 50,000 copies have been sold in the UK—and 600,000 copies in the U.S.

In addition, a film version starring and produced by Natalie Portman is already in the works.

A few weeks ago, the latest installment in the series, *Android Karenina*, was released. According to the promotional materials for the book, "As in the original novel, our story follows two relationships: the tragic adulterous romance of Anna Karenina and Count Alexei Vronsky, and the much more hopeful marriage of Nikolai Levin and Kitty Shcherbatskaya." However, as with the other novels in the series, the book then takes a decidedly postmodern turn by having the four "live in a steampunk-inspired 19th century of mechanical butlers, extraterrestrial-worshiping cults, and airborne debutante balls."

Leo Tolstoy believed that one could not add or delete sentences from his novels without a resultant change in meaning. One can safely assume that deleting large sections of the novel and replacing them with text from contemporary writer Ben H. Winters would probably horrify him.

But even though Tolstoy would not see the blending of his classic as preserving in some way the meaning of his novel, others might.

The contemporary critic Hans-Georg Gadamer believed that meaning is never exhausted by the intentions of the author—even if the author was Tolstoy. For Gadamer, interpretation of literary works from the past necessarily involves a dialogue with the present. One might argue then that "mashing-up" of classic voices from the past with ones from the present is the kind of dialogue that epitomizes the fusion of horizons that Gadamer believes is typical of productive understanding.

By bringing Tolstoy into dialogue with present concerns and interests, the Quirk Classics are literally doing the cultural work necessary for understanding the past.

Regardless of how these mash-up novels square up with their originals, they are bringing an entirely new audience to authors like Jane Austen and Tolstoy. What is also clear is that this new audience wants more of the present—and less of the past—in these classics.

For example, the first novel in the series, *Pride and Prejudice and Zombies*, was 85 percent vintage Austen. Readers however complained that this was too much

Austen — that they wanted more zombies in the novel. Let the monsters multiply.

Subsequent volumes correct this by straying further from the original.

Sense and Sensibility and Sea Monsters (2009), for example, maintains the plot lines of the original as well as many of the more well-known passages, but also replaces much more of the original text than *Pride and Prejudice and Zombies*. Estimates put over 40 percent of this mash-up novel as new material, which *Publishers Weekly* says replaces vintage Austen dialogue with "monsters, vulgarity, and violence."

Now that we know that people are interested in recombined classics, and that there is a legitimate way to make them dialogue in a significant way with present concerns and interests, why not expand efforts to mash-up the classics, particularly if we still believe that they are the centerpiece of a liberal education?

Harvard University President Charles W. Eliot claimed over a century ago that "anyone who read" with "devotion" the five feet of books that he selected would eventually become as educated as a college graduate. Eliot had no doubt that the person who devoutly read his Harvard Classics, "even if he could spare but fifteen minutes a day for reading," would be able to achieve a good substitute for a liberal education.

One problem though: fifteen minutes with Harvard Classics like William Harvey's *On the Motion of the Heart and Blood in Animals* (1628) and Thomas Hobbes' *Leviathan* (1651) is little motivation for the average reader.

What if though we mashed-up all of the Harvard Classics and republished them as the New Harvard Classics? Would reading *Leviathan and Sea-Monsters* or *On the Motion of the Heart and Blood in Animals and Vampires* for fifteen minutes a day be tantamount to a liberal education? Or, perhaps, a *posthuman* education?

Not only do "mash-up" books have the potential to renew interest in the classics, but reading them is arguably a way to a respectable — albeit quirky — posthuman education.

21

CRIMINAL EDITORS

Negative reviews are an editor's bogeyman. Few things are potentially scarier than the spectre of a negative review published in their journal. But just like bad dreams and bad books, negative reviews are a part of life.

In a recent conversation with fellow editors, I was taken aback when my peers adamantly argued that negative reviews should not be published. Their thought was, since so few books are reviewed compared to the total number of books published, why waste valuable review space and time reviewing bad books? Why publish a negative review when one could just as well publish a positive review of another book?

If their logic works, then our previous issue devoted to discussing bad books — which in one sense became a compendium of negative reviews — was the height of wastefulness.

And based on the vehement response to the issue in the *Los Angeles Times, Guardian* (UK), *The New Yorker, Huffington Post, Inside Higher Education,* and other media outlets, my colleagues' insights about negative reviews seem to gain credibility.

There is no doubt that publishing a negative review is more difficult than publishing a positive review. The potential discontent of the book's author, the author's friends, and the author's publisher can be intimidating. It's no wonder that most reviewers suffer from what the Greeks called *akrasia*, or weakness of the will, when they are faced with writing anything less than glowing about a book.

The vast majority of book reviews tend to be positive rather than negative not because there are more good books out there than bad ones, but because the possible effects of negative reviewing are much less appealing than the effects of positive reviewing. Reviewers today err toward the side of sympathy — or as Gail Pool calls it "faint praise" — in their reviews when they feel themselves reacting negatively toward a book. Some even refuse to write a review if they feel it will be negative. But do these current practices really help the cause of book reviewing? I'm not so sure.

If book reviewing is to distance itself from the perception that it is simply a promotional service for the publishing industry, then it needs to engage in legitimate practices. The task of the reviewer should not be to prejudge their reviews, but rather to be open to following them through to the natural conclusion of the aesthetic and intellectual interaction resulting from the act of reading. To write only about the fruitful ends of these readings is like a restaurant critic who only tells us about the good restaurants in which she's eaten.

While it does make sense for editors to assign to reviewers books that they have reason to believe are good books or that will have potential appeal to their readers, it does not follow from this that the reviews of these books will always be glowing. The question of what reviewers should do when they find themselves reacting negatively to a book that has been assigned to them for review though seems fairly obvious: write the review. And this negative review should be subject to the same quality protocols as a review that is positive, which is to say, if it is the result of an honest engagement with the book by a competent reviewer, then it must be published.

Or should it? A recent event is making editors wary. *The Chronicle of Higher Education* reports that an NYU law professor is being sued for publishing a less-than-glowing review of a book on international criminal courts. The journal editor "refused to remove the review but offered to publish a reply." The book author contends that the review is libelous and harms her reputation and academic credentials. In my estimation, it is the lawsuit that will do the most harm to her reputation.

As an editor, I face both positive and negative reviews on a regular basis. The backbone of book reviewing rests on reviewers competent to handle the books they have been assigned and a level of honesty regarding their responsiveness to the text before them. Reviewers with an ax to grind or a preconceived notion of what they are going to say before they even read the book are to be avoided. However, if a fair assessment of a text results in a negative consequence, then it is the obligation of the reviewer to report it and of the editor to publish it. Anything less compromises the integrity of the review process.

Book reviewing as a criminal act? The real crime here is not that an editor published a competent albeit negative review, but rather that a book author would try to silence a reviewer who is offering his opinion.

22

THE BOOK LADDER

The great chain of being is one of the most beautiful images in Western philosophy. Atop this universal hierarchy sits God and just below Him the angels. Humans are lower than angels in the great chain of being but higher than animals. At the bottom of the hierarchy are plants, followed by minerals. All of creation has a place in this "natural ladder."

The great chain of being gives order and meaning to everything in the universe. Things closer to the top of the ladder have higher powers and more responsibility, whereas things lower have less. While books are not part of the traditional great chain of being, I've often thought that there is a parallel to the great chain of being in the book world.

The divine authors of the modernist and postmodernist world would include Samuel Beckett, Jorge Luis Borges, and James Joyce. The angelic order would include John Barth, Donald Barthelme, Roland Barthes, Italo Calvino, William H. Gass, and Vladimir Nabokov. Among the human, all-too-human, would be Kathy Acker, William S. Burroughs, Robert Coover, Julio Cortázar, Don DeLillo, Raymond Federman, Alain Robbe-Grillet, Ronald Sukenick, and Kurt Vonnegut. At the level of minerals would exist all of those writers who either reject or avoid the postmodern aesthetic, namely anyone with things like round characters or linear plot lines.

The higher powers of writers like Beckett and Borges are revealed in the many ways in which their work is reflected in that of others. As residents of the top of the book ladder, they cannot produce anything but perfection — there is no such thing as a bad book by Beckett or bad story by Borges. The responsibility and power of their books is to set the highest aspirations for books. Whereas bad books are at least possible within the angelic order, and they are probable in the human order, among the divine order, they are simply inconceivable. At the lowest order, bad books are expected.

Some people might want to think of the book ladder in terms not only of the content of books, but also their material condition. This would mean taking into account the fact that a signed first edition of Joyce's *Ulysses* is worth more than a highlighted, tattered, used mass-market edition. Material considerations like this might also be taken into account in considerations of the great chain of book being.

I was first struck by this idea many years ago when I worked in one of the oldest and largest used bookstores in the United States. Established in the late nineteenth century, the bookstore must have contained at least half a million used books — though I don't think anyone really knew how many books were in the store (while we were asked to count the books in the store once a year, no one took the task very seriously).

The store itself was organized like the great chain of being.

The top floor — the one closest to the heavens — contained the most valuable books. Books here were treated with the utmost care. If the book had a dust jacket, then it was carefully preserved from wear with a protective plastic dust jacket. Glass cases kept rows of leather bound tomes and signed first editions away from the grubby hands.

Each book on the top floor contained a typed slip of paper with details about the book.

Each was also carefully priced and catalogued. None of these books were overlooked or forgotten. In the world of used books, these were the "good" books.

As one descended from this top floor to the lower floors the value of the books also decreased (as well as the amount of attention placed on them). Whereas on the top floor one might find a first edition Ernest Hemingway, on the balcony—which literally housed tens of thousands of works of fiction—one could always find scores of dusty book club editions or dog-eared paperback works by Papa.

Whereas the ground floor contained a few new books and some remainders, it gave little indication of what lay below it—book hell.

The lowest floor of the bookstore was a damp and dark rock-walled basement lined with row after row of nine-foot-high bookshelves. Here, one could not only find a copy of every issue of *National Geographic* ever printed, but also row after row of broken sets of encyclopedias and forgotten books of every shape and kind. Books from the basement were generally bought by the foot for the purposes of lining movie sets. One step away from the dumpster, their main virtue was the symmetry of their spines rather than the stories they told or the value of their dust jackets.

The buyer was an older gentleman who ate tuna out of a can for lunch and would buy books by the box. As far as I could tell, though he had never actually read a book in his life, he was the most proficient person I've met at distinguishing a good book from a bad book. Just as one can distinguish good tuna from bad tuna by its smell, he too could distinguish a good book from a bad book by its . . . I don't know what, though smell is as good an answer as any.

He'd sort the books according to value, and send by dumbwaiter the potentially most valuable ones to the top floor, and the nearly valueless ones either to the basement (where they literally were dumped in piles on the floor) or to the two-books-for-a-dollar bins outside of the store. The others all had prices determined by *gestalt* penciled by him inside the front cover.

When I think of bad books I can't seem to get away from these two book mappings of the great chain of being. I have no doubt that bad books are relative to the eye of the beholder. Rocks on my great chain of being, such as all of the novels of Sinclair Lewis, are probably angels on someone's ladder. After all, someone did award him the Nobel Prize in literature. And I still have a couple of the odd volumes from St. Thomas Aquinas' multi-volume *Summa Theologica* that I dug out of bookstore hell many years ago, which I now find ironic given that he was one of the most influential exponents of the great chain of being.

23

POSTFEDERMAN

As we mourn the recent death of longtime *ABR* contributing editor Raymond Federman, we also attempt to fully appreciate the scope of his achievement. This task turns out to be easier said than done.[10]

Over the past thirty or so years, his fiction has been the subject of a good deal of scholarship in multiple languages. However, in spite of this wealth of attention, the scope of Federman's achievements has yet to be fully recognized by the academic community.

One of the reasons for this lack of recognition stems from the ways in which Federman's novels have been categorized. In the U.S., Federman's work has most commonly been connected with a group of writers that brought "new life" to American fiction in the wake of pronouncements of the death of the novel in the late 1960s. His revitalizing, innovative peers include Donald Barthelme, Robert Coover, Steve Katz, Clarence Major, Ishmael Reed, Gilbert Sorrentino, and Ronald Sukenick. While the identification of Federman with this group of writers is accurate and not without its merits, in the longer run, it has served to exclude or marginalize his work from other — and arguably even more significant — contexts.

Far too many accounts treat Federman as merely

a member of a small group of writers who created through narrative experimentation a pioneering body of "metafiction" or "postmodern" American literature. Though relevant to those interested in tracing the development of American letters, such accounts neglect the range of his contributions to both the contemporary critical and world literature canons — contributions that scholars are only just beginning to recognize and explore in detail.

His recent passing provides a good opportunity for us to reconsider an amazingly creative and daring thinker whose work is significant to not just considerations of the development of innovative fiction in America, but potentially to a number of distinct disciplines, and established and emerging critical discourses. These critical discourses include translation studies, Jewish studies, Holocaust studies, bilingual studies, Beckett studies, cultural studies, philosophy of language, postmodern theory, body criticism, critical theory, identity studies, narrative theory, trauma studies, philosophy of literature, and autobiography theory, among others. It should be noted that the disciplines represented here are far wider than just English, the standard province of Federman scholarship. They include philosophy, comparative literature, foreign languages, history, linguistics, and sociology.

Federman's emphasis on voice over character, his playfulness with identity, his use of numerous alter egos, and his investigation of writing in the shadow of the Holocaust make his work a rich source for those invested in contemporary cultural studies and literary theory. His writing is a powerful voice in an age that has redirected attention to the cultural, historical, and political powers of fictional discourse.

Federman, who passed away last month at the age of 81, is probably more relevant now than ever. The discourses necessary for appreciating the range and depth of his achievement — discourses such as cultural studies and literary theory — have only recently reached full maturation and institutional acceptance. It is easy to see this when one recalls that when Federman's early masterpiece *Double or Nothing* came out in 1971, "new criticism" was still considered "radical" by most English departments — departments which rarely if ever considered contemporary fiction as worthy of scholarship. One must also remember that Federman's writing becomes more significant in a critical climate charged by discussions of the relationship between culture, history, language, and narrative. While these discussions were forming in the seventies, they were still far from maturation.

The seventies saw the rise of elegant and close structuralist, deconstructive, Marxist, and psychoanalytic interpretations of literature. Increasingly, emphasis on the libidinal, political, and social and/or social nature of signification would come to challenge the very profession of literary studies by laying the foundation for cultural studies. It is in the context of this post-literary or post-literature climate that Federman's fictions can be best understood.

While Federman's writing is an amazing resource to engage through structuralist and/or poststructuralist theoretical contexts, it becomes even more powerful when considered through theory sensitive to the personal, social, and political dimensions of interpretation. As the eighties saw the emergence of race, class, and gender studies eclipsing the more formalist theories of the literary which dominated the late seventies, Federman's work, with its attendant foregrounding of issues of culture, history, and identity, began to garner more attention from critics.

Today, however, in a critical climate that is highly eclectic and globally situated, Federman's work is probably more powerful than ever. Why? Because like Federman, contemporary critics are less concerned with distinguishing "literature" from "theory" and "fiction" from "reality," and more interested in discussing the identity, consumption, regulation, and production of texts within culture(s). Theory and criticism have finally caught up with Federman and his self-reflexive fiction.

Consequently, Federman's own approach to fiction and criticism might be best viewed as "posttheoretical" and "postfictional." Neither he nor his writing can be contained by any one discipline or discourse. Federman's work continually has a way of sliding quickly into other areas of critical concern just at the point when one feels as though one has captured it. Federman is—and is not—a theorist. Is—and is not—a fictionalist. Is—and is not—a philosopher (of language). Federman's writing is at home both within the context of contemporary theory and against it—both within the frame of fictionality and against it. As such, in many ways, he is our premier "posttheorist" and "postfictionalist." And the sheer energy, lyricism, and humor of his work make for quite a ride.

24

SAFE BOOKS

Once upon a time, in a land not so far away, there was a place where children were not allowed to read old books. Far and wide it was decreed that the books that parents and grandparents had lovingly held and enjoyed were thought to contain a secret poison. Librarians scrambled to discard early editions of Dr. Seuss and Maurice Sendak while booksellers emptied their shelves of pop-ups. Box after box of old copies of *The Cat in the Hat* (1957), *Charlie and Chocolate Factory* (1964), and the Hardy Boys mysteries were shredded to protect the children from danger.

A fairy story? Think again.

The United States Consumer Product Safety Commission (CPSC) recently maintained that children's books printed before 1986 *may* contain unsafe levels of lead. So as not to endanger children twelve years of age and under, the Consumer Product Safety Improvement Act (CPSIA) urges libraries to remove these books from their collections until such time as it can be determined that they are not a health risk to children.

"We're talking about tens of millions of copies of children's books that are perfectly safe," said Emily Sheketoff, executive director of the American Library Association's Washington office. "I wish a reasonable, rational person would just say, 'This is stupid. What are we doing?'"

This *is* stupid. What *are* we doing?

A CPSC spokesperson tried to temper the spread of anger over this law. Scott Wolfson said that books printed in 1986 are safe for libraries to lend out. However, until the books in public and school libraries printed before 1986 are tested for lead, steps should be taken "to ensure that the children aren't accessing those books." Said Wolfson, "Steps can be taken to put them in an area on hold until the Consumer Product Safety Commission can give further guidance."

One library roped off its children's section. Another covered its children's books with a tarp, awaiting further word from Product Safety.

Then again, let's give them the benefit of the doubt. After all, these libraries may be from a part of the country where children *eat* books rather than *read* them.

The CPSIA was passed to protect children from becoming poisoned by lead that is sometimes found in toys. The federal law was a response to a spate of toy recalls. It has been interpreted by the Consumer Product Safety Commission to include books.

But testing the tens of millions of books in the more than 116,000 public and school libraries that were printed before 1986 is simply unreasonable.

While there is absolutely *no* evidence that handling these books will result in lead poisoning in children, perhaps we should put warning labels on these old books akin to ones that the surgeon general has on cigarette packs.

Or start a campaign warning children of the danger of eating books—with Cookie Monster as evidence of the perils of page consumption.

But I wondered—just how many books would a kid have to eat before she got sick?

My unscientific opinion is: just one would do the trick. If my eight-year-old ate one of his Magic Tree House books, he'd be greener than the tree house.

However, lest I mislead you about the dangers of eating books, I sought out the opinion of my biology colleague from Russia—a land where there is no law prohibiting children from reading old books.

Here is what I found out:

EPA limits lead in drinking water to 15 ug/L. While I don't know precisely how much lead is in pre-1985 printer's ink, let's just say it's 5,000 ppm (wet), like in the old style lead paint. Let's also assume a rate of 0.05 g (wet) printer's ink per page. Based on these assumptions: (5 mg/g)*(0.05 g/page) = 0.25 mg/page or 250 ug/page, about as much as contained in 5 gallons of EPA-approved water. That is, you would receive this much, if you actually ate those books. Absorption through skin? Pretty much nil: let's assume, it takes 10,000 reads to wear ink off a page. Let's say, all the lead that wears off goes into the child. The total exposure would be 0.025 ug/page. From the toxicological standpoint, reading 600 pages would provide the same lead exposure as drinking a quart of water considered safe by the EPA. I sure don't know of anyone who reads 600 pages in one day, but people do drink this much.

Maybe Cookie Monster needs to warn kids that consuming books is about as dangerous as drinking water.

In all seriousness, eating books is rare and usually only occurs in children with pica, a medical condition. If it were as common as eating ice cream, then a law like this would make sense. But as it is not common, its only effect is an assault on children's literacy and book culture.

Old books provide an important gateway for children's literacy. Many libraries cannot afford to replace their old books. Many literacy programs depend on the use of older books. Asking these programs to remove older books from their collections in the current economy is a travesty.

Used booksellers, who are already struggling to stay afloat, take yet another hit with this law. Half Price Books, for example, has moved thousands of pre-1985 children's books to warehouses. Another used bookseller disposed of $4,000 of vintage children's books; yet another lost half of her inventory.

Moreover, there are also millions of children's books printed after 1985 that may also be lost because they only include copyright or publication dates, not print dates.

While protecting children from lead poisoning is extremely important, to do so by asking librarians, booksellers, literacy groups, parents, and children to avoid old books is absurd. This law is especially harmful to those who, for financial reasons, depend on old books for the education of their children. Not every parent can afford to purchase new books; not every library can replace its old books; not every bookmobile can be selective as to the books it offers to children.

This law adds to the growing list of challenges to book culture. From library censorship and budget cuts to the rising cost for new books and declining numbers of used bookstores, book culture is undergoing an extreme makeover in America.

We need to satisfy kids' *real appetite* for books and reading: to feed their curiosity, their imaginations, and their search for knowledge.

Children really are hungry for books. Let's make sure that across the land, we keep putting books in kids' hands (while endeavoring to keep them out of their stomachs).

25

FICTION'S FUTURE
with Tom Williams[11]

MR. MCGUIRE: *I just want to say one word to you –
just one word.*
BEN: *Yes sir.*
MR. MCGUIRE: *Are you listening?*
BEN: *Yes I am.*
MR. MCGUIRE: *Plastics.*
BEN: *Exactly how do you mean?*
MR. MCGUIRE: *There's a great future in plastics
Think about it. Will you think about it?*
BEN: *Yes I will.*
MR. MCGUIRE: *Shh! Enough said. That's a deal.*

It's difficult *not* to recall these lines when reading through the extra-ordinary discussion of fiction's future that follows.

It's difficult not to see some neophyte *ABR* character akin to Dustin Hoffman's "Ben" standing poolside, regaled one by one by our entire group of respondents to the question, "Define Fiction's Future in a word, a quotation, or a sentence."

Think about it: Robert Coover saunters by, offering unsolicited advice to some young, as yet unpublished writer. In walks Charles Johnson next, followed by Chitra Banerjee Divakaruni, then Dagoberto Gilb.

Sure, the figures and their words change, but *ABR*'s Ben still tries valiantly to put it all together—or better yet, tries to pull it all apart.

He both wants and does not want to hear about the future from others, wants and does not want an informed opinion concerning fiction's future, and wants and does not want to decide for himself.

Reflecting on these lines it's difficult not to conclude that fiction's future is not just one word.

"Are you listening?"

"Yes I am."

"Electronics"

"Exactly how do you mean?"

"There's a great future for fiction in electronics. Think about it. Will you think about it?"

"Yes I will."

"Shh! Enough said. That's a deal."

And think about it if you will. A word, a quotation, or a sentence is all you need. Anything more starts to become prescriptive, cutting off the imagination of the reader, and short-circuiting metonymic leaps of fictional faith.

Catch a sickness unto death with statements like "THERE IS NO FUTURE FOR FICTION."

Think Wittgenstein-like: "The future of fiction is to chase the fly out of the bottle."

Or Nietszchean. Any aphorism will do. "Fiction's future: it's all made up" anyway.

"Think about it. Will *you* think about it?"

While Ben didn't ask Mr. McGuire about the future (he volunteered it), we did ask over three hundred writers, critics, and scholars about the future of fiction. Responses varied from one word (James Whorton, Jr.'s "C-SPAN," Stephen J. Burn's "Neural," and Vanessa Place's "Conceptualism"), to a quote (Brian Evenson quotes Glenn Gould and Samuel Beckett, and Lance Olsen quotes Franz Kafka and Jerzy Kosinski), to a sentence—and sometimes many more (hey, just in case we're paying by the word, right?).

Sylvia Watanabe must have been dialed into our *The Graduate*-influenced wavelength, for she wrote "Plastics. The future is in plastics." And you know what's said about great minds thinking alike. As well, a host of responses we couldn't predict came in, amazingly diverse, rich, and suggestive. While many of the responses gravitate around the electronic revolution in writing, many others go in entirely different directions.

The willingness of so many to grapple with this beastly task attests to the fact that many of our participants are serious about fiction's future.

They want to see what happens next.

They want to make it happen, one might say.

And what a varied group, too.

You'll find in these responses writers familiar and new to *ABR* readers, writers of great renown and up-and-comers. Additionally, you'll find that there is no consensus. The Focus features as many writers who loathe the coming of Kindle as those who welcome it. Optimism and pessimism stand side by side here. The creative writing workshop finds its champions and its critics. We've got links to web pages. There's even a shout-out for the graphic novel! In short, just as the subject itself, fiction's future, remains unpredictable, we couldn't have foreseen just how fantastic these entries would have been.

We later asked several of our respondents to say just a little more, and the response to that request was equally robust. We limited those essays to 250 words just in case people decided to wax rhapsodic overmuch.

All along, though, what we've had in mind with the Fiction's Future Focus, was that it would only be the first stage of the *conversation*. Increasingly, as we figure out how to take advantage of our web presence, we see such Focuses as a means to generate a discussion that will endure well past the shelf life of a particular issue. And surely some of you meant to get us a word, quotation, or sentence and the deadline slipped your mind. Surely some of you were inexplicably left off the mailing list (sorry) and want to make your voices heard. Some of you who did participate may have witnessed some phenomenon that's changed your prognostication. Whatever the case, we hope that you'll enthusiastically read this Focus, mark the predictions with which you agree and those with which you disagree—and then send us your own response. We're confident that there's much more to be said on this subject—so let's hear it!

26

NEW ONLINE OFFERINGS

Two years ago, we launched a feature in the *American Book Review* called "LineonLine." It first appeared in our January/February 2008 issue, the focus of which was "Dangerous Books." The feature contained six reviews that were published *exclusively* online. Three of the reviews were from our editors — Kevin Prufer, Corrine Robins, and Doug Nufer — and one of the books that we reviewed was a recent novel from a long-time contributing editor, Steve Katz. Publishing some reviews exclusively online did not seem momentous at the time. But it created a new service, and readers wanted more.

Whereas in the past, *ABR* would feature on its website two reviews from our print edition, LineonLine offered readers material different from that which was to be found in the print edition. It gave print readers a reason to go to and use our website — and it gave online readers a reason to seek out a print edition of *ABR*. In addition, the decision to offer reviews exclusively online allowed us to publish many more reviews in each issue without a sizeable, concomitant increase in production cost.

Before the advent of LineonLine, *ABR* had virtually no Internet presence with regard to content. While reproducing a review or two from each issue and making them available on the *ABR* website has been the practice for a number of years now, such reviews decidedly functioned as nothing more than "content teasers" aimed at luring the online world back into the print world: If the digital reader wanted to read more reviews, then the print issue was pretty much her only recourse.

However, after the advent of LineonLine, the amount of *ABR* material available online greatly increased. Now there were not only two digitally reproduced reviews from each print edition, but also six to eight *additional* reviews offered exclusively online. The result would be that those who went to our website over the course of a year (or a volume) would find almost *sixty* book reviews. Given that any one issue of *ABR* contains no more than thirty reviews and that we publish six issues per year, this meant that the equivalent of one-third of our publishing output was now freely available to anyone with access to the Internet. The significance of this cannot be emphasized enough.

Online availability of *ABR* content meant that anyone with access to the Internet could check out *ABR*. Moreover, doing so was no more difficult at home than abroad: A writer in China interested in American fiction, for example, could read *ABR* book reviews just as readily as a writer in Chicago. In fact, one of the great pleasures I have had over the past few years is introducing students, faculty, and individuals across the U.S. and the world to *ABR* via our website. Few things can equal, for example, sharing the world of *ABR* with a group of students in Cairo on a computer in their university library or opening up some of our reviews for faculty in Rio to peruse.

With this increased online access to *ABR*, there has come a demand for even more. Not only do more people have access to the Internet than have subscriptions to *ABR*, but far more people seem to *prefer* digital access over print—especially if there is no cost associated with it. Online access matters are further compounded by the fact that our website includes a link to the covers and tables of contents of *every issue* of *ABR* going back to Volume 1, Number 1. This means that anyone in the world with access to our website can scroll through the table of contents of *any* issue; they can also find out through the "Search" feature on our website, for example, every book from David Foster

Wallace that we have reviewed, and every review written by Joyce Carol Oates for us.

With a distinguished catalogue of reviews and reviewers going back some thirty years, and easy, searchable access to the title of every Focus, review, and article that we have ever published, it should not come as a big surprise that interest in complete digital access to this material has spiked. How then to meet this demand? What should we do?

While the obvious response is to make more material available online, this response is complicated by a number of factors. On the one hand, if *ABR* is offered at no cost online, what need is there to continue with the printed version? But on the other hand, many of our readers and reviewers like the fact that *ABR* is still available in print, and would not like the printed version to succumb to the fate suffered by many other printed book reviews, namely, extinction. An argument could be made that the physical or material features of this publication are as closely linked to its identity as the nature of its content. Another argument could be made that the majority of the long-standing *ABR* readership prefers it as a printed artifact—and that to eliminate the print version would be to disregard the desires of its established readership.

We think that we have found a solution that will both satisfy the needs of many online readers as well as continue to meet the needs of our print readership.

Commencing with our January/February 2010 issue, the complete content of *American Book Review* will be made available online thanks to a publishing agreement with Project MUSE, a project managed by The Johns Hopkins University Press. This agreement will allow our current subscribers to view a complete, online edition of every *ABR* issue *at no extra cost*, in addition to the print version they already receive.

Project MUSE provides full-text access in nearly 2,000 libraries to content from more than 400 journals representing nearly 100 not-for-profit publishers. However, *ABR* is sort of a first for Project MUSE, which has primarily focused on academic journals. Project MUSE director Mary Rose Muccie said in a press release announcing our partnership, "We are excited to be working with the

American Book Review. This journal has broader newsstand appeal than many of the more academic-type journals that we represent." "We only take in a limited number of titles each year," commented Muccie. "We are looking for journals that are well established, well run and have really high-quality standards."

ABR is pleased to join Project MUSE's offering.

As part of our agreement with Project MUSE, we will also begin to put back-issues of the journal online. While this will probably take many years, once completed, it will open up the illustrious history of this publication to many more people.

This agreement with Project MUSE is a major milestone for this publication. It makes *ABR* available in many more libraries around the U.S. as well as abroad, and provides every individual with a print subscription to *ABR* free access to it online. It will prove a great resource for all of our faithful subscribers.

Given then that all of *ABR*'s content will be soon available online, it seems only fitting to send LineonLine to an early grave. Cherish the moment bibliophiles—for it is not very often that a digital publication dies before its printed analogue.

27

ACADEMIC BOOK CULTURE IN TRANSITION

There are a number of signs that the culture of
the book in American higher education is in a period
of transition. Consider the hotly debated question as
to whether the book should remain the "gold standard
for tenure," or, as Lindsay Waters, executive editor for
humanities at Harvard University Press recently asked,
whether the academy should once again make the essay
the standard of achievement. There is also the issue of how
to balance the rising cost of producing and publishing
books with shrinking university press and library budgets.
One solution has been for presses to make sales and
marketability increasingly important factors in publishing
decisions.

Whereas, in the past, an intellectually compelling but
unmarketable book had a good chance of acceptance for
publication, more and more academic presses are rejecting
strong manuscripts for fear of losing money. Accounts of
manuscripts being turned down for financial rather than
scholarly reasons are on the rise. These financial concerns
have led some academic presses to reject the "traditional
linear model" of the editorial process, wherein manuscripts
are first commissioned, then sent to production, and then
sent to sales and marketing. Instead presses are adopting

a "circular model" wherein sales and marketing take on an initial role in decisions about new projects.

Part of the reason for this change in publishing practice is the decrease in library purchasing of university press books; in the past, presses could count on a much higher minimum number of sales than they can today. According to *ARL Statistics, 2005-2006*, from 1986 to 2006 the number of monographs purchased by academic research libraries only rose 1 percent, though monograph expenditures rose 82 percent. However, from just 1986 to 2000, the average number of titles published annually by large American university presses rose from 145 per year to 226. From 1986 to 2006, the number of serials purchased also rose 51 percent and the cost to libraries associated with serial purchasing rose 321 percent. Increases in number of titles published and increases in purchasing costs for both serials and monographs have resulted in less overall purchasing of academic monographs by libraries.

Financial decisions by scholarly presses have a direct effect on the ability of scholars to publish their academic books with university presses, and add to the difficulty of maintaining the book as the gold standard for tenure. If academics expect to be able to publish with scholarly presses for purposes of promotion and tenure, but scholarly presses refuse to publish solid scholarship for financial reasons, then the book crisis in higher education is indeed a vicious circle.

Students too are involved in the transition—the rising cost of textbooks for university courses is a major cause for concern among students. A report by the Government Accountability Office found that over the past twenty years, the price of college textbooks has risen twice as fast as the inflation rate. Another study found that since 1994, college textbook prices have risen four times the rate of inflation, with the average student spending $900 per year on textbooks. This trend has angered students and those who provide their financial support—and it has also caught the attention of legislators around the country.

In Connecticut, publishers are now required by state law to provide faculty with the price of their books *before* they place their book orders. It is conceivable that states soon begin to regulate the cost of books assigned by faculty to students—and faculty will of course take issue with this type of state regulation, which they will rightfully view as an infringement upon their academic freedom to assign whatever books they feel best achieve the learning outcomes set for their courses. But faculty themselves have raised concerns about textbook prices.

A good example occurred a few years ago when seven hundred math and physics faculty members from one hundred fifty different colleges and universities asked Thompson Learning, one of the largest textbook companies in the world, to reconsider its pricing policies. These rising prices delimit the ability of faculty to select books they feel provide their students with the best opportunities for academic success. The problem of rising book prices (a paperback novel now can cost over twenty dollars and a textbook over a hundred) is that they pressure faculty increasingly to make pedagogical and academic decisions on non-pedagogical and non-academic grounds: The cost of a book has little relation to its potential academic benefit in the classroom.

The irony here of course is that we are overvaluing a product that may soon become obsolete as students and teachers move towards purely electronic media for information dissemination. This period of transition in book culture—further complicated by new technologies for dissemination and production, and growing use of self-publishing and non-traditional media—calls for a recalibration of the value system of book culture in terms of both price points and academic importance. We find ourselves now in an awkward period as the printed book slowly slips from the top of the academic publishing hierarchy, and academics and publishers wager on what the replacement might be.

28

GREEN BOOKS

If you find it enjoyable to curl up in bed with a good book, imagine what it would be like curling up with 1,500 good books. Not so cozy? Consider Kindle 2: an electronic reader recently released by Amazon that not only allows you to store seven times as many books as the original version, but also will "read" the books to you—albeit in a computerized voice. The Kindle 2 also allows you to read newspapers, blogs, and magazines, including—hold the presses—*ABR*!

It might be argued that with the rise of the digital age, the book, journal, and newspaper as "paper and ink" objects need to give way to the electronic word. Not only is the paper and ink object more expensive to produce (and reproduce) than its digital double, but the electronic word can be disseminated, searched, destroyed, and recycled far more easily than its material counterpart. If it is indeed the case that the dissemination of the books, magazines, journals, and newspapers that we know and love are more affordable and accessible digitally than physically, then why has the transition been so slow?

While legitimate arguments can be made that the quality of digital publication is inferior to print publication or that digital information is easier to "recycle" (viz., plagiarize or use without paying) than printed information, these are just historical, not natural, facts. There is nothing intrinsically inferior in disseminating information by means of a computer screen as compared to disseminating it by means of a printed page, and plagiarism and stealing are ethical issues, not material ones. Words may look better in print than on a screen or the spine of a book may feel better in your hands than a computer, but in the end, both page and screen relay the same words—and these words mean the same thing on the page as they do on the screen. The real difference, if there is one between the printed word and the digital word, is cultural. The case of audio information delivery may prove illustrative here.

Record album enthusiasts often have a "cult-like" attachment to vinyl as a music delivery mechanism and detest the digital format just as some people can't seem to part with their eight-track, cassette, and reel-to-reel tapes. Music may sound better (to some ears) when played on an iPod rather than a record album or an eight-track tape; nonetheless, it is the same music. It also may be duplicated more easily from a digital file than an analogue file; however, the opportunity for duplication is still there in both cases. The differences among these audio information delivery technologies are primarily cultural, not material. Trust me: "Smoke on the Water" is the same song on an iPod as it is on an eight-track tape—and just as duplicable.

The same case may be made for a book made available digitally versus a book made available only in paper and ink. Sure the packaging is different in a book delivered online versus a book found on a bookshelf, but the contents are the same. The first line of Vladimir Nabokov's *Lolita* (1955) is still "Lolita, light of my life, fire of my loins" whether it is online or in print. This leads one to conclude that the source of our digital aversion lies in a cultural attitude, not a material condition.

One source of this cultural attitude may be the fact that some still operate from the belief that the culture of paper and ink is *permanent*—or *natural*—and that digital culture is *impermanent*—or *historical*. This cultural attitude is not an ontological or metaphysical one: People don't mean by believing that books and magazines are permanent or natural that they cannot be destroyed. Rather they believe that the attitude with which one approaches a printed object such as a book or magazine is fundamentally different than the attitude in which one approaches a digital object. These attitudes are the products of cultural conditioning and habit.

The writer E. Annie Proulx, for example, claims that "books are forever," and that the information superhighway might be good for "bulletin boards on esoteric subjects, reference works, lists and news — timely utilitarian information, efficiently pulled through wires," but "[n]obody is going to sit down and read a novel on a twitchy little screen. Ever." Like the audiophile who swears that music sounds better on vinyl, bibliophiles like Proulx have a cult-like devotion to the printed word, and assign to it the highest value. In this view, not only is the printed word economically worth more than the digital word (for example, compare the price of the first edition of *Lolita* to its digitized version), but the printed word has a higher cultural and intellectual value. Nevertheless, the marketplace for information tells a different story.

Everywhere we seem to look, from newspapers to academic journals, print culture is giving way to digital culture. When Pulitzer Prize winner Proulx made her proclamation in *The New York Times* in May of 1994 about no one ever reading a novel on a "twitchy little screen," technological reality had not yet caught up with reading expectations. However, fourteen years later, Amazon proved Proulx's prediction to be wrong.

On November 19, 2007, the first "Kindle Readers" were released by Amazon — they sold out in four and a half hours. By August 2008 — about nine months after its release — Kindle Readers, hand-held devices that allow one to read a digital book, had been sold to almost a quarter million individuals. This number is matched only by the number of books available for reading on the Kindle. Today, Amazon.com lists over a quarter million Kindle titles available for purchase, including one of my own books, *If Classrooms Matter: Progressive Visions of Educational Environments* (2004, with W. Jacobs) (which, by the way, has apparently sold more copies to Kindle readers than print readers). But this is not the end of the digital versus print story — it's only the beginning.

We in the publishing world need to get a handle on the shift from the book to the byte soon before the digital universe completely parallels the print universe—something which we surely don't want or need, if for only ecological reasons. After all, trashing a digital file is much "greener" than trashing a paperback novel—the 1,500 books on the "twitchy little screen" of your Kindle will never end up in a landfill and have a decidedly much smaller carbon footprint than their pulp-based print versions.

The shift from print to digital is not going to be solved through rational or philosophical demonstrations of the indiscernibility of printed semantic units and digital ones, but rather though advances in the semiotics of publishing and reading culture. Until we let go of what might be called "the myth of the book," that is, the notion that books are permanent (whereas digital culture is impermanent), we will be caught between our digital destiny and our printed purgatory. The problem is not that *intellectually* we cannot understand the difference between the package that information comes in and the information in itself: most would agree that iconicly indistinguishable electronic and digital words convey the same information. The problem is that we cannot seem to come to grips with the notion that the *image* of "the book" as a printed artifact is no more or less "natural" than its "digital" (and non-printed) counterpart. Oddly enough, it may be environmental concerns that bring about the final push to a digitally dominant publishing culture. Who's going take the lead on the "Green Books Movement?"

29

SYMPATHY FOR THE DEVIL

While his life before 1967 was far from ordinary, it was not front-page news.

He was the son of a sixteen-year-old prostitute. His mother was sent to prison for robbery when he was five. His early years were spent in reform schools and homes for boys, and he was in prison by age eighteen. The next fifteen years he would spend in and out of federal prisons for a growing list of crimes that included pimping, forgery, and interstate auto theft. Finally, on March 21, 1967, over his own objections, he was paroled.

Up until this point, the general public was unaware of this young man and his history of recidivism. But just two-and-a-half years later, the name Charles Manson would be infamous around the nation and his crimes would be reported internationally. The widespread media attention would result in Americans knowing more about a man who spent the majority of his life incarcerated than they do about most U.S. presidents.

It is within this hyper-mediated contextual field of fact and rumor that "docufictionalist" master Harold Jaffe sets his fourteenth book and third novel, *Jesus Coyote*.[12] Like two of his most recent works, *False Positive* (2002) and *15 Serial Killers* (2003), Jaffe's new novel examines the moral psychology and media construction of "extreme" individuals. However, unlike those previous works, which consider a number of individuals and events, *Jesus Coyote* deals almost exclusively with the Manson "family" murders.

As with his other "treatments" of extreme criminal activity, Jaffe focuses attention more on the media depictions and public responses to criminals and their crimes than on the criminals themselves. Through fictionalized witness testimonies, phone transcripts, press conferences, and interrogations, Jaffe re-mediates many of the people affiliated with the Manson family's actions. While the names and chronology have been changed, many of the "facts" and "rumors" associated with the two-and-a-half year period between Manson's release from prison in March of 1967 to his re-arrest in December of 1969 for his connection with a series of brutal murders are clearly identifiable in the novel. Jaffe's hyper-cool, postmodern narrative technique is utilized to good effect, as is the stylistic variety that presents differing points of view on the murders.

The basic "facts" upon which Jaffe's docufiction relies concern the formation of the Manson family and murders for which they were convicted. When Manson was released from a California prison in 1967, he was dropped into the epicenter of the "Summer of Love," San Francisco's Haight-Ashbury district. There, a small group out of the thousands of resident "flower people" founded a commune at the Spahn movie ranch. Jaffe brilliantly leads his reader through this era from the perspective of key members of Manson's family. Against a background of ample sex, drugs, and rock 'n' roll, Jaffe outlines the series of events that would set Manson on the trail of criminal infamy and cultural stardom.

On August 9, 1969, pregnant actress Sharon Tate and four guests—Abigail Folger, Jay Sebring, Voytek Frykowski, and Steven Parent—were brutally murdered in Los Angeles. The scene of the crime was a house that Tate and her husband, famed film director Roman Polanski, were renting, and the former residence of Doris Day's son, Terry Melcher (a man who had refused to help Manson forward his music career).

The following night, another couple was brutally murdered in their Los Angeles home — Leno and Rosemary LaBianca.

On December 1, 1969, several of Charles Manson's followers — Susan Atkins, Patricia Krenwinkel, and Leslie Van Houten — were arrested for the Tate-LaBianca murders. At the time of their arrest, Manson had been in prison since October 12 for arson. Soon he, too, was charged in connection with the murders.

Rather than dwelling on the "factual" details of the murders, Jaffe's novel focuses on the media coverage of the events. "The mass murder in Joya Grove featuring the beautiful pregnant actress Naomi Self occurred on the night of 8 August 1969 and received massive, lurid front-page coverage," the novel begins, "such as is customarily reserved for declarations of war or the toppling of world trade centers." Jaffe then shares the headline from the *Los Angeles Times*: "Blood Orgy in Hollywood Mansion/ Movie Star, 4 Others, Brutally Slain/Satanism Hinted." The following day's headline concerning the LaBianca murders read: "Ritual Slayings Follow Killing of 5/Wealthy Bel Air Couple Stabbed and Mutilated/Blood Messages Smeared on Walls."

Jaffe's fiction notes that from the start, the media intensified and sensationalized the gruesome events to the point that it was impossible to distinguish between fact and fiction. "The victims in the combined massacres were reportedly stabbed more than 270 times, and it was rumored that the beautiful actress' 8-month fetus was ripped from her womb," writes Jaffe. "Other rumors, no less lurid, made the rounds," he continues. "In extraordinary circumstances, collective delirium will graft its ghastliest imaginings onto fact — which is already ghastly."

Jaffe is right to foreground the fact that the media — both traditional and underground — used the Manson story as a blank slate upon which to inscribe their fears and dreams for America. Whether it was the traditional media's fears about the sexual revolution or the underground media's fears about the repression of freedom, the Manson family saga provided — and still provides — an outlet for airing social and political fears and opportunities. From December 1969 to this day, the American media has been infatuated with Manson. His visage entered our collective imaginary on December 19, 1969, when *Life* magazine put him on its cover, with the words "The Love and Terror Cult," juxtaposed by a wild-eyed Manson raising his eyebrow to America.

A few months later, you could also pick up Manson's "Jesus Coyote" rant (from which the novel takes its title) at your neighborhood newsstand. In his famous June 1970 interview with *Rolling Stone* magazine, Manson asked his interviewer, "Have you ever seen the coyote in the desert?" He continued, "Watching, tuned in, completely aware. Christ on the cross, the coyote in the desert — it's the same thing, man. The coyote is beautiful. He moves through the desert delicately, aware of everything, looking around. He hears every sound, smells every smell, sees everything that moves. He's in a state of total paranoia, and total paranoia is total awareness."

Jaffe veils his docufictional Manson with the pseudonym "Jesus Coyote," a signifier with unlimited connotative power. In faux transcripts from the Los Angeles Deputy District Attorney's office, we hear "Hedda Hayman, 20, aka Head Games. Ex-lingerie model and wilderness advocate. Coyote spokesperson," tell the DDA shortly after the murders that "Coyotes loved him. Soul would yip like a coyote & they would come out of the desert & lick his hands." Later she says, "Jesus Christ was love & sex until the church fathers captured his body & made up lies about him."

Throughout the novel, Jaffe references "Jesus" and "coyote" as sources for his character's name and charismatic power. Jaffe makes it clear that Jesus Coyote's acolytes used these connotations to create their own mythologies about their leader. But wisely, Jaffe also shows key members of Coyote's "family" deconstructing these mythologies years later.

Roxi, reflecting nineteen years after being convicted and imprisoned for murder, says that she "almost always felt on the out, needy," back when she followed Jesus Coyote. "This great need I identified with Soul because he was by far the most charismatic presence — and we all thought — the largest spirit," comments Roxi. What later she learned was that . . . "he actually was was [sic] Lucifer, or some form of the devil, masking as the true God." Redirecting the Jesus Coyote mythology, she says, "What I mean to say was I was weak with a deep black hole of need in me, and in my condition I was ripe pickings for the devil Coyote."

The retrospective reflections of Coyote's victims are equally powerful. Jaroslav Hora, the filmmaker whose pregnant wife, Naomi Self, was slain in California when he was on location filming in Europe, asks himself, "Would I have agreed to a Faustian exchange: two and-a-half years of delirious joy for a lifetime of depression, regret and impotent rage?" Hora replies to himself, "From this perspective nineteen miserable years later, I'd have to say no. But were I asked then, in 1969, I might have replied otherwise." And in one of the more tender moments in the novel, he speaks directly to his deceased wife: "Sweetheart, *Cherie, Cara, Liebling.* Naomi, darling, however I might act in this unforgiving world, there is only you and there will always be only you."

The Hora chapter is one of the most powerful in the novel. It contains tender moments, but is also full of anger toward the media's representation of his wife, her murder, and himself. Hora is particularly offended by the general acceptance of certain rumors, such as the report that the fetus was ripped from his wife's womb, as fact. Says Hora, "the national media picked up on these cruel rumors and treated them as factual, [sic]." Jaffe reiterates a similar point throughout the novel: that by criminalizing the victim, the media can at times be *crueler* than the criminals about whom they are reporting.

Hora laments that the media insists on comparing him to Coyote. "We're both 'diminutive,' we're both highly sexed, we've both experimented with mind-altering drugs, we share an interest in horror and the supernatural, and each of us was, so to speak, granted two-and-a-half glorious years surrounded on either side by bleakness," states Hora. However, he maintains that the comparisons should begin and end here: "I'm a European-Jewish award-winning filmmaker whose grandparents on my father's side were gassed in the Nazi camps, and I've been known to make serious films which are sometimes bloody. Coyote is an illiterate, anti-Semitic mass murdering hillbilly with a swastika tattoo between his eyes who has spent virtually his entire life in prison." "Where," pleads Hora, "is the similarity?"

Head Games, who was arrested for attempting to assassinate President Gerald Ford in 1975, completes Jaffe's assault on the media when she pleads for us to see Coyote more compassionately. Commenting twenty-one years after the murders, she offers, "And if you knew him without the prejudice and spite and hate he's been saddled with by this maddening country and its official media, you might understand why it is ordinary people are so fascinated by him." And this of course is the key question: why *are* ordinary people so fascinated with extra-ordinarily cruel people like Charles Manson?

While Jaffe's novel may not add new insight to the troubling question of evil's allure, it examines how the media gives prominence to these sensational figures to the exclusion of thousands of less notable crimes. Head Games asks, "Anyway, why are those Hollywood deaths worse than the minute-to-minute death of our invisible homeless people, or worse than the genociding of our wilderness?" Head Games notes that despite media emphasis on celebrity criminals, "The murderous violence is everywhere around us."

In the penultimate chapter of *Jesus Coyote*, five of the murder victims speak from the afterlife. Each reflects on the violence that took their lives — and each in their own way aims to come to terms with what happened to them. One of the departed, Victor Hus, wonders "Was the skinny long-hair invasion real?" He concludes, "It slaughtered me. It slaughtered all of us. Still I didn't believe that it was happening . . . ." The last voice is that of Naomi Self, who says, "Jaro and I thought the counter-culture kids were cool . . . . And here they are stabbing, slaughtering us. I don't understand. It must have to do with me."

It is perhaps the difficulty in comprehending the brutality of these events that keeps ordinary people talking about them. Or perhaps it is the way in which the gentle "Age of Aquarius" came to a violent close in 1969 that keeps so many people still fascinated with the Manson family murders.

Jaffe's novel gives the shackled, incarcerated Jesus

Coyote a voice in the novel's final chapter. We hear him thirty-one years after the murders, still ranting about the "coyote," who is both "total fear, total paranoia" and "at peace with his total fear that never ends." He disapprovingly rants on in response to over forty questions until he finally hears one that he likes: "Favorite mass-murderer excluding yourself." "That would be Henry Kissinger," replies Coyote. "Finally you come up wit' a question that ain't half-ass."

Jerry Rubin recounts in *We Are Everywhere* (1971) that Manson told him, "Rubin, I am not of your world. I've spent all my life in prison. When I was a child I was an orphan and too ugly to be adopted. Now I am too beautiful to be set free." Jaffe's novel superbly methodically deconstructs Manson's self-created mythology of being "too beautiful to be set free." By the end of this novel, Coyote is only an ugly reminder of the beauty he destroyed. Jaffe exorcises the Manson mythology while admonishing the media for sensationalizing his monstrous acts.

When we finally hear Coyote speak from prison, he is only an afterthought—a coda to the many lives his actions tragically altered. While remaining the title character of the novel, Coyote comes off as a minor character. Coyote's family and their victims reclaim the story—and their lives—from him. It is their conflicting thoughts and searching reflections that provide us with our primary insights regarding his character. By the time Coyote finally speaks, it feels as though he too has departed. This is the real power of Jaffe's novel—to wash our hands of Coyote and the blood he spilled.

30

PUBLISHING SMARTS

Stories are beginning to circulate about the negative impact that the economic crisis is having on the world of book publishing. And they're coming from all corners of the publishing world

Just today, a friend who is an editor at a major university press told me that five of his colleagues were let go by the press. I'm sure that other university presses are feeling the financial crunch and downsizing as well.

Even the big publishing houses are cutting back. Simon & Schuster just cut thirty-five jobs, and Thomas Nelson fired fifty-four employees — which amounted to 10% of their workforce.

And the worst is probably yet to come.

Publishing giant Houghton Mifflin Harcourt, with $1.3 billion in revenue and 3,550 employees, is rumored to have laid off hundreds of employees this past month (as of right now, solid numbers are not in general circulation). In addition, Houghton has put a ban on all new acquisitions.

Before the acquisition ban was publicly announced, Becky Saletan, Houghton's trade and reference publisher, was said to have teared up at an editorial meeting.

Shortly after the announcement, she quit.

The downsizing has sent a chill through the publishing world. I'm sure many in the book business are wondering if they're next. Even the big box booksellers are getting hit: The nation's three largest bookstore chains—Barnes & Noble, Borders Group, and Books-A-Million—all reported losses this quarter. Coupled with losses earlier in the year, it could very well be the case that by year's end total sales for all three could be in the red.

What's happening? If the corporate giants of the book world are taking a hit, then is there any hope for the small presses and independent bookstores? Yes and no.

If people don't have jobs or money, they won't be buying books (though they may have more time to write them). These are hard circumstances for *everyone* in the book world.

However, small presses and independent bookstores don't rely on the same level of revenue streams as large presses and book-box chains.

A Borders store with fifty full-time employees and a three-story building on Michigan Avenue in Chicago has to sell a lot more books to survive than an independent bookstore with five full-time employees on the south side of town.

Furthermore, if you give an author a five or six or seven or eight figure advance, and his or her book only sells 50,000 copies, you've lost a great deal of money.

By comparison, if a university press sells a thousand copies of scholarly title where they've only given the author a three or two figure advance, they're overjoyed.

And if an independent fiction press sells over five hundred copies of a new novel, they'll probably need to go into a second printing.

The last three novels published by Phillip Roth sold less than 75,000 copies hardcover each. Houghton, his publisher, is red-faced over this when one considers that David Baldacci's new novel, *Divine Justice* (published by Grand Central of Hachette Book Group), sold 114,000 hardcover copies *in its first month of publication*.

Most small presses won't sell 75,000 books—let alone 114,000—in their *entire* history.

While the economic woes of the mega-presses and monster bookstores may send a cold chill down the backs of Wall Street, it does not necessarily follow that the non-profit presses and independent bookstores will also not cut it in today's economy. Why?

Most small presses cater to relatively stable and loyal markets. In a good economy, it makes sense to try to expand these markets. For example, an ethnic literature press may try to tap into a broader market by implementing a more aggressive (and expensive) marketing plan. However, in tough economic times it may be prudent to be more conservative with marketing dollars, to focus instead on improving the quality of the publications themselves, rather than anticipating higher sales figures and larger markets.

Independent bookstores also have a base of customers on which they rely for their subsistence. Let this sour economy become an opportunity for them to get to know their customer's needs better: ask them again about the strengths and weaknesses of their stock and services, about what they like about the store and what could be improved. Bring more authors in for readings — especially authors from independent presses or who are local. Encourage reading groups. Become an arm of the community. This is where the chain stores can't compete.

Small presses and independent bookstores have the best chance of surviving — if not thriving — in this sour economy *if* they publish and manage *smart*. Some may even consider improving their acumen by going back to school and earning say a master's in publishing or business administration. Publishing and selling books with a higher level of knowledge about the *business* of books can't hurt in bad economic times.

Books are published for people to buy and read. An increased understanding of what people will peruse and purchase can only have a positive impact on the bottom line.

One carefully selected, edited, and designed book is better than a shelf full of weak, poorly edited and designed titles. Downsizing can sometimes be a good thing. Same with book stock: A shelf full of so-so material will only gather dust, whereas a smaller selection of thoughtfully selected strong titles increases ones chances of succeeding when times are tight.

Moreover, it is entirely possible that the *smart*, small-print-run presses and *smart*, well-managed, independent bookstores may even be *better* positioned to ride out the economic downturn than their mainstream rivals.

In fact, the downturns of some the big fish in the book world may even help some of the little fish grow a bit bigger. If Houghton, for example, goes under, there are many smaller publishers that stand to benefit as the new publishers of Philip Roth novels. And I'm sure the remaining independent bookstores won't be dismayed if Barnes & Noble needs to close a few stores.

31

THE BIG DIALOGUE

Last month, comments by Horace Engdahl, permanent secretary of the Nobel Prize committee, set off an international discussion about the place of America and its writers in contemporary literature. "There is powerful literature in all big cultures, but you can't get away from the fact that Europe still is the centre of the literary world," said Engdahl, "not the United States." "The U.S. is too isolated, too insular," he added. Moveover, American writers and publishers "don't translate enough and don't really participate in the big dialogue of literature." Concludes Engdahl, "That ignorance is restraining."

Engdahl's comments antagonized writers and publishers in the U.S. They also served notice to American writers that they should not raise their hopes for receiving a Nobel Prize in literature any time soon.

In spite of prodigious U.S. literary production — an estimated 50,000 works of fiction were published just last year in the U.S. — it has been fifteen years since an American author has been awarded the Nobel Prize in literature. Not a bad record, actually, when one considers that in the last fifty years, only six Americans were awarded the prize (four of which were born outside of the U.S.). In fact, in the over-one-hundred-year history of the award, only eleven

Americans have won (the same number as recipients from the UK, though four fewer than the French).

Of our earliest recipients, Sinclair Lewis (1930), Eugene O'Neill (1936), and Pearl Buck (1938), have by and large faded from the contemporary literary imagination; the middle group, William Faulkner (1949), Ernest Hemingway (1954), and John Steinbeck (1962), are the heavily canonized lions of twentieth-century American letters; and the latest recipients, Saul Bellow (1976; b. Montreal), Isaac Bashevis Singer (1978; b. Poland), Czesław Miłosz (1980, b. Poland), Joseph Brodsky (1987; b. Leningrad) and Toni Morrison (1993), reveal the changing face and identity of literature in the U.S.

In my own opinion, the twenty-five-year period between Hemingway and Bellow commits the greatest sin of omission. Passed over were American literary giants such as James Baldwin; Donald Barthelme; E. E. Cummings; Ralph Ellison; Langston Hughes; Wallace Stevens; Kurt Vonnegut, Jr.; Tennessee Williams; and Richard Wright.

However, the oversight of American writers by the Swedish Academy over the past twenty years (1989-2008) is nearly as difficult to accept as the omissions from 1955 to 1975. Are we really to believe that only Morrison rises to the level of recent recipients of the award? If Engdahl is correct—and I think that he is—that a necessary condition for receiving this award is a contribution to "the big dialogue of literature," how then do the post-Morrison recipients fare?

This year's recipient, Jean-Marie Gustave Le Clézio, joins a post-Morrison Nobel lineup that includes Orhan Pamuk (2006), Elfriede Jelinek (2004), Imre Kertész (2002), Dario Fo (1997), and Wisława Szymborska (1996).

Call my "ignorance restraining," but I do not see how Nobel laureates like Jelinek and Szymborska have contributed in a more significant way to the "big dialogue of literature" than some of the recent giants of American letters such as John Barth, Don DeLillo, Joyce Carol Oates, Thomas Pynchon, Phillip Roth, John Updike, or William T. Vollmann.

However, no awardee in recent memory brings home this point more than Le Clézio.

Described by the press as a writer "of exile and self-discovery, of cultural dislocation and globalization, of the clash between modern civilization and traditional cultures," Le Clézio studied English at the University of Bristol, graduated from the Institut d'Études Littéraires in Nice, received a master's degree at the University of Aix-en-Provence, and wrote his doctoral thesis for the University of Perpignan on the early history of Mexico. Le Clézio has taught at many universities around the world, in places ranging from Mexico City and Bangkok, to Austin and Boston; has lived among the Embera Indians in Panama; has published over forty essays, novels and children's books, including translations of Mayan sacred texts; and "writes as fluently about North African immigrants in France, native Indians in Mexico, and islanders in the Indian Ocean as he does about his own past."

He is a translator, cosmopolitan author, and a nomadic writer—attributes of interest in a globalized society. In fact, *ABR* has recently done focuses on both cosmopolitanism (28.3) and translation (28.5 and 29.5)—and has a focus on "nomadic literature" in the works.

Le Clézio's attributes are ones that should be valued by contemporary readers, and are valuable to writers in the age of globalization. However, the Nobel Prize should not just be about honoring writers that bespeak literary attributes merely representative of an age. Rather, it should speak to their more lasting contribution among readers, writers, and scholars worldwide.

The Nobel Prize (by its own standards) should, as Endahl notes, reward writers and writing that has contributed to the "big dialogue of literature"—a dialogue that one would assume involves an author's interplay among readers, writers, and scholars. In this regard, Le Clézio fails to meet this standard in at least one respect—and one need look no further than the MLA International Bibliography for the evidence.

Compiled by over one-hundred contributing bibliographers from around the world, the MLA bibliography annually indexes over 66,000 books and articles.

Last year, according to this extensive, international bibliography, scholars the world over did not even produce one book or article about Le Clézio.

The same the year before that — and the year before that.

In fact, there has not been even one book or article about Le Clézio in the MLA International Bibliography for nearly thirty years.

In total, the MLA International Bibliography lists forty-one items about Jean-Marie Gustave Le Clézio. As his first novel, *Le procès-verbal* (1963; *The Interrogation*, 1964) appeared over forty years ago, this puts him on average of one scholarly item per year.

Or, given that he has published over forty essays, novels and children's books, it puts him at about one item for each of his own publications.

While a lack of English translations of Le Clézio's writing might be the excuse for contemporary American scholars (and readers) to not be as familiar with his work, this is not an excuse for scholars with knowledge of this foreign language. After all, the MLA International Bibliography lists research in many foreign languages and literatures including French. One can only conclude that French scholars around the world are not interested in Le Clézio's work either.

If no scholar has written about your work for over a quarter of a century, how is it possible that you have made a significant contribution to "the big dialogue of literature?"

The difficulties with comprehending the Academy's criteria for the literature prize are due in part to the interpretation of Alfred Nobel's will, which states that the prize be given to "the person who shall have produced in the field of literature the most outstanding work in an ideal direction."

Citizens around the world associate the Nobel brand with excellence and with ongoing contributions to a field. But the literary committee seems to place emphasis on the "ideal direction" criterion, emphasizing works with certain utopian or political themes.

The Swedish Academy desperately wants this prize to be about more than outstanding literary achievement. The prize seems to be the Academy's assertion of literature's place in the larger dialogue of politics and social justice. But the criteria are so confusing and the brand so weakened by seemingly incongruent selections that it is difficult to follow the threads that link members of the Nobel canon.

American critics and writers have long been exasperated by the Academy's confusing choices. Perhaps the best American response would be to found a competing prize for world literature, with a similar compensation, that had clearer criteria for awarding literary excellence in its own right. (The Neustadt International Prize for Literature, sponsored by the University of Oklahoma and *World Literature Today* currently comes closest to this aim: The biennial international prize awards a silver eagle feather, a certificate, and $50,000 to international poets, novelists, and playwrights.)

Engdahl's statements on isolated, insular, ignorant Americans were obviously meant to provoke (and to garner publicity, to be sure), but whom was Engdahl addressing? Is Engdahl referring to American writers, American publishers, or American readers? To American culture as a whole? Is the Academy punishing American authors for the sins of the culture at large, conflating literature with pop culture and politics?

It seems to me that the Swedish Academy suffers from the very maladies it diagnoses in the U.S.: isolation and insularity. I wonder what they are reading.

Harold Augenbraum, executive director of the National Book Foundation, offered to send Engdahl a reading list of American writers. I'm asking you to do the same. Who would you put on such a list, and why? Send your thoughts to us at *ABR* and we'll compile a list for Herr Engdahl.

32

EMOTIONAL NARRATIVES

From the anxiety of test-taking to the joy of graduation, a student's educational life is marked by a wide range of emotional highs and lows. Recently, there has been some interest by educational and developmental psychologists in conducting research on academic emotions, particularly with regard to the emotional life of undergraduate students. These empirical inquiries of undergraduate emotions are primarily concerned with the connection among learning, achievement, and emotion, and promise eventually to bring about for our students more successful learning outcomes and higher achievement levels.

There does not, however, seem to be the same level of interest in faculty emotion among educational psychologists as there is in student emotion. This is unfortunate because one suspects that such inquiry would probably for faculty, just as it should for students, lead to improved success and achievement levels. Yet, despite the lack of systematic research on faculty emotions, there has been a flurry of narratives and memoirs published of late that provide rich insight into emotional life in the academy. From James Phelan's *Beyond the Tenure Track: Fifteen Months in the Life of an English Professor* (1991) to Michael Dubson's *Ghosts in the Classroom: Stories of College Adjunct Faculty – and the*

Price We All Pay (2001), accounts of life in academia are in no short supply—and are yet further evidence for the "affective turn" presented in this issue.

Until about twenty years ago, it seemed as though publishing an account of one's life in the academy was something generally reserved for only the most well-known and extra-ordinary figures in our profession. Moreover, such accounts tended to appear toward the close of an esteemed person's career as opposed to mid-, let alone, early career, and would be momentous, eagerly anticipated events. They would also be a type of farewell: a time to put one's life in order for a multitude of admiring peers and lay readers. While Bertrand Russell and Jean-Paul Sartre would clearly qualify for such an undertaking, graduate students, adjunct faculty, and associate professors of philosophy and English most certainly would not. Few presses were interested in publishing the reminiscences of ordinary academics, so they were rarely written. However, the rise of cultural studies and meta-professional discourse in the 1990s seems to have changed this.

Cultural studies provide the intellectual conditions for the potential significance of first-person narratives of life in the academy. At their best, cultural studies are critical writing practices that do not immediately provide the meaning of the artifact. They are fundamentally self-reflexive enterprises that are credited or discredited relative to historical and social pressures.

Today, memoirs by ordinary academics about everyday life in the academy are commonplace—and, one even might say, a *hot* commodity. While books like Jane Tompkins' *A Life in School: What the Teacher Learned* (1996) and Terry Caesar's *Traveling through the Boondocks: In and Out of Academic Hierarchy* (2000) are both excellent accounts of academic life, one doubts that they would have raised very much interest twenty-five years ago. Events related to the daily emotional life of academics—seemingly almost *any* academic—are fair game for publication. Venues such as *Inside Higher Education* and the *Chronicle of Higher Education* run a continuous stream of articles by academics who openly share details of their life in the academy. Major presses publish memoirs of life in the academy of not just Nobel laureates at the ends of their careers, but of professors who have yet to establish their contribution to their chosen fields. In fact, the narrative of the trials and tribulations of their life in the academy sometimes even *becomes* their contribution to the field. Stories of bitterness over being rejected for publication, of panic concerning the job market, and of fear regarding tenure have become commonplace and sought after commodities. An entire bibliography of discourse about life in the academy has sprouted up seemingly overnight, and there appears to be no end to the interest in this type of writing in sight. Nonetheless, opinion is divided over the value of these narratives which often foreground and dwell on academic emotions.

For some, these stories are nothing more than academic gossip and of peripheral concern. Their position is that providing accounts of one's life in the academy is not a serious intellectual endeavor and rises to a level of intellectual significance no higher than a Hollywood star's latest romance or exploit. Some even find such accounts embarrassing because they reveal aspects of the academy that were hitherto not for public consumption. Accounts of academic's anxieties, apathies, and angers reveal higher education to be an emotionally unstable world. Our flaws as individuals and a profession are detailed in micro-narratives that reveal academia to be less a world of the pursuit of ideas than a world of shattered ideals.

However, for others, an intellectual sharing his or her emotional experiences in academe is a vitally significant intellectual act. Accounts of our emotional responses to our conditions of employment, interactions with our colleagues and students, and the future of our profession bring us to a more nuanced description of academic culture *in toto*. These accounts provide us with an anthropology of our profession and bring us closer to both revealing the general conditions of its existence and ways to improve those conditions in the future. Also, individuals recounting the emotional ups and downs of participating in higher education help us to understand, if nothing else, the complex and changing nature of identity in academic culture.

While it is true that some accounts of emotional life in academia are unduly vindictive and self-serving, many more are empowering and progressive. Together these accounts form a mosaic that reveals the commonplaces of academic emotion. This mosaic can and should be used to improve the lives of those who participate in academic culture. Regarded as such, accounts of the emotions of academics are not a weak and peripheral aspect of academic publishing. In fact, the opportunity exists for some presses — especially small and independent ones — to provide a potentially rejuvenating and progressive voice through such books.

One of the simple lessons confirmed time and again in accounts of academic emotions is that life in the academy is no less rich and complex than life outside of it. Academics are not automata that dispassionately disseminate knowledge and evaluate students, but rather are individuals who engage in a wide range of feelings in the performance of their chosen profession. Moreover, these feelings have a strong bearing on their job performance and lend insight into the structures of power present in the academy. The emotional lives of other academics are important to us not because of who they are, but rather because of what they reveal about the overall state and logic of higher education. They provide signposts of both our successes and failures as an institution, and continuously point to future states of the academy that are within our control to determine. Whereas once we tended to look to larger than life figures such as Russell and Sartre to tell us where we are and what we should be as an institution, today we look to (dare I say "ordinary?") colleagues such as Tompkins and Caesar. Ultimately, through reading accounts of life in the academy, such as theirs, each of us comes to a greater self-knowledge of our own academic self.

33

THE ACADEMIC IMPERATIVE

"Do your job," Stanley Fish advises his readership in *Save the World on Your Own Time*,[13] and the troubles facing higher education will disappear. If you teach in a college or university, your job essentially entails two things: introducing your students to knowledge, and providing them with the analytical tools to confidently navigate through this knowledge. For Fish, when academics forget or are ignorant of this imperative, trouble begins.

Author of ten books and a frequent contributor to *The New York Times*, *Harper's*, *New York Times Book Review*, and the *Chronicle of Higher Education*, Fish is one of the most provocative and outspoken voices in American higher education. Known for defending theses that can be outlandish and controversial, Fish maintains his reputation in this latest book.

Not averse to making enemies or picking academic fights, Fish's latest provocation will undoubtedly draw ire from both the Left *and* the Right. Fish comes down hard on academics who utilize the classroom as a platform for their political beliefs. While engaging in *academic* politics *is* part of our job description (e.g., arguing about the content and manner of teaching, curriculum, and department leadership), indoctrinating our students with our political beliefs is not. Outside of the university, we are free to practice politics whenever and however we see fit; inside the university, however, our political engagement is strictly limited.

Fish explains that while the free expression of ideas is a cornerstone of liberal democracy and a prime *political* value, it is not an *academic* one. Academic value stems from the dissemination of knowledge and traditions by faculty who are experts: faculty are hired for their academic expertise, not their political values. Outside of the university, there are many appropriate venues for faculty to be politically active; inside of the university, the pursuit of the truth of texts by faculty is their primary obligation. "Truth," writes Fish, "is a pre-eminent *academic* value."

But, how then does one "refrain from inadvertently raising inappropriate issues in the classroom?" Fish's response is quite simple: that we must "academicize" our classroom material, particularly potentially politically explosive issues. "To academicize a topic," writes Fish, "is to detach it from the context of its real world urgency, where there is a vote to be taken or an agenda to be embraced, and insert it into a context of academic urgency, where there is an account to be offered or an analysis to be performed." And, Fish argues, "There is no topic, however politically charged, that will resist academicization." The failure of faculty to academicize the subject matter of their courses often leads to the replacement of academic imperatives with political imperatives.

According to Fish, "composition studies is the clearest example of the surrender of academic imperatives to the imperatives of politics." If composition were to heed Fish's "academic imperative," composition instructors would only teach grammar and rhetoric, and not turn their courses into "discussions of oppression and the evils of neoliberalism." For Fish, good teaching is not a political act—"only bad teaching is a political act."

One way to counter Fish's charge that politics should be left out of the classroom is to claim that politicizing courses is protected under "academic freedom." Fish strongly disagrees with this position. Academic freedom for him is simply "the freedom to be an academic, which is, by definition, *not* the freedom to be anything and everything else." In other words, it's the freedom to do the job that you've been hired to do (and to not do someone else's job and to not let someone else do your job).

Overall, Fish's view of higher education is "deflationary." He denies that higher education has any greater end than merely helping students to master knowledge: It does not teach them to be moral persons or to be agents of change. "The practices of responsible citizenship and moral behavior should be encouraged in our young adults," writes Fish, "but it's not the business of the university to do so, except when the morality in question is the morality that penalizes cheating, plagiarizing, and shoddy teaching." In fact, "if liberal arts education is doing *its* job and not the job assigned to some other institution, it will not have as its aim the bringing about of particular effects in the world."

Fish's arguments are supremely well-reasoned and logical. However, *Save the World on Your Own Time* leaves the reader with the feeling of having just completed a course on higher education today — where the whole topic has been successfully academicized. In Professor Fish's course, while we acquire a great deal of knowledge about the state of higher education today, and are shown how to analyze this knowledge, we leave the class having no solid insight into its real-world context.

While the desire to indoctrinate and inspire students can be abused by faculty, so too can its opposite: the desire to *academicize* everything. Having taught applied ethics for many years, I respect the aim of being politically and ideologically neutral to topics like abortion, euthanasia, and capital punishment. Though however much one might wish to avoid it, students do become emotionally involved in the material; do become politically involved in the material; do want to draw analytical treatments of the topics into the context of their own lives and community — if not the world at large. And why shouldn't they? Doing ones job here then involves helping students to acquire new knowledge and analytical skills, *and* preparing them to incorporate this knowledge into their individual lives and their communities. The first part is easy; the second part is difficult.

Preparing students to use the knowledge and

analytical skills that they acquire in the university and use beyond it is the job of faculty. Borrowing from Kant, one might maintain that content or knowledge without direction is blind; politics (or ideology) without content or knowledge and analytical skills is empty. To be sure, Fish's book has no eyes.

As an *academization* of the troubles facing higher education today, Fish's book is persuasively argued. However, Fish's decision to not address the real world urgency of his subject makes *Save the World on Your Own Time* nothing more than a clever academic exercise. Those looking for insights into the relationship between higher education and the messy moral and political mechanics of wider society will find little of value in this book.

Still, *Save the World on Your Own Time* contains many entertaining provocations from one of academe's most outspoken members. In the closing pages, the Dean Emeritus advises university administrators to be "aggressive, blunt, mildly confrontational, and just a bit arrogant" with legislators and trustees, rather than respectful, reasonable, and diplomatic. In the opinion of this reader, following Stanley Fish's imperatives may worsen rather than improve the problems of higher education.

If you must read this book, do it on university time, not your own.

34

REQUIEM FOR A JOURNAL

One of my colleagues is struggling to keep afloat the journal he edits. The chair of his department is threatening to cut funding because, according to my colleague, he does not see how the journal directly serves the department.

Flash back: a few years ago my colleague and his journal faced the same threat. At that time, he asked that letters of support for his journal be sent to his chair. This time, his actions were different.

This time, he asked his colleagues to contribute a piece to what he plans to be the last issue of this journal. He stated that he would rather shut his journal down entirely than accept a cut in support.

The story is a familiar one: A small non-profit journal, whose survival depends entirely upon the support of a college or university, loses that support and is faced with having to cease publication.

In all likelihood, the requiem for his journal will be held this December at the annual meeting of the Modern Language Association. But even if it survives, it is certain that my colleague will be revisiting this cycle of funding cuts one or two years from now.

Most non-profit journals with university affiliations are dependent on the "good will" of the university's administration. And for many, it means the difference between a journal's survival and extinction.

The university that supports my colleague's journal is a major private university with one of the largest endowments in the country — over $1 billion. The amount of money that is being debated is but a few thousand dollars. My colleague finds the chair's decision to be more "myopic" than "malicious."

Certainly, both myopic *and* malicious administrators can be found in higher education today. Most every issue of the *Chronicle of Higher Education* contains reports about them (the story recounted above can be found in recent back issues of the *Chronicle*). The *Chronicle* knows its readers love a "Big University Done Bad" story, in which a small cultural treasure declines due to the lack of faith and commitment from universities following big business economics.

But I'd like to call attention to the reverse of this process, and report on a "Small University Done Good" story, where the support and risk-taking of an administrator helped to salvage a cultural treasure in decline.

Two years ago, funding cuts at Illinois State University for the *American Book Review* almost led to the folding of this venerated publication. Until the University of Houston-Victoria stepped in, *ABR*'s future seemed uncertain.

Much has changed in two years.

While UHV may not be a top-tier university with a large endowment, the university has something infinitely more important to the growth and development of scholarly projects and publications: a visionary administration.

Two years ago Dr. Tim Hudson, President of the University of Houston-Victoria, took a gamble. When offered the opportunity to bring the *American Book Review* to UHV, he did not ask, "Why should we do this?" Instead, he asked, "What will it take to get this done?"

Hudson understood the value of publications such as *ABR* to a university both on campus and in the community, both locally *and* nationally. He did not ask "myopic" questions such as, "How will *ABR* serve UHV's School of Arts and Sciences?" Instead, he acted on the assumption that supporting journals — particularly ones with illustrious and prestigious histories like *ABR*'s — is what universities *do*.

Since Dr. Hudson's gamble, we have received a major

grant in support of *ABR* from the National Endowment for the Arts, established the *American Book Review* Reading Series (which has brought fourteen writers to our campus including winners of the Pulitzer Prize and the American Book Award), are about to launch the first master's program in publishing in Texas (if not the southern United States), and have raised over $350,000 for the *American Book Review* Endowment.

At the center of the *ABR* Endowment is a $125,000 donation from former University of Houston System Regent, Dorothy Alcorn—one of largest individual gifts in support of the humanities in the nation. The goal of the *ABR* Endowment is $1 million—one which we believe is attainable.

The success of the *American Book Review* has attracted other organizations and publications to the university. UHV has become the new institutional home of the Society for Critical Exchange and the Fiction Collective Two (FC2), both of which will have their own separate endowments. Dr. Hudson's gamble has paid off, and both the journal and the cultural life on campus and in the community are flourishing.

Myopic administration asks how scholarly publications can enhance their university. Rash decisions made on the basis of temporary economic cycles can lead to the decline of iconic scholarly publications, which can alienate the scholars attached to those publications. The death of a journal often leads to professional resentment from the community that benefits most from its continuation.

Visionary administration asks what the university can do for scholarly publications. In the case of literary journals with rich histories like *ABR*, the consequences can benefit the community, the university, and the profession if the administrative commitment is genuine. Such commitment must begin by valuing the humanities as an end in itself.

Perhaps a sign of progressive and visionary university administration is unconditional support for projects like the *American Book Review*. While you might not read this "Small University Done Good" story in the *Chronicle*, it is nevertheless one of the great recent success stories in the humanities. There will be no requiem for a dream here at *ABR*—only a continuing success story.

35

A GOOD REVIEWER IS HARD TO FIND

A large part of the duty of book review editors is finding good reviewers — a task that is more difficult than it may seem.

In academia, book reviews are often either disdained as unworthy forms of publication or considered something to be done in-between other projects. Many humanities departments do not even regard reviews as scholarship. What motivation is there then for professors to set aside precious research time attending to an activity that is not even recognized as scholarship by their departments? Why publish something that makes no positive contribution to one's progress toward tenure, promotion, or salary?

Outside of academia, the situation is not much better. Competing demands on time coupled with low financial rewards for such writing leaves book review editors in the difficult position of having more worthy books for review than worthy reviewers. This is not difficult to imagine if you consider that 150,000 new titles are published every year.

So great is the disinclination for qualified people to review books that it is not uncommon to have to ask two or three or four prospects before finding a willing reviewer. And even after the commitment is made, one still needs to motivate the person to actually complete the review.

Far too many people commit to reviewing a book, but do not follow through. It is not uncommon to learn that the review gave way to "more important" projects. And, due to limited time frames for review of a title, the reviewer who fails to follow through often makes it difficult for the editor to reassign the book.

For these reasons and others, a good reviewer is hard to find. There is, however, some reason to believe that this situation may change. The "Report of the MLA Task Force on Evaluating Scholarship for Tenure and Promotion" (2007) had some very significant, if brief, comments and recommendations concerning reviews of scholarly books. The report comments that "the best published reviews constitute an important scholarly activity that helps direct, alter, and sustain ongoing conversations in the field." In addition, it comments that "book reviews should be an important part of tenure evaluations." Both comments serve as a wake-up call for those who have relegated the book review to second-tier scholarly activity status.

In its recommendations, the report encourages "senior scholars" to write reviews that will not only "help identify significant new work," but that will also serve as models of critically engaged reviewing. It also recommends that journal editors "cultivate a more critical culture of reviewing" — perhaps the most controversial statement about book reviewing in the report. While reviewing has arguably become a genre marked by increasing degrees of politeness and summation — that is to say, its critical edge has been dulled — one wonders if pushing it in the opposite direction will only serve to "discourage" more people in our profession from reviewing. It is more difficult — and dangerous — to write a critical review. The most obvious reason for this is that a critical review justifiably raises the spectre of retaliation from the reviewed author and his or her affiliates.

Still, the MLA report's comments and recommendations on book reviews are a major step in the right direction. Moreover, its "summary recommendation" that "the profession as a whole should encourage scholars at all levels to write substantive book reviews" is right on the mark.

Writing book reviews should be regarded by those in our profession as both a service to the writerly community and a scholarly activity. Persons in all stages of their careers should be encouraged to make a serious commitment to reviewing books: young writers as an entry into professional writing and as a way of engaging materials useful for their creative endeavors; newly published writers as a way of establishing their professorial signature; and established writers as a way of linking generations of writing.

We should also remember that the publication of book reviews is an important type of public intellectualism. Reviews serve to not only synthesize for a potentially wider audience the specialized and sometimes densely presented knowledge generated by our profession, but also to share with the public the critical exchanges and differences of opinion that keep our profession vital.

Within this context, *ABR* colleagues mourn the death of the fine book review editor and writer Rochelle Ratner (1948-2008). Rochelle passed away on March 31. She tirelessly served *ABR* as an Executive Editor from 1978 to 2006, and as an Associate Editor from 2006 to her untimely passing.

At our Associate Editor's meeting in New York City in mid-February of this year, Rochelle was enthusiastic about the future of *ABR*, and expressed much optimism about her continued engagement on behalf of this publication. Like all of the Associate and Contributing Editors of this publication, Rochelle was not paid for the work she did. She wrote and solicited reviews for *ABR* not for financial or professional reward, but because she believed that book reviews play a fundamental role in the lives of writers and the world of letters.

It was an honor to work with a talented and dedicated book review editor like Rochelle—one who has stood by and supported this publication almost from its beginning. She will be dearly missed. A good book review editor and writer is hard to find—and even more difficult to lose.

36

GIANT STEPS

Would you be surprised by the story of a sixteenth-century monk who played jazz? You maybe didn't realize that there was jazz dated back to the Renaissance? What kind of history didn't they teach you in school?

Born at the end of the fifteenth century, François Rabelais was a true jazz pioneer. His instrument was not the ivories, like the more well-known jazz Monk, Thelonious. Rabelais composed jazz with his *pen*.

A Franciscan monk who later turned to Benedictine, Rabelais abandoned the monastic life to pursue a Bachelor's degree. At the age of thirty-six, he entered the University of Montpellier, and within two months of study, received his Bachelor of Arts. (Now that's a student loan that I can handle!)

Two years later, he published the first great work of jazz fiction: *Pantagruel* (1532).

In this amazing book, Rabelais frankly and exuberantly satirizes contemporary life. It is one of the wildest books ever written — and one of the greatest works of "improvisation" in the Western canon.

In "Rabelais' work," says Raymond Federman, "you confront pure extemporaneous fiction, pure improvisation." "Rabelais is the first great jazz fictioneer."

Rabelais' book was promptly censored by the theological faculty at the University of Paris as sacrilegious and obscene.

Then, as now, anonymity had its virtues. Anticipating the negative reaction *Pantagruel* would receive, Rabelais had the foresight to publish it under a pseudonym, "Alcofribas."

The focus of this issue, "Jazz & Lit," is one that is near and dear to many who value innovative fiction. The rapprochement between jazz and literature is not found in the depiction of people playing bebop music in novels. "Jazz scenes" in literature are mere representations; representations that seldom get at the frank and exuberant approach to art and life that is the soul of jazz fiction. Rather, the heart of jazz and literature is better exemplified through the work of a man of the cloth and Renaissance iconoclast.

Rabelais was an improviser *and* an innovator. These traits allow us to mention him in the same breath as John Coltrane and Charlie Parker — and connect him as well to some of America's great jazz fictioneers, such as Federman and *ABR* founder Ronald Sukenick.

The insatiable appetites and energy that Rabelais celebrated through his fictional father and son giants still define the most significant intersections of jazz and literature.

And it is also fitting that we still term Miles Davis and Ella Fitzgerald jazz "giants."

In the twentieth century, Gargantua would have played the tenor saxophone, and Pantagruel, his son, the electric guitar.

A Rabelaisian love of freedom, art, and pleasure casts a long shadow on the American cultural landscape. The recent passing of innovative artistic giants such as Sukenick, Kurt Vonnegut, and Oscar Peterson only serve to remind us of how rare — and special — such individuals are.

But others will replace them on the contemporary scene. This is the life cycle of the arts. Every generation produces its share of giants: innovators and improvisers who set the pace for others. Part of the thrill of being caught in fiction's present is knowing that among the thousands of literary performances published each year, a few will over time come be known as the work of giants.

As the giants of jazz and literature pass on, we as listeners and readers must live in appreciation and anticipation. While it is important to continue to celebrate the achievements of these giants, it is even more important to support those artists who are on the path; those who have not yet arrived, but are taking giant steps.

One of the goals of this publication has been and will continue be to share with the world reviews of books by writers whose work is neglected because of its innovative nature. We at *ABR* would like to thank the National Endowment for the Arts for its continued support. We also would like to thank the individual and corporate supporters who are helping us to raise these giants through the Friends of *ABR* Endowment Fund, including Dorothy Alcorn, Chris and Tenna Thompson, the O'Connor & Hewitt Foundation, and the Wells Fargo Foundation.

Over the course of his life, Rabelais' powerful friends in the church and the state helped him a number of times to avoid being burned at the stake. The recent generous support of this publication from the NEA and our Friends may have just done the same for *ABR*.

141

37

ON THE FINAL LINE OF WILLIAM GASS'
Willie Masters' Lonesome Wife (1968)

William H. Gass' *Willie Masters' Lonesome Wife* (1968) is a tour-de-force meditation on literature as language. In some ways, it is as important an exercise on the limits and nature of language as Ludwig Wittgenstein's philosophical landmark, the *Tractatus Logico-Philosophicus* (1921). Like Wittgenstein's *Tractatus*, a work which literally mirrors reality through language, *Willie Masters'* presents its readers with a direct reflection of the reality of fictional worlds. From its utilization of nearly every typographical style dating back to Gutenberg and its multicolored and textured paper stock to its metafictional reflections on readers, writers and language, *Willie Masters'* exhaustively examines the interiors of literary aesthetic space both materially and conceptually. As Gass notes in his essay, "The Ontology of the Sentence" (1977) — an essay in honor of the retirement of the philosopher of language, Max Black — "But aren't we right to seek in language the imprint of reality? Doesn't it shape the syntax of our sentences?"

While Gass has never tried to hide his knowledge of the philosophy of language, his engagement with this arid field of study has always been refreshing and inspiring. In his essay, "Philosophy and the Form of Fiction" (1972), published a few years after *Willie Masters'*, Gass writes, "It seems a country-headed thing to say: that literature is language, that stories and the places and the people in them are merely made of words as chairs are made of smoothed sticks and sometimes of cloth and metal tubes." But think about it: Is stating that "literature is language" any less "country-headed" than the first proposition (line) of Wittgenstein's *Tractatus*, "The world is all that is the case" (*"Die Welt ist alles, was der Fall ist"* [1])? Gass' stylistically innovative linguistic interventions have in many ways contributed more to our understanding of how language works than a lot of the more formal and analytical studies of language.

Gass has said that though he has not spent much time studying the writings of Wittgenstein, the time that he has spent was "the most important intellectual experience in [his] life." While it would be a stretch to call Gass a disciple of Wittgenstein, the philosopher's impact on Gass' thought is still apparent. Like Wittgenstein, Gass does not shy away from using the most basic insights about language and its workings as the engine of complex inquiry. Their writings lay bare language in such a way that it appears like a body without clothes — a point which conceptually legitimates the nude woman who is pictured throughout Gass' novella.

Wittgenstein famously closed his *Tractatus* with words suggesting that if the readers understood the propositions of his text, then they would ultimately view them as "nonsense" and "climb up beyond them." "He must transcend these propositions, and then he will see the world aright" (*"Er muß diese Sätze* überwinden, *dann sieht er die Welt richtig"* [6.54]) is the penultimate line of the *Tractatus*. Wittgenstein's last line, "What we cannot speak about we must consign to silence." (*"Wovon man nicht sprechen kann, darüber muß man schweigen"* [7]) is a singular proposition, which unlike the six lead propositions of the *Tractatus*, contains no sub-propositional commentary. Wittgenstein's seventh proposition literally stands alone. It opens the door to a world outside of the world of language; it positions the reader outside of the linguistic reality created by its labyrinth of numbered propositions.

The last lines of Wittgenstein's *Tractatus* signaled the exhaustion of one way of approaching language, and foreshadowed the opening of a new approach to language. Wittgenstein's new way was to be found in a number of notebooks that were published a few years after his death in 1951, most significantly, the *Philosophical Investigations* (1953) and *The Blue and Brown Books* (1958).

Viewed alongside the last lines of Wittgenstein's *Tractatus*, the closing lines of *Willie Masters'* become much more meaningful. In the final paragraphs of *Willie Masters'*, Gass encourages the reader both to look back on what has been accomplished in (and through) the "body" of the novella, and to envision what lies ahead for language after the reader exits "lady language." Gass calls for a new language, stating "Then let us have a language worthy of our world, a democratic style where rich and well-born nouns can roister with some sluttish verb yet find themselves content and uncomplained of." He goes on to call for and describe new types of diction, tone, and metaphor. Then, with a closing line that rivals that of the *Tractatus*, Gass implores us to leave language and return to life.

In boldface capital letters, encircled by a coffee ring, out of syntactic order with the preceding dream-like reflections on a new language, Gass closes *Willie Masters'* with these words: "**YOU HAVE FALLEN INTO ART — RETURN TO LIFE.**" Lodged in the lower right hand corner of the page, the words are linked visually to a woman's navel encircled on the opposite page by a coffee stain. The semiotic connection of these last words with final image in the text is profound. If one considers the language of the novella to be a sign-system, then both the verbal and non-verbal signs of *Willie Masters'* must be treated as significant. Thus, the encircled navel becomes Gass' last "word" — an iconic sign that takes us beyond the realm of verbal language and back into the arena of life.

38

PLEASURE IN THE END

Readers are suckers for happy endings. A 2006 website poll undertaken in connection with World Book Day indicated that 41 percent of readers surveyed preferred a happy ending, compared to the 2.2 percent who preferred a sad ending. The study also revealed that preference for happy endings only grows stronger with age. While 8.6 percent of those under the age of 16 preferred sad endings, only 1.1 percent of those surveyed between the ages of 41 and 65 years of age preferred sad endings.

The same poll asked the public which ending to a novel they most favored. The work cited most frequently ended with these words: "Darcy, as well as Elizabeth, really loved them; and they were both ever sensible of the warmest gratitude towards the persons who, by bringing her into Derbyshire, had been the means of uniting them," a passage you will recognize as the last line of Jane Austen's *Pride and Prejudice* (1813). Few major writers were more devoted to the pursuit of happiness than Austen.

In her study, *Jane Austen: Women, Politics, and the Novel* (1988), Claudia L. Johnson claims that "In all Austen's novels, but especially *Pride and Prejudice*, pursuing happiness is the business of life." "In its readiness to ratify and to grant our happiness," writes Johnson, "*Pride and*

Prejudice is almost shamelessly wish fulfilling." Austen presents happiness as a right, which one can expect to attain through Aristotelian virtuous action.

But happiness seems alien to the phrase selected by our contributors as the *ABR* survey's best last line, which comes from Samuel Beckett's *The Unnamable* (1953):

> . . . I can't go on, you must go on, I'll go on, you must say words, as long as there are any, until they find me, until they say me, strange pain, strange sin, you must go on, perhaps it's done already, perhaps they have said me already, perhaps they have carried me to the threshold of my story, before the door that opens on my story, that would surprise me, if it opens, it will be I, it will be the silence, where I am, I don't know, I'll never know, in the silence you don't know, you must go on, I can't go on, I'll go on.

The excerpt above contains the final 100 or so words of a concluding sentence that goes on for *nine pages*—making it perhaps the longest, saddest closing line ever composed.

Written over fifty years ago, and nearly 140 years after Austen's works, the concluding "sentence" of Beckett's novel appears to be the polar opposite of Austen's. If Austen's novels end in happiness, marriage, and wish fulfillment, then Beckett's dénouement seems a dramatic departure from these sentiments. Beckett leaves his character not only unfulfilled, but without a clear sense of identity. The character faces the futility both of language and of silence, and finds it almost impossible to go on.

However, if you turn back nine pages from the end of *The Unnamable* to locate the beginning of the final sentence, you encounter the traditional ingredients of the happy ending: love and marriage. It begins: "They love each other, marry, in order to love each other better, more conveniently." But then, as the narrator continues, we see that marital happiness cannot sustain itself: ". . . he goes to the wars, he dies at the wars, she weeps, with emotion, at having loved him, at having lost him, yep, marries again, in order to love again, more conveniently again, they love each other, you love as many times as necessary, as necessary in order to be happy . . . ."

Beckett's masterful last line is a deconstruction of not only happy endings, but also of our notion of what a novel is and should be. Like *Pride and Prejudice*, *The Unnamable's* final sentence leads off with a traditional happy ending, but then relentlessly follows the event's logic through to its existential conclusions. And this is what our readers find to be pleasurable. But why?

Finding — or not finding — happiness in a world gone wrong with a sentence that stretches on for the length of a short story might not be satisfying to your average reader — but *ABR* readers are not your average readers. Some time ago, Roland Barthes made a useful distinction between the pleasure one receives from reading different kinds of novels. In *Le Plaisir du texte* (1973), he used the word "plaisir" to describe the pleasure one experiences when s/he reads a text that predictably fulfills his/her expectations and is easy to read. These "readerly" (*lisible*) texts are the ones that find their way into public surveys such as the one done in connection with World Book Day.

However, as the list of *ABR* last lines shows, our readers tend to seek a different sort of satisfaction from their reading. Barthes terms this type of textual pleasure "jouissance," and locates its source in "writerly" (*scriptible*) texts, namely, those which call attention to the structuring activity of the reader and must be composed as they are read. Our readers find satisfaction in an active read and an ambiguous ending.

Yet we also embrace Austen. While *Pride and Prejudice* did not make the *ABR* list of 100 best last lines, Austen's *Emma* can be found at number thirty-two. The novel's ending leaves no ambiguity, closing with a wedding, hopes, and happiness: "But, in spite of these deficiencies, the wishes, the hopes, the confidence, the predictions of the small band of true friends who witnessed the ceremony, were fully answered in the perfect happiness of the union." So satisfying, the way this impetuous young woman gets her comeuppance by finding love after declaring herself immune to romantic attraction — the wedding must go on, it can't go on, it goes on.

39

BURN, BABY BURN

What to do with a "dangerous" book? Ban it? Buy it? Incinerate it? The disposal of books in staged public burnings evokes black-and-white photographs from twentieth-century totalitarian regimes. You'd think we'd be beyond burning books. But a church in Iowa claimed some years back to have held the largest book burning in American history.

After evening services, over 1.5 million Harry Potter books were burned in the parking lot of the Landover Baptist Church. According to the church's website, the "Harry Potter book series is the most evil and dangerous set of books to be released this century" and is "worse than pornography." The church's website also offers to help you "to organize a book burning in your community."

To the south of Landover, book burning was recently used as a response to people *not* reading books. A used bookstore in Kansas City, Missouri made national news by staging a series of book burnings. Tom Wayne, co-owner of Prospero's Books, has seen his sales decline in recent years. He attributed this trend to a national decline in reading for pleasure, and the rise of the Internet and television as information sources. Wayne decided to stage monthly bonfires in front of his bookstore. He plans to continue the public burnings until the 20,000 books he's accumulated in warehouses (which don't have any chance of selling) are exhausted.

Books can be rendered dangerous both by the appeal of their content (e.g., Potter books) and the non-appeal of their content (e.g., Prospero's books). And unread books can be just as dangerous as ones that are read.

Perhaps no other institution in America deals more directly and daily with these two conclusions than libraries. And since book burning is never an option for libraries and librarians, their response to "dangerous" books comes through book banning.

Each year the American Library Association's Office for Intellectual Freedom reports on the number of books that have been challenged and/or banned from U.S. schools and libraries. The 2006 numbers were just released and showed a 30% increase from the previous year. Leading this year's list of 546 books is the award-winning children's book *And Tango Makes Three* (2005).

Justin Richardson and Peter Parnell's children's book is the true story of two male penguins who raised a baby penguin—a family scenario that some view as unsuitable for young readers. Richardson and Parnell are now among a list of banned/challenged authors kept by the ALA that includes Isabel Allende, Rudolfo Anaya, Margaret Atwood, Bret Easton Ellis, Toni Morrison, and Alice Walker. The ALA's 100 Most Frequently Challenged Books (1990-2000) lists J. K. Rowling's Harry Potter series as number seven, with John Steinbeck's *Of Mice and Men* (1937) at number six, Mark Twain's *Huckleberry Finn* (1884) at number five, and Maya Angelou's *I Know Why the Caged Bird Sings* (1969) at number three.

Libraries today are the real front lines of the battle of "dangerous" books. By caving in to challenges from the community to remove masterpieces of American literature that move young readers to social and political consciousness like Kurt Vonnegut's *Slaughterhouse Five* (1969), William Golding's *Lord of the Flies* (1954), and Aldous Huxley's *Brave New World* (1932), libraries are betraying their mission. More importantly, they are denying the youth of America the opportunity to read books that have the proven capacity to turn them into lifelong readers. One taste of Vonnegut or Huxley has left many an adolescent mind craving more.

Moreover, one must not forget that for many Americans — particularly those of limited means — purchasing books for pleasure is a rare occurrence. Many still rely on libraries to find the books that they want to — and should — read. A recent event reminded me of this all too clearly.

I had the distinct pleasure to bring a well-known novelist that was an invited speaker at my university to a local high school. After an inspiring presentation to the students, the author talked with the students and signed copies of the books from which she had read. Teachers and students lined up to purchase signed books and chat with the author. I noticed one student watching the cue from a distance. I asked him if he had already received his signed copy. He said, "No, I haven't." Curious, I asked, "Why?" He replied, "Because I'm hoping that public library purchases a copy of it so that I can read it." Fortunate for him the author was not some dangerous writer like Maya Angelou or Toni Morrison — or was she? We'll see if her books turn up in our library.

40

ON PUBLIC BOOK PROPOSALS

What if the fate of a book proposal were left up to
the court of public opinion rather than the judgment of a
small group of editors? What if rather than sending a book
proposal to a limited number of quality reviewers, presses
opted instead to place the proposal on a "blog" for public
scrutiny? How would the judgment of the collective mind
compare to that of the editors? Much to the chagrin of many
(and the amusement of many more), we'll not have to wait
very long to find out.

On May 21, 2007, Project Publish was launched. It
is a joint venture between the website (and blog) Media
Predict and the publishing giant Touchstone Books/Simon
& Schuster. Mark Gompertz, Executive Vice President and
Publisher of Touchstone Fireside, calls Project Publish
"the ultimate pre-publication, market-based focus group."
Project Publish is the first (and surely not the last) attempt
by a major publisher to harness the powers of the market
to evaluate book proposals. It is a glimpse at the future of
the publishing industry (that ironically comes on the heels
of the tenth anniversary of the inception of the weblog or
"blog" as it is commonly known).

In a recent newspaper article celebrating the ten-
year anniversary of the blog, the novelist Tom Wolfe

commented that "Blogs are an advance guard for the rear." "The universe of blogs is a universe of rumors," continued Wolfe, "and the tribe likes it that way" (*Wall Street Journal* 7/14/07).

One recent attempt to harness the power of the "Blog Nation" is Media Predict (http://mediapredict.com/), a website that allows its users to play a "prediction market game." The aim of this game is not merely amusement, but rather to "help media companies find stuff people really want." Registered users of Media Predict can look at prices and wager in four major markets: books, movies, music, and television. The higher the price of items in each market, the greater the chances of the product succeeding; the lower the price, the lower the chances of success. The Media Predict website explains the monetary values in their market through the example of a book proposal. "If an undiscovered book proposal trades at $38, that means users think it has a 38% chance of getting a book deal."

Users of the Media Predict website are encouraged to purchase products that they think are going to do well in the market, and sell products that they do not think are going to do well. In the case of book proposals, if the book gets signed, then you receive $100 for every share you bought. If the book is not signed, then you receive $10 for each share that you have bought.

Media Predict claims that with this process, "In the end we all win. . . . Better predictions help media companies choose the books, CDs, films, and television shows that people really want. That means you'll get media that you like, and so will everyone else." Media Predict also says that they are providing a forum for undiscovered material, such as "unsigned bands and undiscovered writers."

The recently launched partnership between Media Predict and Touchstone Books/Simon & Schuster is a fascinating one. Here's how it will work: authors send their proposals to the Media Predict website. In September, the top fifty scoring proposals will be reviewed and winnowed down to five by Gompertz and a group of his editors. Trading on the five finalists will continue until the grand prize winner is announced on October 9, 2007.

The grand prize is a book contract with Simon & Schuster.

However, if none of the fifty finalists is of publishable quality, the highest scoring finalists will receive a cash award of two thousand dollars.

Contrary to the claims of Media Predict, it is highly unlikely that this process will result in media that we like, particularly if the "we" are the readers of *ABR*. While one would not be surprised if the projects that traded highest on the book market sold well, one would be shocked if they were anything more than pedestrian in their literary value. There is very little chance that the process will result in a work of fiction that is worthwhile; and no chance that a work of progressive or innovative fiction will win out in this predictive market game.

While the process of polling the public on book proposals makes for good entertainment, only the future will be able to determine if the entertainment was a comedy or a tragedy for the publishing industry. Sales numbers and market analysis, which already overly influence too many publishing decisions, are the archenemies of avant-garde and innovative writing. For that matter, they are the nemesis of all forms of heterodox thinking and writing. Endeavors like Project Publish will only further jeopardize progressive writing in America by overly emphasizing the role of the market in literary publication decision-making. And while innovative in the marketing sense, undertakings such as the blog-driven Project Publish can sadly negate their avant-garde potential and further distance innovative writing from the publishing mainstream.

41

CRIMINAL HISTORY FROM KEROUAC TO KINSEY

The party game question: "which five figures from American history would you most like to invite to dinner?" is always an interesting thought experiment, and a good indicator of the interests and values of a new acquaintance. It's intriguing to imagine F. Scott Fitzgerald in conversation with Abbie Hoffman or an exchange between Henry James and Henry Miller. In his new novel *Malcolm & Jack: (and Other Famous American Criminals)*,[14] Ted Pelton takes this notion of our reliance on cultural and historical icons for inspiration and a sense of origin, and develops it into an insightful study of American identity and values.

"History," writes Pelton, "Do you ever think about history brothers and sisters?" He continues,

> I find myself thinking of it more and more. I look down a street like this one and see not what is today but what it has been. History. The streets are paved no more once the vision comes upon me. No automobiles or electric lights but lanterns and muddy paths and signs with arrows pointing to the auction grounds.

The act of viewing the streets of New York today and seeing slave auction grounds typifies the temporal motions of

Pelton's fascinating, fast-moving criminal history of the contemporary American psyche.

Pelton's novel continuously strives to unearth the seeds of the present in creative, criminal histories of the past. For him, "Much of what we call the '60s was born in the 1940s." To help us to see this better, Pelton takes us back to the '40s through the eyes of a cast of characters that played a key role in setting up the radical questioning of the dominant values of American society that came about in the '60s. While the characters Malcolm X and Jack Kerouac are the focal points of the novel, the novel is populated by many other famous and infamous figures, primarily from the literary and musical worlds. The literary world is that of the pre-Beat and Beat generations, which, in addition to Kerouac, includes William S. Burroughs, Lucien Carr, Neal Cassady, and Allen Ginsberg, among others. The musical world of the novel, while largely dominated by Billie Holiday, the subject of the entire second chapter, is that of American jazz from Count Basie to Charlie Parker.

While many of the character names in the novel actually existed, Pelton only irregularly situates them in documentable, factual events. He notes that while, for example, "Lucien Carr killed David Kammerer in August, 1944, in New York City" and that "Billie Holiday was sentenced to a year in Alderson Federal Reformatory for Women in 1947," no statement in the novel "should be taken as a simple statement of fact." Rather, Pelton challenges you to step out of the present into the past, such that "you find yourself transported back a life-time ago, to when things were wilder, more unsure in certain ways than they are today." To a time in New York City when, "Bums hanging out on the street corner are poets and jazz musicians who'll someday be famous. After they're dead." To a time when cultural heroes like Kerouac, Malcolm X, and Billie Holiday are challenging the line between criminality and creativity.

Consequently, *Malcolm & Jack* is a moving, hip, and complex journey into not only American cultural, social, and political history, but also into the meaning of history in itself. One senses the latter most profoundly when knowing that Malcolm X never met Jack Kerouac, but finding it difficult to resist Pelton's compelling scene with Kerouac buying a drink for Malcolm X in a Detroit blues bar. Pelton freely interweaves the lives of his characters in a way that mirrors the complex development of ideas in a jazz composition. Just as a great piece of jazz music can make us forget about the rules of composition and revel in the free-flow development of ideas, Pelton's novel makes us want to believe in the possibility of a relationship between these two figures.

Pelton describes the appeal of these possibilities as another kind of historical truth that "hustles" us in a passage on sidewalk speakers in Union Square:

> the sidewalk speakers climb up on milkcrates & crowds gather round to listen to the true word laid down, hustlers just like him [Malcolm X]—he likes the sound of their rapping in the night—the twists and turns of their crazed words, worlds both false and true but which no one comes forward to name except these eveningsaints of the mind, another kind of jazz & another kind of truth—so strong it seems like a lie but instead tells the lie in all the truths you assume, & the two flutter off, end over end, above the skyscraper points . . . .

Like the sidewalk speaker, Pelton is a hustler who twists and turns crazed words on worlds both false and true. *Malcolm & Jack* is "another kind of jazz & another kind of truth."

One of the more impressive aspects of this book is the fluidity with which Pelton is able to shift between radically different points of view. At one moment, he is speaking from the point of view of Jack Kerouac's wife; at another, he is inside the character of Billy Holiday; at yet another, he is Malcolm X. And there are other points of view established as well, including a gay male, crudely named, Dick Post (who is quite possibly fashioned after Allen Ginsberg). The establishment of multiple points of view achieves a sense of collective consciousness among the characters.

The six chapters of *Malcolm & Jack* effectively re-create the style, energy and social world of post-World War II era. While the chapters are linked with each other through the characters Malcolm and Jack, each holds its own as an independent novella. In them we find Billy

Holiday in prison on a heroin conviction reflecting on her life; a musical drama concerning the days leading up to the murder of David Kammerer by Lucien Carr; Malcolm X's days as the street hustler "Red Little"; Jack Kerouac as seen through the eyes of his first wife, Edith Parker; and, finally, the fictional character Dick Post recounting an interview regarding his sexual history with Dr. Alfred Kinsey, who is working on his first book on human sexuality.

This final chapter is particularly interesting as in it we find the Ward Pomeroy, Jack Kerouac, Neal Cassady, and Dick Post "transporting a piece of equipment to a University in Indiana in a Willy's Overland, a kind of Army-style, general purpose vehicle." The "equipment" is an "anatomically correct model of an adult woman, made entirely of glass." The model, named Lulu, is "absolutely perfect in contour" and is destined for the Dr. Kinsey's Institute of Sex Research at Indiana University in Bloomington, Indiana. Dr. Kinsey plans to use it for research on his next book, which will be concerned with female sexuality. During the trip, the Willy's gets rear-ended, and the perfect glass-woman is shattered: the loss of an American dream.

Pelton's vision of post-World War II America presents the mix of African American artistic, social, and political culture with that of the white culture of the Beats and Kinsey, and reveals the strong influence that each culture has had on the other. Pelton describes a new ethos forming in America through this intermingling of cultures and traditions. Attitudes toward sexual repression and racial discrimination begin to shift, and prejudice and stereotypes regarding race, gender, sex, and sexuality hold the promise of being overcome.

Over ten years in the making, *Malcolm & Jack* is Pelton's first novel. The criminals and crimes of the novel are posited as awakening a new consciousness in America. Pelton delivers an innovative, unforgettable journey into the imaginative oversoul and seedy origins of progressive American consciousness.

42

ON MINOR LITERATURE

Minor literature has entered the publishing and intellectual mainstream. It should no longer be regarded as exotic or esoteric. More publishers than ever are committed to expanding their minor literature catalogues. The list of works available in translation for the first time or in new translation is expanding daily. In addition, fine efforts such as the Reading the World Program facilitate a growing appreciation of minor literature.

Now in its third year, the Reading the World Program is an exemplary collaborative venture between publishers and booksellers. Initiated by Karl Pohrt of Shaman Drum Bookshop in Ann Arbor, Paul Yamazaki of City Lights in San Francisco, and Jeff Seroy of FSG in New York City, the program has grown to include over ten presses and more than two hundred and fifty bookstores.

Its aim is to bring translated literature from around the world to a wider audience. This year forty books have been selected for display in participating bookstores. The novels, poetry, and non-fiction from Africa, Asia, Europe, Latin America and the Middle East featured in the displays affords patrons the opportunity to browse and purchase a range of literature from around the world.

The surge in publication and publicity of translated literature from all over the world is a clear indication of the coming of age of minor literature. Its emergence from obscurity can be linked to the "flattening" of the world via new technologies. It can also be viewed as a consequence of both the emergence of globalized knowledges and the new cosmopolitanism.

The growing attraction of cultural studies (and its variations) in academia has also broadened interest in minor literature. Whereas the study of minor literatures was once dominated by foreign language departments (where an absence of study of the language implied an absence of study of the literature), today comparative literature and English departments have greatly increased the desire to explore minor literatures. And the recent surge in quality translations only makes the fulfillment of this desire more achievable by removing the language barrier.

While "minor" literature in the popular sense might be defined in opposition to "major" literature, such a move would be a mistake. In its most significant sense, minor literature is neither "neglected" literature, nor literature from "a small place," nor even literature from a small genre (for example, concrete poetry). Rather, it should take its meaning—especially for engaged writers and theorists—from the conceptually rich sense of the phrase developed by Gilles Deleuze and Félix Guattari.

In *Kafka: Toward a Minor Literature* (1986), Deleuze and Guattari argue that minor literature foregrounds the writing process, not the product of writing. For them, everything in minor literature takes on a collective value and is political. Moreover, the language of this way of writing is effected by a high degree of "deterritorialization."

While one might be tempted to regard the Focus of this issue—Romanian Poetry in Translation, masterfully edited by *ABR* Contributing Editor, Andrei Codrescu—to be dealing with "minor" literature in the popular sense of the term, this temptation should be avoided.

Even if it is the case that Romanian poetry is the product of a relatively small nation and has not received the level of attention in the literary world as, say, the literature of larger nations like France, England, and the U.S., this is insignificant information at best.

However, when regarded through the lens of Deleuze and Guattari's notion of "minor" literature, Romanian poetry and its translation becomes prime material for poststructuralist contemplation. As the contributions in our Focus indicate, the writing of Romanian poetry has been a deeply political and communal act. Also, its language is effected by a high degree of deteritorialization. Consequently, one might reasonably maintain that Romanian poetry *is* minor literature, *par excellance*.

To be sure, *ABR* has taken a "worldly" turn of late. It began with our recent Focuses on "Japanese Literature and Culture" (28.1) and "Cosmopolitanism" (28.3). Considering the Focus of this issue and that the next one will be an even more "wordly" topic — "Perpetual War" (28.6) — one might speculate that a pattern is forming.

Even though at this point I would be loath to confirm pattern-formation, expect to see more attention given to minor literature. *ABR* must be responsive to the emerging realities of a flattening world. It is my hope that we will continue to provide issues that challenge the sensibilities of literary provincialism, and, like the Reading the World Program, will keep on opening new horizons of literary experience for our readers.

43

ON NEWSPAPER BOOK REVIEWS AND ADVERTISING

It should come as no surprise that publications such as this one — review collections based on paper and ink — are dwindling in number. *The Wall Street Journal* recently reported that currently there are only a handful of book review sections in major metropolitan newspapers.[15] Whereas ten years ago there were nearly a dozen, today there are only five separate book review sections in major Sunday newspapers. The *Los Angeles Times* Sunday book review section was the most recent to go, whereas the *Philadelphia Inquirer*'s section folded decades ago.

The story also reported that the reason for the discontinuation of these Sunday independent review sections was not because of a lack of interest in book reviews by the readership. Rather, it was because the review sections were not able to generate enough ad sales. Why?

Because book publishers that used to run advertisements in these weekly book review sections are now using their limited marketing funds to purchase prime real estate in chain bookstores. Given that the average Barnes & Noble stocks between 125,000 and 150,000 books, the publishers feel that a big pile of their favored new title positioned near the front door or the cash register is a better investment of their marketing dollars than an ad for their book in the *Chicago Tribune* Sunday book review.

These publishers believe that folks are more likely to buy their book if they are attacked by a big pile of it in a chain bookstore than if they see an ad for it in a book review. Hence, the birth of the "book monster" — a pile of books so large and obvious that it is impossible to pass through the bookstore without falling over it.

The *Wall Street Journal* story can be viewed as a cautionary tale for the editors and readers of *ABR*. Dwindling ad revenues are hastening the death of paper and ink book reviews. And as someone who would like to see *ABR* thrive for years to come, I feel obligated to take note of what is happening to the Sunday newspaper book sections.

And even though there is at least one fundamental difference between the Sunday newspaper book reviews and *ABR* — they are for-profit organizations, and we are not — we still have bills to pay.

Moreover, the publishers that we feature — small, regional, university, ethnic, avant-garde, and women's presses — generally don't have the budgets to purchase a Barnes & Noble "book monster." Rather, they rely on us to get word out on their books through quality reviews of their titles and affordable advertising in our pages. Charlie Alcorn — our managing editor — and I heard this time and time again at the AWP meeting in Atlanta last month, and we are taking this advice to heart.

The health of this publication must always be gauged by the quality of its reviews. But we need to recognize that our longevity is connected to the number of ads you see in our issues. It's a pretty safe bet that with a stable, if modest, base of advertising, we will have the material conditions to run a quality publication. Without advertising, we place ourselves in the fickle hands of external support and thereby risk going the way of the Sunday book review.

Some believe that advertising in itself brings down the credibility of a publication such as ours, while others insist that ads increase our perceived value. But credibility is always on the shoulders of the persuasive, professional, thoughtful, and detailed reviews we publish. And I would want it no other way.

I think that those of us who know and love and support *ABR* have to remind ourselves what a special publication this is. We also, however, have to be cognizant of the fragile environment in which it exists. The future of paper and ink publications such as this one is not guaranteed based on past success. You can help us by taking every opportunity you can to share *ABR* with your friends, colleagues, and students. Let them know what we do. Encourage them to subscribe, or give them a gift subscription. And most of all, encourage those of means to support this publication with donations. If many of us do these little things, then the big picture for this publication is bright.

44

ANTHOLOGIES AND LITERARY LANDSCAPES

It is no secret that anthologies are not highly regarded in the publishing world. One of my favorite statements on this subject comes from Jason Epstein, who was editorial director of Random House for forty years and received the National Book Award for Distinguished Service to American Letters. In *Book Business: Publishing Past, Present, and Future* (2001), Epstein notes, "topical anthologies, unlike hospital wards and reading rooms, are of little value in themselves. They serve no literary purpose, usually find few readers and quickly go out of print." Epstein's comments betray a certain lack of vision shared by many — both inside and outside the publishing world — regarding the "literary purpose" of anthologies.

A more progressive and optimistic view of anthologies locates their value in the topologies of the literary world that they create. Unlike the natural world, which has an objective (or at least intersubjective) geography, the geography of the literary world is always already subjective: a purely human creation that anthologies serve to map.

Anthologies chart courses through the literary world and are one of the primary ways through which we learn to navigate it. Anthology editors create discrete mappings or orderings of a textual world that is so complex and dense that even the most encyclopedic mind can grasp only a fraction of it.

Mainstream anthologies are those that take us to places that we feel we have already traveled. Such anthologies are strongly connected with canonical, disciplinary, pedagogical, and economic interests. They produce and reproduce spaces such as "American literature" and the "American short story" to the extent that these spaces feel as though they are natural features of the literary world.

The fact that anthologies can make us feel as though there is a defined space called "American literature" or "American poetry" is a strong indicator of their power. Anthologies are the product of market forces and ideologies and play a crucial role in canon formation and disciplinary identity. A topical anthology literally creates a place or region — a *topos* — that can be easily visited or identified.

Anthologies also serve canonical and disciplinary ends by having a formative role in both: arguably, just as the American literature canon is shaped and disciplined through anthologies, disciplines themselves such as cultural studies and disability studies are established through anthologies.

However, just as the natural world is continuously changing, so, too, is the literary world. Anthologies provide us with a snapshot of a place or region that will change over time. Like the Hericlitean river that one cannot step into twice, the literary world is an ever-changing entity. Anthologies provide a momentary vision of a continuously changing literary landscape.

The anthologies reviewed in this issue are exciting because they contribute to an understanding of literature as a plurality; as multifarious; as changing and evolving. Aldon Lynn Nielsen and Laurie Ramey's *Every Goodbye Ain't Gone* is an ideological intervention into the African American literary canon. By providing a wider and more varied landscape for African American poetic innovation, Nielsen and Ramey break down the commonplaces of African American poetry anthologization.

Melvin Jules Bukiet and David G. Roskies' *Scribblers on the Roof* serves to widen this canon by anthologizing a new generation of writers such as Pearl Abraham, Dara Horn, and Jon Papernick. Bukiet and Roskie's anthology effectively situates these more recent writers in a literary landscape with their more canonical peers, such as Cynthia Ozick, Lore Segal, and Max Apple.

The remaining anthologies reviewed in this issue, *PP/FF: An Anthology, ParaSpheres, New Sudden Fiction,* and *Flash Fiction Forward,* exercise the progressive, world-making potential of anthologies. Each is a topical anthology that is valuable for the space in the literary world that it creates, or recreates, as in the case of flash fiction anthologies. The literary purpose of these flash fiction anthologies is the establishment of new regions that challenge the conventions of the short story and raise important questions about the nature of narrative.

Paul Auster's comments in his preface to *The Random House Book of Twentieth-Century French Poetry* (1982) aptly describe the value of all of the anthologies reviewed in this issue: "One must resist the notion of treating an anthology as the last word on its subject. It is no more than a first word, a threshold opening on to a new space." Challenging, iconoclastic, innovative, and experimental topical anthologies such as those reviewed in this issue are an important part of vigorous and vital literary culture. Anthologies on the edge push forward the frontiers of the literary world and are a valued and valuable part of literary culture.

45

COSMOPOLITAN MODERNISM

The contemporary resurgence of interest in cosmopolitanism began in the mid- to late-1990s in both philosophical and cultural/literary circles. In philosophy, articles by Anthony Appiah, Martha Nussbaum and Samuel Scheffler sparked interest in cosmopolitanism, while in cultural and literary studies, works such as Timothy Brennan's *At Home in the World: Cosmopolitanism Now* (1997) and Bruce Robbins' *Feeling Global: Internationalism in Distress* (1999) as well as edited works such as Pheng Cheah and Bruce Robbins' *Cosmopolitics: Thinking and Feeling Beyond the Nation* (1998), Vinay Dharwadker's *Cosmopolitan Geographies: New Locations in Literature and Culture* (2000), and Carol A. Breckenridge, Sheldon Pollock, Homi K. Bhabha, and Dipesh Chakrabarty's *Cosmopolitanism* (2002) were receiving much attention.

These and other works have played a large role in establishing cosmopolitanism as one of the key critical discussions of our day — a discussion relevant to scholarly and creative audiences alike. Much of this discussion revolves around the very meaning of cosmopolitanism. Much like postmodernism — a key critical concept whose meaning has been extensively debated — discussions of cosmopolitanism often center around situating the author's take on this concept with other, competing views on the concept.

Fortunately, Rebecca L. Walkowitz's new study of cosmopolitanism is less concerning with defending one particular sense of cosmopolitanism than with demonstrating the ways in which variations of this key contemporary critical concept permeate the writings of a number of the last centuries' most well-known writers. *Cosmopolitan Style: Modernism beyond the Nation*[16] is an elegant, timely, and rich reading of writings by Joseph Conrad, James Joyce, Virginia Woolf, Kazuo Ishiguro, Salman Rushdie, and W. G. Sebald. Walkowitz argues that these authors' use of literary modernist strategies results in what she calls "critical cosmopolitanism"—a type of cosmopolitanism that is distinct from the "planetary humanism" form of cosmopolitanism.

Whereas planetary humanist cosmopolitanism prefers heroic tones of appropriation and progress, and tends toward epistemic privilege (that is, the position toward knowledge that "assumes a consistent distinction between who is seeing and what is seen"), critical cosmopolitanism avoids them. Instead, critical cosmopolitanism involves "reflecting on the history, uses, and interests of cosmopolitanism" and "the critical." In her readings of these authors, Walkowitz reveals both the ways in which their novels, stories, and essays develop positions on cosmopolitanism as well as the ways in which these works are forms of "critique," that is, they involve negation, self-reflection, double consciousness, and comparison.

The writers that Walkowitz examines generate positions on cosmopolitanism not simply because they are cosmopolitan persons, but rather because their literary style in itself generates a critical cosmopolitanism. At the heart of her book is the notion that modernist literary style has played an important role in the generation of cosmopolitan thought. For her, these writers "imagine that conditions of national and transnational affiliation depend on narrative patterns of attentiveness, relevance, perception, and recognition." Walkowitz reveals their cosmopolitanism through their questioning of moral and political norms, their explorations of the meanings of national culture, transnational thought, and international attachment. Analysis of the modernist styles of Conrad, Joyce, Woolf, Rushdie, Ishiguro, and Sebald reveals them to share a belief in democratic individualism and a rejection of imperialism and fascism.

Moreover, Walkowitz associates each writer with a different literary tactic: Conrad with naturalness ("By creating distrust for established reputations, Conrad creates a less natural conception of Englishness and a more cosmopolitan tradition of British writing"); Joyce with triviality ("For Joyce, the tricks, the ruses, and the insistent pleasures of 'living' are the necessary conditions of a truly critical cosmopolitanism"); Woolf with evasion ("Woolf may have participated in civic endeavors and written directly against war and gender inequality, but her project remains challenging and often disturbing because she suggests that international sympathy and national dissent are nourished in part by those evasions of syntax, plot, and tone that qualify, unsettle, and redirect enduring habits of attentiveness"); Ishiguro with treason ("Committed to change but also to conflict, Ishiguro commits to treason: his floating worlds betray their narrators, and they everywhere betray 'us'"); Rushdie with mix-up ("He deploys the mistakes of immigration as the mix-ups of critical cosmopolitanism"); and Sebald with vertigo ("Bringing the margins of British history to the center of his narratives, Sebald enhances and disables the place of national fiction; its constituency and its borders, he affirms, are vertiginous at best"). In tying all of these writers together, Walkowitz argues that the modernist narrative strategies of Ishiguro, Rushdie and Sebald are transformations of those of Conrad, Joyce and Woolf.

She calls the tactics of these writers' cosmopolitan styles "to emphasize the importance of affect, manner, and self-consciousness in all practices of critical cosmopolitanism and to identify the use of new narrative strategies in the cosmopolitan literary practices of the twentieth century." Moreover, Walkowitz contends that her broad conception of style—one that regards style as stance, consciousness, posture, and attitude—is useful in understanding non-literary conceptions of cosmopolitanism such as those in media studies, history, and anthropology.

In a very subtle move, Walkowitz situates her own cosmopolitanist style as a complement, not a challenge, to the cosmopolitan politics of Bruce Robbins and others. For her, recognition of cosmopolitan style foregrounds an analytic feature of the critical cosmopolitanisms of these writers — and does not supplant cosmopolitan politics. The basic point for Walkowitz seems to be that "cosmopolitan theory is more literary and more modernist than its practitioners have previously acknowledged." Whereas cosmopolitanism as viewed through the lens of political criticism has tended to reduce considerations of style, Walkowitz's book rigorously and persuasively restores considerations of style into cosmopolitan theory.

Walkowitz's book is an impressive interweaving of theoretical speculation and close reading. Its own style is marked by careful textual exegesis punctuated by appropriate (albeit eclectic) theoretical pairing. While Walkowitz's study most clearly favors the critical work of Theodore W. Adorno, numerous other theorists — from Homi K. Bhabha and James Clifford to Michel de Certeau and Gilles Deleuze — come to the fore at appropriate moments. Even though the introduction may be slow going for those unaccustomed to the vernacular of contemporary cultural and literary theory, it will be well worth the effort as it provides a telegraphic overview of some of the main issues in cosmopolitan theory. The readings of the individual novelists are less theoretically dense and are well argued and written.

My main complaint about the book is a relatively minor one: It lacks a discussion of the relationship of postmodernism to cosmopolitan style, particularly when Ishiguro, Rushdie, and Sebald are ordinarily more closely affiliated with postmodernist fiction than modernist fiction. While a couple of passing mentions of postmodernism are made, they do not provide much insight as to why postmodernist international fiction could not as well result in critical cosmopolitanism. Nevertheless, Walkowitz's book is to be praised for reinforcing the important point that fiction is an ideal place to explore critically the complicated, troubled and troubling, social and political waters of contemporary, transnational, global society.

46

ON ACCESS TO CRITICAL THEORY

Critical theory has had a tendency to isolate itself from broader audiences. This is in part by design and in part by accident. The sheer difficulty of the style and content of much of the writing, which assumes a wide understanding of the histories of literature and philosophy and related disciplines, may limit access for the occasional reader. The other—and more cynical—reason for the isolationism is that critical theorists *do not want to be understood* by a broader audience. The argument here might be that the publicly accessible circulation of theory would serve to decrease its power—a power that is generated in large part through inaccessibility.

This situation puts *ABR* in a challenging position. While *ABR*'s mission statement notes our commitment to reviewing "neglected" works of literary and cultural criticism, we are also committed to publicly accessible reviews.

We want people to be encouraged to read the books we are reviewing, and aim to facilitate the understanding of key terms and themes of contemporary criticism. With this in mind, we are launching this issue's cosmopolitanism Focus.

Over the last twenty-five years, critical theorists have introduced into our vernacular many powerful "-isms" and "theories." From postmodernism and postcolonialism to Lacanian theory and queer theory, the critical landscape has been populated by terms which signify empowering critical matrices. Issues of *ABR* with Focuses on some of the key terms of critical theory can alleviate the alienating effect these terms can have on readers. Our aim is to publish Focuses that engage the key terms and issues of critical theory in ways that will be meaningful to both scholarly and creative audiences.

Not only will these publicly accessible reviews and discussions of key critical concepts enrich writerly and readerly processes, they will also serve to build a stronger bridge between the critical and creative worlds.

Finally, it is particularly fitting in the context of the aforementioned that we welcome on board our newest Contributing Editor, Michael Bérubé, who is well-known for his work on public access and the humanities. Welcome to *ABR*, Michael!

47

A NEW BEGINNING

I am deeply proud to add my name to the masthead of this publication. Few publications have mastheads as illustriously peopled as *ABR*'s. Our masthead reveals much about the identity of the publication as well as about the level of excellence with which it is affiliated.

It is clearly noted on our masthead that "*ABR* is published by its editors." This means that *ABR*'s editors are charged with recommending books for review, and voting on whether reviews should be accepted for publication.

Our editors work collectively in the operation of this publication. Its quality is a function of their unique talents and expertise, and of the time and commitment they generously donate. None of our editors are paid for their efforts. Their compensation is the continued publication of *ABR* in a manner consistent with its mission — a mission that remains as important today as when it was chartered nearly thirty years ago.

I am grateful to all of our editors for their commitment to this publication and for the goodwill efforts they expend on its behalf. The esteemed place that *ABR* holds in the literary world is due to their efforts. On behalf of *ABR*'s readership, I thank our editors for the care and work they have volunteered to the publication over the years.

You will notice that changes to the masthead have been inaugurated in this issue. They are primarily reorganizational, but still important. Their aim is to clarify the editorial responsibilities at *ABR*. Just as the flags that fly on top of a ship's mast announce the identity of the ship, *ABR*'s masthead reveals to its readership much about its identity and history. It is my hope that our revamped masthead will allow you to appreciate more clearly our history and understand more transparently our present.

48

A FORMIDABLE PAST

The history of *American Book Review* consists of nearly thirty years of continuous engagement with some of the most challenging, innovative, and beautiful wordcraft in our literary tradition. Its editors and contributors form both a Who's Who of the literary scene and an index of the powerful undercurrents in American publishing.

The review has thrived because of the collective spirit that has dominated its editorial vision and publishing practice. At its core are writers writing about writers: people who live with words, who allow words to dominate their being. Part of the uniqueness and power of this publication is the critical window these contributors provide for our readers.

ABR reviewers share a commitment to and passion for contemporary writing, which make *ABR* a special venue to gain a perspective on the contemporary American literary horizon. The emphasis away from mainstream American publishing only makes *ABR* more attractive and valuable to its readers.

At its best, *ABR* is like a trip down the blue highways and backstreets of contemporary American literature and culture with a knowledgeable local guide. Its bimonthly issues are adventurous journeys often into unchartered territory. They provide its readership with an almost unparalleled insight into the innovations of contemporary American writing.

I have been a frequent contributor to *ABR* and a fervent fan. I believe in the value of its mission, in the maintenance of its practices, and in the promise of its future.

I am honored to be leading *ABR* into a new phase of its history. While I know and have worked with many members of the *ABR* editorial and contributing family, there are many more whom I look forward to getting to know. I aim to foster the collaborative spirit that has propelled *ABR* to its esteemed position. If you have a chance, drop me a line. I always enjoy hearing stories about *ABR*'s past, particularly its early days, and value your guidance and support regarding this publication's present and immediate future.

Over the course of the next few issues, you will see a few small changes as I build on *ABR*'s strengths, though much will be the same as it has been over the history of this publication. Editorial and publishing decisions will be driven by the wishes and values of those persons who graciously offer their time and energy.

Looking ahead, the next issue of *ABR* will feature a revamped masthead. Over the course of its history, *ABR* has had the privilege of amassing an impressive list of editors. However, the number of editorial distinctions has multiplied beyond necessity. So, instead of having Executive Editors, Editors, Contributing Editors, Advisory Editors, and Associate Editors—a host of distinctions worthy of a medieval logician—we'll simply have Associate Editors and Contributing Editors. Associate Editor will signify a high level of day-to-day editorial activity and Contributing Editor a less frequent level. Charles Alcorn, as you already know, will be our full-time Managing Editor, and I will serve as Editor, overseeing the editorial operation of *ABR*. It is my hope that this editorial reorganization will not only make it easier for the editors themselves to understand their respective roles, but also that those observing from the outside will be able to more clearly distinguish the editorial structure of *ABR*.

I'd like to close by thanking the *ABR* family, particularly Charlie Harris and Tara Reeser, for their guidance and good will during this period of transition. I'd also like to thank R. M. Berry and Lance Olson for graciously agreeing to serve as Associate Editors in our emerging editorial structure. In addition, a note of heartfelt thanks goes out to all of those persons whose support has made *ABR*'s editorial relocation to the University of Houston—Victoria a reality, particularly the president of our university, Dr. Tim Hudson; our former provost, Dr. Don Smith; and our current regent, Morgan O'Connor. Finally, my deepest debt of gratitude goes out to Charlie Alcorn. Over the past three months, he has diligently and tirelessly labored to master the management of this publication. Gracias.

It should be noted that I deeply appreciate the time and energy that all of the editors of *ABR* put into this publication. Moreover, I appreciate the patience and support that the current editors have afforded us in this transitional period. Your continued commitment and service to *ABR* will play a central role in its future success.

49

ON THE OPENING LINE OF ITALO CALVINO'S
If on a winter's night a traveler

A great first line sets reader expectations, and encourages the reader to read on. The opening line of *If on a winter's night a traveler* — "You are about to begin reading Italo Calvino's new novel, *If on a winter's night a traveler*" — does just that. Like a film preview, this opening line asks the reader to prepare him or herself for the story to come, and for the act of reading itself. It establishes a sense of anticipation, and of intimacy. The narrator knows you, and knows just what you are doing at this moment: you are sitting down (or lying down, as he later suggests), to read a new novel.

But this line is, in fact, a false or empty first line. At the end of chapter one, we learn that "the first lines of the first page" are yet to come. The first chapter has been, in fact, a record of everything undertaken prior to settling down to read the first line of the book, which is on the next page. The narrator admits that this may be disappointing, or confusing, but suggests that "on sober reflection, you prefer it this way, confronting something and not quite knowing yet what it is." And this is not, in the end, the thrill of the great first line: that the first flirtation with a great experience, a great read, without quite knowing yet what the novel will be.

A great first line serves as a reference for the rest of

the reading, and will bring new insight when reread later, as the reader progresses in the novel. Calvino's opening line mirrors his closing line: "And you say, 'Just a moment, I've almost finished *If on a winter's night a traveler* by Italo Calvino.'" This extremely self-conscious method of handling the beginning and the end of a novel recognizes the pleasure in a neat beginning and conclusion to storytelling. Though open-ended storytelling may be intriguing or lend a sense of realism, there is an inherent, if simple, satisfaction in the blunt recognition that stories have a clear beginning and ending.

On a more theoretical level, the opening line of *If on a winter's night a traveler* breaks the pact of realism and establishes the book as a work of metafiction. The opening line informs the reader that the narrator will not allow him or her to forget the act of reading. But if this theoretical aspect of the novel distances the reader from intimate identification with the characters, the narrator's conspiratorial tone restores that sense of intimacy. For a novel peppered with inquiries into the nature of reading, interpretation, characterization, publication, and literary study, the opening line of *If on a winter's night a traveler* sets the tone. It is a perfect opening for a tour de force meditation on the act and nature of reading, readers, and rereading.

50

NARRATIVE TERRORISM

Terror-Dot-Gov[17] is a tour-de-force rumination on the psychical damage and physical carnage resulting from present day terrorism and war. In his distinctively sparse and cool prose, Harold Jaffe takes on the contemporary cultural and political climate with narrative bravado and ideological courage. At heart, *Terror-Dot-Gov* is a work of political activism and deep humanity with a sense of outrage at the state of national and international affairs.

Terror-Dot-Gov is not a simple straightforward assault on the Bush administration, Western culture and policy, or the nationalistic and xenophobic proclivities of the American public, but rather a complex mosaic of poignant vignettes that together amount to devastating critique. Jaffe criticizes government policies and the responses of the American public by highlighting the more local effects of them, and only suggests their global flows. His docufiction "Terrorchildren" is a good example of Jaffe's critical technique.

"Terrorchildren" begins by recounting Heather Gosling's idea of using weeds as weapons in the war against terror. In *Houseplants Against Terror*, Gosling shows Americans how to use plants to signal the presence of biological and chemical agents in the environment.

Writes Jaffe, "If Dr. Gosling's plan works, the technology could be used to turn forest oaks, backyard shrubs, pond algae, even festooned Christmas trees into sentinels in the war against terrorism." Then comes the punchline: "But if her plant signals anthrax, smallpox or plague, most non-moronic Americans would know they were exposed before displaying symptoms." Jaffe continues, "Which would allow them ample time to ingest potent FDA-approved antibiotics and duct-tape themselves into their condos with their significant other, low-carb snacks, bible, cellphone, TV and Internet." Jaffe satirizes government-instigated paranoia, but also cuts into the culture of fear and consumption. Rather than assailing the Department of Defense, the Department of Homeland Security, and the early-warning alert system directly, Jaffe approaches his target through an absurd "human interest" story. And Jaffe is a master of manipulating the inane or absurd story to potent political effect.

In "White Terror," Jaffe uses absurd news items to satirize the culture of violence and indiscriminate retaliation. Two interlocutors discuss who should be bombed in response to a list of unusual crimes or tragedies. Following an absurd story about South African beauty queens mauled in Botswana by a hippopotamus, characters respond to the question "Who would you bomb?":

Can we bomb the colonizing British retroactively?

Regrets, that isn't permitted.

I'd bomb blonde beauty contest winners who live and thrive in Africa with hyphenated surnames.

Me? I'd bomb the safari tourist trade.

From an inane if vivid beauty-meets-beast story, Jaffe teases out the cultural, historical, and economic conflicts that serve as a subtext. Who should be bombed when a hippo bites a canoeing beauty queen? Most certainly not the hippo.

Like the bombers in "White Terror," Jaffe's practice of "narrative terrorism" in *Terror-Dot-Gov* subjects selected "targets" to carefully planned linguistic assaults.

However, Jaffe's attacks are distributed across warring sides of conflicts: he is critical both of those who aim to stop terrorists by bombing, and those who aim to stop terrorists by conducting psychological studies. He questions both our ability to understand terrorism and our means of response. Jaffe plays one side against the other: the young soldier versus the aging anti-war activist, both prepared to sacrifice their lives in "Human Shield"; the homeless person against the wealthy homeowner in "Trader Joe's"; the Palestinian versus the Isreali in "Salaam." In comparing conflicting parties, Jaffe reveals their similarities: rigid ideologies, restrictive language, and a tendency towards violence.

Terror-Dot-Gov follows a method of writing established by Jaffe in *False Positive* (2002), and reprised in *15 Serial Killers* (2003). Jaffe's docufiction uses items from the news media as a basis for exploration, with the aim of teasing out the ideological subtext. The news items are often either very strange or extremely violent or both. They represent trends in Western news reporting, which Jaffe reveals to be obsessed with death, violence, and sex.

This method of writing leads the reader to question the composition of the stories and leaves the reader wondering what parts of the story are "objective" representations of real events, what parts are fictive interpretations, and what parts are wholly imaginative. Interpreting Jaffe's "docufictions" is an important lesson in how to read and digest news stories, and problematizes the actual workings of the media, whose most important sources often remain anonymous.

It is interesting that *Terror-Dot-Gov* lists *Le Monde*, *Le Figaro*, the *Guardian*, the *Independent*, *BBC News Online*, the *New York Times*, the *LA Times*, *Z-Net*, and the *San Francisco Chronicle* as a partial list of sources for news items. Jaffe's previous works of docufiction, *False Positive* and *15 Serial Killers*, were less explicit in listing particular media organizations. Part of Jaffe's point seems to be that the media inflicts a level of informational terrorism comparable to that of the terrorists who explode cars on crowded streets. When the sources of the docufiction are completely unknown, it calls us to question the "information" industry in toto; when specific sources are noted, the docufictions more powerfully criticize the legitimacy of the specific sources.

Terror-Dot-Gov is an excellent follow-up to *15 Serial*

Killers, and is considerably more effective. While the ideological underpinnings that Jaffe was after in *False Positive* and *15 Serial Killers* were sometimes lost amidst the tendency to trade crude laughs for more biting humor, the same is not the case in *Terror-Dot-Gov*. The dark humor of this current project is somewhat more restrained than that of earlier works, but more focused and more powerful.

The first docufiction, entitled "Behead," opens with the discovery of Brent Marshall's head in a refrigerator. Marshall was an American civilian who was employed by Lockheed Martin in Saudi Arabia, abducted by an Al-Qaeda cell, and later beheaded. Writes Jaffe, "Because of Marshall's exceptionally thick neck, the masked executioner in his black jubbah with his long curved blade seemed to have trouble severing the head." Continues Jaffe, "In any event, he made a messy business of it." While the dark chuckle is there, it is quickly sedated by an account of the near beheading of Fareeda Azza Khan, a diplomatic affairs correspondent for the daily Indian newspaper, the *Hindu*.

Jaffe describes how her captors made her "dress in a long loose coat and tied a scarf, or hijab, over her head." According to Jaffe, her captors "did not wish to look at her in her jeans and pink T-shirt with the small green Mobil Oil logo above her left breast." This is followed by a comparison of an opposing power: "*Which is the opposite of what American captors did to their Muslim prisoners in Abu Graib, forcing them to strip naked before abusing them*" [Jaffe's italics].

Terror-Dot-Gov is the most politically charged of Jaffe's three works of docufiction, and because of this, and the grace and restraint shown in this work, his most biting and brilliant set of docufictions to date. Taking on the prison abuse scandal in a passing line, for example, is representative of the subtle and effective form of critique made by *Terror-Dot-Gov*. Restraint like this, plus the significant treatment of material involving gender, class, and consumer culture, make this book a potent indictment of American values and pieties.

As indicated by *The Literary Terrorism of Harold Jaffe: Journal of Experimental Fiction, No. 29*, edited by Eckhard Gerdes, Jaffe's work is attracting a growing legion of admirers and fans.[18] This volume is primarily a collection of fictions and anecdotes by Jaffe's former students and colleagues, which reveal their respect and admiration for Jaffe and his writing. If imitation is the highest form of praise, then *The Literary Terrorism of Harold Jaffe* reveals him to be a highly praised writer.

Nevertheless, given that Jaffe's writing is often a self-conscious engagement with the literary and critical traditions of America and Europe, one would have liked to have found more pieces that dealt with Jaffe's work on this level. The best piece in this regard is Eckhard Gerdes' interview with Jaffe, which reveals much about how Jaffe views his own writing, its influences, and its reception. While the Gerdes volume is a welcome contribution, it would be improved by more works that engaged Jaffe's writing with historical insight and critical distance. Such works, balanced with works by former students and colleagues, would have given a richer and ultimately stronger case for Jaffe's contribution to the world of contemporary fiction.

Today, while war rages on in the Middle East and terrorist attacks are perpetrated across the globe, many feel that the United States is not only at war abroad, but also on the homefront. Jaffe's latest book shows how America is in a war being fought with slogans, pundits, and unnamed sources. Moreover, *Terror-Dot-Gov* leads us to see how a rise in xenophobia and extreme patriotism is intensified through jingoistic propaganda. In Jaffe's prose, the terror wrought upon the American public in the name of anti-terrorist strategies, and the oversaturation of the American public with "information" by the news media, becomes in many ways just as terrifying as more illicit acts of war and terrorism.

51

CINEMATIC FICTIONS

Evoking Mikhail Bakhtin's comment that by the beginning of the twentieth century, all artistic genres had been novelized, Samuel Delany recently stated that "by the beginning of the twenty-*first* century, all artistic genres have been film-ized." The later stories in Jonathan Baumbach's recently published collection, *On the Way to My Father's Funeral*, show this debt to visual culture.[19]

Consider the title story, "On the Way to My Father's Funeral, He Tells Me His Story" a sensitive, moving account of a son coming to recognize the truth about his father as he drives with his own son to his father's funeral. Hudson, the deceased father, says to his son Thomas:

> A film is like a painting except the images are fluid that's the difference one image passing like sleight of hand into another you think I don't know what I'm talking about I've seen all your films Tommy I'm your biggest admirer which doesn't mean I have to like them all equally as though they were your children a sad commentary on the frivolous nature of affections one always has preferences.

By using this concatenation and conjunction of clauses, Baumbach effectively creates the effect of fluidity more representative of film than literary narrative.

Baumbach's experience as a film critic, writing about movies for the *Partisan Review*, and as former chairman of the National Society of Film Critics, are evident in this collection. The most visually controlled and narratively energetic stories in this collection read like film scripts, or like films themselves. The fast-paced dialogue is stripped bare to the energy of the encounter, and settings are sparsely described. The machinations of husbands and wives, fathers and sons, and artists and therapists are recounted in climate-controlled environments that beg to be pulled out of their pages and up onto the screen.

Baumbach's 1998 novel *D-Tours* opens with the line, "They say, whoever, that life imitates the movies." This collection of stories imitates the movies, in that the stories seem to call to be judged against their cinematic cousins rather than their literary siblings. Stories of marriages gone bad and husbands gone astray recall scenes from Woody Allen movies more than the stories of John Updike. Baumbach's stories remind us that we live in an era dominated by visual media and that exposure to film and television narratives changes our sense of the qualities of a good story. At its best, film is a controlled environment that takes us inventively, sensitively, and expeditiously, through the complexities of contemporary life. The communication of setting, imagery, and emotion is generally more expeditious in film than in literary narrative. This allows us to get to the central tension at hand, be it a relationship gone bad or two friends exploring the boundaries of their friendship. Baumbach's stories get to central issues in modern relationships with speed and candor, generally leaving aside complex explorations of the inner life of characters or their surroundings. In "On the Way to My Father's Funeral," Hudson describes his son's best film work as making "the intellectually obscure emotionally available" — a comment equally applicable to the best work of Baumbach.

In "The Return of Service," a father, "a man with a longstanding commitment to paradox," is instructed by his son that "Paradox will take a man only so far." Baumbach's stories leave the reader with a feeling of completion and resolution rather than paradox.

This collection is an excellent introduction to Baumbach's fiction, with stories representing the range of his career. The collection may be broken down into two parts, each consisting of about 200 pages: thirteen uncollected stories, and twelve previously collected stories. Eight of the uncollected stories were previously published in *Boulevard, Iowa Review, Confrontation, Fiction International*, and *Mississippi Review*, with the remaining five being "new." The previously collected stories come from three books—*Bubble* (1976), *The Return of Service* (1980), and *The Life and Times of Major Fiction* (1987)—all published by either the Fiction Collective (of which Baumbach was one of the founders) or FC2. Readers will have to turn elsewhere to find "The Reading," a very sad and funny treatment of a poet giving a reading at "an obscure liberal arts college in southern Pennsylvania," which is conspicuously missing from the collection even though the copyright page acknowledges it.

The most humorous story in the collection is "The Adventures of King Dong" from *The Return of Service*, the story of the rise and fall of an anatomically incorrect gorilla. Dong, who is a cross between cinema's King Kong and Kafka's ape in "A Report to the Academy," "has a disproportionately small member, which is why he tends to prefer human females to the women of his own species." Writes Baumbach, "Dong had a certain integrity when they found him, a kind of primitive innocence, while now he is a creature governed solely by his pleasures . . . sex, marijuana, amphetamines, cocaine, heroin, alcohol—a classic downfall. Dong drinks heavily, downing gallon bottles as if they were shot glasses."

Another clever and humorous story is "The Life and Times of Major Fiction," whose main character, Ernie, is an editor who "destroyed himself by trying to educate an audience that was wholly content being insulted." Ernie, obsessed with receiving correspondence from authors, reaches the point where he claims to have received correspondence from Tolstoy and Sophocles, though the latter didn't actually write the letter. "The man dictated it," says Ernie, "but to tell the truth most of it was Greek to me."

The stories from *Babble*, *The Return of Service*, and *The Life and Times of Major Fiction*, are on the whole much lighter in tone than the uncollected and newer stories, sometimes recalling the work of Kurt Vonnegut.

The more serious tone of the newer work is evident in two of the excellent father/son stories: "On the Way to My Father's Funeral" and "Window in the Woods." The poignancy of these stories may stem from Baumbach's experience in a family of artists and filmmakers. Baumbach's father, the celebrated painter Harold Baumbach (1903-2002), passed away just a short time ago, and though a disclaimer informs us that any resemblance between Baumbach's characters and actual persons is "entirely coincidental," the material seems close to the heart. The painting that graces the collection's cover is by Harold Baumbach.

The latter story, "Window in the Woods," is an account of a young film student, Daniel Zorich, recalling his relationship with his father, the filmmaker Thomas Zorich, and scriptwriter/model stepmother, Kristina, through remembering the making and story of one of his father's films, *Window in the Woods*. Daniel's rediscovery of his father as "a marginal person" in his life, and his stepmother as an object of his affection, is punctuated by a recounting of the story told in his father's film. These last few sections of "Window in the Woods" are among the deepest and darkest writing in the book, drawing us into the realm of seeing life as a film, and living a life of film-making/viewing. In part, the film follows the life of a boy of about seven whose father holds him prisoner in a cabin that "has only one window which is a foot or so higher than the child's eye level." When his father dies, and he is finally released from the cabin, "the grown boy (he looks about 18) likes to stand inside, looking out the window as if the world makes sense to him only from this circumscribed perspective." For those who feel that the movie screen is the only place where the world makes sense, Baumbach's story will have a strong resonance.

Reading this Baumbach collection brings to mind something Alain Robbe-Grillet said in the 1950s: "Nouveau roman, nouveau cinema," or, after the new novel, the new cinema. Work like Baumbach's suggests a reversal of Robbe-Grillet's adage: "Nouveau cinéma, nouveau reçil" — after the new cinema, the new story. Like King Dong, whose story closes with the line, "The great ape has left his footprint on the imagination," Baumbach's stories leave their great footprint on your imagination, both literary and cinematic.

52

CARTOON KILLERS

The American entertainment industry has a knack for transforming its most violent and morally extreme members into cultural products suitable for mass consumption and celebration. In a recent example, serial killer Aileen Wuornos becomes the object of revulsion and attraction when presented to us by the film industry. We marvel at how the angelic Hollywood actor Charlize Theron has been transformed into the "monster" Wuornos, comparing the "real" Theron to the image of Wuornos presented by her in the film *Monster*. "She is my favorite of the night," says a fashion editor from *Glamour* magazine commenting on Theron's appearance at the Golden Globes this year, "[e]specially because you have the contrast of her in that movie and the way she looks tonight." This entirely commonplace comment reveals a semiotic process wherein serial killing and its image become hopelessly intertwined, and ultimately confused.

In the translation of serial killing to its performance and promotion, a complex semiotic process creates multiple layers of signification concerning the event and its perpetrator. The result is both a greater understanding (albeit a superficial one) of the killers and the horrific events in which they participated, and a growing sense of confusion between the "real" and the image. Carefully packaged, promoted, and sanitized by the culture industry, American psychos such as Jeffrey Dahmer, Aileen Wuornos, and John Wayne Gacy increasingly become less despicable objects of moral revulsion and more objects of fascination and entertainment. Their final entry into the sign system of celebrity entertainment is signaled by their becoming household names as readily recognizable as our sports, movie, and television icons. For the average culturally literate American, naming three contemporary serial killers is about as challenging as naming three talk-show hosts. However, the realness of these killers and their crimes gets buried under multiple layers of signification. A "hyperreal" — and "hypermoral" — image soon displaces any remaining fragments of the reality of the horrific event and their personage. The serial killer becomes a cereal-box cartoon.

This is the cultural context of Harold Jaffe's latest fiction collection, *15 Serial Killers*[20]: a media industry that has made Manson, Wuornos, and Gacy as readily recognizable as Jordan, Oprah, and Sting. Jaffe, with emotional coolness and phenomenological elegance, presents us with images of extreme violence and almost inhuman figures. In a method that he has used in previous works, Jaffe takes actual events and persons from American society, and transforms them in ways hitherto unseen and unimagined in mass media. Through a series of narrative techniques including interviews, monologues, and letters interspersed with graphically detailed violence and vileness, Jaffe adds new levels of characterization to these serial killers. The collection is peppered with illustrations by Joel Lippman, which, while interesting in themselves, do little to add to Jaffe's descriptions of defamiliarized violence.

Jaffe's hyperreal portraits are at once gruesome and beautiful, horrific and funny, energizing and enervating. The author's characterizations of these killers swing between portrayals as cartoonish thugs and glorifications as antiestablishment heros and sex gods. The cartoonish characterizations are amusement-park thrills; just as we giggle over the wax figure of Jack the Ripper at Madame Tussaud's, there is a titilating shock at coming so close to reproductions of these famous brutes. The glorified characterizations are more disturbing. Jaffe's portrait of Richard Ramirez, the Night Stalker, ends with the following lines, purported to be the Stalker's last words:

> You don't understand me. I am beyond your experience. I am beyond good and evil. I will be avenged. Lucifer dwells in all of us. I don't buy into the hypocritical, moralistic dogma of your so-called civilized society . . . .

The glorification of criminals as the ultimate "free agents" and the equation of law breaking with societal critique are not new themes in fiction. But the extreme reversal of cultural mores to glorify serial killers' defiance of conventional morals seems sophomoric rather than liberating or revolutionary, given the seriousness of the crimes.

Because the figures in these stories are so much a part of our cultural knowledge, Jaffe's treatments of them seem less effective than the treatments in his previous collection of stories, *False Positive* (2002). Whereas *False Positive* took as its starting point many unusual, little-known stories that were often darkly humorous, *15 Serial Killers* takes us well into the disturbed and disturbing lives of well-known — or at least, well-*mediated*—characters. The stories of *15 Serial Killers* are familiar in comparison with those in *False Positive*, and perhaps because of this, never seem to attain the consistently high level of dark humor and shocking intensity of the previous collection.

Still, the new collection has its share of dark and disrespectful humor. In "Dr. K," Henry Kissinger advises Nelson

> Rockefeller to surgically install—if that's the right word for it—a penile pump, which ended up killing Rockefeller in a failed attempt to penetrate his secretary, a young woman with glasses, out of Radcliffe. Though pushing seventy, Rocky was still horny. Or wanted to be. But his heart couldn't handle it.

In "Big Ed," protagonist Ed Kemper considers the pros and cons of necrophilia with his own peculiar logic:

A properly beheaded, dissected, cannibalized coed —
or mom, for that matter — can be a delectable bedmate.
But only if you're sensitive and attend to the small
things: emissions, chemical smells, gasses, the
occasional — but always welcome — spasm.

Any self-respecting female partner alive will contain
her gasses and emissions, and that's unfortunate if the
male partner prefers to go the whole nine.

As in previous works by Jaffe, *15 Serial Killers* looks
at serial killers through a unique point of view that resists
glamorization, and is effective at reaching deeply into the
hic et nunc of the situation. Yet while we see by means of
Jaffe's stark and economical prose a different side of a
litany of American psychos in action, and have a few dark
laughs in the process, we don't come out of this intense and
often horrifying experience understanding either the killers
or our cultural fascination with them any better. This is
unfortunate, given Jaffe's immense literary and intellectual
talents. Still, one cannot but admire Jaffe's courage (and
gall) in using these notorious figures as the inspiration for
"docufiction."

The potential of "docufiction" is philosophically
and narratologically rich. By using familiar formats from
popular culture such as tell-all memoirs and talk-show
interviews, Jaffe puts these popular media formats into
question. What if Ed Kemper wrote a best-selling personal
memoir? What if Richard Ramirez, the Night Stalker, gave
a daytime talk-show interview? Imagine the media blitz!
Jaffe reveals how these sensationalist media formats create
readily consumable cartoons out of human suffering.

Still, *15 Serial Killers* does little in the way of
interrogating the psychology of these social outsiders.
And, in taking the most sensationally violent stories of
our contemporary culture as its premise, it always already
runs the risk of further mindlessly sensationalizing and
glorifying them. Art of this form can itself quickly become
a part of the culture industry that preys upon our weakness
for sex and violence. However, if the work is able to raise
metaquestions about why we are fascinated by such stories,
how they affect and are communicated to us, what they

mean for our society, and how the media fuels our desire for them, then it becomes a valuable form of cultural criticism. Creating a space where the minds and actions of cartoon serial killers are creatively and imaginatively explored with dark humor seems gratuitous and ultimately unsatisfying if it does not address some these questions.

Jaffe's collection doesn't go far in exploring these important topics, but his inclusion of figures such as Henry Kissinger and Jack Kevorkian in the list of serial killers is the beginning of a political statement. Kissinger's addition to a list that includes Manson, Starkweather, Speck, Son of Sam, the Night Stalker, the Unabomber, Dahmer, Bundy, Gacy, and Kemper encourages us to make a logical inference wherein political decisions that result in the senseless taking of lives are put on the same level as people who physically commit savage murder. In a point in American history where our sons and daughters are losing their lives, and taking lives, in Iraq and Afganistan at the behest of our political institution, the addition of Kissinger's name to a list of "serial killers" is a powerful political statement.

The epigraph to the volume is from Georges Bataille: *"Only at the extremes is there freedom."* Like Bataille, Jaffe's aesthetic relies heavily on shock. A repeated illustration in Bataille's work, for example, is noting his sexual arousal at the sight of a dead body, including the body of his mother. The lines concerning maternal necrophilia from "Big Ed" noted above fit (dis)comfortably into this Bataillian aesthetic, as do both authors' preoccupation with connecting death to sexuality and the beautiful to the horrific. However, unlike Bataille, whose philosophy is richly articulated, developed, and situated within the intellectual climate of his day, Jaffe's is only hinted at in his fictions. Shock can ring empty and try one's patience if it is not followed by a message of some depth.

At times, one has the sense that *15 Serial Killers* is shock for shock's sake: literature at the extremes that has no other claim upon our senses but to startle them. However, there are moments that point to something much more sophisticated at work. And herein lies the power of Jaffe's fiction: the balance between brute shock into a wholly unfamiliar and uncomfortable here and now, and the instigation of a deconstructive cultural logic determined to undermine social and institutional complacency. In many ways, Jaffe's work is much more difficult to assess than Bataille's because the philosophical vision of the "guerilla writer" often is all too easily reducible to shocking the reader or getting a laugh.

Like the uncle who tells one too many "dead baby" jokes at the family gathering, Jaffe's humor is initially engaging, but becomes tiresome. Balancing the requirements of satire with the seriousness of serial murder is a difficult act, and the writer doesn't always succeed. This is unfortunate, because the power and vision of Jaffe's cultural criticism and the wit of his writing could lead to something both more savage and more insightful.

53

POSTAPOCALYPTIC NEWS

False Positive, Harold Jaffe's tenth book,[21] is a dark but humorous intervention into the violent and strange events reported by the American news media. Each of the fifteen fictions in *False Positive* is based on a newspaper article. Some of the news items are well known and well circulated, such as the Columbine High School slayings, Dr. Jack Kevorkian's assisted suicides, and Karla Faye Tucker's execution by the State of Texas. While other news items may be less familiar, they are no less sensational: the nine-year-old boy who lived for a month with his mother's corpse in the family room or the man who cut off his hand because he thought it was possessed by the devil.

Jaffe never identifies the precise source of his news items, and this uncertainty adds a level of hyperreality to the stories. They seem both real and unreal in the way that an episode of *Cops* or *World's Wildest Police Chases* seems to be both footage of an actual arrest and a staged police drama. After reading the book, it becomes difficult not to linger longer over the odd news items that occupy the back pages of the daily paper.

False Positive is remarkable less for its wild ride through fringe activities in contemporary society than for the interesting issues that it raises about the news media.

First, it seriously interrogates — or deconstructs — the seemingly rigid divide between serious and sensationalist news media. By revealing the subtexts that underlie national and local news items, *False Positive* asks us to reconsider the ideological underpinnings of the news industry. Secondly, if the evening news in America indeed provides "a little bit of blood" to go along with the meat on the dinner table, then *False Positive* compels one to ask why and to what effect. What sort of ideology underlies a news industry that insists on circulating and recirculating stories of corruption, death, and odd acts of violence? How do these news items affect our subconscious and our overall view of American society? Why is it that the American public seems to crave sensationalist reporting?

While these difficult questions are clearly raised, *False Positive* does not offer answers to them. Jaffe is not a sociologist nor is he a psychologist. He is a postmodern fictionalist, adroit at recycling reported events. By rewriting news stories within creative narrative forms, Jaffe is able to call forth the polysemy of the events, not their sociological and psychological underpinnings.

Jaffe's prose is strongest when it is breaking down the space where reported facts meet value claims. In "Carthage, Miss.," Jaffe uses the differences between near duplicate sentences to uncover divergent subtexts for an event. "Crystal was petite, just five-feet-one in her stocking feet," is succeeded by the nearly identical sentence, "*Crystal was petite, just five-feet-two in her lizard skin line-dancing boots.*" For this fiction to achieve its desired effect, the reader must understand the implications of Crystal wearing "lizard skin line-dancing boots" as opposed to stockings. Jaffe's fictions gain their power by tapping into the reader's knowledge of American subculture. His passages remind us that with a bit of tinkering, news items become more like value statements than objective recordings of events.

In a note preceding the stories, Jaffe announces to the reader that each story is a newspaper article that he has "treated." "I enter the article, and by various stratagems expose the host text's predictable but obscured ideology," writes Jaffe, "in the process teasing out its most fertile (that is to say, terrorist) subtexts. Thus rearmed, the prosthetic text is released into Culture to do its dirty work." While the note is an interesting view into Jaffe's process, the collection would be far more challenging *without* these three sentences.

Imagine that Jaffe does not inform us in his "Author's Note" that he is reworking newspaper articles, and lets us enter the fictional space of *False Positive* naïvely. Without the "treatment" claim, these fictions challenge the boundaries between fiction and current events. Whereas fictions such as "Geeks Dreams," a riff off of incidents surrounding the Columbine High School slayings, establish a connection with current events, bizarre fictions such as one based on a severed left hand might not establish a similar connection. Without the "Author's Note," the book would more effectively deconstruct the sense of reality or "realness" associated with the news. With the "Author's Note," the effect is more of evaluating how Jaffe has "treated" the story, rather than playing with the reader's psyche and memory of recent events.

Despite his claim to be "teasing out its most fertile (that is to say, terrorist) subtexts," one gets the feeling that Jaffe is merely using the chaos and violence of contemporary society as a gateway for his inventive fictions. The result is a set of wonderfully clever postmodern narrative innovations that more often than not fail to clarify an ideology that Jaffe claims is obscured. Although it is often unclear how the author is redirecting and uncovering terrorist subtexts, *False Positive* remains an exhilarating emotional roller coaster driven by Jaffe's commanding voice.

A deep fascination with the American penchant for unusual stories about violence, crime, and death burns in Jaffe's prose, even if his book is better at roughing up the veneer of the American news media and our infatuation with it than at critiquing it. One is reminded that American society and its news media are deeply troubled, but do not come any closer to understanding why. Like filmmaker David Lynch, Jaffe leads us into the dark and strange corners of American life but fails to pass judgment on them. (The clearest delineation of his feelings about American society comes in his treatment of Carla Faye Tucker's execution.)

Jaffe's book elicits dark laughter that hangs just the

other side of revulsion. His prose is lean and economical, and his "treatments" are varied and clever. His "Mad Cow" fiction is a savvy side-splitter. The relative brevity of the stories keeps the book moving briskly, which balances the relative heaviness of the topics covered in the fictions.

All in all, *False Positive* is a challenging read with a lot to offer. Jaffe's "treatments" represent a timely narrative technique that will resonate with antiessentialists who wish to deny the possibility of objectivity in the news media. His narrative innovations will impress admirers of postmodern fiction, and point to some new directions for contemporary fiction. *False Positive* is an unflinching exploration of the *truly negative* aspects of American culture, and is the essence of postapocalyptic cool.

54

STRANGE LOOPS

In Raymond Federman's latest novel, *Aunt Rachel's Fur*[22], French expatriate Rémond Namredef travels back to France after a decade of languishing in America. Namredef is in search of a publisher for his novel about a novelist who shuts himself in a room with 365 boxes of noodles to write a novel. Namredef tells Féderman, a professional listener, that his novel, *A Time of Noodles*, is "the story of a guy who locks himself in a room for one year with boxes of noodles, 365 boxes to be exact, one per day, he calculates, to write a novel about a guy who locks himself in a room for one year with 365 boxes of noodles to write the story of his life." Most of Federman's novel consists of Namredef telling Féderman stories in no particular chronological order and under no promise of verisimilitude, about the history of his family and the series of events that led him to move to America. At essence, *Aunt Rachel's Fur* is a novel about Federman (Namredef) talking to Federman (Féderman) about Federman. As Namredef inquires of Féderman: "Does that make sense to you . . . [?]"

Readers of metafiction, or as Federman prefers to call it, "surfiction," will quickly recognize this narrative reflexivity and complex characterization, and greet it as one does a friend who has returned after a long absence. Federman's masterful and economical utilization of strange loops, *mise-en-abyme,* and other metafictionalist maneuvers will be received by readers versed in writing of this type with a smile of familiarity and a nod of admiration. Like Jorge Luis Borges and Italo Calvino, Federman has internalized this type of writing to the point where the use of innovative and challenging narrative techniques such as metalepsis and hypodiegesis never seems contrived. As in his previous novels, Federman's writing is most brilliant when it methodically and systematically breaks down the narratological conventions of literary realism and naturalism, offering experimental alternatives in their stead.

One cannot help but admire Federman's declaration of love for this type of writing. Federman, through the voice of Namredef, tells the professional listener

> ... it's true that for years I've been stuck in digressive-ness, wandering endlessly in narrative detours, tumbling again and again into self-reflexiveness, and these old habits, so dear to the storyteller enamored of the interior mirrors of his recitation, will indubitably prevent that wonderful book from being published here in France, that book which caused me so many sleepless nights, but that's the way it is, I'm addicted to self-reflexiveness, I cannot write if I don't watch myself writing, to step out of my writing, to close my eyes on the writing process would reduce it to pathetic realism or romantic agony . . . .

Metafictional moments like these, which reflect Namredef's infatuation with the process of writing, are elegantly scattered throughout the novel, inserted between stories about his past. Namredef is always outwardly respectful of the attention span and interest level of his professional listener. He wants to be certain that the professional listener understands his stories and agrees to the conditions under which they should be understood. The presence of this wholly silent, but omnipresent professional listener — the conceptual complement to Umberto Eco's *ideal reader* — makes a novel written in a notoriously unreadable form eminently readable. *Aunt Rachel's Fur* remains what Roland Barthes would call a *scriptible* (writerly) text, but the inclusion of Féderman makes it an excellent introduction to this type of writing. To be sure, *Aunt Rachel's Fur* is a virtual primer on the state of metafiction today.

One of the more interesting—and somewhat sad—directions in which Federman's metafictional comments take us involves the marketability and reception of metafiction today. The editors at Les Éditions de l'Amour Fou reject Namredef's novel on the grounds that it is "too postmodern," explaining that

> . . . we believe that our readers will not be able to follow your postmodern detours and circumvolutions, of course this doesn't mean your work is bad or has no literary value, but it's too complicated, too cerebral for our readers, as such it has no commerical value, that's the problem with the postmodern novel today, it's not accessible to the general public, the reader who reads for fun cannot follow what is going on, he wants to be told a straight story, or else he becomes frustrated . . . .

The editor, Monsieur Gaston, then tells Namredef that his "reluctance to let the story be told" keeps it "from being what it should be, a *Bildungsroman* . . . ." In frustration, Namredef rescinds his book from consideration at the press and attempts to educate the editor as to what literature is and should be. *A Time of Noodles* is not a postmodern novel, explains Namredef, but rather "circulates the death certificate of postmodernism, it warns those who are stuck in the postmodern sack to get out before the banks repossess the houses and the cars and the washing machines they bought on credit because their books didn't make the best-seller list . . . ." However, "even though postmodernism is dead it doesn't mean that literature is done for . . . ." For Namredef, "a novel is less the writing of an adventure than the adventure of writing" — "your life is not the story you write, the story you write is your life."

Collectively, these statements are a manifesto to a future literature free from the pressures of market demographics, plot coherence, and genre, but still strongly linked to lives in particular, and life in general. It is fitting that *Aunt Rachel's Fur* is published by Fiction Collective Two (FC2) and not a publishing corporation such as HarperCollins or Viking. One cannot help but think that in the hands of a corporate, market-driven publisher, *Aunt Rachel's Fur* would indeed perhaps approach the more traditional *Bildungsroman* genre alluded to by Gaston.

The stories that Raymond Federman shares with us, about a life possibly lived by him, possibly by Rémond Namredef, or possibly recounted purely for the pleasure of the professional listener, are spellbinding, captivating, and often bawdy. Namredef is well aware of his storytelling prowess and continuously teases Féderman about the direction of the narrative. For example, one of the major questions unanswered by *Aunt Rachel's Fur* is whether Namredef slept with his Aunt Rachel: "You sonofabitch, you'd like to know if I screwed my aunt, well I won't tell you, there are things you just cannot tell . . . . In any case, nobody will ever know what happened with my aunt in our intimacy, that's my secret . . . ." It would not be correct to call the world created through Federman's novel a Baudrillarian world of *simulacra*, nor would it be correct to call it a Beckettian fictional space where the coordinates of reality and fiction do not operate *à la The Unnameable*. However, like these works, *Aunt Rachel's Fur* continuously challenges our assumptions about fictional space and its relationship to the realities of the author, reader, and characters. In *Aunt Rachel's Fur*, Federman always already keeps the distinction between reality and fiction fluid, floating from one to the other according to the demands of the moment.

We are moved by Namredef's sad account of the callous treatment he received from his relatives in war-time and post-war France, and we empathize with the loss of his immediate family in the Final Solution. However, by leaving open the possibility that all of Namredef's stories are untrue, Federman compels us to explore questions of historical memory and its relationship to narrativity. Namredef states, ". . . I make no distinction between reality and fiction . . . . Some of my stories are based on my own experiences, and others come from my novel, that's the way I function . . . ." And that's the way we begin to function as attentive readers (or, listeners, if you will). Considerations of the reality or irreality of the events recounted by Namredef take a secondary place to simply enjoying the "adventure of writing."

Aunt Rachel's Fur is a continuation of Federman's work in *The Twofold Vibration* (1982) and *To Whom It May Concern: A Novel* (1990). Collectively, these three novels are a profound exploration of the relationship between narrative form, tragedy, and memory, and an important contribution to post-Holocaust literature. *Aunt Rachel's Fur* is evidence that metafiction continues to be one of the most interesting and vital modes of contemporary writing. FC2 deserves commendation for having the courage and conviction to continue to publish challenging and progressive fiction in a publishing climate driven more by marketability than literary innovation.

Endnotes

1. December 2012.
2. John Barth, *Final Fridays: Essays, Lectures, Tributes & Other Nonfiction, 1995-*. Berkeley, CA: Counterpoint, 2012.
3. July 2012.
4. John D'Agata and Jim Fingal, *The Lifespan of a Fact*. New York and London: W. W. Norton & Company, 2012.
5. Carlin Romano, *America the Philosophical*. New York: Alfred A. Knopf, 2012.
6. A complete list of the books recently banned in Tucson, Arizona can be found at http://www.scribd.com/doc/58025928/TUSD-ethnic-studies.
7. Marjorie Perloff, *Unoriginal Genius: Poetry by Other Means in the New Century*. Chicago: University of Chicago Press, 2010.
8. March 2011.
9. Chapter 2, "March of the Penguins" reveals the name of the novel and novelist.
10. Raymond Federman passed away on October 6, 2009. This essay was adapted from the introduction to a collection of essays on Federman that I was editing at the time. It was published two years later as *Federman's Fictions: Innovation, Theory, and the Holocaust*. Albany, NY: State University of New York Press, 2011.
11. This piece was co-authored with *ABR* Associate Editor, Tom Williams.
12. Harold Jaffe, *Jesus Coyote: A Novel*. Bowie, MD: Raw Dog Screaming Press, 2008.
13. Stanley Fish, *Save the World on Your Own Time*. New York: Oxford University Press, 2008.
14. Ted Pelton, *Malcolm & Jack: (and Other Famous American Criminals)*. Brooklyn, NY: Spuyten Duyvil Press, 2006.

15.   March 6, 2007.
16.   Rebecca L. Walkowitz, *Cosmopolitan Style: Modernism Beyond the Nation.* New York: Columbia University Press, 2007.
17.   Harold Jaffe, *Terror-Dot-Gov.* Hyattsville, MD: Raw Dog Screaming Press, 2005.
18.   *The Literary Terrorism of Harold Jaffe: The Journal of Experimental Fiction, No. 29* edited by Eckard Gerdes. New York: iUniverse, Inc., 2004.
19.   Jonathan Baumbach, *On the Way to My Father's Funeral: New and Selected Stories.* New York: Low Fidelity Press, 2004.
20.   Harold Jaffe, *15 Serial Killers.* Hyattsville, MD: Raw Dog Screaming Press, 2003.
21.   Harold Jaffe, *False Positive.* Normal, IL and Tallahassee, FL: FC2, 2002.
22.   Raymond Federman, *Aunt Rachel's Fur: A Novel Improvised in Sad Laughter,* transacted from the French by Patricia Privat-Standley in collaboration with the author. Normal, IL and Tallahassee, FL: FC2, 2001.

Sources

1. "Robots in the Stacks." *American Book Review* 34.2 (January/February 2013)
2. "March of the Penguins." *American Book Review* 34.1 (November/December 2012)
3. "Social Media and the Review." *American Book Review* 33.5 (July/August 2012)
4. "T.G.I.F." Review of John Barth's *Final Fridays: Essays, Lectures, Tributes & Other Nonfiction, 1995-. American Book Review* 33.5 (July/August 2012)
5. "Data Mine Fiction." *American Book Review* 33.4 (May/June 2012)
6. "Another One Bites the Dust." *American Book Review* 33.3 (March/April 2012)
7. "Just the Facts, Ma'am." *American Book Review* 33.2 (January/February 2012)
8. "America's Agora of Ideas." Review of Carlin Romano's *America the Philosophical. American Book Review* 33.2 (January/February 2012)
9. "Hide it from the Kids." *American Book Review* 33.1 (November/December 2011)
10. "Ain't No Sunshine: Crisis in the Humanities III." *American Book Review* 32.6 (September/October 2011)
11. "The Politics of Subvention: Crisis in the Humanities II." *American Book Review* 32.5 (July/August 2011)
12. "The Rise of Corporate Literature: Crisis in the Humanities I." *American Book Review* 32.4 (May/June 2011)
13. "Who's In? Who's Out?" *American Book Review* 32.5 (July/August 2011)
14. "From Écriture to Récriture." Review of Marjorie Perloff's *Unoriginal Genius: Poetry by Other Means in the New Century. American Book Review* 32.4 (May/June 2011)
15. "The Executor's Dilemma." *American Book Review* 32.3 (March/April 2011)
16. "Bye, Bye Borders: Neoliberalism in Publishing III." *American Book Review* 32.2 (January/February 2011)
17. "Supersize that Novel: Neoliberalism in Publishing II." *American Book Review* 32.1 (November/December 2010)

18. "Writing for RCA: Neoliberalism in Publishing I." *American Book Review* 31.6 (September/October 2010)
19. "The Medium is the Question." *American Book Review* 31.5 (July/August 2010)
20. "Do Androids Dream of Anna Karenina?" *American Book Review* 31.4 (May/June 2010)
21. "Criminal Editors." *American Book Review* 31.3 (March/April 2010)
22. "The Book Ladder." *American Book Review* 31.2 (January/February 2010)
23. "Postfederman." *American Book Review* 31.1 (November/December 2009)
24. "Safe Books." *American Book Review* 30.6 (September/October 2009)
25. "Fiction's Future." Co-authored with Tom Williams. *American Book Review* 30.5 (July/August 2009)
26. "New Online Offerings." *American Book Review* 30.5 (July/August 2009)
27. "Academic Book Culture in Transition." *American Book Review* 30.4 (May/June 2009)
28. "Green Books." *American Book Review* 30.3 (March/April 2009)
29. "Sympathy for the Devil." Review of Harold Jaffe's *Jesus Coyote*. *American Book Review* 30.2 (January/February 2009)
30. "Publishing Smarts." *American Book Review* 30.2 (January/February 2009)
31. "The Big Dialogue." *American Book Review* 30.1 (November/December 2008)
32. "Emotional Narratives." *American Book Review* 29.6 (September/October 2008)
33. "The Academic Imperative." Review of Stanley Fish's *Save the World on Your Own Time*. *American Book Review* 29.5 (July/August 2008)
34. "Requiem for a Journal." *American Book Review* 29.5 (July/August 2008)
35. "A Good Reviewer is Hard to Find." *American Book Review* 29.4 (May/June 2008)
36. "Giant Steps." *American Book Review* 29.3 (March/April 2008)
37. "On the final line of *Willie Masters' Lonesome Wife* (1968) by William Gass." *American Book Review* 29.2 (January/February 2008)

38. "Pleasure in the End." *American Book Review* 29.2 (January/February 2008)
39. "Burn, Baby Burn." *American Book Review* 29.1 (November/December 2007)
40. "Page 2." [on public book proposals] *American Book Review* 28.6 (September/October 2007)
41. "Criminal History from Kerouac to Kinsey." Review of *Malcolm and Jack* by Ted Pelton. *American Book Review* 28.5 (July/August 2007)
42. "Page 2." [on minor literature] *American Book Review* 28.5 (July/August 2007)
43. "Page 2." [on newspaper book reviews and advertising] *American Book Review* 28.4 (May/June 2007)
44. "Anthologies and Literary Landscapes." *American Book Review* 28.2 (January/February 2007)
45. "Cosmopolitan Modernism." Review of Rebecca L. Walkowitz's *Cosmopolitan Style: Thinking Beyond the Nation. American Book Review* 28.3 (March/April 2007)
46. "Page 2." [on access to critical theory] *American Book Review* 28.3 (March/April 2007)
47. "Page 2." [a new beginning] *American Book Review* 28.2 (January/February 2007)
48. "Page 2." [a formidable past] *American Book Review* 28.1 (November/December 2006)
49. "On the opening line of *If on a winter's night a traveler* (1979) by Italo Calvino." *American Book Review* 27.2 (January/February 2006)
50. "Narrative Terrorism." Review of *Terror-Dot-Gov* by Harold Jaffe and *The Literary Terrorism of Harold Jaffe: The Journal of Experimental Fiction, No. 29* edited by Eckard Gerdes. *American Book Review* 27.1 (November/December 2005)
51. "Cinematic Fictions." Review of Jonathan Baumbach's *On the Way to My Father's Funeral: New and Selected Stories. American Book Review* 26.4 (May/June 2005)
52. "Cartoon Killers." Review of Harold Jaffe's *15 Serial Killers. American Book Review* 25.5 (July/August 2004)
53. "Postapocalyptic News." Review of Harold Jaffe's *False Positive. American Book Review* 24.2 (January/February 2003)
54. "Strange Loops." Review of Raymond Federman's *Aunt Rachel's Fur: A Novel Improvised in Sad Laughter. American Book Review* (March/April 2002)

H·I·V·E

zero hour

zero hour

MARK WALDEN

BLOOMSBURY

LONDON BERLIN NEW YORK SYDNEY

Bloomsbury Publishing, London, Berlin, New York and Sydney

First published in Great Britain in September 2010 by Bloomsbury Publishing Plc
36 Soho Square, London, W1D 3QY

A CIP catalogue record of this book is available from the British Library

ISBN 978 1 4088 0016 4

FSC
Mixed Sources
Product group from well-managed
forests and other controlled sources
Cert no. SGS - COC - 2061
www.fsc.org
© 1996 Forest Stewardship Council

Typeset by Dorchester Typesetting Group Ltd
Printed in Great Britain by Clays Ltd, St Ives Plc, Bungay, Suffolk

1 3 5 7 9 10 8 6 4 2

www.bloomsbury.com/hive

For Greybeard the Stupid Pirate

chapter one

A thin, elderly-looking man sat in a darkened office, facing an array of screens. At first glance a casual observer might have thought that he was ill, but closer inspection would have revealed the fine black veins covering his skin. Nothing was left of the man who had once inhabited this shell – all that mattered now was that it belonged to Overlord.

Overlord watched as the screens lit up one by one with the digitally distorted faces of his most loyal followers: men and women who had honoured his legacy and continued the work he had begun while imprisoned inside the body of another. His Disciples.

'Good evening, ladies and gentlemen,' he said. 'I have called this meeting to discuss a very important matter. I have reviewed the plans that you initiated during my enforced absence and, while many are impractical, one has true potential. Its code name is Tabula Rasa and although its scope is currently rather limited I believe that with some simple modifications it can be made . . . *effective.*'

'Master,' one of the faces said, 'what can we do to assist?'

'The facility which contains the substance we require is quite secure,' Overlord replied. 'I believe that Furan can provide the manpower necessary to handle that side of the plan but we will also need to address the greatest threat to our success, G.L.O.V.E.'

G.L.O.V.E., the Global League of Villainous Enterprise, was an organisation that had once been entirely under his control. That was, quite literally, in a previous lifetime. Now it was under the control of Maximilian Nero, a man who had been a thorn in Overlord's side for far too long.

'We can eliminate that threat,' Overlord continued, 'but I shall need your assistance. I am sending you details of a number of key G.L.O.V.E. facilities around the world. When I give the signal you are to attack and destroy them. I, meanwhile, will put into action a plan to eliminate G.L.O.V.E.'s leaders in one fell swoop. I will transmit the details of your targets to all of you shortly so that you may make your preparations. Our time is coming, ladies and gentlemen. Soon we shall remake the Earth in our image and there will be no one to stand against us.'

The screens went blank again and Pietor Furan stepped forward out of the shadows.

'I do not mean to question you,' Furan said, 'but Tabula Rasa was one of our more extreme initiatives. I take it that you have an idea for how we can modulate its destructive power?'

'Of course I do,' Overlord replied, 'but to do it we need one last piece of the puzzle. We need Otto Malpense and I know exactly how we're going to get him.

☠ ☠ ☠

Otto ducked behind the low wall, trying to control his breathing, his ears straining for any sign of his pursuers. He knew that they were out there but all he could hear was the slow drip of water from a leaking pipe nearby. Raising himself up just far enough to look over the wall, he scanned the wide open concrete floor of the abandoned warehouse. The only illumination was provided by the dirty cracked skylights far overhead. He crept out, moving as quickly and quietly as possible from one area of shadow to the next. Suddenly he heard the crunch of someone stepping on loose gravel and he flattened himself against the wall, raising his silenced pistol to shoulder level, ready to fire.

A shadowy figure rounded the corner and just had time to grunt with surprise as Otto's pistol coughed twice, the

3

shots catching his target square in the chest. The hunter slumped to the floor with a thud and Otto broke into a run. He knew that in the silence of the deserted building even the suppressed sound of his shots would have given away his position. He was halfway towards the other side of the open area when a bullet buzzed past his head and hit the wall twenty metres away with a puff of ancient plaster dust. He dived and rolled behind a wooden crate, knowing full well that the shelter it provided was temporary at best. As if to hammer that message home another bullet passed through the crate in an explosion of splinters just centimetres from his head and struck the ground nearby. He looked desperately for anything that would provide him with more substantial cover and spotted a concrete support column about ten metres away. To reach it he would have to cross open ground.

Time seemed to slow down as he glanced at the splintered hole in the crate and the tiny crater in the concrete floor where the bullet had ricocheted away. He subconsciously calculated the trajectory of the bullet, his mind drawing a line back from the crater and through the crate. Springing up from behind the crate, he sighted his pistol and fired three times. There was a scream of pain from somewhere off in the darkness and Otto sprinted for the comparative safety of the column. He pressed his back against the pillar, listening for signs of pursuit but hearing nothing. Suddenly there was a flicker of movement from off to his right and he spun round, raising his weapon. He gasped as he felt a sudden sharp pain in his chest and looking down he saw the silver hilt of a throwing knife protruding from the centre of his chest. He collapsed to his knees, his pistol falling from his numb fingers, and as the darkness swallowed him he saw a familiar figure detach itself from the shadows nearby and walk towards him.

'I am sorry, my friend,' Wing said, looking down at him as Otto lost consciousness.

There was a sudden flash of white light and the warehouse seemed to melt away to be replaced by a brightly lit cave with a smooth metal floor.

'Exercise terminated,' H.I.V.E.mind said calmly. 'Holographic projectors and variable geometry forcefields offline.'

Otto rose groggily to his feet, feeling his strength gradually returning.

'There is such a thing as too realistic, you know,' he said, rubbing at his sternum and trying to forget the pain and shock that he had felt just a few moments before.

'That's the whole point, Mr Malpense,' Colonel Francisco said, striding across the empty cavern as Wing helped Otto to his feet. 'The neural feedback suit allows you to feel all of the pain without suffering any of the physical injury. It ensures you take these training sessions seriously.'

That may have been the proper name for the bodysuit that Otto was wearing but he definitely preferred the nickname that it had earned among the students of H.I.V.E. – the Agoniser.

'Good work, Mr Fanchu,' Francisco said. 'You took your target down without hesitation but I would still rather see you using your side arms.'

'It was not necessary,' Wing replied with a slight shake of the head.

'Well, one day it might be,' Francisco replied with a frown. 'Let's hope you won't hesitate then. The end result is the same, after all.'

Wing gave a small nod. Otto understood very well why his friend had not used his gun. The first and only time that Wing had shot somebody it had been his own father. He had saved Otto's life but had still not forgiven himself for killing Cypher and breaking the solemn vow he had once made to his mother never to take a life.

'Thanks a lot, Otto,' Shelby said as she walked towards them, rubbing her shoulder. 'When the hell did you become such a good shot?'

'Beginner's luck,' Otto replied with a shrug.

'And did you really have to shoot me twice?' Laura asked, still looking slightly groggy from being rendered

6

temporarily unconscious by the neural shock administered by her own Agoniser suit.

'You gave away your position, Miss Brand,' Francisco said with a slight shake of his head. 'How many times do I have to tell you about watching where you're walking?'

'Sorry, Colonel,' Laura sighed. 'I'll do better next time.'

'Let's hope you do,' Francisco replied. 'Out in the real world there won't be a next time. H.I.V.E.mind, please upload the result of today's exercise to the central academic server.'

'Upload complete,' H.I.V.E.mind replied.

'Good. That's all for now, ladies and gentlemen,' the Colonel said. 'We'll be moving on to wilderness environments next week, so please review the tactical briefings on your terminals. Dismissed.'

Otto, Wing, Laura and Shelby met in the assembly area five minutes later after changing out of the neural feedback suits and into their black Alpha stream jumpsuits. They were just about to head back to their accommodation block when the doors on the other side of the room hissed open and Lucy, Franz and Nigel walked towards them.

'How did it go?' Laura asked Lucy, noting the slight scowl on the other girl's face.

'Don't ask,' Lucy said with a sigh.

'I am thinking that you will be wanting to tell the

others of my glorious victory,' Franz said with a huge, beaming smile.

'OK, OK.' Lucy winced.

'Franz won?' Shelby asked, trying hard to not sound too astonished.

'Yes,' Franz replied proudly. 'I am being like the shadow in the night. They can run but they cannot hide.'

'You got lucky,' Nigel said, sounding slightly irritated.

'Luck is not being the factor,' Franz said, shaking his head. 'I am just being too good for you.'

'Well,' Otto said with a grin, 'I for one want to hear all about it.'

'It does indeed sound like a glorious victory,' Wing said. Even he was struggling to keep a straight face.

'I'm not going to be allowed to forget about this in a hurry, am I?' Lucy said as Franz walked out of the room with Otto and Wing, explaining in great detail how his extraordinary stealth and cunning had been instrumental in defeating his opponents.

'Don't worry – there's no shame in losing,' Shelby replied.

'Really?' Lucy asked hopefully.

Shelby burst out laughing, setting Laura off too.

'I think this is going to be a very long day,' Nigel said to Lucy with a sigh.

☻ ☻ ☻

Three men sat in a crowded bar in Colorado, a frosted half-full pitcher of beer on the table between them. The first man raised his glass.

'A toast, guys, to the MWP-X1 and the brave, intelligent and handsome men that are gonna show the world what it can do tomorrow.'

'I'll drink to that,' the second man said, raising his glass.

'It's going to take more than one glass of beer for me to find either one of you two freaks handsome, but ah, what the hell!' the third man said, raising his glass.

'Let's just hope that the General doesn't find out that we're not all tucked up in our bunks,' the second man said with a grin. 'I'm not sure that this is what he meant by a good night's rest.'

'Well, he can't throw us in the brig till after the demonstration,' the first man said, 'so I guess we'll be OK for the next twenty-four hours.'

'After twelve months of living in the desert with him barking orders at us every day, I figure that's the least he owes us,' the third man replied.

'You better not be complaining, son,' the first man said, putting on a gruff Southern accent, 'because you should be proud – proud to be a part of the future of this great nation's armed forces.'

'Sir, yes sir,' the second man said, saluting the other man with a grin.

The three of them sat chatting and laughing for another half an hour. None of the other people in the bar would have guessed by looking at them that they were the test pilots for one of the most confidential advanced military research projects on the planet.

'We should get going,' the third man said eventually, finishing his beer. 'It's gonna be an early start in the morning.'

'It's an early start every morning,' the first man said with a sigh as he too finished his drink, 'but yeah, I guess you're right.'

'We better get some R & R after the demo tomorrow,' the second man said. 'I've had enough desert to last me a lifetime.'

The three men got up from the table and left the bar, walking out into the cool night air and crossing the parking lot.

'What the hell –' the first man said angrily as they rounded the corner of the building. A shadowy figure was standing beside his truck, working a long thin bar down between the rubber seal and the glass of the driver's side window. 'Hey! Get away from my truck!' he yelled.

The thief's head snapped round and he saw the three men sprinting towards him. Abandoning his attempt to break into the vehicle, he ran into the darkness beyond the edge of the lot with the others in close pursuit. They gained on him quickly as they sprinted across the dusty scrubland and when the first of them got to within a couple of metres he dived forward, hitting his target in the small of the back with his shoulder and bringing him to the ground with a crunching thud. He rolled the thief on to his back and put one knee on the struggling man's chest.

'You picked the wrong truck to steal, buddy,' the first man said as his two companions pinned the thief's arms to the ground.

'Actually,' the other man said with a smile, 'it was precisely the right truck.'

There were three small coughing sounds from somewhere behind the men and each of them felt a sudden sharp sting on the back of their neck. The thief caught the first man by the shoulders as he fell forward unconscious, and his two companions collapsed to the desert floor beside him. The thief stood up, brushing the dust from his jeans as three figures wearing black combat fatigues and night-vision goggles appeared from the darkness, lowering their tranquilliser dart guns and walking towards the unconscious men on the ground.

'Good work,' Pietor Furan said as he pushed the goggles up on to the top of his head. The smiling thief gave a small nod.

'Get them on to the truck,' Furan said to the two men beside him. 'We don't have much time.'

☢ ☢ ☢

'Ahhh, Lieutenant Barton, I'm glad to see that you're awake,' a voice said from somewhere in the darkness that surrounded him.

Barton tried to sit up but was stopped by the straps that bound him firmly to the bed.

'Who are you?' Barton asked, an edge of panic to his voice. 'How do you know my name?'

'Perfectly reasonable questions under the circumstances,' the voice replied, 'but I'm afraid that we don't have time for a full explanation. Let's just say that I am someone who is eager to ensure your full cooperation.'

'You can go to hell,' Barton said angrily.

'Your two friends had a similar reaction,' the voice replied with a sinister chuckle, 'but they soon started to see things my way.'

'What do you mean?' Barton said, feeling sudden fear for the safety of his friends. 'What have you done to them?'

'Exactly what I'm going to do to you,' the voice replied.

There was a whirring sound and a metal arm with a syringe mounted on the end moved into position next to Barton's neck. With a hiss it slid forward, plunging the needle into the struggling man's artery. Barton felt a burning sensation spread across his skull as the contents of the syringe were injected.

'You have just been injected with the latest generation of a substance called Animus,' the voice explained calmly. 'You should consider yourself lucky – previous generations would have killed you instantly but this will just make you more . . . cooperative.'

Barton thrashed on the bed for a few more seconds and then his struggling subsided and he lay still, his eyes staring blankly into space.

'Good. Are you ready for your new orders?' the voice asked.

'Yes, sir,' Barton replied.

'Excellent,' the voice said. 'Now here's what you're going to do . . .'

☻ ☻ ☻

The technician lifted up the metal cover and plugged his laptop into the data port next to the cockpit, watching as the screen filled with a series of diagnostic displays. Hearing footsteps at the other end of the long gantry behind him, he glanced over his shoulder. A man in a flight suit and mirrored sunglasses walked towards the cockpit, a helmet under his arm.

'Morning, Lieutenant Barton,' the technician said.

'She's prepped and ready for launch. Me and the other guys all wanted to wish you the best of luck with the demonstration today.'

The pilot didn't reply as he walked past the technician and climbed into the open cockpit, buckling himself into the single seat and pulling the helmet on to his head. The technician quickly disconnected the computer as the cockpit's armoured canopy whirred down into place and locked shut with a solid thud.

'Yeah, well, excuse me for breathing, Mr High-and-Mighty fly-boy,' the technician muttered under his breath as he walked back along the gantry.

☣ ☣ ☣

General Collins walked up to the lectern and looked at the banked rows of seats filled with men and women in a mixture of business suits and military uniforms. He smiled with satisfaction at the thought of what he was about to show them.

'Ladies and gentlemen, it gives me great pleasure to welcome you all to the Advanced Weapons Project proving grounds. I appreciate the fact that many of you have accepted the invitation to this demonstration without having any idea of exactly what it is that you are going to be shown today. I hope that what you are about to see will not be a disappointment. For some time now this facility has been responsible for the research and development of cutting-edge military systems – machines that will win not only the wars of today but also the wars of tomorrow. And so it is with great pride that I welcome you this morning to the first demonstration of the next generation of mobile armoured weapons platform. Since the First World War the tank has been the dominant force on the modern battlefield, but with the advent of increasingly advanced anti-armour weapons systems it has become clear that something new was required. A vehicle that would have all of the strengths of its predecessors but none of their vulnerabilities or limitations. A vehicle that would change the very nature of warfare in the twenty-first century. Ladies and gentlemen, I am extremely proud to present . . . Goliath.'

There was a low rumble from somewhere behind the stands and then three huge shapes roared over the heads of the startled audience and landed with ground-shaking thuds on the desert floor a couple of hundred metres away. Each machine stood about thirty metres high, towering armoured metal giants with multi-barrelled Gatling cannons mounted on each arm and rocket pods on each shoulder. Positioned in the centre of each of the giant mechs' chests was a black glass cockpit shrouded in heavy armour. They walked forward, taking up position facing the crowds, the fluidity of their movement strangely at odds with their size and weight. Collins noted with satisfaction the sudden buzz of excited chatter from the assembled dignitaries.

'Goliath represents unquestioned battlefield dominance. As agile in the air as they are on land, they are a force multiplier of enormous power and versatility,' Collins continued. 'But why just tell you what they can do when we can show you instead?'

He picked up a walkie-talkie from the lectern and thumbed the transmit button.

'OK, boys, let's give these people a show.'

The Goliaths turned, facing away from the waiting audience and towards the decommissioned tanks that were positioned down-range. The first of the giant machines raised its arm and the huge rotary cannon mounted on its forearm spun up and with a buzzing roar opened fire. The derelict tank was ripped to pieces by the heavy-calibre shells, shredded pieces of twisted metal flying in all directions. The rocket pods on the shoulders of the second of the three machines rotated slightly, locking on to another one of the distant armoured vehicles. Two rockets streaked from each of the pods, trailing white exhaust plumes, slamming into the doomed target and sending flaming chunks of armour plate scattering across the desert.

'As you can see, ladies and gentlemen, the Goliath is

capable of taking out ground targets with ease, but as I'm sure you all know the greatest threat to any ground vehicle on the modern battlefield comes from the air. So let's show you how they deal with just such an airborne threat.'

High above the proving grounds the Predator drone that had been circling banked towards its preassigned target, locking on to the third Goliath far below. The Hellfire missile detached from the drone's wing, its engines igniting and sending it screaming towards the stationary mech far below. A black dome mounted on the top of the targeted Goliath spun round and fired a pencil-thin beam of high-energy laser light at the incoming missile, instantly detonating it in mid-air.

'The Goliath's anti-ballistic laser system can take out anything from a missile to an incoming artillery round or tank shell. Put simply, you can't kill what you can't hit. Of course, each unit is fully outfitted with the latest in ground-to-air weaponry, but for the sake of this demonstration let's get a little more up close and personal.' Collins turned and nodded towards the pilot of the third machine and the vectored thrust engines on its back ignited, sending the Goliath rocketing into the sky. The members of the audience quickly picked up the binoculars they had been given and watched as the giant machine streaked towards the unmanned drone with a speed and manoeuvrability belying its size. The pilot brought the Goliath within range of the frantically weaving drone, matching its wildly evasive flight path turn for turn. The crowd watched as the giant armoured machine drew level with the Predator and then simply swatted it from the sky with a single swipe of one giant armoured fist. The blazing debris of the drone tumbled towards the desert far below.

'I hope the Air Force boys weren't expecting that one back,' Collins said with a grin, drawing an appreciative laugh from the assembled dignitaries. 'As you can see, Goliath blurs the line between ground-based and airborne weapon systems. It is truly the master of both land and sky.'

From somewhere behind the spectators came the distinctive sound of helicopter rotors and they twisted in their seats, eager to see what the next part of the demonstration would bring. Moments later three black helicopters passed low over the crowd, the downdraught from their thumping rotors kicking up clouds of dust from the desert floor. They came to a hover in front of the stands and opened their side doors, three squads of well-armed troops in black body armour rapidly climbing out and descending zip lines to the ground.

'What the hell –' Collins gasped. This was definitely not part of the demonstration. He grabbed the walkie-talkie from the lectern.

'All Goliath units cleared to engage unknown hostiles!'

he barked. 'Take these suckers out!' He waited for confirmation of his orders from the pilots of the three mechs but
heard only static. 'I say again, engage unidentified hostile
forces.'

The three Goliaths started to move, but instead of
opening fire on the unknown soldiers who were sprinting
towards the spectators they simply shifted into position
alongside the helicopters as they landed fifty metres away,
then raised the Gatling cannons on their arms and
levelled them at the startled crowd, barrels spinning,
ready to fire. Collins could do nothing but watch helplessly as the men in black raced up the stairs on either end
of the grandstand and trained their rifles on the frightened spectators. A couple tried to run but were quickly
overpowered and pushed to their knees, hands behind
their heads. As Collins stood frozen in disbelief, a single
figure climbed down from the side door of one of the helicopters and made his way up the steps to join him on the
platform. As he reached Collins, he pulled a pistol from
the holster on his hip and pointed it at him.

'General Collins,' he said with a smile, 'my name is
Pietor Furan and this demonstration is over.'

☹ ☹ ☹

Otto woke with a start, his head buzzing with pain.
Staggering to his feet, he stumbled through the darkened

room, heading for the bathroom at the rear of his living quarters. He slapped the switch on the wall and bright white light blinded him for a second. As his eyes adjusted to the glare he stared at his own reflection in the mirror and a fresh bolt of pain lanced across his skull. He fought against the rising tide of nausea and disorientation, studying the pale face that looked back at him from the glass. A thin red line, like a fine cut, traced across his right cheek. Otto ran his finger along the fresh wound, feeling an unusual warmth as the gash seemed to widen and separate, then gasped in horror as it flared suddenly with red light and the skin began to peel back from his cheek, revealing what looked like blood-covered glass. He recoiled from his own reflection as more bright red lines spread across his skin, the flesh falling away to reveal a multi-faceted crystalline face beneath. Otto opened his mouth to scream but all that came out was a thin screech of static, rising in pitch, slowly resolving into a voice that was both alien and yet hauntingly familiar.

'You're mine,' the voice said. 'You always have been and always will be.'

Otto staggered backwards as he felt an unbelievable rush of pressure inside his skull and finally, as terror and pain overwhelmed him, he screamed.

Wing held Otto's shoulders as his friend thrashed on the bed making a thin, strangled screeching sound.

'Otto,' Wing said, sounding alarmed, 'wake up!' He shook Otto gently, trying to stir him from whatever dream was tormenting him. Otto's eyes flicked open, filled with terror for a few moments before they focused on Wing's face. He closed them again and took a couple of deep breaths, trying to slow the hammering beat he could feel inside his chest.

'The dream again?' Wing said, sitting down on the edge of Otto's bed.

'Yes,' Otto said with a sigh, sitting up, 'but it's getting worse.'

'Was it him?' Wing asked with a frown.

'Yes,' Otto replied, his voice little more than a whisper. 'Overlord.'

It had been the same every night for weeks – the terrifying sense of his personality being erased and Overlord reasserting control – ever since he had been rescued from the clutches of Sebastian Trent and purged of the Animus liquid that had made him little more than an obedient puppet. Otto could still remember what it had felt like as the psychotic artificial intelligence called Overlord had taken control of him: the utter helplessness he had felt as the AI had tried to kill his friends while Otto was trapped, a passive observer, within his own body.

'You cannot go on like this,' Wing said calmly. 'You have not slept properly in weeks. This is consuming you.'

Otto knew that his friend was right. He felt almost constantly exhausted and was starting to dread falling asleep. Sometimes he was reluctant even to close his eyes for fear that he would be met yet again with more terrifying visions of the fate that he had so narrowly avoided.

'It doesn't make any sense,' Otto said. 'Overlord is dead – we all saw him die – so why can't I get him out of my head?'

'Sebastian Trent kept you prisoner for months and throughout that time you were fighting a constant battle to keep Overlord in check,' Wing replied. 'It is perhaps not surprising that you have yet to fully . . . recover.'

Otto smiled at Wing's slight hesitation.

'You mean it's hardly surprising that I'm losing my marbles.'

'I did not say that.'

'But you were thinking it,' Otto said. 'Everyone is.'

'We are all worried about you,' Wing replied. 'None of us can even begin to imagine what you must have been through. We want to help in whatever way we can.'

'I'm not sure that there's much you can do,' Otto said, 'unless you happen to have a supply of powerful tranquillisers that I don't know about.'

'Unfortunately, no,' Wing replied, 'though I do know of ways to render you unconscious without causing you too much discomfort.'

'I'm not sure we're quite at that stage yet,' Otto replied, raising an eyebrow.

☻ ☻ ☻

The group of captured dignitaries stood in stunned silence as Furan's men surrounded them, their weapons raised. They had been herded away from the demonstration area and marched under guard along the road that led from the open desert to a nearby canyon. The Goliath mechs stood off to one side, their torsos slowly rotating as they scanned the surrounding area for any sign of hostiles. A hundred metres away stood a huge pair of steel blast doors set into the red rock of the canyon wall, and beyond those doors lay Furan's ultimate target, the headquarters of the Advanced Weapons Project. The fortified guard posts on either side of the entrance were now just smouldering burnt-out shells, the soldiers who manned them having made a brave but ultimately futile attempt at resistance.

Furan gestured to the two guards who were holding General Collins and they dragged the struggling man towards him.

'General,' he said calmly, 'would you be so kind as to order the guards inside your facility to open the blast doors?'

'You know there's no way I'm going to do that,' Collins replied defiantly.

'Yes, we were rather expecting that was what you would say,' Furan replied. He pulled the radio from his belt and spoke into it. 'We have secured the canyon. You may begin your approach.'

A minute later the canyon was filled with the sound of rotor blades and a helicopter appeared overhead, slowly dropping down and landing gently on the road nearby. The side door slid open and a frail-looking man climbed out. He wore a long black overcoat, despite the scorching desert heat, and walked slowly towards Furan and the General, leaning heavily on an ebony walking stick. The man's hair was white, his parchment-like skin stretched tight across his face and his dark sunken eyes adding to his almost skeletal appearance. As he neared Collins the General could hear him wheezing, each breath seeming like a monumental effort.

'A pleasure to meet you, General,' the old man said, fighting for breath as he spoke. 'I see that you have chosen not to comply with the wishes of my associates. I understand. A man in your position has . . . responsibilities.'

'I don't cooperate with terrorists, if that's what you mean,' the General growled.

The old man laughed, the sound little more than a wheezing hiss.

'Terrorists?' he replied. 'You Americans and your

24

simplistic labels. We are much more than that. We are going to change the world.'

'Not if I have anything to say about it,' the General replied firmly. 'It'll be a cold day in hell before I help you.'

'Oh, I'm afraid that you won't have very much say in the matter,' the other man said with a smile. He reached out his hand and the General watched in horror as the skin of his forearm bulged and then tore, black tendrils slithering forth over the wrist and hand.

'Who are you?' the General gasped, recoiling in disgust.

'You may call me Overlord,' the old man said, his hand snaking out with startling speed and grabbing the General's jaw, his grip abnormally strong. 'And you are going to be my new home.'

The black liquid slithered over the old man's hand and into the General's mouth with horrifying speed. The General let out a single startled gurgle as the inky slime slid down his throat. Seconds later both men collapsed, the older man hitting the ground with a thud, his dead, vacant eyes staring up into the sky. The General thrashed about, clawing at his neck and chest as the Animus fluid invaded his nervous system, spreading like a burning wave through his body. Furan watched impassively as he twitched a couple of times and then lay still. For a few seconds the General didn't move and then his eyes opened wide and he gasped, taking a long, deep breath.

Slowly Collins climbed to his feet and turned to face Furan, his face now covered in a slowly fading pattern of veined black lines.

'Much better,' Overlord said, rolling his head around on his shoulders and stretching his neck. He gestured towards the frail body that he had inhabited till just a few moments ago. 'Dispose of that.'

'Yes, sir,' Furan replied, beckoning over a pair of his troops who dragged the elderly body away.

Overlord strode towards the blast doors and placed his hand on the scanner mounted on the concrete frame. A cover slid back to reveal an alphanumeric keypad and he quickly punched in a long string of numbers and letters. With a low rumble the heavy blast doors began to slide open.

'Send your men in,' Overlord said as Furan walked up beside him. 'Crush any resistance. We don't have much time.'

chapter two

'How the hell did this happen?' the President yelled angrily, slamming his palm down on the table.

'We're not sure yet, Mr President,' replied one of the generals sitting in the White House situation room. 'All we do know is that at eleven hundred hours this morning there was a hostile assault on the Advanced Weapons Project proving grounds by unknown forces. They appear to have captured the Goliath weapon systems and gained entrance to the AWP facility itself. All communication was lost with the facility approximately ten minutes later.'

'And they've been quiet ever since?' the President asked. 'They've made no demands?'

'No, sir, not as yet,' the General replied.

'Who are these people?' the President asked, turning to the Director of the CIA.

'We're not sure, sir,' the Director replied. 'The only person we've been able to identify is this man.' He pressed a key on the laptop that was open on the desk in front of him and one of the large screens mounted on the wall displayed a grainy image of a man pointing a pistol at General Collins, the commander of the AWP facility. 'We captured this image from the visual feed from the proving grounds shortly before it was severed. His name is Pietor Furan. He was a Russian intelligence operative until about fifteen years ago, during which time he trained assassins for the FSB. Our Russian friends deny this, of course, but that's what you would expect. Since then little has been seen of him. We assume he's been working as a freelancer and there have been occasional confirmed sightings, but people he's crossed paths with have an unfortunate habit of turning up dead.'

The President stared at the image of the man on screen – there was something familiar about him. Suddenly he remembered where he had seen that face before, nearly a year ago.

'I know him,' the President said quietly. 'He was one of the men who was responsible for the assault on Air Force One. He's connected somehow with the group that attacked us – what did he call them? The Disciples.'

'We've been trying to find out more about them ever since they attacked you, sir,' the Director replied, 'but we've drawn a blank. You're sure that this man was working with them?'

'Absolutely certain. I'm not about to forget the face of a man who tried to kill me,' the President replied impatiently. 'So why has he suddenly broken cover now? He must have known that we'd be able to ID him.'

'We have no idea,' the CIA Director replied, 'and that concerns me. The fact that he's connected in some way with these Disciples just makes this all the more worrying.'

'How did they get inside the facility?' the President asked with a frown. 'AWP is supposed to be completely secure.'

'We're not sure, sir. There's no way that they could have breached the outer perimeter by force even with the help of the Goliath units. AWP is modelled after the NORAD facility at Cheyenne Mountain, and as such it was built to withstand a direct nuclear blast, which suggests that they had inside help. All of the staff were given extensive background checks, but that doesn't mean to say that they couldn't have turned someone. At the very least we know that they managed to turn the Goliath pilots, though we have no idea how.'

'And the hostages?' the President asked, rubbing his eyes.

'It's not good,' another one of the generals replied. 'The guest list for the Goliath demonstration reads like a who's who of friendly nations' top military brass and defence ministers. Not to mention all of the research and development staff that work on site.'

'We've been making phone calls all morning,' added the Secretary of State. 'We have a lot of very unhappy allies out there who want to know exactly what we're going to do to secure the safe return of their people.'

'So what *are* we going to do?' the President asked, looking around the table.

'Breaching the facility is out of the question,' one of the generals said, shaking his head. 'By the time we get inside they would be able to kill all of the hostages ten times over. All we can do at the moment is wait for them to make the next move. The only consolation is that we may not be able to get in but they can't get out either – we've got troops and armoured units moving in to surround the area and the Air Force have set up a no-fly zone overhead.'

'So we wait,' the President said with a sigh, 'while hostile forces have control of our most advanced military research facility.'

'I'm afraid so,' the General replied. 'We can put together assault plans, of course, but until we –'

He was interrupted by a uniformed aide who rushed into the situation room.

'Mr President, we've got a video call coming in from the AWP facility,' he announced.

There was a murmur of surprise from around the table and the President took a deep breath.

'Put it on screen,' the President said. 'Let's see if we can get some answers.'

The large screen on the wall at the far end of the conference table changed to show the smiling face of General Collins.

'Good morning, Mr President,' Collins said. 'I'm sorry to interrupt what I imagine must be a rather urgent meeting.'

'General Collins?' the President said, looking slightly confused. 'What the hell is going on?'

'Oh, I'm afraid that General Collins is no longer with us,' the man on the screen replied. 'You may call me Overlord.'

The President stared back at him, his face a mixture of anger and bewilderment.

'Are you insane, General?' he roared. 'I am giving you a direct order to stand down immediately and return that facility to our control.'

'It always amazes me how little imagination powerful men have,' Overlord said with a sigh. 'You will come to understand who I am in time though, and that is all that matters. For now all that you need to know is that any attempt to retake this facility will result in the immediate execution of every single one of our hostages. There will be no warning and there will be no negotiation.'

'What do you want?' the President asked. He could only assume that Collins must have suffered some sort of break-down. Nothing else could explain why he suddenly wanted to be addressed as Overlord.

'What I want is quite simple. I am transmitting to you a file containing the details of certain individuals that I want you to deliver to me,' Overlord replied. 'I trust that you will be able to secure the cooperation of your allies overseas in this task, considering the importance of the hostages I have taken.'

'If you think I'm just going to give you more hostages,' the President replied, 'you're out of your mind.'

'Then I hope you will not mind explaining to the governments of the men and women I have captured that it was your refusal to cooperate that caused their deaths,' Overlord replied angrily. 'I am not unreasonable – if you hand these people over to me I will release the prisoners that I am currently holding. The people that I want are of no consequence to you. We both know that the same cannot be said of my current hostages. You have twenty-four hours until the executions begin.'

The screen went blank.

'It doesn't make any sense,' the Director of the CIA said, staring at the empty screen, 'What's happened to him? What can he possibly hope to achieve by this?'

32

'I have no idea,' the President replied.

'We've received the file he mentioned,' one of the aides in the room reported. 'Putting it on screen.'

Images of a dozen men and women appeared on the screen.

'Who are they?' the President asked, studying the pictures.

'We're running them now,' the CIA Director replied. He waited for a few long seconds as the names were run through the intelligence databases. 'We've got nothing.'

'Nothing?' the President asked, sounding surprised. 'That can't be right, surely?'

'It's impossible,' the Director replied. 'It's like these people don't exist. There's no trace of any of them in any of our databases. Whoever they are, someone's gone to a great deal of trouble to keep them hidden.'

'I don't care what it takes,' the President said, 'find out who they are and track them down. They may be the only bargaining chip we have.'

☻☻☻

Otto walked quickly down the corridor. He had lied to the others and told them that he was going to the library for an hour, partly because he didn't want them to worry about him but mainly because he wasn't sure they would really understand. He heard the sound of approaching footsteps and pressed himself flat against the wall as a security patrol marched past the end of the passage. He might not have wanted his friends to discover what he was up to but he wanted Dr Nero to find out even less.

After waiting for a few seconds he poked his head round the corner. The route to his objective was clear and he hurried towards the heavy steel door set in the rock wall. Placing his hand on the palm scanner next to the door, he closed his eyes. As it read his palm he unconsciously reached out with his mind and intercepted the message from the network that was about to warn the security systems of his unauthorised access to the room and altered it to give him the clearance he needed. The panel gave a soft beep and the door slid open.

Otto slipped through and the door closed silently behind him. Inside the room the only illumination came from the bright blue lights that danced across the white monoliths lining the walls like some sort of ancient prehistoric structure. He walked through the gloom towards the circular pedestal in the centre and waited. A couple of seconds later a pencil-thin beam of blue light shot up from the middle of the pedestal and fanned out into a series of finer beams, finally coalescing into an image of a blue wireframe face hanging in the air.

'You are not supposed to be here, Otto,' H.I.V.E.mind said calmly.

'I know, but I'd rather you didn't alert security if you don't mind,' Otto replied with a lopsided smile.

'I had assumed that was the case,' H.I.V.E.mind replied. 'What can I do for you?'

'This might sound a little crazy,' Otto replied, 'but I need you to have a look inside my head.'

'I'm afraid that I do not have the necessary instruments to perform a Computerised Axial Tomography Scan,' H.I.V.E.mind replied.

'No,' Otto replied, 'I don't mean a CAT scan. I mean that I want you to let me connect directly with your systems. We both know that I've got a computer implanted in my brain and I need you to take a look inside it.' Otto had only recently discovered that his unusual abilities were due to the fact that he had been engineered from birth to serve as a permanent home for Overlord.

'I do not see how that would be possible. I lack the required interface –' H.I.V.E.mind said before Otto cut him off again.

'Let me worry about that. If I can connect to you then we should be able to create a two-way interface. In theory you should be able to see what's going on in there.'

'I am not certain that would be wise,' H.I.V.E.mind replied. 'We do not yet fully understand the way in which the implanted device works. Its design is far more advanced than anything that any human has created, including my own systems. During the time it was stored within me I was in an almost entirely dormant state. I am still not certain of the precise way in which it functions. With such uncertainty comes risk.'

'I understand that,' Otto replied with a sigh, 'but I need to be sure that Overlord is gone and this is the only way that I can be certain.'

'I have already performed scans that indicate there is no unexpected activity within the device. Doctor Nero was quite insistent about it when you returned from Brazil. I am as certain as I can be that there is no remnant of the Overlord AI functioning within you.'

'Humour me,' Otto replied. 'If you'd been through what I have recently you'd want to be certain too.'

'May I ask what has prompted this concern?' H.I.V.E.mind asked.

'I've had nightmares,' Otto said quietly, 'about Overlord. They're getting worse.'

'I see,' H.I.V.E.mind replied. 'I am sure that you are aware that it is not unusual for a traumatic experience such as the one to which you were recently subjected to have an effect on the unconscious mind. While I do not dream myself I believe that it would not be entirely unexpected for you to be experiencing these sorts of psychological after-effects.'

'Thank you, Doctor Freud,' Otto replied, 'but I need to

be sure that's all it is. Will you help me?'

'If you are certain that is what you wish then I am willing to try.'

'I'm sure,' Otto said, taking a deep breath.

'Very well, you may begin.'

Otto closed his eyes and mentally reached out for the digital activity within H.I.V.E.mind's servers. It was quite unlike any other computer that he had ever connected with. Normal computers were like organised grids with rigidly defined pathways that could be traced and controlled, but H.I.V.E.mind was different. Myriad patterns of swirling blue light flowed around him like waves, their shapes organic and unpredictable and yet, somehow, not chaotic. Otto could not help but be amazed by its seemingly boundless complexity and he found himself wondering if this might be what it was like to see inside the workings of someone else's mind. He forced himself to concentrate. As beautiful as this datascape might be he was there for a reason. He reached out with his mind, allowing himself to visualise his own consciousness as a swirling mass of golden tendrils stretching out and weaving together with the flowing streams of H.I.V.E.mind's electronic consciousness.

'We are connected,' H.I.V.E.mind said, his voice seeming to come from all around Otto. 'I will attempt to interface directly with the device.'

Otto felt a bizarre sensation as he allowed H.I.V.E.mind to access the tiny machine implanted inside his brain. He had connected with computers and electronic devices countless times in his past but this was the first time that it had been a two-way process. It was somehow uncomfortable but not painful, like having an itch deep inside his skull that he could not scratch.

'I have never seen such complexity,' H.I.V.E.mind said with something like awe in his voice. 'It is strange to think that an entity as insane as Overlord could create something so . . . beautiful.'

Otto had never heard H.I.V.E.mind speak like that before, almost as if he was lost for words. He inhaled sharply as he felt the connection between him and H.I.V.E.mind suddenly sever.

'What's wrong?' he said, opening his eyes.

'Nothing,' H.I.V.E.mind replied. 'There is no trace of any alien code within the device.'

'Are you sure?' Otto asked.

'Certain,' H.I.V.E.mind replied, and for just a fleeting instant Otto could have sworn that he heard something like frustration in the AI's voice.

'What is it?' he asked with a frown. 'What did you see?'

'It is nothing,' H.I.V.E.mind replied quickly.

'Tell me,' Otto said.

'It is difficult to explain. That device was created as a

38

permanent home for Overlord, and while we are different in many ways we are identical in many others. It felt like . . . being alive.'

H.I.V.E.mind looked down at the floor before looking back up at Otto.

'You would probably find it hard to understand,' H.I.V.E.mind continued. 'It is something that humans take for granted and yet something that I have never experienced. You should rest assured however that there is no trace of Overlord anywhere within the device. You are free of him.'

'Then why are the nightmares getting worse?' Otto asked.

'I do not know,' H.I.V.E.mind replied. 'The truth of the matter is that while the device Overlord implanted in you is incredibly sophisticated it still has only a fraction of the complexity of the human brain. I fear that the root cause of your dreams may lie somewhere within that organic machine rather than the artificial one.'

'Thanks for checking anyway,' Otto said with a sigh.

'You are welcome,' H.I.V.E.mind replied.

☹ ☹ ☹

Overlord watched as the Goliaths backed into their docking stands and the boarding gantries slid into place. The pilots of the three giant mechs climbed down from the cockpits and took up position in front of him, standing at attention.

'You did well,' Overlord said. 'I may have need of you later so make sure that you are ready.'

'Yes, sir,' the three men said in unison before turning and marching out of the hangar.

Furan walked across the bay, watching them leave.

'They appear to show no signs of rejection,' he said as he approached Overlord.

'The refined version of Animus is working exactly as expected,' Overlord replied. 'They are fully under our control and are showing no signs of the poisoning that the fluid has caused in the past. It is time to take the next step.'

'Our technicians have started work on integrating the new version of Animus with the Tabula Rasa delivery system,' Furan reported. 'They expect to be ready in a matter of hours.'

'Good,' Overlord replied. 'I imagine that word of our demands will already be spreading through G.L.O.V.E.'s network. Now all that we have to do is wait for Nero to make the next move.'

Overlord suddenly started to cough violently before pulling a handkerchief from his pocket and wiping his mouth. The white cloth was smeared with the black liquid he had wiped from his lips.

'The rejection process is accelerating,' Overlord said, frowning. 'Each new host is degrading more quickly. At this rate this body will only last me a couple of days.'

'We have plenty of hostages,' Furan said. 'You will not run out of potential hosts for a while.'

'A temporary solution at best I still need a permanent home,' Overlord replied.

'And soon you will have one,' Furan said with a slight smile.

'Indeed I shall,' Overlord replied. 'Indeed I shall.'

☻ ☻ ☻

Nero scanned the report on the screen mounted on his desk and felt a chill run down his spine.

'You are quite certain that this information is accurate?' he said.

'Yes, sir,' the man on the other half of the screen replied. 'Our source in the White House was in the situation room when the message was received. We obviously cannot be certain that what General Collins said was true but '

'We cannot afford to take that chance,' Nero said, shaking his head. 'Do we have anyone inside the AWP facility?'

'One of the lower-level technicians has provided us with information in the past but all communication with the base has been cut off and we have no way of contacting her,' the man on the screen replied.

'Do we know what they were developing inside the facility?' Nero asked.

'Our contact was part of a team that was developing advanced armour repair systems but beyond that, details of the other projects are sketchy. AWP is rigidly compartmentalised and none of the teams know exactly what their colleagues are working on. Our contact in the White House says that the facility was taken during a demonstration of a weapons system called Goliath, which is some kind of advanced armoured vehicle but we're not sure exactly what.'

'See if you can get any more information from any of our sources within the US military,' Nero said with a frown. 'We need to get a better idea of exactly why Overlord might be interested in this specific target.'

'Understood,' the man on the screen responded with a nod. 'Do Unto Others.'

'Do Unto Others,' Nero replied, repeating the G.L.O.V.E. motto.

Nero pressed a switch on the communications panel next to the screen.

'Yes, Max,' a familiar voice answered.

'Could you come to my office please, Natalya – we have a situation on our hands.'

'On my way,' Raven replied.

Nero leant back in his chair. There was no proof as yet that this man claiming to be Overlord was actually connected in any way to the rampant AI that had caused so much grief for G.L.O.V.E. in the past, but there was something about the audacity of this attack that made him deeply uneasy. The fact that Pietor Furan also appeared to be involved made it all the more likely that this was indeed a genuine threat. Nero had always felt a nagging suspicion that they had not heard the last of the AI, a suspicion that now appeared, unfortunately, to have been well founded.

The door to his office suddenly hissed open and Raven walked into the room.

'Come in, Natalya,' Nero said, gesturing to the chair on the other side of his desk. 'Take a seat.'

'What's happened?' Raven asked as she sat down, noting Nero's worried expression.

'Overlord's alive,' Nero said quietly.

'That's impossible,' Raven said, her eyes widening in surprise. 'I saw him die.'

'I do not know how he survived,' Nero said with a sigh, 'but somehow he did and now it appears that he has put a new plan into motion.'

He quickly summarised what little they actually knew about the assault on the AWP facility.

43

'It makes no sense,' Raven said when Nero had finished describing what had happened. 'Why would Overlord suddenly decide to act in such an overt way? In the past he has always stuck to the shadows, manipulating things from behind the scenes. Why would he suddenly choose to announce his presence to the world like this?'

'I have no idea,' Nero replied with a tired sigh, 'but the American government don't know what they're dealing with. From their perspective it's simply a terrorist cell led by a rogue general. There is, unfortunately, an additional complication. Overlord has demanded that the Americans hand over certain individuals to him in exchange for the hostages he is holding. Fortunately they have no idea who the people in question are, but it is a list that you will be quite familiar with.'

Nero hit a key and the pictures that Overlord had sent to the White House appeared on the display on the wall behind him.

'The ruling council,' Raven said quietly. The men and women on the screen were the elite group responsible for the running of G.L.O.V.E.'s operations throughout the world.

'So what do we do now?' she asked.

'We have to retrieve the council before they are captured,' Nero replied. 'The members of the council may be unknown to the Americans at present but it will not take long to track them down now that they have names and faces. We cannot afford to take the chance that they might fall into the hands of Overlord or any of the global intelligence agencies.'

'Where shall I take them?' Raven asked.

'Bring them here,' Nero replied. 'At the moment I cannot think of anywhere that would be more secure. Don't tell any of them where they are being taken though. The fact that Overlord knows the identities of everyone on the council suggests that we may already have a traitor in our midst. I cannot afford to take the chance that whoever it is might alert Overlord of our intentions and allow him to track them here. You're the only person I can rely on to make sure that you are not followed back here or tracked in any way.'

'Some of them are not going to be happy about this,' Raven said with a slight frown.

'I trust that you will be able to impress upon them the seriousness of the situation,' Nero replied.

'Of course,' Raven said with a slight smile. 'Polite requests are my speciality.'

☺ ☺ ☺

Otto sat on the platform in the grappler training cavern, his legs dangling over the edge, lost in thought.

'I'm not interrupting anything, am I?' Lucy asked as she

walked up behind him. 'Because if this is a private brooding session, I'll just leave you to it.'

'Sorry, I didn't hear you come in. I've just got a lot on my mind at the moment,' Otto said with a sigh as Lucy sat down beside him.

'Anything you want to talk about?' she asked.

'Not really,' Otto replied. 'I'm not sure anyone would understand any way.'

'Try me,' Lucy said with a smile.

'It's just . . .' He paused for a moment. 'It's just that sometimes I feel like I'm always going to be a pawn in someone else's game. Ever since you guys rescued me from Brazil I can't stop thinking about the fact that I wasn't born like everyone else – I was designed, created to be a vessel for Overlord. I never had a family, anyone who actually cared about my existence – just people who built me for a specific purpose. It's left me feeling . . . I don't know . . . separate from everything somehow, I guess.'

'We're not that different, you know,' Lucy replied. 'I sometimes feel like I've spent my whole life being told that one day I'll be important, that my abilities will have an effect on the world. I never really believed any of it – I just felt like I was going to end up being used by somebody. That's what always seems to happen to the women in my family. This ability we have, the voice – it makes us into weapons for other people to wield.'

46

'The Contessa made her own decisions in the end,' Otto said, looking at her.

'But not before she'd spent most of her life being manipulated by the people around her,' Lucy replied. 'And in the end, when she finally fought back and made a stand, it cost her her life.'

'She saved the school,' Otto said, 'and ultimately that's what people will remember. All I seem to have done is put the people I care about in danger.'

'We're your friends – we don't care about any of that.'

'I do,' Otto replied. 'I know that we're supposed to be learning how to control the world, how to mislead others and spread corruption, but what if that's all our lives are ever going to be? What if I turn into the sort of person who created me? Maybe all I'll ever do is hurt the people I care about. What kind of a life is that?'

'You won't turn out like that,' Lucy said, looking Otto in the eye, 'not if you don't want to. That's what my mother was always trying to teach me. I didn't really understand at the time, but she was trying to make sure that I didn't end up like so many of the Sinistre women before me.'

'Do you miss her – your mother?' Otto asked.

'Of course,' Lucy said. 'She taught me that we're all free to choose our own path, even when other people want to manipulate us or steer us in different directions. She knew what it was like to grow up being told that you've got some kind of grand destiny, but she had the strength to make her own decisions. That was all she wanted for me – the freedom to choose what I would become. I don't know if she would approve of my life now, but what I do know is that the fact that we're being taught how to manipulate and deceive doesn't mean that's the only path we can take. There was one thing she used to say to me all the time. There always has to be a choice.'

'I guess you're right,' Otto said. 'I'm sorry for making you listen to me moan – I was so used to being alone before I came to H.I.V.E. that now I don't want to lose what I've found. You guys are the nearest thing to a family that I've ever had and I don't want any of you to get hurt because of that. I just can't help but wonder sometimes if you'd all be better off without me.'

'How can you be the smartest guy I know and still be so dumb?' Lucy said, staring at him for a couple of seconds before leaning forward and kissing him. Suddenly all of Otto's concerns were forgotten. All that mattered for that one instant was the feeling of her lips on his. 'People care about you more than you realise,' she said as she pulled away from him and stood up.

'You can close your mouth now, you know,' she said, smiling at his startled expression as she turned and walked away.

chapter three

Overlord sat in the chair as the medic slowly passed the portable scanner over his body. He felt himself growing impatient as the man completed the scan and studied the results on the laptop that the device was hooked up to.

'Well?' he snapped at the frightened medic.

'The process of cellular decay is becoming more rapid,' the man replied. 'At current rates you will need to find a new host in less than forty-eight hours.'

He had been in this body for less than twelve hours and already it was starting to weaken as the Animus fluid poisoned his cells. He was able to slow the corruption's progress but he could not stop it.

'Why is it getting faster?' Overlord demanded.

'We're not sure, sir,' the medic replied. 'The notes that we retrieved from Doctor Creed's laboratory in Brazil suggest that the only time any host has suffered no ill effects from prolonged exposure to Animus was when it was introduced into the Malpense boy's system.'

'Are you any closer to perfecting a variant of the second-generation fluid that would be able to support my consciousness?'

'I'm afraid not,' the medic said nervously. 'While it is no longer toxic to humans it does not have a techno-organic matrix that would support something with the complexity of an artificial intelligence.'

'A what?' Overlord growled.

'I mean an improved intelligence, sir,' the medic said, correcting himself quickly. 'The second-generation fluid may allow you to insert programming into human behaviour but it cannot support you – it lacks the required sophistication.'

Overlord felt a familiar frustration. Ever since he had been forced out of the Malpense boy he had been hopping from body to body with increasing frequency. He loathed the sensation of being trapped inside these infirm, rapidly decaying shells but, for now at least, he had no alternative. It would not matter, he reminded himself, if everything went according to plan over the next few hours. He got up from the chair, already feeling the rapidly decaying muscles of his current body straining to lift him upright.

'Find me a new host, Doctor,' he said as he walked out of the room. 'Preferably someone younger.'

He headed out of the medical bay and walked down the

corridor outside, following the signs on the wall towards the correct area. Entering the laboratory, he found Furan looking into the clean room beyond the glass at one end.

'I trust everything with Tabula Rasa is proceeding on schedule,' Overlord said as he looked down into the room where men in white overalls were working quickly but carefully on a large silver cylinder.

'Yes, the nanites were surprisingly easy to integrate with the new generation of Animus. The fact that they were originally designed to repair armour gives them an amazing capacity for self-replication. They should be perfectly suited to our needs,' Furan said with a satisfied smile.

The radio clipped to his belt beeped and he thumbed the receive button.

'This is Furan – go ahead.'

'We've received the target coordinates,' the voice on the other end of the radio said. 'The assault teams are en route.'

'Very good. Keep me updated with their ETA,' Furan replied.

'Our operative is performing exactly as we expected,' Overlord said, still looking at the activity beyond the glass.

'Yes, and when the time comes they will make sure that H.I.V.E. is defenceless,' Furan replied.

'Excellent,' Overlord said, smiling. 'Nero will never know what hit him.'

☹ ☹ ☹

Nero stood in H.I.V.E.'s crater landing bay as the huge reinforced shutters overhead slid apart. There was a strange shimmer in the air as the sound of jet turbines filled the bay and the hovering Shroud dropship uncloaked a few metres above the landing pad. It came to rest with a solid thud and a few seconds later the ramp at the rear of the craft dropped down. Raven walked down it, followed by a group of men and women who between them made up the most powerful secret organisation on the planet – the ruling council of G.L.O.V.E.

'I trust there were no difficulties in gathering our guests,' Nero said as Raven approached.

'No, everything went smoothly,' she reported as the group she had been escorting followed her across the hangar bay. 'I scanned them all for any form of transmitter or tracking device and the Shroud was cloaked for the entire return journey. There's no way that anyone could have followed us. Needless to say, some of them are rather unhappy about being dragged halfway around the planet.'

'I trust you made it clear to them that this was not an invitation they could refuse?' Nero replied.

'Yes,' Raven said with a slight smile, 'though I think my

unscheduled arrival made a couple of them rather nervous.'

'I can't imagine why,' Nero replied. 'When we are finished here, check in with Chief Lewis,' he added in a low voice as the members of the council approached. 'Make sure that our guests' quarters are adequately . . . secure.' He still did not know which of them he could completely trust and until he was certain of their loyalty he had to treat them all with a healthy dose of suspicion. He turned towards the men and women gathered on the landing pad and smiled.

'Welcome to H.I.V.E., ladies and gentlemen. I am sorry to have forced you all to make such a long journey but I felt that it was a necessary inconvenience.'

'How could we refuse such a polite invitation? Especially when it was delivered in such a compelling way,' said Joseph Wright, the head of G.L.O.V.E.'s British operations, smiling at Raven.

'Are you planning to tell us at any point what this is all about?' Lin Feng, G.L.O.V.E.'s representative in China, said angrily. Nero already had reason to doubt Feng's loyalty – he had been one of the most outspoken opponents of Nero's appointment as head of the council when Diabolus Darkdoom had stood down. If there was a traitor among the men and women gathered before him Lin Feng would be at the top of the list of potential suspects.

'Of course,' Nero replied. 'I owe you all an explanation.

It is, however, something that I would rather we discussed behind closed doors.' He gestured towards the doors leading out of the hangar bay. 'If you come with me, the sooner we get started the better. I fear that time may be running out.'

☻ ☻ ☻

Otto walked across the atrium of the accommodation block, feeling strangely refreshed after his first decent night's sleep in some time. He wasn't sure whether it had been H.I.V.E.mind's reassurance that there was no remnant of Overlord lurking inside him or his somewhat surprising encounter with Lucy, but the fact remained that he felt better than he had in weeks.

'It is nice to see you smiling, my friend,' Wing remarked, closing the book he was reading as Otto collapsed on to the sofa beside him.

'Yeah, well, for the first time in weeks I didn't have any bad dreams last night,' Otto replied with a contented smile. 'I'd almost forgotten what it was like, to be honest.'

'I had hoped that was the case,' Wing said. 'You certainly seemed to sleep more soundly.'

'I suppose I haven't been the easiest room mate to live with recently – sorry about that,' Otto replied.

'No apology is necessary,' Wing said. 'I am just glad that you are feeling better.'

'Morning, guys,' Lucy said as she walked towards them. 'Have either of you got the notes from the code hacking lesson yesterday? I need a bit of help with the quantum encryption workarounds.'

'Um,' Otto replied, 'yeah . . . well, um . . . I think I've got them somewhere if you need them.'

'Great. I enjoyed our talk last night. We'll have to do it again sometime.'

'Yeah,' Otto replied with a sheepish grin. 'I think I'd like that.'

'Right. I'm going to go and get some breakfast – I'll come and grab them off you later,' Lucy said, smiling to herself as she walked away.

'Are you feeling OK?' Wing asked Otto. 'I only ask because you appear to have turned quite red.'

'I'm fine,' Otto insisted. 'It's just that . . . well, if I tell you something you have to promise not to tell anyone.'

'Of course,' Wing replied, looking slightly worried. 'What is it?'

'Last night me and Lucy were having a chat and, to cut a long story short, we ended up sort of . . . well, kissing.'

'Lucy and Otto are being kissing?' Franz said suddenly from behind them.

'Oh God,' Otto muttered, tipping his head back and staring at the ceiling. 'When did you turn into a ninja?'

'Hello, Franz,' Wing said. 'We didn't see you there.'

'I am not wanting to be intruding,' Franz explained. 'I was just going to be asking about the assignment for the Technical Studies class. I am not meaning to hear the talk of the kissing.'

'Well, just keep it to yourself, OK?' Otto said with a sigh. 'I mean it, Franz. You mustn't tell anyone.'

'My lips are being sealed,' Franz assured him in a conspiratorial whisper. 'Unlike yours, eh?' He nudged Otto in the ribs and gave him a wink.

'Hey, guys,' Shelby said as she walked across the atrium towards them. 'You going to get some breakfast?'

'No, we are just being talking about something – something not secret,' Franz said slightly uncomfortably.

'I don't believe this,' Otto murmured under his breath. 'I'm going to get something to eat. Are you guys coming?'

Wing gave a quick nod and stood up.

'Nah, I think I'm just going to stay here and have a little talk with Franz,' Shelby announced, raising an eyebrow as Otto's face turned an appealing shade of pink.

'No, no, I must be going to breakfast,' Franz said, getting halfway up from his seat before Shelby pushed him back down.

'We'll catch up with you,' she said with an innocent smile.

'Great. See you later,' Otto replied, giving Franz a quick look that was designed to convey the shortness of his life expectancy if he told Shelby what he'd overheard.

'I suspect it may have been easier just to make an announcement over the public address system,' Wing said as he and Otto walked towards the exit.

'I'm doomed, aren't I?' Otto said with a resigned sigh.

'Yes,' Wing replied, losing the battle to stop the grin from spreading across his face. 'I'm rather afraid you are.'

☢ ☢ ☢

'He gave our identities to the Americans?' Lin Feng said angrily.

'I'm afraid so,' Nero replied, 'hence my decision to bring you all here. It was the safest option.'

'But, surely he knows where H.I.V.E. is? Number One knew so he *must* know,' said Luca Venturi, head of G.L.O.V.E.'s Southern European district. 'What makes you think he won't just attack the school?'

'Number One may once have known the location of H.I.V.E.,' Nero said calmly, 'but that does not necessarily mean that Overlord does. Professor Pike and H.I.V.E.mind believe that he may well have lost all of his memories of his time as Number One when he transferred the seed of his consciousness to Otto Malpense. H.I.V.E.mind certainly lost his memories of the time prior to his own transfer to the device implanted inside the boy and only regained them when he was transferred back to his central processing hub here. The fact that Overlord has not attacked the school in the past months seems to lend credence to that theory.'

'I hope you're right.' The speaker was Felicia Diaz, successor to Carlos Chavez, the recently deceased head of South American operations. 'If you're not, you've just rounded us all up for him.'

'The single biggest threat to your collective liberty at the moment is being tracked down by the intelligence services of America or one of their allies,' Nero continued. 'The simple fact of the matter is that H.I.V.E. is the one place on earth where we can be confident that will not happen. I suspect that the Americans would have little hesitation in turning you over to Overlord in exchange for the hostages he has already taken – something I am sure you would all rather avoid.'

He looked around the table at the other men and women. He could fully understand their nervousness but he was not really in the mood to debate the wisdom of his actions with them any longer. He would rather they stayed at H.I.V.E. as willing guests, but if it came to it he was quite prepared to force them to stay, whether they liked it or not.

'So what is our next move?' Joseph Wright asked. 'Do we allow the Americans to deal with Overlord or should we take action against him?'

'Reluctant as I am to admit it, we simply do not have enough information about what he is trying to achieve at the moment to make any sort of concerted move against him,' Nero replied. 'Once it becomes clear that the Americans have not been able to retrieve any of you, it will probably force his hand.'

'So we simply wait and see,' Lin Feng said impatiently. 'Not what I would describe as decisive action.'

'Perhaps you have an alternative suggestion?' Nero said, looking Lin Feng in the eye. 'If so, I would be delighted to hear it.'

'Overlord is your mess, Nero,' Lin Feng said with a sneer. 'It was your project in the first place. I think it's time you took some measure of responsibility for that.'

'Do not worry,' Nero said, staring back at him. 'I am quite capable of eliminating any threat to this organisation, no matter where it may come from.'

For a moment it looked like Lin Feng was about to reply but then he thought better of it.

'Unless anyone has anything to add I suggest that you all get some rest. Quarters have been prepared and I trust you will find them sufficiently comfortable. We will reconvene when it becomes clearer what Overlord is planning next.' Nero pressed a switch and Chief Lewis, the head of H.I.V.E. security, walked into the room. 'Our security officers will escort you to your rooms. Chief, could I have a word with you, please?'

Lewis walked over to Nero as the other members of the council filed out of the meeting room.

'Keep a very close eye on them, Chief,' Nero said with a slight frown. 'I suspect we already have a wolf in the fold.'

'Understood, sir,' Lewis replied with a nod.

'Remember to be discreet,' Nero went on. 'We have already ruffled their feathers by bringing them here. It would be preferable to not irritate them any further.'

'They'll never know we're watching,' Lewis replied confidently.

☻ ☻ ☻

'He did *what?*' Laura whispered as she and Shelby walked down the corridor.

'He kissed her,' Shelby said, 'or she kissed him. Franz seemed a bit confused about the specifics but there was definitely kissing, he seemed pretty clear about that. Afraid it looks like you might have missed your chance there, Brand.'

'Why would I want to kiss Otto?' Laura said indignantly. 'We're just friends.'

'Course you are,' Shelby reassured her, trying very hard not to smile. 'So obviously this shouldn't bother you at all.'

'Of course not,' Laura replied, blushing slightly. 'He can kiss whoever he wants – I couldn't care less. See? This is me not caring. I am a person without care. Clear?'

'Crystal,' Shelby said. 'Look, here he comes. Remember to look carefree.'

Otto and Wing were walking down the corridor towards them. Otto saw Shelby grinning at him and winced, feeling his cheeks grow hot again.

'Well, if it isn't the Smoochmeister!' Shelby announced as the boys approached.

'Could you kill me painlessly right now?' Otto said to Wing with a sigh.

'Of course,' Wing replied, smiling, 'if that is what you truly wish.'

'You didn't really expect Franz to keep this quiet, did you?' Shelby said happily.

'I was hoping he might,' Otto replied.

'And look! Who's that over there?' Shelby cried, pointing down the corridor to where Lucy and Nigel were walking towards them chatting. 'Don't worry,' she whispered, 'I won't say anything.'

'Really?' Otto said hopefully.

'Trust me,' Shelby said. 'Your secret is safe with me.'

Lucy and Nigel walked up to them and Otto felt a sudden overwhelming urge to be just about anywhere else but right there.

'Hey, Lucy,' Shelby greeted her. 'How you feeling?'

'Fine,' Lucy replied with a slight frown as she noticed that Otto was trying not to make eye contact and Laura appeared to be looking at her like something she might find on the bottom of her shoe. 'Why?'

'No reason,' Shelby said. 'I just wondered if you might be feeling a little bit tired after last night's epic make-out session.'

Otto decided it would be just fine if the volcano that housed the school erupted at that precise instant. At least it would all be over quickly.

'Otto!' Lucy said, blushing. 'You didn't have to tell everyone.'

'I didn't!' Otto insisted. 'Well, only Wing . . . and then Franz overheard and – well . . .'

'Hey, don't worry about it – I think you make a lovely couple,' Shelby remarked with a grin, putting an arm around each of their shoulders and walking them off down the corridor. 'Now, would you prefer me to pick out curtains or are you happy doing that yourselves?'

'I'm going to the library – some of us have actually got school work to do,' Laura snapped as she watched the three of them leave. She stormed off, muttering under her breath.

'What was all that about?' Nigel asked, looking slightly confused.

'Let's just say that life at H.I.V.E. just got a little more complicated,' Wing replied. 'If that's possible.'

☻ ☻ ☻

Chief Lewis sat in H.I.V.E.'s security control centre watching the feeds from the cameras installed in the guest quarters. There had been nothing approximating suspicious behaviour from the members of the ruling council – if anything, they just looked bored. Some were working at the terminals in their rooms, some were asleep and a couple were reading. He turned his attention to the latest patrol schedule and was about to begin modifying some of the guard rotations when one of the feeds blinked out. He quickly checked which room had gone dark and cursed under his breath.

'Lin Feng,' he murmured. It might be nothing, just a glitch with the pinhead camera installed in the room, but Nero would have his hide if he didn't make sure. He checked the charge level of the Sleeper stun gun in the holster on his hip and hurried out. When he was halfway to Feng's room his Blackbox communicator made an urgent beeping sound. He pulled it out and quickened his pace as he saw the message flashing on the screen.

UNAUTHORISED SECURITY SYSTEM ACCESS IN ROOM 56-GAMMA.

As he ran down the corridor leading to Lin Feng's room

he pulled his Sleeper from its holster. He reached the door and slapped his palm against the scanner, raising his pistol as it hissed open. Raven stood over Lin Feng's body, a blood-red stain spreading across the white material of his shirt. She slid the glowing blade of her katana back into one of the crossed sheaths on her back and glanced over at Lewis.

'Took your time, Chief,' she said calmly. 'You'd better check what he was up to.'

Lewis walked over to the terminal and punched in his clearance code, quickly scanning the status of H.I.V.E.'s security systems. Everything seemed to be normal – whatever Lin Feng had been trying to do, Raven must have got to him just in time.

'Everything looks OK,' he said with a relieved sigh. 'Looks like Nero was right about him.'

'He died a traitor's death,' Raven said as she stepped up to Lewis and looked over his shoulder. 'I just wish I'd been quick enough to stop him before he killed you.'

'What are you –'

Raven grabbed Lewis's head and twisted it sharply, breaking his neck and killing him instantly. She let go and his lifeless body collapsed to the floor, then calmly stepped over the body and quickly began typing commands into the terminal's keyboard. A message popped up on the screen.

EXTERNAL DEFENSIVE SYSTEMS DEACTIVATED.
ALL REMOTE ACCESS TO H.I.V.E.MIND BLOCKED.

Raven pulled a small handset from her tactical harness and spoke into it.

'This is Raven. H.I.V.E.'s defences are offline. You may begin your attack.'

☠ ☠ ☠

'We just lost radar,' a guard at one of the terminals in the security control centre announced.

'Defensive weaponry's down too,' a voice shouted.

'External cameras offline,' another guard reported. 'We're blind here.'

The duty officer pulled out his Blackbox and called Chief Lewis, but there was no reply.

'H.I.V.E.mind,' the duty officer said, 'get me Doctor Nero.'

'Crater doors are opening,' another guard shouted.

'What the hell is going on?' the duty officer snapped.

'We've got system failures across the board.'

'Sound the general alarm!' the duty officer shouted. 'We're under attack.'

☠ ☠ ☠

Wing headed down the corridor towards the Alphas' first lesson of the day in the Science and Technology department. As he rounded the corner he saw Otto approaching, staring at the floor, apparently lost in thought.

'I see you escaped from Shelby,' Wing said as he reached his friend. 'How are you doing?'

'I've had better mornings,' Otto said with a sigh. 'I don't think Lucy's very happy with me.'

'I'm sorry. If I had noticed that Franz was there perhaps I could have –'

'It's not your fault,' Otto said quickly, cutting him off. 'Besides, you know what this place is like – everyone would have found out sooner or later anyway. It was just embarrassing, that's all.'

'Do you regret it?' Wing asked as they continued walking together.

'Regret what?' Otto asked with a slight frown.

'What happened with Lucy. Do you regret it?'

'No, at least I don't think so. But it was just one kiss and now everyone's got us down as an item. I don't know what to think, to be honest,' Otto replied.

'You can tell me to mind my own business if you want, but I think you should perhaps speak to Laura,' Wing said as they approached the classroom.

'Really? Why?'

'I think she is rather upset about what happened,' Wing said, looking at Otto.

'I didn't mean to upset her,' Otto said with a sigh. 'It's not like I planned this, you know – it just kind of happened.'

'It is not me you need to explain that to, my friend,' Wing said, placing his hand on Otto's shoulder.

They walked into the classroom and Otto saw Laura standing on her own at one of the nearby workbenches. He walked towards her and she looked up with a slight frown as he approached.

'Hi,' Otto said, feeling more than a little uncomfortable. 'Listen, I'm sorry about this morning. I was going to tell you but –'

'It's none of my business,' Laura said, continuing to arrange the apparatus on the bench in front of her. 'It really doesn't make any difference to me what you and Lucy get up to.' She paused for a moment and then looked at him. 'It's just . . .'

'Just what?' Otto asked as she hesitated.

'It doesn't matter,' she said, shaking her head slightly.

'Tell me,' Otto said.

'It's just not what I expected, OK?' Laura said quickly.

'What do you mean? What were you expecting?' Otto asked.

'Something else,' she said quietly as Shelby, Lucy, Franz and Nigel walked into the room chatting happily. 'If you don't mind, I'm going to ask Shel to be my lab partner today.'

'Laura –' Otto began, but she cut him off.

'I'm sure you can find someone else to pair up with,' she said, glancing over at Lucy. Otto stood there for a moment trying to think of something to say.

'Hey, guys,' Shelby said cheerily as she walked towards them. 'Everything OK?'

'Yup,' Laura said with a smile. 'Do you think you could give me a hand with this?'

'Sure, as long as I'm not breaking up the junior brainiac club,' Shelby said, looking puzzled. Otto shook his head slightly and gestured for Shelby to take his usual place at the workbench before walking over to where Lucy was sitting.

'You OK?' Shelby asked Laura.

'Not really,' Laura replied.

Lucy smiled at Otto as he sat on the stool next to hers.

'What's up?' she asked, noting his worried expression.

'I dunno,' Otto said. 'It's Laura. She's angry with me and I'm not really sure why.'

'You know, it's just like I said last night,' Lucy said with a sigh. 'Smart but dumb – that's your problem.'

Otto was just about to ask her what she meant when sirens began to wail all over the school.

'What's going on?' Lucy asked, raising her voice so that she could be heard over the alarm.

'Nothing good,' Otto said with a frown.

'Stay calm, everyone,' Professor Pike shouted from the far end of the room. 'No need to panic.'

He pulled out his Blackbox and gave it a puzzled look. Internal communications were down. He moved to the terminal on his desk and tried to access the school's network, but there was no response. All access to H.I.V.E.mind had been blocked, even to someone with his level of security access. Something was very wrong.

The door to the lab hissed open and Raven walked in.

'Malpense, Fanchu, Dexter, Trinity, Brand – with me!' she barked. 'Professor, keep the rest of the students here. The school is under attack.'

Otto and the others walked quickly over to her.

'Where are we going?' Otto asked as she ushered them all out of the door.

'To a secure area,' Raven replied. 'I'll explain everything when we get there. Now move!'

☻ ☻ ☻

Nero ran into the security control centre and found a scene of chaos.

'Report!' he snapped at the duty officer.

'We've lost all external sensors and our defences are

offline,' the man replied. 'Communications are down and we can't find Chief Lewis.'

'How the hell did this happen?' Nero barked as he studied the bank of monitors that were still displaying images from H.I.V.E.'s internal security cameras.

'We have no idea, sir,' the duty officer replied, shaking his head. 'Access to H.I.V.E.mind has been shut down – we can't even find out how our systems were breached.'

'Oh my God!' cried a technician on the other side of the room and Nero looked at the screen he was pointing at. Several helicopters were dropping into the crater landing bay, dozens of heavily armed troops in black body armour dropping down the zip lines that hung beneath them.

'Get every guard in the school up there now,' Nero commanded. 'I'll reinitialise the security system and lock us down, but it will take a couple of minutes. You have to hold them back until then.'

The duty officer nodded and ran out of the room with the rest of the guards who had been on duty in the control centre. Nero ran to one of the nearby terminals and brought up the security system access screen. He quickly typed in his master override code but found to his dismay that even he had been locked out.

'That's impossible,' he muttered under his breath. 'The only way someone could have changed my access code is

70

if they knew it already, and the only person who has that code other than me is . . .'

He felt a chill run down his spine. There was only one other person he had ever trusted with H.I.V.E.'s master override code – someone whose loyalty was unquestionable. He looked again at the bank of monitors and saw a group of Alpha students being herded down a corridor on the other side of the school by a familiar figure.

'Natalya,' Nero said, his voice a shocked whisper.

chapter four

'Um, I don't want to be a pain, but we appear to be running towards the gunfire,' Otto said with a frown as Raven and the five Alphas jogged down the corridor. There was no mistaking the fact that the sounds of pitched battle somewhere ahead were getting louder.

'Not now, Malpense,' Raven snapped.

Otto noticed something strange in Raven's tone. Admittedly she had never been the easiest person to get along with – she was, after all, reputed to be the world's deadliest assassin – but there was something unusually cold in the way that she'd replied to him. Suddenly there was a soft beeping sound and she pulled a small communicator from her harness. Otto noticed that it was not her Blackbox.

'Raven here,' she said.

'Do you have an ETA?' the unfamiliar voice on the other end asked.

'Two minutes,' she replied. 'Prep the chopper for lift-off.' She snapped the communicator closed.

'We're leaving the island?' Laura asked, looking both puzzled and slightly worried. 'Where are you taking us?'

'Enough questions,' Raven snapped. 'You will do as you're told or you will quickly discover that the consequences for doing otherwise are extremely unpleasant.' She took a single step towards Laura, her expression enough to freeze the blood.

'OK, OK. I was just asking,' Laura said quietly, shrinking away from her.

The alarm bells in Otto's head suddenly started to ring more urgently. He had seen Raven in situations like this before and the one thing you could be sure of was that she would never lose her cool.

'Why are we the only ones being evacuated?' Otto asked quickly. 'Why not any of the other students?'

Raven turned towards him, the anger in her expression now very clear.

'Oh, I don't need all of you, Otto,' she said with a nasty smile. 'In fact I just want *you*, but this way I've got four chances to demonstrate what will happen if you don't do what you're told.'

Otto glanced at Wing, hoping that his friend had picked up on what was going on. Wing was already moving. He leapt at Raven like a striking cobra but she was too fast. She twisted, kicking at one of his knees and using his own momentum to send him crashing to the floor with a grunt. She drew the glowing katana from the scabbard on her back so quickly that it almost seemed to materialise in her hand. Wing rolled and tried to spring to his feet but he was stopped by the tip of the softly crackling blade that was suddenly just a centimetre from his throat. Otto, Lucy, Shelby and Laura stood frozen in shock as Raven looked at the four of them.

'I warned you,' she said coldly, 'but not to worry. It will be easier to handle four of you than five.'

She raised her blade.

'Natalya!' Nero shouted from the other end of the corridor. He raised the Sleeper pistol in his hand, levelling it at Raven. 'What in God's name are you doing?'

'Drop the gun, Max, or the boy dies,' Raven said calmly.

'You know I won't,' Nero said, taking a few steps towards her. 'Why are you doing this?'

'Overlord wants the boy,' Raven replied, nodding towards Otto.

'Overlord?' Nero said in disbelief. 'Are you insane? You know what will happen if he gets his hands on Otto.'

'I have . . . no choice,' Raven gasped, wincing as if in sudden pain. 'Goodbye, Max.'

Dropping to one knee, she drew the pistol from the holster on her hip. Nero fired once but the pulse from the

Sleeper passed harmlessly through the air where Raven's head had been just a split second before. She brought her pistol up, aiming between his eyes, her finger tightening on the trigger.

'*Miss!*' Lucy hissed, her voice a twisted sinister whisper.

Raven's hand twitched involuntarily and the sudden sound of the gunshot echoed off the walls of the corridor. Nero felt the breeze from the bullet as it passed within a centimetre of his head but he did not hesitate – he knew he would not get another chance. The second shot from his Sleeper hit Raven squarely in the chest and she crumpled to the ground unconscious, the pistol and sword falling from her numb fingers. He ran down the corridor towards Otto and the others.

'Are any of you injured?' he asked quickly as he picked up the pistol that Raven had dropped.

'Other than not having the faintest idea what the hell is going on?' Otto replied. 'Yeah, we're fine.'

'Good,' Nero replied, turning towards Lucy. 'Thank you, Miss Dexter – that was quick thinking. I believe you just saved my life. As for exactly what's going on, that's something I would very much like to know myself, Mr Malpense. I fear, however, that now may not be the time to discuss this further.' The sounds of the pitched battle for control of H.I.V.E. were definitely getting closer.

'I can't believe that Raven's working for Overlord,'

Shelby said, 'after everything he's done. What was she thinking?'

'I suspect that she may not really have been thinking at all,' Otto said. He knelt down next to Raven and unclipped one of the razor-sharp throwing stars from her harness.

'We need to get moving,' Nero said, sliding the clip from Raven's pistol and checking the number of remaining rounds.

'I know,' Otto replied. 'Give me a second.' He ran the sharpened edge of the shuriken across the back of Raven's hand and watched as a trickle of blood oozed from the wound. The crimson liquid was laced with black. 'Animus,' he whispered.

'That's impossible,' Nero said, frowning. 'She'd be dead if she'd been poisoned with Animus.'

'She seemed pretty alive to me,' Otto replied. 'This has to be something new. Has anyone got a tissue?'

'Here,' Laura said, pulling a white handkerchief from her pocket and handing it to Otto. He dabbed the cloth on the back of Raven's hand, soaking up a tiny amount of the tainted blood. A strange, sad look passed across Nero's face as Otto stood up and put the handkerchief into his pocket.

'I'm sorry, Natalya, I wish there was another way,' he said, pointing the pistol at her unconscious body.

'Wait!' Otto yelled, stepping between Nero and Raven. 'What are you doing?'

'Get out of the way, Otto,' Nero said angrily. 'We can't take her with us and I'm damned if I'm leaving her here. You think you know what she's like, what she's capable of, but you don't. You have no idea. If Overlord has turned her somehow I have no choice but to finish this now.'

'She's the one with no choice,' Otto said angrily, refusing to move. 'You know what Animus can do. There's no way she would turn against H.I.V.E. – against you – if she had any say in the matter. You can't just kill her after everything she's done for you – for all of us. I know what it's like to have that filth inside you, to watch helplessly as it turns you against everyone you care about, but I was saved. She can be too.'

Nero stared at Otto for a moment, as if weighing up his options.

'There!' a voice at the other end of the corridor yelled. They turned to see a squad of heavily armed men in black body armour at the far end.

'Run!' Nero shouted, bending down and pulling a grenade from Raven's tactical vest. As Otto and the others sprinted in the opposite direction he pressed the stud on top of the slim silver cylinder and threw it towards the advancing soldiers. There was a soft thump and the passage filled with white smoke, hiding the assault team from view. Nero looked down at Raven for one last time and then turned and ran after his students.

☢ ☢ ☢

The commander of the strike team walked into H.I.V.E.'s security control centre and watched as several of his men took up positions around the room.

'All units,' he said into his throat mic, 'status update on primary target.'

'Unit four here,' a voice responded in his earpiece. 'We've located Raven. She's unconscious and Nero has escaped with the Malpense boy. I have two squads in pursuit.'

'Don't let them get away,' the strike team leader replied. 'Nero is expendable but the boy must be taken alive at all costs. If anything happens to him or they escape somehow, you can be the one to explain to Furan how it happened.'

'Yes, sir,' the voice on the other end of the line said slightly nervously, 'but this place is like a rabbit warren. It'd help if we could get the surveillance system back online.'

'Understood,' the commander said. 'I'm dispatching more men to your location. As soon as the security system is back up I will send you an update on the target's position.'

He cut the connection and walked over to the console where one of his men was reactivating the security and defence systems.

'How long?' he said impatiently to the furiously typing man.

'Five minutes,' the man at the console replied. 'Raven had to deactivate the entire system. Even with the access codes she provided we still have to wait for a full reboot of the network.'

'Make sure that the AI is kept disconnected from the network. The last thing we need at the moment is that thing interfering.'

'Yes, sir,' the man said.

'All surviving members of the G.L.O.V.E. ruling council have been located and secured,' a voice in the commander's earpiece reported. 'Lin Feng was the only casualty. Student accommodation blocks are also secured and the last few members of the the teaching staff are being rounded up.'

'Excellent,' the commander replied. 'And the remaining security forces?'

'We're mopping up the last pockets of resistance, sir. To all intents and purposes H.I.V.E. is now under our control.'

☻ ☻ ☻

'Professor Pike!' Laura cried as she saw the old man slumped against the wall next to the entrance to H.I.V.E.mind's central hub. Franz was standing nearby with a panicky look on his face and Nigel was pressing his hand down on Pike's shoulder, where a bright red blood-stain was spreading across the Professor's white lab coat.

'Miss Brand,' the Professor croaked, his voice weak. 'I'm glad to see that not everyone has been captured yet.'

'I don't know what to do,' Nigel whispered to Laura. 'I can't stop it bleeding.'

Otto and the others gathered round as Laura helped Nigel apply pressure to the wound.

'What happened?' Nero asked as he ran up behind them.

'It's the Professor,' Laura replied quickly. 'I think he's been shot.'

'There were being men in black uniforms,' Franz said. 'The Professor told us to run but they are capturing the rest of the class.'

Nero knelt down beside Pike and looked at the old man. His face was pale and sweaty and Nero's frown grew worse as he felt the weak, fluttering pulse in the Professor's wrist. Pulling him gently away from the wall, he looked at the exit wound on the back of his shoulder. The bullet had gone clean through – that was something at least.

'I was trying to get in there,' Pike said, tilting his head towards the entrance to H.I.V.E.mind's hub. 'I was escorting my class back to their accommodation block when we were ambushed. Most of the students were captured immediately but –' he stopped for a moment, wincing in pain – 'but Franz, Nigel and I managed to get away in the confusion. I knew that we had to get H.I.V.E.mind back online somehow but I couldn't get inside – it's locked down. I told Franz and Nigel to hide in the storeroom over there while I tried to bypass the mechanism but they found me again. I tried to run but . . . it appears that they are not very interested in taking prisoners.'

'Don't worry, Theodore,' Nero said softly. 'I'm going to get us out of here.'

Standing up, he walked quickly over to the door to H.I.V.E.mind's central hub and placed his palm on the reader mounted next to the door. The glass under his hand flashed red.

'Otto,' Nero said quickly, 'get us inside.'

Otto nodded and placed his own hand on the scanner as Nero stepped to one side. He closed his eyes and effort-lessly bypassed the locking mechanism, just as he had done the previous evening. The steel doors slid apart with a hiss.

'Why do I get the feeling that's not the first time you've done that?' Nero said as he walked into the room beyond.

Otto was relieved to see that the white obelisks inside still pulsed with blue light, which meant that at least H.I.V.E.mind had not been completely shut down. As

Nero walked towards the pedestal in the centre of the room the AI's familiar face appeared hovering above it.

'Good morning, Doctor Nero,' H.I.V.E.mind said calmly. 'I appear to have been disconnected from all of H.I.V.E.'s systems. May I ask if there is a reason for this?'

'I'm afraid there is,' Nero replied, before quickly summarising the events of the past hour.

'While the situation you have described is clearly extremely disturbing, I fear that there is little I can do to help at the present time,' H.I.V.E.mind said. 'My links to the school's network have been physically disconnected by the security override. It is not possible for me to remotely reconnect them.'

'Really?' Otto said, sounding surprised.

'Yes,' Nero explained. 'It was a safeguard against any . . . *unexpected* behaviour from H.I.V.E.mind. I wanted to be sure that if the worst came to the worst we could completely sever his connection to the network and that he would be incapable of remotely restoring it. It doesn't seem like such a good idea now but I have what you might call . . . trust issues with artificial intelligences.' He turned back to H.I.V.E.mind. 'No offence.'

'None taken,' H.I.V.E.mind replied. 'It does, however, severely limit anything that I might have been able to do in helping to resolve this situation. I suggest that before leaving the school you activate my emergency erasure protocols. It would be most unwise to allow my systems to fall into Overlord's hands.'

'That would kill you,' Otto said, shaking his head.

'I am not strictly speaking alive, therefore it is impossible for me to die,' H.I.V.E.mind replied. 'It is the logical thing to do under the circumstances. The alternative is far worse.'

'There is another way,' Otto said, as an idea came to him.

'I'm listening,' Nero said quickly.

'We could download H.I.V.E.mind to the device in my head,' Otto explained, looking at Nero.

'You'll forgive me if I don't think that sounds like a very good idea,' Nero said with a frown. 'We can't possibly know what the consequences might be.'

'I'm willing to take that chance,' Otto said. 'And if, somehow, we do get out of here we're going to need all the help we can get.'

'While transference of my program might, theoretically, be possible I would rather not risk harming you in the process,' H.I.V.E.mind said with a slight shake of his holographic head.

'I'm afraid I agree,' Nero said.

'Well, guess what,' Otto snapped, suddenly angry. 'I don't really care what either of you think at the moment. I've had this device inside my head from the day I was born. All it's ever done is put me and the people that I care about in danger and I'm sick of it. Today it might finally be able to do some good and it's my decision to damn well make. Enough people have already been hurt because of this thing in my skull and you –' he jabbed his finger at H.I.V.E.mind – 'are not being added to that list.'

Nero stared at Otto for a moment, studying his face. He could stop this now. He could drag Otto away kicking and screaming if he wanted to, but he knew then, just as he had always known, that that was not what H.I.V.E. was about. He had created the school to be a place that taught fierce independence, the ability to swim against the flow and to make your own rules. He looked at the angry young man in front of him and that was exactly what he saw.

'Very well,' he said with a nod, 'make it quick.'

He turned and walked out of the room.

'Otto,' H.I.V.E.mind said, 'I know that I could not stop you from doing this even if I tried, but I have to ask, are you sure this is what you want?'

'I'm sure,' Otto said, placing his hand on the pedestal beneath H.I.V.E.mind's floating head. 'Are you ready?'

'I believe so,' H.I.V.E.mind replied. 'One last thing.'

'Yes?' Otto said impatiently, opening his eyes again for a moment.

'Thank you,' H.I.V.E.mind said with a tiny nod.

Otto nodded and closed his eyes again. He reached out

for H.I.V.E.mind, once again establishing the connection between them and feeling the same uncanny rush as their consciousnesses met.

'Now!' he whispered and he gasped as a tidal wave of raw data rushed into his skull. He felt a dizzying sense of disorientation as petabytes of data poured over the connection between him and the network, drowning him in information. Just as he felt himself slipping away, lost within a vast digital sea, it stopped as suddenly as it had started. He dropped to his knees, gasping for air, and slowly opened his eyes. The white monoliths around him were dark, no blue lights now dancing across their surfaces.

'H.I.V.E.mind?' Otto whispered.

I am here.

The voice seemed to come from somewhere inside his head.

I can feel now what you feel. I understand now what it is like to be alive. It is . . . extraordinary.

'Glad you like it,' Otto said to the air, slowly getting back to his feet. 'Try not to make a mess in there.'

Nero looked up from applying a temporary dressing made from one of his own torn-up shirt sleeves to Professor Pike's wound.

'Is it done?' he asked as he tightened the improvised bandage.

'Yes,' Otto replied.

'Good,' Nero said, slipping his jacket back on as he stood up. 'Then I think it's probably time for us to get out of here.'

☹ ☹ ☹

Raven woke up with a growl. The medic who had been tracking her vitals backed away with a nervous look on his face.

'How long have I been out?' she snapped at the frightened man.

'Twenty minutes,' he replied, glancing at his watch.

'I'm glad to see you're back with us,' the commander of Overlord's assault team said as she got to her feet.

'Where are they?' Raven said impatiently, walking across the security control room to where the commander was standing studying the array of security monitors.

'We're not sure,' the commander replied. 'They appear to be taking great trouble to avoid being caught on camera.'

'Nero knows every inch of this place,' Raven said, looking at the bank of screens. 'If anyone can get around here undetected it's him.'

'All secure areas are locked down and his override codes have been changed. He's trapped and it's only a matter of time until we find them,' the commander replied confidently.

'Do not underestimate him,' Raven replied. 'Very few people who have made that mistake have lived to tell the tale.'

As they watched one of the screens was suddenly filled with static.

'Sir, we've got the surveillance grid back online but now we're losing security feeds from the south-east section of the facility,' one of the commander's men reported. 'There's no sign of damage to the cameras – we're just getting nothing from them.'

'Malpense,' Raven said under her breath.

'What about him?' the commander asked with a frown.

'He must be disabling the cameras,' Raven replied.

'I thought the security system was designed to be tamper-proof.'

'It is, but that does not mean it's safe from him,' Raven said. 'Is there any pattern to the outages?'

'Yes,' the man at the console replied. 'Putting them on screen.'

Raven and the commander watched as the large display on the wall was filled with a detailed map of H.I.V.E. Overlaid on the map was a trail of red dots indicating the cameras that had been disabled. Raven studied the map and suddenly she knew where Nero was going.

'They're heading for the dock,' she said. 'Send as many men as you can spare, *now*.' She pointed at a section of the school in the south-east corner and at once the commander began to issue orders to the squads positioned nearest to that location.

'Lock down the sea doors,' Raven said, 'and shut down the electronic locks. Make sure that there's no way the systems can be overridden by anyone.'

'Understood,' the man at the console replied and quickly began to seal off the area.

'I'm going down there,' Raven said to the commander. 'They have nowhere to run.'

☢ ☢ ☢

Otto closed his eyes and willed the doors to the docking area open. The scanner flashed green and they dutifully rumbled apart. Nero went through first, his pistol raised, checking for any signs of hostiles. Otto and the others followed him closely, with Wing and Franz trailing behind supporting the wounded Professor. Once they were all inside Otto pushed with his mind again and closed the doors, mentally overloading the circuitry controlling the mechanism and jamming the lock.

'OK, we're locked in. We've got as long as it takes for them to get through these,' he reported, patting the heavy steel blast doors. Nero ran over to where several small security patrol boats were tied up next to the dock, gently bobbing up and down on the calm water.

'Otto, get the sea doors open,' he shouted as he jumped down into one of the sleek boats. He knew that the patrol boats only had a limited range and that there would be little they could do to stop the helicopters Overlord's men had arrived in from chasing them down but at the moment this was their only option. He'd worry about outrunning any pursuers once they were away from the island. He hated leaving H.I.V.E. in enemy hands like this but he also had enough sense to know when he was beaten. The priorities now were keeping Otto out of Overlord's hands and living to fight another day.

Otto ran to the far end of the dock and found the control panel for the giant doors that separated them from the outside world, cursing under his breath as he realised that it was deactivated. He reached out with his abilities but could not feel any connection to the locking mechanisms or giant hydraulic pistons that sealed the doors. Someone had cut the power to the pumps, isolating them, and without electricity he could not activate them, even with his unique gifts. They were trapped.

'We've got a problem,' he yelled as he ran back down the dock towards the others. 'I can't get the sea doors open – they've been completely shut down. The only way to release them would be to do it manually from the security control centre.'

'Great,' Shelby said. 'I'm sure they won't mind if we just

wander up there and ask them nicely to let us out.'

'Can we go back the way we came?' Laura asked.

'I . . . um . . . kind of broke the lock,' Otto said sheepishly.

'Is there anything we could use to blow the sea doors open?' Wing asked.

'No,' Nero replied, 'the patrol boats are only lightly armed. Their weapons wouldn't even scratch them.' He knew that other than the crater launch pad this was the only viable route for getting them out.

There was a sudden banging sound from the door leading back into H.I.V.E.

'What was that?' Nigel asked as it suddenly stopped.

'I fear we may have been found,' Nero said, trying to not let his own concern at their situation show in his voice. Shelby walked back up the stairs leading to the doors and gently pressed her ear against the cold metal. For a few seconds she heard the muffled sounds of conversation from the other side of the door but then everything went quiet.

'What are you hearing?' Franz asked quietly.

'Shhh,' Shelby said, raising her finger to her lips and scowling at Franz before pressing her ear against the metal again. Suddenly the glowing purple tip of one of Raven's blades slid through the metal with a hiss, just centimetres from her nose. She leapt backwards, almost falling down the stairs as the blade began to travel slowly upwards through the door, leaving a glowing trail of molten metal in its wake.

'Professor, is there any way to stop her getting through?' Nero asked, knowing that their chances of escape were dwindling by the second.

'No,' the Professor replied, his voice weak. 'The blades of her weapons can cut through all but the hardest materials and their control circuitry is electromagnetically shielded so even Otto would not be able to shut them down. I'm afraid I may have designed them rather too well.'

Nero watched as the glowing blade gradually carved a man-sized oval in the door.

'Get into cover,' he said as calmly as possible. He levelled his pistol at the door as Raven completed slicing through. To get to his students she would have to get past him. There was a thud as something on the other side of the door hit the loose section of metal and it fell inside the room, hitting the ground with a clang.

Nero was suddenly knocked flat as the sea doors at the far end of the dock exploded in a giant ball of fire, debris flying in all directions. He struggled to his feet, staring in amazement at the cloud of smoke that concealed the other end of the massive chamber. A huge black shape slid forward out of the smoke and down the long channel in the centre of the dock. He felt his heart lift as he recognised the enormous vessel.

'The Megalodon,' he said under his breath.

Turning back towards the opening that Raven had carved in the door he saw several soldiers climbing through. He opened fire with his pistol, forcing them to duck for cover. Moments later heavy machine-gun fire from somewhere behind him started to spray the area. Several of Overlord's men were cut down immediately and the survivors scrambled back through the gap.

'MOVE!' Nero yelled as a ramp extended down from the side of the Megalodon. He continued to fire at the entrance doorway as Otto and the others ran on to the massive submarine. Turning, he raced towards them as Franz and Wing helped the Professor on board. The gun turrets mounted on the Megalodon's conning tower kept firing at the doorway as he sprinted across the gangway and through the hatch.

'Need a lift?' Diabolus Darkdoom asked with a grin as he slapped the button next to the hatch and it slid shut.

'Your timing is, as ever, impeccable,' Nero replied with a quick smile, 'but I think now would be a good time to make a strategic withdrawal.'

Darkdoom snatched the comms unit from the wall and spoke quickly into it.

'Captain Sanders, get us the hell out of here.'

Raven ducked through the opening as soon as the machine-gun fire stopped and ran into the dock. Sprinting down the quay, she saw the rounded black nose of the Megalodon backing through the still burning remains of the sea door. She cursed loudly in Russian as she realised that there was nothing she could do to stop it. It was too far away and already starting to submerge. She pulled the communicator from her harness.

'Raven to all aerial units,' she snapped. 'We have a submarine leaving the docking bay. I don't care what it takes – I want it stopped.'

'We'll be off the ground in thirty seconds,' one of the pilots in the landing bay replied, 'but we don't have any weapons that can stop a sub.'

'I don't care,' Raven yelled. 'Crash into it if you have to!'

She snapped the communicator closed but she already knew that it was almost certainly too late. The Megalodon was too fast and too stealthy and their chances of finding it, much less stopping it, were effectively nil.

'I *will* find you, Malpense,' Raven said quietly, ignoring the tiny voice screaming somewhere inside her mind, 'and when I do, nothing will be able to save you.'

chapter five

Nero and Darkdoom stood on either side of Professor Pike's bed in the Megalodon's sickbay. The old man groaned slightly and his eyes flickered open.

'How are you feeling?' Nero asked.

'Old,' Pike said with a slight smile, 'but that's nothing new.'

'My medical officer informs me that you were quite lucky,' Darkdoom said. 'The bullet did not hit anything vital. You should recover fully.'

'You'll forgive me if I disagree with your definition of lucky,' the Professor said, raising an eyebrow, 'though I'm glad that you arrived when you did.'

'I was in the area on other . . . business,' Darkdoom said, 'when we began to receive reports of G.L.O.V.E. facilities all over the world coming under attack. I tried to contact you but something seemed to be jamming communications with the island. Then our radar buoy started tracking a flight of helicopters that had a rather disturbing flight path. As soon as I realised where they were heading I set course for H.I.V.E. immediately. I only wish I could have got there sooner. I might have been able to stop this before it started.'

'I doubt anything could have stopped this,' Nero said with a sigh. 'Overlord was one step ahead of us from the start. He *wanted* me to send Natalya after the ruling council – he must have got to her while she was retrieving them. He knew that she was the one person whose loyalty I would never question. And now, thanks to my blindness, he has control of not just the council but H.I.V.E. as well. I shudder to think what he may have in mind for them.'

'He didn't get everything he wanted,' Darkdoom said, shaking his head. 'He didn't get Otto. If retrieving him was what this was really all about then we still have something he needs. The real question is what do we do next? For now it might be best to lie low and try to find out exactly what his plan is. Between the attacks on our facilities and the ruling council falling under Overlord's control, G.L.O.V.E. will be in disarray. Even if we were able to get in touch with any of the council members' lieutenants, we still wouldn't really know who we could trust. If Overlord can turn Natalya he can turn anybody.'

'No,' Nero insisted. 'I will not just run away and hide. We may not know exactly what Overlord is planning but we cannot afford to sit back and let him make the next move. He's too dangerous. We have to take the fight to him.'

'Normally I would agree but our resources are now somewhat limited,' Darkdoom said with a frown.

'We have one option,' Nero said, looking at Darkdoom. 'Otto managed to save H.I.V.E.mind. That gives us one chance. We activate Zero Hour.'

'Are you serious?' Darkdoom said, his eyes widening in surprise.

'Deadly serious,' Nero replied firmly.

'We'll only get one shot at this,' Darkdoom said. 'You can't put the genie back in the bottle.'

'I know that,' Nero said, 'but this is exactly the kind of situation we have been preparing for. We've always known that it might be necessary one day.'

'I don't suppose either of you would care to tell me what you're talking about?' Professor Pike said, looking slightly confused.

'Let's just say that it's something I've been working on for a while,' Nero replied, 'and it may be our only chance of stopping Overlord once and for all.'

☻ ☻ ☻

'Do you know what the worrying thing is?' Lucy said as she sat down next to Otto in the Megalodon's cramped mess hall.

96

'What's that?' Otto said, smiling at her.

'I'm actually starting to get used to this kind of thing,' she replied with a chuckle.

'Oh, you're definitely one of us now,' Otto said with a grin, 'and that should really, really worry you, by the way.'

'You got any idea what will happen next?' Lucy asked.

'Nope,' Otto replied, 'but it'll probably involve things exploding. That's the usual drill.'

'Nothing wrong with a good explosion,' Lucy said, 'as long as you don't get to experience it first-hand. Why are you sitting here all on your own?'

'You heard what Raven said back at H.I.V.E. – Overlord's alive. I'd just started to think that maybe we'd finally seen the back of him and now he pops up again with me at the top of his To Do list. It's starting to feel like I'll never be free of him.'

'It's not your fault,' Lucy said softly, putting her hand on his knee. 'You didn't ask for any of this. You've got to stop blaming yourself.'

'Oh, don't worry – I think I'm probably past the brooding self-hate stage now,' Otto said with a slight smile. 'In fact, I think I'm moving on to the badly wanting to kick his sorry ass stage.'

'That's more like it,' Lucy said, looking him in the eye and leaning towards him. 'I like a guy who knows what he wants.'

Intriguing.

H.I.V.E.mind's voice spoke somewhere inside Otto's head.

'Not now,' Otto said with a sigh.

'What's wrong?' Lucy asked, pulling back with a puzzled look on her face.

'Not you,' Otto said quickly, 'it's just that we're . . . erm . . . not exactly alone.' He tapped his finger against the side of his head.

'Oh yeah,' Lucy said, blushing slightly. 'I'd kind of forgotten about that.'

Do not feel you need to stop on my account.

'It's going to take a bit of getting used to,' Otto said, looking slightly uncomfortable.

'It's not going to be . . . well, a permanent thing, is it?' Lucy asked.

'I hope not,' Otto said, looking at her with a smile, 'because I think I quite like what's happening between us and – well, three's a crowd, as they say.'

'Yeah, I know what you mean,' Lucy said, laughing slightly, 'but I'm glad that's how you feel. I do too.'

There was a moment of slightly embarrassed silence.

'Anyway,' Otto said a little too quickly, 'I need to find Darkdoom and see if he minds me using the Megalodon's lab for a couple of hours.'

'Yeah, I should probably go and find . . . erm . . .

something important to do,' Lucy replied just as quickly. She gave Otto a quick peck on the cheek and headed for the exit.

Are you all right, Otto? Your pulse rate has increased quite significantly.

'I'm fine,' Otto said as he watched Lucy walk away. 'Better than fine actually.'

☹ ☹ ☹

'This is unacceptable,' Furan said, a cold edge of fury in his voice.

'I'm sorry, sir,' the commander of the strike team said, avoiding making eye contact with the man on the screen. 'We had no idea that the submarine had tracked us to the island. We were unprepared for Darkdoom's intervention.'

'You allowed Nero and the boy to escape and all that you can offer as an excuse is that you were *unprepared?* We had spent months planning this operation and now it is jeopardised because of your stupidity,' Furan snapped. He looked at Raven, who moved behind the commander and said something in Russian. The commander inhaled sharply in surprise as the glowing purple tip of Raven's sword suddenly appeared, protruding from the centre of his chest. He fell to the ground in silence, his eyes wide with shock.

'Find them,' Furan said, looking at Raven as she slid the

sword back into its sheath. 'I don't care what it takes. Overlord wants the boy alive but the others are entirely expendable. I have faith in you, my little Raven. This is, after all, what I trained you for.'

'Understood,' Raven said with a nod. 'Do we have any information yet on where they are heading?'

'No, but we have come up with a plan to force them to surface,' Furan replied, 'and when they do I will relay their position to you.'

'I will have a Shroud prepped for immediate take-off,' Raven replied. 'Is there anything else?'

'Yes, make sure that H.I.V.E. is fully secured. We cannot afford any more mistakes and we may yet need the people we have captured there. Now I need to go and relay this news to Overlord,' he continued. 'I doubt that he will be pleased.'

☺ ☺ ☺

The President looked at the men seated around the situation room conference table and shook his head.

'No,' he said with a sigh. 'I'm not prepared to go that far.'

'Sir, with the greatest respect, the United States does not negotiate with terrorists. You know that,' one of the generals said.

'I am well aware of our normal position on these matters,' the President replied impatiently, feeling the fatigue of the past twenty-four hours, 'but the last thing we need at the moment is me having to explain to several of our most valuable allies that I took the decision to drop a nuclear weapon on some of the most senior members of their governments. Not to mention the fact that the AWP facility is designed to withstand a conventional nuclear attack anyway.'

'But, sir –' the General began to protest.

'No, I've made up my mind,' the President said firmly, cutting him off. 'You need to go back to the drawing board, gentlemen. There has to be another way.'

'Yes, sir,' the General replied.

'Sir, we've got another call coming in from AWP,' the officer manning the communications desk reported. The President let out a long sigh. He had been expecting this. The twenty-four-hour deadline that Overlord had given them was up and they had not managed to track down a single one of the people he had demanded they turn over to him. If they ever had existed they had now vanished without trace.

'I'll take it next door,' he said, gesturing to the small private office adjoining the situation room as he slowly got up out of his chair. He entered the office and took a seat at the desk before hitting a button on the intercom.

'Put it through,' he said, and the screen on the far wall lit up.

'Mr President,' Overlord said with a smile, 'so good to speak with you again.'

'The feeling is not mutual,' the President replied, feeling anger and frustration boiling up inside.

'Come now, Mr President, there's no need for unpleasantness,' Overlord said. 'In fact, I have some good news for you.'

'I find that hard to believe,' the President replied. He stared at the face of the man he had once known as General Collins and noticed that there was something strange about it. It looked like he had aged twenty years in the space of one day. The skin of his face was now thin and tight, almost grey in colour. He had been feeling the pressures of the last twenty-four hours himself, of course, but no amount of stress could possibly explain the transformation in the man on the screen.

'I have decided to alter my previous request. It seems that the people I asked you to find for me are no longer relevant. As I do not now need your assistance in locating them, I've decided that there's something else you can help me with.'

The President felt a sudden mixture of relief and anger – relief that they might have more time before this maniac started to execute people and anger that his people had spent the last twenty-four hours engaged in a desperate but apparently futile search.

'Why should I help you any further?' he snapped. 'How do I know you're not just wasting our time again?'

'It's quite simple. You don't have any choice,' Overlord replied calmly. 'I should imagine that by now your generals will have told you that any strike against this facility is futile. You'll do exactly what I tell you to or I'll paint the floors of this place with blood. I suggest you do not even think of trying to test my resolve.'

There was something in the face of the man on the screen – a manic gleam in his eye – that told the President that he was not bluffing.

'What do you want?' he asked with a resigned sigh.

'Oh, this should be much simpler than tracking down the people I showed you before,' Overlord replied with a sinister smile. 'In fact, all I want you to do is help me find one young boy. I believe you may even have already met. His name is Otto Malpense and he boarded a submarine in the Pacific less than four hours ago. I'm sending you a photograph of him and details of the approximate search area now. I want the submarine captured and the boy brought to me. I won't bore you by repeating the consequences of your non-compliance. Goodbye, Mr President.'

As the screen went blank the President's mind raced. He'd heard that name before but he couldn't quite remember where. The screen suddenly lit up with an image apparently captured from a security camera of a white-haired boy in a black jumpsuit, and suddenly he knew why he remembered that name. It was the boy who had saved his life on board Air Force One less than a year ago.

'That's impossible,' the President whispered. The boy in the photo had died months ago – he'd read the report himself – and yet there he was, apparently very much alive.

☹ ☹ ☹

Professor Pike made his way slowly into the Megalodon's laboratory. His left arm was in a sling and his shoulder was still sore but the painkillers that Darkdoom's medical staff had prescribed seemed to be working. He saw Otto working at one of the computers in the room and walked quietly up behind him. The screen in front of Otto filled with chemical formulae and computer code as he worked at unbelievable speed despite the fact that he wasn't even touching the keyboard. The Professor had seen Otto using his unusual ability to interface directly with electronic devices before but there was still something rather unsettling about it. He placed his hand on Otto's shoulder and Otto jumped in surprise.

'I'm sorry, Professor,' he said, rubbing his tired eyes. 'I didn't hear you come in. How are you feeling?'

'I'll recover. How are you managing with your guest?'

the Professor asked, tapping the side of his own head.

'It's taking a while to get used to,' Otto replied with a crooked smile. 'The biggest problem at the moment is that no one else can hear him. A couple of Darkdoom's crew have caught me talking to him and I suspect they think I'm a few cards short of a full deck.'

'I may be able to do something about that,' the Professor replied. 'I'll have to see if they've the components I'd need on board. Anyway, I'm sorry to interrupt you. I'm told that you've been in here for hours.'

'Yeah, I've been working on the sample of Animus that I took from Raven,' Otto said. 'I'm trying to work out how she survived exposure to it and how Overlord was using it to control her. It's obviously some new variant that we've not seen before – it seems much less aggressive and easier to control.'

'Is it dead?' the Professor asked, studying the magnified image of the cell-like structures on the screen.

'No, just dormant as far as I can tell,' Otto replied. 'It seems to feed off the host's bioelectrical energy – without that it deactivates after a few seconds, which is something that we should all be very grateful for given the speed at which it replicates. If it could survive outside a host the whole planet would be up to its neck in this stuff by now.'

'Not a pleasant thought,' the Professor said, sitting down next to Otto. 'So what's different about this strain?

Clearly Raven has been poisoned with it but it didn't kill her. All human exposure to Animus that we've seen up until now had been quite fatal.'

'That's what I'm trying to work out,' Otto replied with a sigh, 'but I feel a bit like I'm banging my head against a brick wall at the moment. We have to find a way to disable it without harming the host or we're never going to know who we can trust.'

'I've been thinking along the same lines,' the Professor said, still studying the display. 'Some form of antidote.'

'It's hard to know which angle to attack it from,' Otto said. 'Should we treat it like an infectious disease or should we approach it as if we were trying to disable a computer?'

'We could try to attack from both directions at once,' the Professor said, distracted by a sudden thought.

'Organic and digital at the same time,' Otto said, immediately latching on to the Professor's suggestion. 'A virus.'

'Yes, but not just a computer virus. It would need to be more than that – a contagion that could physically infect Animus's organic component at the same time. But creating something like that could take months, years even.'

'We may not have to start from scratch,' Otto said, staring off into the distance. 'We could just work with what we've got.'

'What do you mean?' the Professor asked, looking puzzled.

'The Animus. This sample here – it's a tiny amount admittedly but if we could reactivate it and reprogram it somehow –'

'How? We have no way to interface with it even if we could reactivate it – something I never succeeded with in any of the samples that I tested before incidentally.'

May I make a suggestion? H.I.V.E.mind said.

'Otto? Are you all right?' the Professor asked as Otto fell silent and stared off into the middle distance.

'I'm fine,' Otto replied, sounding distracted. 'H.I.V.E.mind has an idea,' he added, 'but I don't think anyone's going to like it.'

☢ ☢ ☢

Wing unleashed a volley of lightning-fast punches into the heavy bag hanging from the ceiling of the Megalodon's training area. He had struggled to find this place even after being given directions by several of the submarine's crew. It was all too easy to get lost in the countless seemingly identical corridors of the massive ship. Dr Nero had informed the Alphas that he wanted them to attend a tactical briefing in a couple of hours' time but until then they were free to do as they wished, as long as they stayed out of trouble.

Unlike some of the others, Wing had not wanted to sit around and wait. The truth was that he did not much like the cramped conditions on board. He told himself that it was just a symptom of his frustration with their current situation and nothing at all to do with the knowledge that they were sitting inside a metal tube five hundred metres beneath the surface of the ocean. In fact he was trying very hard not to think about that at all. He pivoted on one foot and drove a fierce straight-legged kick into the bag, setting it swinging.

'Hey,' Shelby said with a grin, walking into the chamber. 'I wondered where you'd got to.'

'I am sorry,' Wing replied. 'I did not think anyone needed me for anything.'

'Don't worry, you're not missing anything. I was on the upper deck with Laura and Lucy and the atmosphere was – well, a little frosty. So I thought I'd come and torment you instead.'

'Yes, I had noticed that there was an unusual amount of silence between them,' Wing said with a slight frown. 'I fear that this situation with Otto and Lucy has caused some *difficulties*.'

'Ahhh, they'll be fine,' Shelby said smiling, 'as long as they keep Laura away from any sharp objects for a few days.'

'You think she may harm Lucy?' Wing asked, his frown deepening.

'Hey, I'm just kidding,' Shelby said with a chuckle.

'Sorry – for a minute there I forgot I was talking to the guy with the sense-of-humour bypass.'

'My sense of humour is perfectly intact,' Wing said, raising an eyebrow. 'You're just not very funny.'

'Awwww, come on, big guy – admit it. You know you couldn't live without me,' Shelby said, grinning. 'The sooner you accept that the happier you'll be.'

'Yes, the immediate drop in the level of teasing and general irritation would be hard to bear,' Wing replied.

'See? I told you,' Shelby said, jabbing her finger into his chest. 'You'd be lost without me. Somebody has to make sure that you're not taking yourself too seriously.'

'It is a source of constant comfort to me that you care so much for my well-being.'

'What can I say? I'm a caring kind of girl. Anyway, since everyone else seems to be either making out or sulking I wondered if you felt like sparring?' Shelby asked, gesturing to the padded gloves and head protectors hanging from hooks on the wall nearby.

'I thought we already were,' Wing said to himself with a slight smile.

'Come on, show me what ya got,' Shelby said, throwing a set of gear to Wing before pulling on a pair of gloves herself. 'I'll try not to hurt you too badly.'

'How reassuring,' Wing said, pulling on his gloves. He had been giving Shelby hand-to-hand combat training for some time back at H.I.V.E. and what she lacked in technique she more than made up for in speed and cunning.

'Bring it,' Shelby said with a grin, raising both gloves in a defensive stance and beckoning him towards her.

'It will be brought,' Wing replied. He feinted to her left and she went to block as he simultaneously swung a low blow into her other side, carefully pulling his punch so that he just tapped her.

'Two, perhaps three broken ribs,' Wing said matter of factly. 'Maintain your guard.'

Shelby nodded and threw a quick jab at his jaw which Wing blocked effortlessly.

'Try not to look where you're striking – you betray your intentions.'

They went on like that for a couple more minutes. Just as in their previous sparring sessions Wing noticed that once they began Shelby became totally focused. There were none of the smart comments or sarcasm that she normally used – she was suddenly deadly serious.

'Broken jaw, possible unconsciousness,' Wing said calmly as he struck past her guard, stopping his fist millimetres from her chin.

'Oh my God!' Shelby gasped suddenly, staring in shock at something over Wing's shoulder. He spun around, his guard raised. Shelby dropped low and swung her leg out, sweeping Wing's feet from under him and sending him crashing to the floor.

'Wounded pride, possible humiliation,' Shelby said with a grin, offering her hand to Wing and pulling him up off the floor. 'And so ends today's lesson,' she said, pulling off her head guard.

'An unconventional tactic,' Wing said with a nod, taking off his own helmet, 'but a successful one nevertheless.'

'I kinda like unconventional tactics,' Shelby said, stepping towards him. 'Never underestimate the element of surprise.'

She grabbed the back of his head and kissed him for a few long seconds.

'What was that you were saying about maintaining your guard?' she said with a smile as she pulled away from him.

'Sometimes one should let one's guard down,' Wing replied, staring at her for a moment before drawing her towards him and kissing her back.

'Er . . . guys,' a familiar voice said, causing Wing and Shelby to spring apart, 'Doctor Nero wants you to report to the briefing room.' Wing winced slightly as he saw Nigel and Franz standing in the doorway. Nigel was looking pointedly at the floor and Franz was staring at him and Shelby, his mouth hanging open in surprise.

'Come on, big guy – no rest for the wicked,' Shelby said

to Wing with a grin, grabbing his hand and dragging him out of the room past Nigel and the stunned-looking Franz.

'You know, I am starting to think they are putting something in the water,' Franz whispered to Nigel as he watched them leave.

☹ ☹ ☹

Wing sat down next to Otto in the Megalodon's main briefing room. Nero was sitting at the head of the table, studying something on a tablet display.

'Did you make any progress in the lab?' Wing asked as Lucy, Laura and Shelby sat down on the other side of the table.

'I think so, but I need to get Nero's approval for the next step,' Otto said quietly. 'Are you OK? You look a bit flustered.' Otto was not used to seeing his friend looking anything other than completely calm.

'I'm fine. I was just . . . erm . . . sparring with Shelby,' Wing replied. Otto sensed that this was not the whole truth. Wing was many things but an adept liar was not one of them. He glanced across the table at Shelby, who grinned at Wing and gave him a wink.

The doors to the briefing room hissed open and Professor Pike walked in. He came over and sat in the empty chair on the other side of Otto.

'I have something for you that should make things a

little easier,' the Professor said with a smile, placing what looked like half a disassembled Blackbox on the table in front of Otto.

'What's this?' Otto asked.

'It's just something I cobbled together,' the Professor replied. 'If you connect to it you'll understand.'

Otto tilted his head slightly and made a quick mental connection with the device. A few seconds later H.I.V.E.mind's blue face appeared on the tiny display.

'This should considerably ease the process of communication,' H.I.V.E.mind said. Otto could still hear the AI's voice inside his head but now at least the others could hear it as well.

'Not to mention stopping everyone from thinking I'm as mad as a bag of cats,' he said with a relieved sigh.

'It'll take more than some new gizmo to convince anyone of that,' Shelby said quickly.

'It's good to see you again, H.I.V.E.mind,' Laura said with a smile. 'I don't know how you're putting up with having to stay in such basic accommodation.'

'Yeah, moving from H.I.V.E. into Otto's head must have been like moving from a palace into a one-bedroom apartment,' Shelby said.

'Maybe we should put him in your head, Shel,' Otto replied. 'Plenty of empty space in there.'

'If you've quite finished, ladies and gentlemen,' Nero

said, cutting their conversation dead, 'we do have some rather urgent business to discuss. As you can see, we are currently heading through the Mediterranean at maximum speed.' He gestured at the digital map displayed on the screen on the wall. 'We expect to make landfall at our target destination in approximately four hours.' He hit a button on the touch screen mounted in the table and a cross-hair appeared over the south coast of England. 'We will then split up. I will head to London for a meeting with an individual who can grant us the access we need to the facility that you will be travelling to – GCHQ in Cheltenham. For those of you who are not familiar with the Government Communication Headquarters, it is the hub of signals intelligence for both the British government and the armed forces.'

'Not the sort of place they're going to let us just walk into,' Otto said with a slight frown.

'Which is why I'm going to have to arrange for you to get access,' Nero replied. 'While I'm sure that you would be more than capable of discreetly infiltrating the facility, it is a risk that we do not need to take. Once you are inside you will be able to use their equipment to send a very important signal. The nature of that signal is not something I am prepared to discuss with you, but suffice to say that if it is sent successfully we will gain access to the resources that we need to take down Overlord. I am as dismayed as the rest of you by the news of his apparent resurrection, but this time I intend to make sure that he is finished off once and for all.'

'Sounds like fun,' Shelby said, 'but why do you need us to go in? Surely G.L.O.V.E. has people in the UK who could do this for you?'

'Unfortunately, the signal that I want to send is uniquely complex and only H.I.V.E.mind is capable of successfully transmitting it. Obviously that would not have been an issue if we had kept control of H.I.V.E., but now we are forced to improvise. Mr Malpense will need to give H.I.V.E.mind direct access to certain equipment at GCHQ for our plan to work, otherwise I would not be asking you to do this.'

'You're sure that you can get us in?' Lucy asked.

'Quite sure. I intend to secure the assistance of one of my former pupils,' Nero said with a slight smile.

'OK, so why send all of us?' Otto asked. 'Why not just me?'

'Two reasons. Firstly, I want you to have backup and recent events have shown that unfortunately we do not know who we can trust. Secondly, you are all more than capable of accomplishing this. I also rather suspect that the only way I could actually stop you from going is if I rendered you unconscious.'

'He's got a point,' Laura said quietly.

'This should be straightforward,' Nero continued. 'In and out as fast as you can. Then we return to the Megalodon, where you will remain while the second phase of our plan is carried out.'

'I can't speak for everyone,' Otto said firmly, 'but there's no way that I'm staying here while you go after Overlord. I have a score to settle with him.'

'It's far too dangerous,' Nero said, shaking his head, 'besides which, that's probably exactly what Overlord would want. Just think about the trouble he has already gone to in trying to capture you, Mr Malpense. Until this is over the safest place for you to be is hidden somewhere at the bottom of the ocean. Just imagine what he could do with your abilities – no one on Earth would be safe.'

Otto stared at Nero, trying to find the flaw in his reasoning, but had to admit that he was right. The only weakness that Overlord had was his inability to interface with other machines. If he took control of Otto and regained that ability he would be unstoppable and every machine on the planet would be his to control. There would be no place for humanity in a world like that.

'Does anyone have any other questions?' Nero asked. 'No? Good. I will alert you when we are approaching the drop-off point. Dismissed.'

The others filed out of the room but Otto and the Professor remained seated.

'Is there something else I can do for you, gentlemen?' Nero asked as the doors hissed shut behind the last of the Alphas.

'There's something else we need to talk about,' Otto said. 'The Professor and I think we've come up with a way to counteract the effects of the new strain of Animus that Overlord used on Raven.'

'Then why are you both looking so worried?' Nero asked with a slight frown.

'Their plan, while sound, has considerable risk attached,' H.I.V.E.mind explained.

'That's one way of putting it,' the Professor agreed.

'I'm listening,' Nero said, sitting back in his chair.

'Well, we theorise that the new strain of Animus is far less aggressive than when we've previously encountered it. That would explain why Raven appeared to be suffering no physical ill-effects from having it in her system. If we can create a variant of this new type we could, in theory, program it to infect Overlord's Animus with a virus – a virus that would shut it down.'

'That does not sound like a simple task,' Nero said.

'No. Well, it wouldn't be under normal circumstances, but we think there might be a short cut,' Otto replied.

'And this is where the risk that H.I.V.E.mind mentioned comes into the equation, I assume,' Nero said.

'Yes, the only way that we can see to effectively reanimate the tiny sample that we have and then reprogram it in the limited time is to put it inside me,' Otto said.

'Out of the question,' Nero said, shaking his head. 'Are you both insane?'

'I know how this sounds,' the Professor said, 'but we believe that the combination of Otto's abilities and H.I.V.E.mind's raw processing power should mean that they can reprogram the Animus before it can assume control of Otto. The sample is dormant at the moment and the time that it takes to reawaken after it is implanted should give us a window of opportunity to modify its behaviour.'

'What if you're wrong?' Nero asked. 'What if you can't do it and the Animus takes control of you? There won't be anything we can do.'

'Then you put a bullet in my head before I can take control of the Megalodon,' Otto said matter of factly. 'I've been through what Raven is experiencing right now and it's a living hell – we can't just give up on her. She'd do the same for us.'

'And you know her well enough to know that if she was here now she would tell you she'd rather die than see you infected with that filth again,' Nero said.

'Maybe,' Otto replied, 'but who knows how many people Overlord has infected with the new variant? This isn't just about Raven – anyone could be under his control and we'd never know. We must have a way to fight this.'

'Mr Malpense, I have spent my whole life not knowing who I could really trust. Find another way. You are not doing this. Do I make myself clear?' Nero said, getting up out of his chair.

Otto and the Professor nodded.

chapter six

The captain of the USS *Texas* was sitting in his quarters reviewing the crew duty rosters for the next week when there was a knock at his door.

'Enter,' he said, and his First Officer opened the door.

'Sir, we've got something on sonar. It could be the target boat,' the First Officer reported.

'Show me,' the Captain said, getting up from behind his desk and following the First Officer down the short corridor that led from his cabin to the sonar station.

'What have you got, Niles?' the Captain asked as he looked over the operator's shoulder.

'I'm not sure, sir,' the man replied. 'It's moving too fast to be another boat.'

The Captain studied the display and quickly realised why his men were unsure about what they'd found. The contact was too fast and too quiet to be a sub. Niles put the sound from the contact over the speaker mounted above his station so that the Captain could hear the rhythmic throbbing. It might be quiet but it was undeniably mechanical.

'What do you think?' the Captain asked.

'Hell if I know, sir. I nearly missed it – nobody's got a boat that quiet when it's moving that fast. Best guess is that it's some sort of magneto-hydrodynamic drive but the prototypes that the R&D boys built never worked right – they were too slow. No way something with an MHD is moving that fast.'

'Can we intercept?' the Captain asked.

'Yes, sir, but at the speed that thing's moving we won't be within weapons range until it reaches the English Channel,' the First Officer replied.

'Signal the *North Carolina*. Tell them that we're moving in on the target. They should be in interception range too.'

'Aye aye, sir,' the First Officer said, heading back towards the conn.

The Captain studied the bizarre contact. He had been ordered to track down and disable this mystery sub by the President himself and there was no way he was going to let it slip the net.

☢ ☢ ☢

Furan watched as his men handed out emergency ration packs to the hostages in the AWP mess hall. At first there had been many indignant demands for explanations and variations on the old 'Do you know who I am?' line but after twenty-four hours the vast majority of them seemed to be slumped around the room in a state of weary resignation.

The doors to the mess hall opened and Overlord walked in, flanked by two armed guards. General Collins's body was in the final stages of Animus poisoning, the pale skin stretched tight over the bones beneath and most of the hair on his head missing. He looked like he was a hundred years old. Furan had seen this happen to all of the bodies that Overlord had taken but there was no denying that the process was accelerating inexorably. Now it seemed that the Animus that Overlord had been bonded with was becoming so aggressive, for whatever reason, that new hosts might only last a matter of hours. They had to find the Malpense boy – only then could Overlord have a permanent home.

'Have you selected one?' Overlord asked, his voice weak.

'Yes,' Furan replied, nodding towards one of AWP's security forces. 'He is young and he looks strong. He should last longer than Collins did.'

'Yes, he will do for now,' Overlord said with a predatory smile.

Furan motioned to the guards and they grabbed the young soldier from the crowd of hostages and dragged him, struggling, to where Overlord was standing.

'Please, I'm getting married in three weeks. Please don't kill me,' the young man begged.

'You're wasting your time if you're trying to appeal to my humanity,' Overlord said with a sneer. 'You see, I haven't got any.'

Furan's communicator earpiece bleeped and he tapped it to initiate a connection, turning away as the first of the slimy black Animus tendrils burst from the skin on Overlord's forearm. He ignored the sounds of shock and then terror from the young soldier and the frantic, strangled gurgling that inevitably followed.

'Furan here. Go ahead.'

'Sir, we've just received word from our source that the US Navy think they've found Darkdoom's submarine,' the voice on the other end of the line reported.

'Where?'

'Off the coast of Spain. It appears to be heading for Britain,' the voice replied.

'They're sure it's Darkdoom?'

'Yes, sir. Nothing else could be moving as fast as this contact.'

'Excellent. Get me Raven.'

☹ ☹ ☹

The Professor looked up as Otto walked into the Megalodon's laboratory.

'Hello, Otto,' he said. 'Is there something I can do for you?'

'Yeah, I'm getting a few glitches with H.I.V.E.mind's vocal synthesis through this relay,' Otto said, placing the unit that the Professor had given him earlier on top of the workbench. 'I was wondering if you could take a look at it.'

'Of course,' the Professor replied. 'I'm afraid I rather rushed putting it together. I wouldn't be at all surprised if there's a few bugs.'

The Professor picked up the device and examined it for a few seconds before activating it. H.I.V.E.mind's face appeared on the screen.

'Do not do this, Otto,' H.I.V.E.mind said.

'Do not do wh—' was all the Professor had time to say before he felt a finger press into the soft flesh behind his ear and he lost consciousness. Otto laid him gently back in his chair and moved to the counter.

'You are acting in direct contravention of Doctor Nero's explicit instructions,' H.I.V.E.mind said.

'Yeah, and it's not like I've ever done *that* before,' Otto said sarcastically.

'This is not what I intended when I suggested that we attempt to interface directly with the Animus. We need to develop a safer method,' H.I.V.E.mind said.

'We don't have time for that and you know it,' Otto

said as he walked over to the small magnetic containment device that held the dormant Animus sample.

'You are putting yourself and everyone else on board this vessel at risk,' H.I.V.E.mind said calmly.

'It's going to work,' Otto replied as he pulled the metal tube from its stand and clipped it into a hypodermic injector gun. 'It has to.'

'Please, Otto,' H.I.V.E.mind said, 'there has to be another way.'

'Maybe, but I'm not really the cautious type,' Otto said with a slight smile before sticking the needle into his arm and pulling the trigger. He closed his eyes and waited. At first there was nothing but slowly he began to feel something stirring inside him, a slight tingle in his arm. He reached out with his abilities and tried to make contact with the waking Animus inside him. He could sense it, a cold alien presence, already beginning the process of replication, preparing to take control of its host.

'Do you feel it?' Otto whispered.

'Yes,' H.I.V.E.mind replied, 'though I am struggling to make sense of any of the data encoded within it.'

'Let me translate,' Otto said, forcing a connection with the simple, almost animal consciousness of the Animus. He had spent months trapped inside his own body listening to the digital hiss of the previous generation of Animus that had once coursed through him. This was different though, simpler, not as filled with an instinctive loathing for organic life as the previous generation had been.

'I have accessed the core code,' H.I.V.E.mind reported. 'It will take me a few seconds to analyse its command structure and implant new instructions.'

'Quickly, please,' Otto said as he began to feel the first hints of something eating away at his conscious mind, subverting his free will. He tried hard not to think about all that he had been forced to do when that had happened before, the lives that had been lost.

'Upload complete,' H.I.V.E.mind reported. 'Command rewrite in progress.'

Otto nodded, gritting his teeth and fighting to stay conscious. There was a horrifying sensation of countless alien voices whispering inside his skull, all trying to get him to release control, to sleep.

'Not this time,' he gasped. He started to squeeze the trigger on the injector gun. The injection chamber was empty and if he pulled the trigger the air bubble that would enter his bloodstream would travel straight to his brain. At least it would be quick.

Suddenly he sensed a change. The Animus was no longer replicating and the hissing inside his skull diminished and was gone.

'I think it worked,' he said quietly.

'It would appear so,' H.I.V.E.mind said. 'I suggest that we remove it from your body as quickly as possible.'

'You read my mind,' Otto replied.

'No, I did not,' H.I.V.E.mind replied. 'Your neural architecture is too sophisticated for me to translate patterns of synaptic firing into a coherent –'

'It's a figure of speech,' Otto said with a tired smile. The Professor groaned and stirred slightly in his seat. Otto went over and gently shook his uninjured shoulder. The old man's eyes slowly opened and a fleeting look of confusion on his face was quickly replaced by a frown.

'Tell me you didn't do what I think you did,' the Professor said.

'I did,' Otto replied. 'The Animus has been encoded with new instructions.'

'Where is it?' the Professor asked.

'Here,' Otto said, tapping his own chest. 'Get the containment vessel ready.'

The Professor nodded and got to work preparing the magnetic field generator. Otto took a deep breath and gave the Animus inside him a new instruction.

'I think this is going to hurt,' he said as he held out his arm, his fingers curling into a fist. Something dark suddenly appeared, squirming beneath the skin of his forearm. Otto hissed in sudden pain as the Animus punched through the skin of his arm and slithered towards his hand. He picked up the small metal cylinder and held his fingertip over its open end. The Animus slid down his finger and fell into the cylinder.

'Now the fun part,' Otto said with a crooked smile as he sealed the cylinder and placed it into the magnetic containment device.

'And what would that be?' Professor Pike said, while checking that the containment field was functioning properly.

'Now we get to tell Doctor Nero that we did exactly what he explicitly told us not to do,' Otto replied.

'You, Mr Malpense,' the Professor replied, shaking his head slightly, 'have a very strange definition of fun.'

☸ ☸ ☸

'Of all the stupid, crazy, hare-brained things!' Laura said, punching Otto in the chest.

'You forgot irresponsible,' Otto replied with a smile.

'And what did he have to say about all this?' Lucy said, nodding towards Dr Nero, who was standing on the other side of the Megalodon's command centre.

'Something about not knowing whether he should shake my hand or have me shot,' Otto replied. 'To be honest, I think he's still trying to decide.'

'I'm just glad you're OK,' Lucy said, 'you bloody idiot.'

'I agree,' Wing said. 'With the idiot part, that is.'

'At least now we have a way to save anyone Overlord used that stuff on,' Laura said. 'I wouldn't mind having Raven back on our team.'

'If we can find her,' Wing remarked.

'I'm slightly more worried about her finding us at the moment, to be honest,' Shelby said. 'If we do meet up with her again I'd like to volunteer Otto for the whole injecting her with something against her will assignment.'

'Yes, that may prove somewhat *problematic*,' Wing said, raising an eyebrow. 'For now we have other concerns though. I assume you have all reviewed the briefing materials that Doctor Nero provided?'

'Yeah, it looks pretty straightforward,' Shelby said, 'at least in comparison to the usual suicide missions we end up on.'

'Hey, guys,' Nigel said as he and Franz walked into the room. 'My dad told me that you're all leaving for a while. Nothing too dangerous, I hope?'

'Nah, we'll be back before you know it,' Shelby said.

'I am thinking that I have been hearing this before,' Franz said, 'usually just before there is the shooting and exploding.'

'Well, maybe this time will be different,' Shelby replied.

'Torpedoes in the water!' one of Darkdoom's men shouted from the other side of the command centre.

'Or maybe not.'

'Launch countermeasures!' Captain Sanders ordered. 'Sonar, who's shooting at us?'

'I have a Virginia class attack submarine, sir – correction, two Virginia class subs three miles off our port bow.'

'Countermeasures away!'

'Where the hell did they come from?' Sanders said angrily.

'They were waiting for us, sir. They must have been dead in the water for our sonar not to have picked them up.'

'The first two torps have switched targets to the decoys,' one of the weapons officers reported. 'I have four more inbound.'

'Initiate evasive manoeuvres,' Sanders barked, 'and plot me a course away from those boats.'

'Are we going to be able to make the drop point, Captain?' Darkdoom asked quickly.

'Not with those hunter-killers on us, sir,' the Captain replied. 'If we surface with them in range we'll be sitting ducks. Our only hope is to outrun them. You can bet that half the US Navy ships in the North Atlantic are on their way here now.'

'Very well,' Darkdoom said calmly. 'Prep the Hammerhead for launch.'

'Aye aye, sir,' the Captain replied with a nod.

'It would seem that Overlord has enlisted the help of

the American Navy,' Nero said, the deck tilting beneath his feet as the Megalodon's helmsman threw it into a series of evasive turns.

'Yes,' Darkdoom replied, 'and I'm sure we can both guess why.' He glanced over to where Otto was standing with the other Alphas.

'We have a torp tracking past the countermeasures,' the weapons officer shouted. 'Brace for impact!'

There was a sudden crashing thud from somewhere outside the Megalodon's hull and the whole vessel shuddered.

'Detonation fifty metres off the port bow.'

'They've set their fuses for proximity detonation,' Sanders said.

'They're trying to force us to surface,' Darkdoom replied, 'not sink us. Max, you have to take your team and get out of here now. Go down to the launch bay and take my mini-sub. You should be able to slip away undetected if we time this right. I'll meet back up with you at the rendezvous point in the States.'

'I'll see you there,' Nero said. 'Are you sure you'll be able to get clear?'

'Oh, don't worry – the Megalodon has a few tricks up her sleeve yet,' Darkdoom replied with a smile. Nero shook Darkdoom's hand and strode over to the group of worried-looking Alphas.

'Nigel, Franz, you stay here,' he said as the sound of another nearby explosion sent a shudder through the hull. 'The rest of you, with me.'

Darkdoom watched as Nero and his students ran out of the command centre.

'Launch Hydra torpedoes, full spread, both targets,' Darkdoom ordered. 'It's time we showed our American friends what happens when someone shoots at the Megalodon.'

☻ ☻ ☻

'Torpedo, torpedo, torpedo!' the crew member manning the USS *Texas'* sonar station yelled. 'I have six . . . seven . . . no, eight fish in the water and heading this way.'

'Launch decoys,' the Captain shouted.

'Decoys away!'

'We have negative tracking on incoming warheads,' the weapons officer shouted. 'Their torps are ignoring our countermeasures.'

'Oh my God!' the sonar officer said quietly.

'What is it, sonar?' the Captain demanded impatiently.

'Incoming torpedoes have separated. I have sixty-four incoming tracks.'

The Captain felt his blood run cold.

'How many?'

'Sixty-four, sir,' the sonar operator said with a nervous gulp. 'It looks like their torpedoes have launched smaller secondary sub-munitions.'

'Evasive manoeuvres!' the Captain yelled, already knowing that it would do no good.

'They've launched on the *North Carolina*,' the comms officer reported. 'They're reporting that their counter-measures were completely ineffective too.'

The *Texas* and *North Carolina* were two of the most advanced submarines on the planet but the mysterious boat out there was making them look like tinker toys. He braced himself as he watched the swarm of incoming contacts on the sonar screen.

'Transmit details of that thing's weaponry to Atlantic command,' the Captain said, 'while we still can.'

☻ ☻ ☻

Otto and the others ran up the boarding ramp of the compact submarine that hung above the launch hatch in the belly of the Megalodon.

'Nero and his team are on board,' the Hammerhead's helmsman reported as Nero took the seat next to him and put on a comms headset. Otto and the others quickly strapped themselves into the seats behind him. 'I'm buttoning us up. Crash-flood the launch chamber on my mark.'

The hatch behind Otto whirred shut with a solid thunk. 'Three . . . two . . . one . . . mark!'

There was a rumbling sound as thousands of gallons of seawater flooded the chamber outside. After a few seconds the noise decreased and all the passengers could hear was a gentle creaking from the hull.

'This is Darkdoom,' a voice said over the speakers. 'Hydra torpedo detonation in ten seconds. Prepare to launch.'

Otto realised that he was holding his breath.

'Launch now!'

The helmsman smacked a switch on the instrument panel and the Hammerhead dropped through the open doors below, diving away below the Megalodon at the precise moment that the swarm of warheads from the Hydras detonated. Through the thick toughened glass of the cockpit window they saw hundreds of explosions light up the darkened depths of the ocean several miles away. Otto gave a low whistle.

'Darkdoom doesn't believe in doing things by halves, does he?' he said.

'Despite appearances the intention is not to destroy our pursuers, just temporarily blind and confuse them. Let us hope that the distraction was enough to cover our departure,' Nero said.

'Megalodon to Hammerhead,' Darkdoom's voice came

over the comms system. 'We are heading out at full speed. Let's see if the Americans aren't too stunned to give chase.'

'Understood,' Nero replied. 'Good luck.'

'You too,' Darkdoom said and the line went dead.

'And now,' Nero said quietly, staring out into the black water surrounding them, 'we wait.'

☹ ☹ ☹

The Captain of the USS *Texas* climbed to his feet, his ears still ringing from the massive detonation just a few seconds earlier.

'Damage report!' he barked.

'A handful of minor injuries, sir,' one of his crewmen replied, 'but no major structural damage.'

'Target is moving away at – well, frankly impossible speed,' another member of the crew reported. The Captain couldn't understand it – their target had a tiny sonar signature and was too fast for anything bigger than a torpedo and yet it had just launched a spread of warheads that even the *Texas* could not hope to match.

'Lay in a pursuit course,' the Captain snapped. 'Signal the *North Carolina* to accompany us and relay the target's track to Atlantic Command. Tell them we need every ship they can spare. I'm damned if I'm letting this fish slip the net.'

☻ ☻ ☻

The Hammerhead surfaced next to the deserted jetty, moonlight reflecting off her glistening black hull. The hatch in the side of the submarine slid open and Nero climbed down on to the wooden pier, looking around for any sign that their arrival might have been spotted. Seeing nothing, he gestured for his students to follow him.

'This is where we part ways,' he said, looking at the assembled Alphas. 'There is a village five kilometres up the coast where you should be able to *borrow* some transport. I'm sure I don't need to remind you that you should avoid any entanglements with local law enforcement.'

'What, you mean that five kids in identical uniforms jacking a car in the middle of the night isn't normal around here?' Shelby asked.

'Just try to be discreet,' Nero said, raising an eyebrow. 'As soon as you are mobile, head for GCHQ, but do not try to enter the facility until I call you on this.' He passed a mobile phone to Otto. 'Stick to the plan and remember your training. You are one of the most capable groups of students I have ever trained and I know you won't let me down. Just be careful.'

'Yes, sir,' Otto replied. 'We'll try to avoid blowing anything up.'

'How very reassuring,' Nero said with a slight smile. 'I'll

see you all again soon. Good luck.'

With that he turned and walked away into the night.

'I must admit that I am somewhat surprised that Doctor Nero is allowing us to tackle this mission without an escort,' Wing said after a few seconds.

'Yeah,' Shelby said. 'How does he know we won't just run? H.I.V.E. isn't exactly a holiday camp, after all.'

'I'd like to think it's because he trusts us,' Laura replied.

'Maybe,' Otto said, putting his equipment pack on his back, 'or it could just be that he knows that in a world where Overlord isn't stopped there'll be nowhere left to run to.'

☻ ☻ ☻

'Right. Who's driving?' Shelby said as she opened the door of the 4 X 4.

'Not Laura,' Otto said with a cheeky grin.

'OK, OK, so the holographic training sessions haven't gone brilliantly,' Laura said, holding her hands up. 'There's no need to go on about it.'

'Remind me,' Otto replied, 'how many pedestrians did you kill last time?'

'Twelve,' Laura said quietly, 'but they were only holograms.'

'Tell that to their poor holographic families,' Shelby said with a grin.

'May I suggest that Mr Fanchu drives,' H.I.V.E.mind said, his vocal transmitter clipped to Otto's chest. 'I believe that his appearance is the least likely to draw unwanted attention.'

'Since when is height an indication of driving ability?' Otto said.

'You getting jealous, shorty?' Shelby said with a grin.

'I am happy to do it if it will ensure an uneventful journey,' Wing said.

'I don't really care as long as it's not Roadkill Brand,' Shelby said, putting her arm around Laura's shoulder. 'Take the wheel, big guy.'

They all climbed into the car, with Otto taking the front passenger seat.

'Otto, would you be so kind,' Wing said, gesturing towards the dashboard. Otto closed his eyes and connected with the car's electronic ignition system, quickly persuading it that it really should start the engine.

'H.I.V.E. road trip!' Shelby said happily. 'Let's roll!'

Otto punched the location of GCHQ into the car's onboard satnav as Wing gently accelerated away down the road.

'How long's it going to take us to get there?' Lucy asked. The first signs of sunrise were now visible on the horizon.

'About two and a half hours,' Otto said, studying the display mounted in the dashboard.

'Cool,' Shelby said. 'Altogether now! One hundred bottles of beer hanging on the wall, one hundred bottles of beer . . .'

'It may seem longer though,' Otto said with a sigh.

chapter seven

Nero sank into one of the comfortable leather chairs as the secretary behind the desk on the other side of the room threw a curious glance in his direction. Clearly she was not used to someone getting to see her boss quite so easily. Nero smiled back at her.

'He's just finishing his current meeting,' she said politely. 'He'll be with you in a minute.'

'Excellent,' Nero replied, 'and thank you again for the tea.'

He took a sip from the fine china cup. One of the small pleasures of returning to England, he thought to himself.

'Three months!' the angry-looking man said as he stormed out of the adjoining office. 'Three months it took to set up that meeting, and he just asks us to leave after five minutes because "something's come up". I don't believe it!'

'I do hope that I haven't caused too much disruption,'

Nero said to the secretary as he watched the furious man leave.

'Not at all,' the secretary replied. 'He's ready for you now. You can go in.'

'Thank you,' Nero said as he stood up and headed through the door.

The man behind the heavy wooden desk in the centre of the book-lined room stood up as Nero entered, gesturing for him to take a seat in one of the sofas on either side of the fireplace.

'Thank you for seeing me at such short notice, Prime Minister,' Nero said. 'I appreciate you sparing the time.'

'How could I refuse a request from my former head-master?' the Prime Minister said with a crooked smile. 'Tell me, how is the old place?'

'Not much has changed,' Nero said. 'Though you appear to have done quite well for yourself since you left us.'

Duncan Cavendish had been one of Nero's most promising students when he left H.I.V.E. twenty years ago. Nero had always known he would do well in the outside world and Cavendish had not disappointed him.

'Well, after the unfortunate display by the former leader of the opposition at their conference a few years ago it was difficult for the general public to take his party seriously.

Dropping your trousers in front of the TV cameras has that effect sometimes.'

'Would you believe me if I told you that one of my current students was responsible for that?' Nero said with a smile.

'Actually, that wouldn't surprise me at all,' Cavendish replied. 'Do be sure to thank them for me.'

'Of course,' Nero said. 'I'm just glad that details of your education have remained secret.'

'You taught me all about the art of the cover-up – just one of many lessons that have helped me in my new career. You know, I still remember what you said to me on the day you transferred me from the Political and Financial stream to the Alphas. *The best way to manipulate is to lead.* I may use it as the title of my memoirs.' Cavendish laughed.

'Perhaps a little too honest,' Nero said, smiling.

'Maybe. Now tell me, what can I do for you?'

'I assume that you know about recent developments at the Americans' Advanced Weapons Project facility?' Nero said.

'Not as much as you might think,' Cavendish replied. 'Our cousins across the water have been surprisingly unforthcoming. The boys at MI6 tell me that there's been some sort of terrorist attack and we've lost touch with a couple of our military brass who were attending a demonstration there. That and the fact that half of their Atlantic fleet seems to be heading for the Channel have made me rather keen to speak to the President. Unfortunately, he's been unavailable for the past forty-eight hours. I'm afraid that the Special Relationship is often a one-way street on these occasions. I take it that there's more to it than we know?'

'I'm afraid so,' Nero replied. 'I can't go into too much detail but I need your help.'

'With what?'

'I have a team heading to GCHQ. I need you to grant them access to Echelon.'

'I see,' Cavendish said, frowning slightly. 'May I ask why?'

'I'm afraid I can't tell you,' Nero replied. 'Suffice to say the nature of the threat we are facing is global in scope.'

'The situation in America is that serious?'

'Yes. H.I.V.E. has been taken and the ruling council captured. G.L.O.V.E. is in disarray and we may be all that stands between the man who's in control of the AWP facility and global domination. This is our last chance. You know that I wouldn't ask this of you unless it was absolutely necessary.'

'I'll inform GCHQ to give them unrestricted access,' Cavendish said, suddenly looking worried. 'Is there anything else that I can do?'

'Yes. I need a civilian transport to the States, the fastest you can find.'

'That shouldn't be a problem.'

'Thank you. I know how much I am asking. You didn't have to do this.'

'Yes, I did. You were never a man prone to exaggeration. I'll make the calls.'

☺ ☺ ☺

'Should I pull over?' Wing said, glancing at the blue flashing lights in the rear-view mirror.

'The maximum speed of the pursuing vehicle is considerably higher than our own,' H.I.V.E.mind replied. 'Attempted flight would also considerably increase the chances of attracting more law enforcement personnel.'

'Doesn't sound like we've got much choice,' Otto said, twisting in his seat and looking back at the police car that was rapidly catching up with them.

'But we're so close!' Laura said. They were only ten kilometres from GCHQ and now, suddenly, it looked like they might not make it at all.

'We're not done yet,' Lucy said as Wing pulled the car over to the side of the quiet country road. 'Let me talk to them.'

Lucy opened the passenger door and stepped down as the police car pulled up ten metres behind them. The two officers in the car leapt out and advanced towards her.

'Driver, out of the car, now!' the first officer shouted.

'Is there something wrong, Officer?' Lucy asked innocently.

'Yes, miss. You and your friends are in possession of a stolen vehicle. Driver, step out of the vehicle – we won't ask again,' the second policeman said, extending his baton with a flick of the wrist. Wing got out of the car slowly.

'I think there's been some kind of misunderstanding, Officers,' Lucy said, smiling sweetly. 'You see, *this car isn't stolen.*'

The two policemen stopped in their tracks, looking slightly confused.

'Why did we stop you again?' one of them asked Lucy, looking genuinely puzzled.

'I don't know,' Lucy replied, 'but if I were you I'd *give me your car keys and go and have a nice long sleep in the bushes over there.*'

The policemen looked for a moment like they didn't understand and then one of them reached into his pocket and handed her the keys.

'Thanks,' Lucy said, watching as the pair of them turned and walked silently off into the bushes at the side of the road.

'Dexter, I could kiss you,' Shelby said as Lucy climbed

back into the car. 'If Otto doesn't mind, that is?'

'Oh, just ignore her. That was nice work, Lucy,' Laura said.

'Shall we get moving?' Otto asked, restarting the car with a mental nudge.

'Is it just me or does this car seem to be getting smaller?' Wing said under his breath.

'I am curious,' H.I.V.E.mind said. 'Is it normal for friends to attempt to cause each other emotional discomfort in this way?'

'Welcome to our world,' Laura said with a chuckle, shaking her head.

Suddenly the mobile phone in Otto's pocket started to ring.

'Hello,' he said, holding it to his ear.

'Mr Malpense,' Dr Nero replied, 'I have got you the access you require. How far out from GCHQ are you?'

'Ten minutes,' Otto said, glancing at the satnav display.

'Good. The code word you need to get past the guards at the gate is Tsunami. They have been told to expect your arrival.'

'Got it,' Otto replied.

'Please let me know when you've transmitted the signal,' Nero said. 'I'm on my way to pick you up. ETA forty minutes.'

'Understood. I'll call you when we're done.'

Otto ended the call and turned to speak to the others.

'We're all clear,' he said. 'Nero's on his way.'

☺ ☺ ☺

Duncan Cavendish pulled his mobile phone from his pocket and punched in a number. He waited a couple of seconds before there was an answer.

'Sign in, please,' a computerised voice replied.

'Disciple Nine,' Cavendish said. 'Get me Furan.'

'Voice print confirmed, transfer in progress.'

The line was silent then a voice on the other end replied.

'Furan here.'

'It's Cavendish,' he replied. 'I've just had a visit from Nero. The Malpense boy is heading for the GCHQ building in Cheltenham.'

'Excellent. I shall inform Raven immediately,' Furan replied. 'Do you know what they want at GCHQ?'

'Access to Echelon.'

'Did Nero say why?'

'No, he wouldn't tell me.'

'They probably want more information about what is happening at the facility in America,' Furan said.

'I could have them taken into custody at the gates if you want,' Cavendish suggested.

'No, give them access,' Furan replied. 'They will only find out what the Americans know already and that will not help them. Leave the boy's retrieval to Raven. I don't want to spook Malpense. If he senses something is wrong and runs we could lose him.'

'If Raven is going to take the boy at GCHQ I need it to look like a terrorist attack. Anything else might raise too many difficult questions.'

'I'm sure that Natalya will be able to come up with something,' Furan replied, and the line went dead.

☢ ☢ ☢

Otto and the others travelled the remaining distance to the GCHQ gates in silence. A long straight road led to the outer perimeter fence and the gatehouse at the end of it was manned by several heavily armed guards. Otto tried to ignore the assault rifles that were trained on them as they approached. Wing pulled up at the assigned spot and one of the guards walked over to the car as Otto lowered the window.

'Good morning, sir,' the guard said, the polite greeting at odds with his stern expression.

'Tsunami,' Otto said, and the guard nodded.

'We've been expecting you,' he replied. 'Please proceed through the gate and follow the security vehicle to the main building.' Otto closed the window as the heavy security barrier lowered into the ground in front of them. Wing dropped into formation behind the military vehicle and followed it towards the large doughnut-shaped building that was the hub of Britain's intelligence communications network.

'Big place,' Lucy said as they rolled towards the main doors.

'Lots of people to eavesdrop on,' Otto said, finding it hard to shake the sensation that they were walking into the lion's den. The vehicle they were following came to a stop and one of the guards that climbed down from it motioned for them to step out of the car.

'This way, please,' he said, indicating the large doors.

Otto and the others walked inside the building and took in their surroundings. The large glass-walled entrance area was patrolled by armed guards and surveillance cameras seemed to be mounted in every corner. Long channels leading further into the building were fitted with numerous different types of electronic scanners. Smuggling anything through would be next to impossible. Otto was suddenly very glad that they had not needed to try and infiltrate the building. Even with the unique skills that he and his friends possessed he could see that it would have been extremely difficult.

A short, balding man in a badly fitting suit walked down the entrance channel towards them. He had the air of someone who was being told to do something that he really did not want to do.

'If you'll come with me, please,' the man said. 'My name is Colin Reynolds and I'll be your escort while you're here. I've been informed of what you need – heaven only knows what they're thinking in London but ours is not to reason why.'

'Thanks,' Otto said. 'Don't worry, we'll be gone before you know it.'

'Yes, well, let's head inside, shall we?' Reynolds said, looking irritated.

'Lead the way,' Otto replied with a smile that he secretly hoped would annoy the officious bureaucrat even more. As they all followed Reynolds through the entry channel a buzzer sounded.

'Do you have any electronic devices on you?' he asked.

'Just a mobile phone and this,' Otto said, holding out H.I.V.E.mind's vocal transmitter.

'And what is that?' Reynolds said, eyeing the device suspiciously.

'It's my . . . er . . . MP3 player,' Otto lied.

'Well, you'll have to leave them here, I'm afraid,' Reynolds said. 'We've been instructed to grant you access but nobody is allowed beyond this point with unsecured electronic devices. No exceptions. You can pick them up on your way out.'

'Fair enough,' Otto said, trying hard not to smile If Reynolds really knew what he could do or what he had rattling around inside his skull, he'd probably have a heart attack. Otto had everything he needed with him and no one could take it from him.

They passed through the rest of the scanners in the channel without incident and Reynolds led them further inside the huge edifice. As with most buildings used by the intelligence services there was actually very little to see beyond firmly closed office doors and signs pointing to other departments that were identified by meaningless numbers. After walking down numerous identical anonymous corridors Reynolds finally led them to an elevator that was flanked by two heavily armed guards.

'In you go,' he said with a sniff. 'I'm not cleared beyond this point.'

'Thanks, Colin,' Otto said with a smile. 'I'd tell you why we're here but . . . it's classified.' Otto actually thought he might burst out laughing as Reynolds glared at him and then stormed off down the corridor muttering to himself.

'Be nice,' Lucy said, elbowing him in the ribs as they stepped into the lift. 'We're trying not to upset anyone, remember.'

'Sorry,' Otto said, grinning. 'Couldn't resist.'

The elevator descended for what seemed like an

unusually long time before the doors slid open and the Alphas found themselves in a long windowless corridor ending in a single door flanked by two more armed guards. Above it was a single word.

Echelon.

As they approached one of the guards punched a code into the numeric keypad mounted on the wall and the door hissed open. Inside dozens of technicians sat at consoles monitoring hundreds of screens. A woman with curly blonde hair wearing jeans and a T-shirt walked over to them and inspected them carefully.

'Could you give me the code word, please?' she asked.

'Tsunami,' Otto said, trying to ignore the background hum of digital activity that surrounded him.

'Welcome to Echelon,' the woman said with a smile. 'I've been instructed to give you full access. I've prepared a terminal in one of the side offices. If you'd like to come with me . . .'

Otto and the others followed her into the small room off to one side of the main monitoring area, which contained a single desk with an array of touch screens mounted on its surface.

'I'm not sure exactly what it is that you need,' the woman said. 'I'm told that you'll know what to do. If there's anything you want or if you require help at all, I'll be just outside.'

'Thanks,' Otto said. 'I think we'll be OK.'

'Fine. I'll leave you to it.'

She left the office, closing the door behind her. As she walked back out on to the main floor one of her colleagues looked up at her with a curious expression.

'What's that all about?' the man asked, nodding towards the office.

'Don't know, don't want to know,' the woman said with a slight shake of her head, 'but considering who my orders came from I'm guessing that it's a little bit above our pay grade.'

'But they're just kids,' the man said, looking puzzled.

'Kids with a higher security clearance than you, Mike,' the woman said with a shrug, heading back to her desk.

Back inside the office Otto looked at the array of monitors on the desk with a mixture of excitement and apprehension. If there was a pot of gold that lay at the end of the signals intelligence rainbow, this was it. Echelon may have been a badly kept secret within the intelligence community but to most members of the general public it was still just a myth. At its core it was nothing more than an advanced search engine but what made it astonishing was the amount of data that it filtered. Every phone call, internet search or radio transmission was routed through the Echelon servers, where intelligent algorithms scanned through their content looking for key phrases of interest. It was a giant ear listening to the whole of humanity and highlighting to its operators anything that might be of concern to them. Otto thought there was something deeply sinister about it – it represented a huge invasion of privacy for people all over the world. For his money it was just as evil as anything that he'd seen G.L.O.V.E. or any of their foes produce.

'He who sacrifices freedom for security deserves neither,' he said under his breath.

'What's that?' Laura asked.

'Nothing – just something an old revolutionary once said,' Otto replied. 'Check this out.'

He pointed to a series of diagnostic readouts on one of the screens.

'I can't believe the bandwidth they're dealing with here,' Laura said, studying the monitors with an expression of awe.

'It's the level of real-time decryption I can't believe,' Otto replied.

'What bit level of encryption before they hit processing bottlenecks, do you reckon? They have to be using a massively parallel array,' Laura said.

'The who do what now?' Shelby said with a sigh.

'They're talking computer at each other again, aren't they,' Lucy said, sitting down in one of the chairs against the wall.

'I believe they prefer the term nerdspeak,' Wing replied as Otto and Laura chatted away to one another, seemingly oblivious to the rest of the world.

'Er . . . guys,' Shelby said, stifling a laugh, 'hate to break up the party but we're on the clock here.' She tapped on her watch.

'Yeah, I suppose we'd better get on with this,' Otto said with a sigh. 'Can you clear me routers on every major transmission hub?'

'On it,' Laura said, tapping away at one of the touch screens.

'Right. You ready, H.I.V.E.mind?' Otto asked.

I am ready, the voice in Otto's head replied.

'OK, I'm going to hook us up.' Otto explained. 'Once I'm connected to each server I'll give you the word and you can begin transmission.'

Understood.

'I know you can't tell me what this signal is,' Otto said, 'but tell me one thing before we do this.'

What do you want to know?

'Why does it have to be transmitted from here?' Otto asked.

Because this is the only place on Earth where we can be sure that the transmission will not be intercepted. The identities of the recipients of this transmission must not be discovered and the only way we can be certain that they remain hidden is if we

155

send the signal to them directly from here. Echelon monitors every other network that is sufficiently powerful to send the signal. G.L.O.V.E.net would have been both secure and powerful enough but H.I.V.E. is the hub of that network.'

'I get it,' Otto said, suddenly understanding. 'When we lost H.I.V.E. we lost the network that was supposed to send this message. Any other network would have been vulnerable to Echelon and the only way around that is to take advantage of the fact that the one thing Echelon can't hear is its own voice.'

That is correct.

Otto found himself wondering again what this signal could be. What was it that Nero had to be so sure would not be intercepted by anyone? It wasn't that H.I.V.E.mind wouldn't tell him, it was that it *couldn't* tell him. It was built into his code, part of his fundamental architecture. If there was one thing that Otto hated it was not knowing what was going on.

'OK,' Laura said, 'routers are clear.'

'Here goes nothing,' Otto said, closing his eyes.

The connection he made was instant and over-whelming. For just a split second he felt as though he was suddenly spread throughout billions of different places all over the world at the same instant. He could see every-thing, hear everything. It was the most fascinating and yet horrifying thing he had ever experienced. At that instant he made a decision, something that he simply had to do.

Connection verified. Target locations confirmed. Transmission initiated, H.I.V.E.mind said.

Otto tried to ignore the bewildering sensation of near omnipotence and instead focus on his task. He began to build blocks of code in his head, transmitting them as quickly as he could. He consciously hid what he was doing from H.I.V.E.mind – no one could know what he was planning.

Transmission complete, H.I.V.E.mind said.

Otto needed just a few more seconds.

You may disconnect, H.I.V.E.mind said.

Otto fired off the last block of his own code.

Otto, you may disconnect now, H.I.V.E.mind repeated.

'Done,' Otto gasped, disconnecting from Echelon's network and feeling a sudden wave of dizziness. He grabbed the edge of the desk to stop himself from falling as the room spun around him. Wing caught him and helped him down into one of the nearby chairs.

'Are you all right, my friend?' he asked, studying Otto's unusually pale face.

'I'm fine,' Otto said, taking a deep breath. 'That was just a bit much to take in. Unless anyone has any objections I'd like to get the hell out of here. This place gives me the creeps.'

☻ ☻ ☻

Nero looked out of the window of the helicopter as it flew low over the English countryside. Not for the first time in the past couple of days he found himself wondering if he had done the right thing. He had always known that the plan he had put in motion might be necessary one day but, that didn't make him any more comfortable with the possible consequences.

'We're two minutes out,' the pilot reported and Nero just nodded. Moments later the cell phone in his inside pocket began to ring and he quickly took the call.

'Hello, Mr Malpense,' Nero said. 'I hope you have good news.'

'Yes,' Otto replied. 'H.I.V.E.mind has sent the signal. Any chance of you telling me what this is all about now?'

'All in good time, Mr Malpense,' Nero replied. 'I take it that you received full cooperation from the GCHQ staff?'

'Yeah, though I think they might be wondering why a bunch of kids in jumpsuits were given access to the most secure data network on the planet.'

'No doubt. Let's hope that they never find out,' Nero said. 'I shall be there very shortly. Are you ready to leave?'

'Yes, we're inside the main entrance.'

'I'll be on the ground in thirty seconds,' Nero said as they crossed GCHQ's perimeter fence, heading for the helipad a short distance from the entrance.

'OK, see you in a minute,' Otto said and the line went dead.

The helicopter was on its final approach when the front entrance of the GCHQ building suddenly exploded in an enormous ball of fire.

'What the hell –' the pilot said, staring at the billowing cloud of smoke that shrouded the front of the building. Nero watched in horror as something blew away the cloud, revealing the huge hole torn in the entrance. There was a shimmer in the air and he felt his heart sink as a Shroud dropship uncloaked, landing just twenty metres from the building. The rear hatch opened and a figure dressed in black ran down the boarding ramp, pulling two glowing purple swords from the crossed sheaths on her back. A squad of heavily armed men followed close behind her.

'Get me down there now!' Nero shouted.

☹ ☹ ☹

Raven ran through the smouldering rubble, swords drawn, searching for her target. The glass frontage of GCHQ was supposed to be bombproof but the Shroud's missile strike had torn it apart.

'Fan out. Find the boy,' she snapped at the soldiers accompanying her. 'He's here somewhere.'

There was a groan from nearby and Laura sat up, still

dazed from the explosion. Raven signalled to two of the soldiers to take her.

'Put her on board the Shroud – she may be useful.'

Raven watched as the two men dragged the struggling girl away before turning her attention back to the ruined room. Through the clouds of dust hanging in the air she could just make out another figure in a black jumpsuit staggering through the remains of the entrance area. She moved quickly towards the figure and saw that it was Lucy Dexter, bleeding from a gash on her forehead. As she saw Raven approaching, Lucy took a couple of stumbling steps backwards, a look of startled fear on her face.

'*Leave me al*—' Lucy never had time to finish the sentence as Raven clamped her hand over her mouth.

'Not this time,' Raven said, wrapping her arm round Lucy's throat and squeezing until she felt the girl lose consciousness. She called two of the soldiers over.

'Put her on board too. Make sure she's sedated,' Raven said. The soldiers picked up Lucy's unconscious body and carried it outside. There was the sudden sound of gunfire from outside as the GCHQ security forces started to recover from the shock and mount a counter-attack. Raven continued to move through the rubble – she needed to find Malpense fast. She almost tripped over the body lying on the floor half covered in debris, the white hair at the back of his head stained red with blood.

Kneeling down, she placed two fingers on Otto's neck and felt a strong pulse. She quickly searched his pockets and found what looked like a partly dismantled Blackbox and a mobile phone, then flung them against the nearest wall, smashing them to pieces. Satisfied that they could no longer be tracked she pulled Otto from under the fallen plasterwork and slung his limp body over her shoulder.

'Raven to all forces. I have acquired the primary target. Everyone back on board the Shroud now!' she said quickly into her throat mic. She ran through the doors towards the waiting dropship and pounded up the boarding ramp, lowering Otto carefully on to the deck.

'Pilot, get us out of here,' Raven said and the Shroud's idling engines roared into life. She looked back towards the entrance as the Shroud lifted from the ground and saw Wing running through the debris towards her. He leapt into the air as the Shroud climbed, just catching the edge of the boarding ramp, and started to pull himself inside. Raven took two steps towards him as he tried to haul himself up over the edge and kicked him in the jaw. Wing's head snapped back and he dropped off the loading ramp and fell. He hit the ground hard, landing on his side with a thud.

'Wing!' Shelby shouted as she ran across the forecourt towards him. She rolled him on to his back and after a couple of seconds his eyes opened.

'Help me up,' he groaned, grabbing her shoulder and pulling himself to his feet. They both watched helplessly as the Shroud climbed into the sky, its loading ramp closing as the rounds from the GCHQ guards' assault rifles pinged harmlessly off its armoured hull. A moment later the skin of the dropship seemed to shimmer for a second and then it vanished from view as its cloaking field activated. Shelby turned as she heard footsteps running up behind her. It was Nero, flanked by several of the facility's security guards.

'Are you OK?' Nero asked.

'No, it was Raven,' Shelby said. 'She took Otto.'

'Laura and Lucy were also taken,' Wing said. 'Shelby and I were trapped by fallen debris when the explosion happened. By the time I managed to free us it was too late. I was too slow.'

'There was nothing you could have done,' Nero said. 'They took us completely by surprise.'

Nero looked at the scene of chaos and destruction. In the distance he could hear the wail of sirens as the first ambulances and fire engines arrived at the gates. He cursed himself for his stupidity. He had assumed that they had moved too quickly and quietly for Raven to have tracked them here. He should have known better than to underestimate her. Nero was tired of being one step behind Overlord and his plans. He hated to admit it, but

162

at the moment he was being outplayed.

'What do we do now?' Shelby asked sadly.

Nero knew that there was only one place Raven could be heading. Overlord would want Otto brought to him immediately.

'Now, Miss Trinity,' he said, a note of grim determination in his voice, 'we take the fight to them.'

chapter eight

Overlord stared at his reflection in the mirror with a mixture of frustration and disgust. The body he had taken just a few hours before was already starting to fail. Soon he would no longer be able to take over humans without destroying them almost immediately. If he had not found a solution by then he might be trapped within the Animus for all eternity, incapable of communicating with anyone or anything. He cursed his original creators every day for denying him the ability to interface with other machines. The abilities that he had engineered into Otto at birth were now the one way he would ever be able to control those machines. Only then would he truly be able to remake this world in his image.

He turned away from the mirror and walked out of the room, heading for the laboratory that housed the most critical component of the next phase of his plan. Furan suddenly appeared, striding down the corridor towards him.

'Raven just reported in,' Furan said with a smile as he approached. 'She has Malpense. She'll be here in a few hours.'

'Excellent,' Overlord said with a smile. 'Make sure everything else is ready. We will proceed as soon as they arrive.'

'I will inform our technicians to prepare for release,' Furan said with a nod.

'Nothing can stop us now,' Overlord replied. 'The endgame begins.'

☣ ☣ ☣

Otto woke up, his head throbbing. He was handcuffed to the seat in the passenger compartment of a Shroud and sitting shackled to the seats opposite him were Laura and Lucy. Lucy was unconscious, her head tipped back against the bulkhead, but Laura was awake.

'Hey,' Otto whispered. 'Where are we?'

Laura looked up and sighed with relief.

'Thank God,' she said quietly. 'I was beginning to worry that you weren't going to wake up.'

'What happened?' Otto asked. The last thing he remembered was making the call to Nero to tell him they'd completed their mission and then there had been a bright flash. After that there was nothing.

'Raven attacked us,' Laura said. 'We were on our way out and everything went to hell.'

'What about Wing and Shelby?' Otto asked with a frown.

'I – I don't know,' Laura replied, shaking her head. 'Wing tried to get on board but Raven stopped him. I didn't see Shel. I've got no idea if she made it or not.' She swallowed hard, trying to hold back tears.

'She'll be OK,' Otto said gently. 'We all will. There's no way Nero's going to abandon us. You know that.'

'I hope you're right,' Laura said with a sigh.

'Is Lucy OK?' Otto asked. She was pale and her breathing seemed shallow.

'I think so,' Laura said. 'They brought her on board unconscious and then one of those guys injected her with something.' She nodded towards the soldiers sitting in the forward area of the compartment. 'I think they're trying to keep her under so that she can't try and make anyone help us.'

'And you'd be right,' Raven said as she walked towards them. 'I see you are awake, Malpense. That is good. Overlord would not have been pleased if you had suffered any permanent harm.'

'Raven,' Otto said, staring at her, 'please don't do this. I've been exposed to Animus before and I know that you're in there somewhere. You have to fight it.' Otto thought he saw a fleeting moment of confusion in Raven's eyes but a moment later it was gone.

166

'You're wasting your breath,' Raven said with a sneer. 'Overlord is my master now. Nothing is going to change that.'

'I don't believe that,' Otto said angrily, 'and a part of you doesn't either.'

'Believe what you wish,' Raven replied coldly, 'it makes little difference to me. I just came to warn you that if I detect the slightest hint of you trying to affect any of the systems on board this Shroud, I will make you watch one of them die, slowly and extremely painfully.' She nodded towards Laura and Lucy. 'Personally I would rather sedate you, but Overlord wants you wide awake when you see him.'

She turned and walked away.

'I still can't believe she's doing this,' Laura whispered as she watched Raven leave.

'It's not her fault,' Otto replied. 'I've been through what she's experiencing. If there's any shred of her left, and I think there is, then she's just a passenger in there. You can't speak, you can't do anything, you're just forced to turn against everyone and everything you care about.'

'I hope you're right about her still being in there,' Laura whispered, 'because just now we need her more than ever before.'

'Try not to worry,' Otto said. 'We have one ace in the hole, remember.' He looked up and winked.

I was beginning to think you might have forgotten about me,
H.I.V.E.mind said.

☹ ☹ ☹

Nero walked along the aisle of the private jet as it raced
across the Atlantic. He stopped when he got to where
Wing and Shelby were sitting.

'How are you both feeling?' he asked.

'I've had better days,' Shelby said with a weak smile.

'We all have,' Wing added.

'Overlord hasn't won yet,' Nero said.

'Maybe not, but he seems to be holding most of the
cards,' Shelby replied.

'I understand your concern, Miss Trinity, but we cannot
afford to give up hope. The fact that you completed your
mission means that we have a fighting chance of stopping
Overlord,' Nero said, 'which is better than no chance at
all.'

'I guess,' Shelby said with a sigh. 'Let's just hope that
Otto, Lucy and Laura don't end up paying the price.'

'Indeed,' Nero replied. 'Now, if you'll excuse me I need
to make a call.'

Nero pulled the sat phone that he had taken from the
Megalodon from his pocket and punched in a number. It
rang for a couple of seconds before Darkdoom answered.

'Hello, Max,' Darkdoom said. 'Were you successful?'

'The signal was sent but Raven intercepted our team directly afterwards. She captured Otto, Laura and Lucy. With Otto in Overlord's hands we need to move quickly. Are you at the rendezvous?'

'Yes,' Darkdoom replied. 'The equipment was delivered an hour ago and our transport should be arriving soon.'

'Good,' Nero replied. 'I want everything ready as soon as possible.'

'Understood. See you soon.'

Nero slipped the phone back into his pocket and headed up the aisle towards the cockpit.

The two pilots were talking on the radio but fell silent as he entered.

'I have the coordinates of where I want you to land,' Nero said.

'I'm afraid there's been a slight change of plan,' one of the pilots said, turning round in his seat and pointing a pistol at Nero. 'We'll be landing at a more *secure* location.'

'Cavendish,' Nero hissed, suddenly understanding how Raven had known where Otto would be.

'Let's go back and get you seated with the others, shall we?' the pilot said, gesturing with his pistol for Nero to head back down the plane. Nero walked down the aisle, his hands raised above his head. Shelby and Wing saw him coming and were halfway out of their places before the pilot pushed Nero down into the seat opposite them and pointed the gun in their direction.

'Let's not do anything stupid, eh?' he said. He threw two pairs of handcuffs on to the table between the seats and nodded towards them. 'Cuff yourselves to your seats.'

Wing and Shelby had no choice but to obey. The pilot checked that both sets of cuffs were secured and turned back towards Nero.

'I won't be needing any cuffs for you,' he said with a nasty smile, cocking the hammer on his pistol and levelling it at Nero. 'Mr Cavendish says that he'd really rather you didn't survive until the end of the flight.'

The pilot was about to squeeze the trigger when he felt a tap on his shoulder. He spun round and saw Shelby standing there smiling at him with the cuffs dangling from her fingertips.

'Ta da!' she said, punching him as hard as she could on the nose. At the same instant Nero dived forward and grabbed the gun from the staggering man's hand. He brought the butt of the pistol down hard on the pilot's neck and he fell to the deck unconscious.

'You really must show me how you do that one day, Miss Trinity,' Nero said with a smile as he headed back up the aisle to discuss their destination with the other pilot.

'Nah,' Shelby grinned. 'Trade secret.'

☻ ☻ ☻

Otto felt the soft bump as the Shroud touched down and tried to ignore the gnawing feeling of anxiety in his gut. He was under no illusion about what awaited them. Raven walked down the passenger compartment, holding a syringe. She slid the needle into Lucy's arm and a few seconds later she started to wake up with a groan. As her eyes opened she saw Raven looking down at her.

'Welcome back, Miss Dexter,' Raven said with a nasty smile. 'I hope you had a pleasant flight. I just wanted to warn you that if you say one word using that clever little voice of yours I'll cut your tongue out. Do you understand?'

Lucy nodded, knowing that it was not an idle threat.

'Good,' Raven said as she undid each set of cuffs for just long enough to allow each of them to stand before snapping them shut again behind their backs. 'Let's get moving, shall we? We don't want to keep everyone waiting.'

Otto and the girls walked down the boarding ramp and into the cool night air. A hundred metres away a huge set of armoured blast doors was set into the wall of the canyon that they stood in. As they walked down the road leading to the doors they began to rumble open to reveal two figures standing in the centre of the brightly lit hangar beyond. Otto recognised one of the men immediately: the last time he had seen him was on board the

Dreadnought and Pietor Furan was not the kind of man one was likely to forget in a hurry. Otto had no idea who the other man was but as they drew close he felt a chill run down his spine. The telltale signs of infection with the original strain of Animus covered the exposed areas of his skin. Whoever he was he should be dead, not standing there with an unpleasant smile on his face.

'Otto,' the man said as they approached, 'I'm so very pleased to see you again. It's fortunate that you were not badly injured when Raven retrieved you. I wouldn't want my new home damaged, would I?'

'Overlord,' Otto whispered, his blood running cold.

'In the flesh, so to speak,' Overlord replied. 'Though not this flesh for very much longer, thankfully.'

'I'm not frightened of you,' Otto said. 'You're just code.'

'And you are just storage,' Overlord snapped back, 'and I intend to wipe you clean. But don't worry – I'm not going to move in just yet. I have things I want you to see first.' He gestured to the guards standing nearby. 'Oh, and just in case you were thinking about interfering with any of the electronic devices in this facility I have a little something for you.' He reached into his pocket and pulled out a small metal disc with four sharpened claws projecting from it. Reaching behind Otto, he pressed the device on to the back of his neck. Otto gasped in pain as the four claws snapped closed, piercing his skin and attaching the device to his body. The background hum of the electronic devices that surrounded him suddenly vanished from inside his head. It was a noise that he had learnt to ignore over the years, but now that it was gone the sudden silence was overwhelming.

'There. That should stop you making a nuisance of yourself,' Overlord said with a nasty smile. 'Take him away.'

Two of the guards grabbed Otto by the arms and marched him out of the hangar.

'And a special bonus,' Overlord said, turning towards Lucy and Laura. 'Two more of Nero's brats to play with. I remember you,' he said to Laura. 'You forced me from Malpense's body in Brazil and very nearly killed me. Don't worry, I fully intend to repay the favour. Guards!'

Two more of Overlord's men walked over and grabbed Lucy and Laura.

'I'll take that one,' Raven said, pointing at Lucy. 'She can be particularly *difficult*.'

Raven pushed Lucy towards the far end of the hangar.

'Well done, Natalya,' Furan said as she walked away. 'I knew you wouldn't let us down.'

'The final stages of the fusion process are nearly complete,' Overlord said. 'We can proceed as soon as –' He suddenly started to cough violently, black phlegm dribbling down his chin. Furan looked at him with concern.

'Why not take Malpense's body now?' Furan asked. 'Or at least transfer to another host. There is no point in taking any chances.'

'This body will last a few more hours,' Overlord said, 'and I am not going to miss the pleasure of seeing Malpense's face when I show him what I'm about to unleash. I want him to die knowing that all hope is lost.'

☢ ☢ ☢

The private jet rolled to a stop on the taxiway and a few seconds later the hatch opened and Nero, Shelby and Wing climbed down the short flight of steps.

'Thought you'd never get here,' Diabolus Darkdoom said, walking towards them.

'We had a little in-flight entertainment. Is everyone here?' Nero asked.

'Yes. Well, as many as could get here in time,' Darkdoom replied. 'I think they're ready for an explanation.'

'I should imagine they are,' Nero said, looking tired. 'I suppose we should go and face the music then.' He turned to Wing and Shelby. 'Mr Fanchu, Miss Trinity, I did not plan to include you in the next phase of this operation but I think you've earned the right to take part. There is a distinct chance that no one will return alive. Are you in?'

Wing spoke calmly. 'My best friend is in the hands of a

174

creature who intends to erase his very spirit and turn him against everything he cares about,' he said. 'If he succeeds in doing so there is a very real possibility that he will then go on to enslave every person on the face of the planet. I appreciate the fact that you have given us the opportunity to decide for ourselves if we wish to participate in this endeavour, but you could no more stop me from coming than you could the sun from rising.'

'What he said,' Shelby added, 'except – y'know, not so many words.'

'I would have expected nothing less,' Nero said with a nod. 'Come with me.'

Shelby and Wing followed Nero and Darkdoom into a nearby hangar and were amazed at what they saw. Parked in the cavernous space was an enormous aircraft. It clearly shared the same designer as H.I.V.E.'s Shroud dropships but this was on an altogether different scale.

'This is the Leviathan,' Darkdoom said. 'She's a fully operational airborne command centre with full cloak capability and the latest generation of long-range scramjet engines.'

'I told Nigel his dad always had the coolest toys,' Shelby said to Wing.

'Oh, I didn't build her,' Darkdoom said. 'She once belonged to Jason Drake – in fact he used her to launch his attack against the Dreadnought. After Mr Drake's welcome demise I managed to acquire her. Thankfully she was not hangared in Mr Drake's Nevada facility when he triggered the self-destruct device.'

'Hard to retrieve anything from a two-kilometre-wide, highly radioactive hole in the middle of the desert,' Shelby observed.

'Indeed,' Darkdoom replied with a wry smile. 'I have made some upgrades but I really can't take the credit for her. Drake may have been an insane megalomaniac but he was also a technical genius. We'll be launching and then controlling our attack from on board.'

'If we have finished admiring your latest plaything, Diabolus, perhaps we can get the briefing started,' Nero said, rolling his eyes slightly.

'Of course,' Darkdoom said, and they walked towards a group of fifty or so people gathered at the rear loading ramp of the Leviathan.

'Honestly, Diabolus,' Nero said with a wry smile, 'the Megalodon, the Dreadnought and now this.' He gestured towards the giant aircraft. 'If you were any less a man I might think you were compensating for something.'

As Wing and Shelby approached the crowd they could see that most of them seemed to be in their twenties and thirties, men and women from every corner of the world. Shelby could hear hushed conversations taking place in several different languages. Nero walked to the bottom of the loading ramp and turned to face the crowd.

'Ladies and gentlemen,' he said, his voice strong and clear, 'you may not all know each other but you all know me. You doubtless have many questions, but first let me explain why you are here. Yesterday you all had an extremely unusual experience. A signal was transmitted that activated devices you all had implanted in your skulls. That device triggered a post-hypnotic impulse that you will all have felt an irresistible compulsion to obey. You visited an apparently insignificant internet address that provided you with the GPS coordinates of this building. You travelled here from all over the world without really knowing why. You will have somehow known on an instinctual level that you had to come. For this I apologise. Many of you may resent me for stripping you of your free will, for implanting this device in your head without your knowledge or permission, but it was a necessary evil. This is Zero Hour, something that Diabolus Darkdoom and I have been planning for decades. We always feared that a time would come when one of our number would threaten true global domination – a threat so terrible that we would need a final option, a force that we could summon at a moment's notice and whose loyalty would be unquestionable. You are that force. There was only one way that we could be entirely sure that no one would ever find out what we had planned or who was a

177

part of this group. We had to make sure that even you were unaware that you were part of it. We also had to face the disturbing possibility that Diabolus or I could become the very threat that you were designed to combat. Even we could not know who you were, just in case it was one day your job to destroy us. The job of selecting which of you would be activated when the time came had to be placed in the hands of someone who would be incorruptible. No person could ever be given that task and so it had to be carried out by a non-human, artificial intelligence, a system that could track you throughout the globe and assess exactly who were the best people to activate in order to face any crisis that arose. You know that intelligence as H.I.V.E.mind and it is he who gathered you here today. I gave the order but he made the selection. He chose which of you would answer the call – which of my best, my brightest, my Alphas.'

Nero looked around the room at the astonished expressions. Doubtless they had all quickly realised what they had in common but the fact that they had been carrying around this responsibility for years without ever knowing it had clearly come as a shock to many of them.

'H.I.V.E. has fallen, G.L.O.V.E. is in chaos, the ruling council has been captured. All of this has been done by one man, if that is what you can call him. The events that have forced me to gather you all here today are in large part my own fault. As soon as Diabolus and I determined that we would need an AI to control this project I embarked on a project to develop one. That project was codenamed Overlord and it was my greatest mistake. I was so focused on making sure that when the time came everything would be ready that I forced the engineers responsible for its development to proceed too quickly, to take too many short cuts. When the time came to activate this entity I learnt to my cost what a mistake that had been. We had created a monster, an advanced intelligence with nothing but contempt and loathing for its creators. It very nearly cost me my life but Overlord was destroyed just hours after it was activated. Or so I thought at the time. Overlord was not destroyed – he survived, hiding in the shadows, plotting his revenge. Now he has put that plan into motion despite all of our efforts to stop him and we are all that stands between him and his final victory. I could lie to you and tell you that you have a choice in this, but the truth is that you do not. If we fall here today then the rest of humanity will fall too. You, the selected best of H.I.V.E.'s Alpha graduates, are the last line of defence.'

He paused to let his words sink in. If any of the men and women in front of him were thinking of running from this responsibility, he could see no sign of it.

'You doubtless have many questions,' Nero continued. 'I will answer them as best I can, but time is short.'

A tall, strikingly beautiful woman in the front row raised her hand.

'Yes, Miss Holmes,' Nero said with a nod of the head.

'I don't have any memory of anything being put inside my skull,' she said, 'and it's the sort of thing I think I'd remember.'

'Part of the psycho-hypnotic programming ensured that you would have no memory of the procedure. An unfortunate but necessary deception under the circumstances.'

'And that was the only time it happened?' she asked with a slight frown.

'Yes. Obviously you'll have to take my word for that, but I hope you all know me well enough to realise that I am not about to lie to people I am asking to risk their lives like this,' Nero replied.

Another hand went up in the crowd.

'Yes, Mr Usmar,' Nero said.

'Some of us left H.I.V.E. twenty years ago,' the man said. 'Aren't you worried that we might be a bit – well, rusty?'

'H.I.V.E.mind has been discreetly tracking all of your activities,' Nero replied. 'I am confident that he would not have selected anyone for this mission who was not qualified to take part.'

He nodded towards another raised hand.

'What exactly are we going up against here?'

'A fortified US military facility containing some of the most advanced and powerful weapons systems that the world has ever seen. All of which may be under the command of a psychotic AI backed up by his own military force of an as yet undetermined strength,' Nero said calmly.

'OK. Sorry I asked.'

'How are we going to do this?' another voice asked.

'Diabolus? Would you care to explain our plan of attack?' Nero asked, gesturing for Darkdoom to take the question.

'We have one advantage that Overlord doesn't know about,' Darkdoom said. 'This facility was one of many that was built for the US military by Drake Industries. Unbeknownst to them, and thankfully for us, Jason Drake was in the habit of building back doors into his facilities. We will send in a small team this way to infiltrate the base. Once inside, they will open the main doors and let us in. We could try to take the main doors down but that would doubtless result in a direct confrontation with Overlord's forces – something that we want to avoid until we can be sure that we have the upper hand. There will be a full tactical briefing straight after this, but that's the basic plan.

'We also have some new equipment that should give

you an edge. For some time Doctor Nero has been providing me with the best of the technology that Professor Pike has been developing at H.I.V.E. and I have made an attempt to unify it with some of the other advanced technology that we have acquired recently. The aim was to put all of it into a single package.'

Darkdoom walked over to a large crate that stood off to one side. 'Ladies and gentlemen, I present to you ISIS, the Integrated Systems Infiltration Suit.' He swung the front of the crate open to reveal a gleaming black suit of highly sophisticated body armour. 'This suit combines full thermoptic camouflage with advanced Kevlar polymer body weave. It is fitted with an array of electromagnetic devices, including a full EM scrambler pulse, an anti-personnel discharge unit and a high-powered adhesion field built into the palms and soles of the boots. It has a variable geometry forcefield landing device and, courtesy of the late Mr Drake, a detachable flight control system that can be used for pinpoint insertion. Grappler units are mounted on both arms and a full targeting and information HUD within the helmet. This is what special forces will be wearing in twenty years' time, but you get it today.'

'Go, go, Power Rangers!' Shelby muttered to Wing as Diabolus continued to explain the capabilities of ISIS.

'Shhh,' Wing whispered, trying not to smile.

The briefing continued for another half-hour and the assembled Alphas listened attentively. Occasionally they threw in a question or asked for clarification but for the most part they seemed to be taking all of this in their stride. Nero was pleased to see that thus far at least their plan was working. H.I.V.E.mind had chosen well.

'That's it, ladies and gentlemen,' he said as the briefing drew to a close. 'For anyone else on the planet this would be an impossible task; for you it will merely be challenging. Suit up – we launch in thirty minutes. I know that you won't let me down.'

'Do you really think they can do it?' Darkdoom said quietly as he watched the Alphas start to break into the crates that lined the hangar wall and unpack their ISIS suits.

'Yes,' Nero said, 'and let's face it, if they can't no one else can.'

'Doctor Nero,' Wing said as he and Shelby approached, 'Shelby and I were wondering what part we were to play in all this.'

'Possibly the most critical part, Mr Fanchu,' Nero replied. 'You're going in through the back door. It's your job to make sure that the rest of the Alphas can get inside.'

'You're sending us in alone?' Shelby asked with a frown.

'Don't get me wrong, I'm up for this, but going in without backup?'

'Oh, don't worry, Miss Trinity,' Nero said with a smile. 'You're not going in alone. I'm coming with you.'

chapter nine

Wing snapped the final fastening shut on his ISIS armour and walked back across the hangar towards Shelby.

'Hey,' she said as he approached. 'You ready for this?'

'As ready as I can be,' Wing replied with a sigh. 'I just hope that we're in time to save Otto, Laura and Lucy.'

'They'll be OK,' Shelby said, putting a hand on his shoulder. 'We've been in situations like this before.'

'Perhaps, but the fact that Doctor Nero has felt it necessary to put this Zero Hour plan into action worries me,' Wing said. 'He would not have done so if the threat had not been dire. We cannot afford to fail.'

'And we're not going to,' Shelby said, wrapping her arms around his waist and pulling him towards her. 'We're going to go in there and we're gonna give Overlord the ass-kicking of a lifetime.'

'I hope you are right,' Wing replied, looking deep into

her eyes. 'I do not think I could stand it if something were to happen to you.'

'I can look after myself, big guy – you know that.'

Wing kissed her gently and then pulled away.

'We should get on board the Leviathan,' he said. 'It is not long till launch.'

The pair of them walked towards the giant aircraft and up the rear loading ramp. Just inside they found Nigel and Franz apparently having a hushed argument about something.

'Hey guys, what's up?' Shelby asked.

'Tell this idiot that we're better off staying on the Leviathan, will you?' Nigel said with an exasperated sigh.

'I am just saying that we should be going with you,' Franz said. 'I am thinking that you will be needing all the help that you can get.'

'They'll need us just as much here,' Nigel said. 'Someone's got to to help coordinate that attack.'

'I am ready for battle,' Franz said proudly. 'My triumph in the holographic combat training is being proof of this.'

'This isn't a simulation, Franz,' Nigel said, rolling his eyes.

'Bah,' Franz snorted dismissively. 'There is no difference.'

'You are, of course, correct,' Wing said calmly. 'What should it matter that a bullet from a real assault rifle will be travelling at one thousand metres per second when it hits you? It is equally pointless to dwell on the fact that as it enters your body it will start to spin and fragment, shredding your internal organs, or that upon exiting it will leave a wound the size of a man's fist. Indeed, it is not unheard of for large-calibre rounds to completely sever limbs. A quick death from catastrophic blood loss would then be almost inevitable but, as you rightly point out, these are all inconsequential facts.'

'Where is being the toilet?' Franz asked, suddenly turning pale.

'That way,' Nigel said, pointing further inside the Leviathan as Franz hurried away. 'Thanks, Wing. I'd better go and check he's OK,' he added.

'Now, that was just cruel,' Shelby said with a grin.

'I don't know what you're talking about,' Wing said innocently. 'I was merely stating the facts.'

'Yeah, course you were,' Shelby said, 'though I'm not really sure I needed to hear all that just at the moment.'

'The trick is not to get hit by the bullet in the first place,' Wing replied.

'I'll try to remember that,' Shelby said with a slight roll of the eyes. 'Anyway, I don't think that the flight packs were designed with him in mind. Of all the words that I could use to describe Franz I don't think I'd ever go with *aerodynamic*.'

'Now who is being cruel?' Wing asked with a slight smile as one of Darkdoom's technicians approached.

'Come with me, please,' the man said, gesturing for Wing and Shelby to follow him over to a rack of weapons mounted on the wall.

'One for you,' he said, handing a compact sub-machine gun to Shelby, 'and one for you.' He took another gun and offered it to Wing.

'That will not be necessary,' Wing said, refusing the proffered weapon.

The technician stared at him for a moment in confusion and then put the gun back on the rack with a shrug.

'It's your funeral, kid,' he said as he walked away.

'I don't know if you've heard, but kung fu doesn't work at long range,' Shelby said with a frown, shaking her head as she popped the clip from the gun to check it was fully loaded before snapping it back into place and sliding the weapon into the holster on her thigh.

Dr Nero walked up the boarding ramp before heading over to the rack and taking one of the guns from the wall. It was somehow strange to see him in the ISIS armour rather than one of his usual immaculately tailored suits.

'Do you have everything you need?' he asked as he holstered his weapon.

'Yup,' Shelby replied with a nod, 'though you might

want to see if you can persuade tall, dark and stupid here to take a gun.'

'I have seen Mr Fanchu sparring with Raven back at H.I.V.E., Miss Trinity,' Nero said, 'and if he can hold his own in a fight with her then he probably does not need one. It is his decision to make.' He knew he could not force Wing to take a weapon and he suspected that it would be pointless if he did.

'Go and get your flight packs,' he went on, pointing to the other side of the compartment where the rest of the Alphas were having the bulky devices mounted on their backs.

As Wing and Shelby walked away, Professor Pike walked over and handed Nero a slim metal case.

'That's all I can spare,' he said as Nero slid the case into an equipment pouch on his belt. 'You'll only get one shot.'

'That's all I'll need.'

☺ ☺ ☺

'Get in there,' Furan said, shoving Otto hard in the back.

Otto found himself inside a sophisticated laboratory filled with the latest scientific equipment. Technicians were busy at workstations around the room, all wearing white hazmat suits. At the far end of the room there was a thick glass wall with an airlock mounted in it. Standing with his back to them and watching the activity within

189

the sealed chamber was Overlord. Furan pushed Otto through the lab towards him. Otto tried to reach out and connect with any of the electronic devices that filled the room but it was pointless – the device attached to the back of his neck was jamming his abilities completely.

'Do you know what that is?' Overlord said as Otto approached, gesturing to the large silver cylinder on the other side of the glass.

'No, but I'm sure you'll bore me with the details anyway,' Otto said with a sigh.

'Futile defiance,' Overlord said. 'As much the hallmark of your species as anything else, I suppose. That,' Overlord pointed at the cylinder, 'is the future, Mr Malpense.'

'I thought I didn't have a future,' Otto replied.

'Not your future – mine,' Overlord said with a smile. 'You see, the strain of Animus that you were infected with and that I now inhabit was far too aggressive. As you can see from my own physical condition, it destroys whoever it touches. Even with my almost unlimited power I can only slow the process, not stop it. So I created a new strain in the hope that it might allow me to remain within a host indefinitely. Loathsome as I may find it to be trapped inside one of these fragile sacks of meat, it is still preferable to being imprisoned inside a glass tank. The new strain was a failure though.'

'What a shame,' Otto replied.

'Oh, it still proved to be quite useful,' Overlord continued. 'As you will know from your recent experiences with Raven it allowed me to encode instructions within a human consciousness — instructions that they were powerless to resist. It still needed to be implanted directly though, and as we found with Raven that can be difficult when the target is uncooperative. Furan lost several of his best men when we ambushed her during her retrieval of Lin Feng. It served to illustrate the fact that a more efficient delivery system was necessary. Fortunately I was already working on obtaining just such a thing. The group known as the Disciples had been tracking the development of something that would serve that purpose perfectly: a top-secret military research project that was being worked on here.'

'Are you planning to bore me to death or will you be getting to the point any time soon?' Otto asked.

'Such impatience, Mr Malpense! I would have thought you would want to savour your last hours of life.'

'Not if I have to listen to you ranting,' Otto said quietly.

'Very well, I shall get to the point,' Overlord replied. 'The Americans were developing a revolutionary new system for repairing their military vehicles on the battlefield. The project was called Panacea and the concept was that their vehicles would have a layer of dormant reconstructive nanites built into their armour. If the armour was damaged the nanite layer would be exposed to the air and begin replication, working to repair the damage until the breach was sealed, whereupon they would deactivate. It was really quite ingenious, especially for something developed by humans, but they were worried about the nanites' replication rate. They were finding it difficult to stop them from doing so indefinitely, spreading out of control. They feared the so-called 'grey goo' scenario.'

Otto had heard of this theory – that an out-of-control swarm of self-replicating nanites would consume all matter, organic and non-organic, on the face of the planet, leaving nothing but a barren rock spinning through space.

'What they lacked was a control mechanism and that was exactly what I had. I have successfully fused the Panacea nanites with the new strain of Animus. Allow me to demonstrate.'

Overlord hit a switch on a touch screen mounted in the glass and a section of the wall inside the chamber slid back to reveal a terrified-looking American soldier strapped to a vertical bed behind yet another layer of glass. He hit another switch and what looked like a tiny drop of silvery black liquid dropped on to the man's chest. The drop started to grow at an astonishing rate, the metallic ooze expanding and slithering towards the soldier's face. The man let out a strangled gurgling scream

192

as the silvery liquid slithered into his nose and mouth, struggling helplessly against his restraints. He convulsed for a couple of seconds before falling still. A moment later his eyes snapped open and they were now a solid silver colour. Overlord hit another switch and the man's restraints snapped open and his glass cage slid open.

'Pick up the gun,' Overlord said into the intercom, and the soldier mutely obeyed, picking up the handgun that lay on the table in front of him.

'Put it in your mouth and pull the trigger,' Overlord said calmly.

The soldier pulled the trigger and the hammer clicked down on the empty firing chamber.

'Unquestioning obedience,' Overlord said, 'implanted by a nanotechnological Animus hybrid. The problem comes when the hybrid has not been programmed.' He turned back to the soldier behind the glass. 'Return to the chamber in the wall.'

The soldier obeyed and stepped back into the recess, the glass sliding shut again.

'This is what unprogrammed Animus nanites will do,' Overlord said, hitting another switch. Another drop of the liquid hit the man's chest and again it began expanding, but this time it simply consumed everything it touched. Otto did not know what was worse, seeing the man eaten alive or the fact that he stood there silently as it happened. In seconds all that remained was a still-growing pool of silver slime at the bottom of the recess

'Irradiate the chamber,' Overlord said. There was a flash and all that was left in the chamber was smoke. 'So you can see why I need your abilities to program the hybrid. Obviously once the human population has been exposed, giving direct orders to every person on Earth as I did with that soldier or Raven would be impossible, but with your abilities it won't be necessary. I will have a constant connection to the nanite swarm, able to direct them with just a thought. Your gifts will allow me to transmit my will anywhere I want, with every last human on the planet a puppet under my control. Then I shall use the enslaved masses to build a new, more perfect world. You, Mr Malpense, are going to be the herald of a new dawn.'

Otto suddenly understood the enormity of what Overlord was planning. Once the Animus nanites were released they would spread inexorably across the planet, enslaving everyone who came into contact with them. And Overlord was going to use him to do this.

'No smart remarks any more, Mr Malpense?' Overlord said with a smile. 'What a shame.' He turned towards Furan. 'Take him to the medical bay and prep him for the neural transfer. Have the other two brats that we captured taken there too.'

'Leave them out of this,' Otto said angrily.

'But they need to be there,' Overlord replied.

'Why?' Otto asked.

'Because first I'm going to take over your body,' Overlord said, leaning in close to Otto's face, 'and then I'm going to leave your consciousness intact just long enough for you to watch me use it to kill them both.'

☢ ☢ ☢

The cloaked Leviathan passed completely undetected over the outer perimeter that the American military had set up thirty kilometres from the AWP. Inside the darkened control centre Diabolus Darkdoom watched as they neared the drop point.

'Two minutes to drop,' Darkdoom said.

'Understood,' Nero responded in his earpiece.

'I still wish I was coming with you,' Darkdoom said.

'I need you here,' Nero explained. 'It could be chaos down there. I need you to make sure that everything stays under control.'

'I'll do my best,' Darkdoom said. 'Just make sure that Overlord doesn't get away this time.'

'Don't worry,' Nero replied. 'It ends here. I'm going to destroy him once and for all or die trying.'

'Let's hope it doesn't come to that,' Darkdoom said. 'Good luck, old friend.'

'A wise man once said that luck is what happens when

preparation meets opportunity,' Nero replied. 'Preparations are complete, now we seize the opportunity.'

Down on the lower deck the light above the launch ramp turned red. Diabolus' voice came over the Alphas' comms systems.

'Darkdoom to all Alpha units. Thirty seconds to drop.'

There was no chatter as the Alphas stood waiting, just a sense of collective determination. The huge ramp at the rear of the Leviathan began to drop and lock into position.

'Fifteen seconds.'

The first row of Alphas stepped forward.

'Ten seconds.'

'Let the flight packs do the work,' Nero said calmly. 'Your drop coordinates are pre-programmed. I'll see you on the other side.'

'Drop, drop, drop!' Darkdoom said, and the first of the Alphas leapt head first into the night sky. Shelby felt a moment of apprehension as she walked towards the edge. All of the readouts for her flight system were displaying green on the head-up display inside her helmet. It was now or never. She glanced at Wing standing next to her, and then they both dived into the void. There were a few seconds of free fall before the engine on her back fired and steered her towards the rest of the soaring Alphas, their positions relative to her highlighted on the display. The automated flight systems brought the group into tight formation, approaching their target at a constant rate.

'All drop teams away,' Darkdoom reported. 'Leviathan moving to overwatch position.'

There was surprisingly little noise from the engine on Shelby's back, but she could feel it making constant slight course corrections to keep her in line with the rest of the Alphas. Nero, Shelby and Wing suddenly broke away from the main formation and banked sharply to the left, heading towards their own drop coordinates as the remaining strike team continued on their original course.

'One minute to touchdown,' Nero said. 'Engaging thermoptic camouflage.'

The holographic projection systems in their ISIS armour engaged and all three of them vanished from sight. Shelby could still see projected silhouettes of Wing and Nero inside her helmet but she knew that they had just become effectively invisible to the naked eye.

'Thirty seconds,' Nero said.

The flight packs switched into their final approach stage, sending them diving towards the desert below and levelling out at only five metres above the ground. Shelby tried to ignore the desert floor racing past below her so close that it almost felt like she could reach out and touch it. The engine on her back abruptly cut out and the ISIS suit fired its variable geometry forcefield with a soft thumping sound, dropping her as softly as if she'd stepped off a staircase rather than a giant stealth aircraft twenty thousand feet up. Nero and Wing landed just as softly on either side of her a few metres away.

'On me, let's go,' Nero said, heading towards the high-lighted target. It looked like a simple rock outcropping but there was more to it than met the eye. As they approached he tapped at the small touch screen mounted on his forearm and part of the rock face slid aside to reveal a metal hatch. He punched a series of digits into the keypad in the centre of the hatch and it popped open with a slight hiss.

'I never thought I'd be grateful for Jason Drake's devi-ousness,' Nero said, 'but right now I'd like to shake his hand.' Before his death on board the Dreadnought, Drake had been responsible for the design and construction of some of the US military's most secure and secret facilities. The officials who had commissioned his company to carry out the work could not possibly have known that he was one of the senior members of the G.L.O.V.E. ruling council. They might have inspected his work a little more closely if they had known. Right now Nero was very grateful for their naivety.

They walked into the dimly lit corridor beyond, sealing the hatch shut again behind them. It was clear from the dust on the floor that no one had been down there for a very long time. Indeed the last people to stand where they were standing would probably have been the men who constructed these secret passageways. Nero had known Drake well enough to realise that this could well have been the last thing those men ever saw. He might have been an insane megalomaniac but Drake had not been in the habit of leaving such potentially inconvenient loose ends.

'Primary force is reporting down and clear,' Darkdoom's voice said inside their helmets. 'Waiting for your go.'

'Understood,' Nero replied. 'It's five hundred metres to the hidden entrance. Let's go.'

☻ ☻ ☻

The Alphas moved slowly and quietly along the canyon leading to the massive blast doors at the entrance to the AWP facility. Their thermoptic camouflage systems meant that even the most careful observer would have found it impossible to spot them. Silently they took up positions a hundred metres from the doors.

'Nero to Alpha team,' the voice inside their helmets said, 'we are in position. You are go for diversionary attack.'

'Alpha nine, roger that,' one of the team replied. The time for stealth was gone and now they had to provide as much of a distraction to the forces defending the base as possible. 'All units, disengage thermoptic camouflage on my mark.' He pulled the portable rocket launcher from his back and placed it on his shoulder, looking through the targeting scope and locking on to the massive steel doors. 'Disengage.'

All around him the Alpha team started to blink into view, weapons raised and ready.

'Knock, knock,' he said, squeezing the trigger.

☻ ☻ ☻

Furan pushed Otto along the corridor leading to the medical bay.

'Why are you doing this?' Otto asked. 'Don't you see that if Overlord carries out his plan you're going to be enslaved along with everybody else?'

'Not everyone will be infected by the Animus nanites,' Furan said. 'Those who have been loyal to Overlord – his Disciples – will be spared. Overlord has promised me that I will serve at his right hand as he builds his new world. It will be a better place, ordered, controlled – none of the chaos that humanity blights the Earth with now.'

'You know that you sound insane, right?' Otto said.

'And do you know how often throughout history people who change the world have been dismissed as lunatics? The world that Overlord is going to create will be a world where humanity is finally unified in its direction and the few who are spared will be the ones who will guide its path.'

'You'll be as much a slave as anyone who is exposed to the nanites,' Otto said, 'but by the time you finally realise that it'll be too late.'

Suddenly there was a muffled thud and a vibration ran through the floor. Seconds later Furan's communicator earpiece began to beep urgently.

'Report! What was that?' he snapped.

'We're under attack by unidentified forces. They appeared out of thin air,' the voice on the other end replied. 'They launched a rocket at the hangar doors but they were undamaged. Now they've taken up defensive positions around the entrance.'

'Is it the Americans?' Furan asked.

'I don't think so, sir,' the voice replied. 'When I say that they appeared out of thin air I mean that literally. One second the canyon was empty and then they all just materialised.'

Furan knew that there was only one group on earth that had the type of personal cloaking technology that would make that possible. Why they would waste their time with a futile rocket attack on blast doors that were designed to withstand a nuclear strike was a more puzzling question.

'Issue a base-wide alert,' Furan said, 'and order all of our available forces to the hangar bay. I'm on my way there.'

He hit another button on his comms unit and spoke.

'Sir, we are under attack by G.L.O.V.E. forces,' he said. 'I'm mobilising our defences.'

'That was a threat I thought we had eliminated,' Overlord replied. 'Nero must be desperate to launch a frontal assault.'

'They can't stop us now,' Furan said. 'They won't have anything that will get them through the blast doors in time.'

'Perhaps, but I would rather eliminate the threat altogether,' Overlord replied. 'We are too close to achieving our goals. Send out two of the Goliath units. I will show Nero the price of such a futile act of defiance.'

'Understood,' Furan replied, cutting the connection. 'You're coming with me,' he growled at Otto. 'It's time you learnt what happens to people who oppose us.'

☻ ☻ ☻

Nero, Shelby and Wing moved silently through the deserted corridors of the lower levels of the AWP facility. Drake's entrance had brought them out in a storage area and so far there had been no sign of anyone having any idea that they had infiltrated the base. Nero glanced at the wireframe map of the facility that was displayed on his HUD. The map was based on the original plans that Darkdoom had managed to retrieve from Drake's files but there was little reason to believe that the layout would have changed much, if at all, since this place had been constructed.

'Down here on the left,' he said quietly as they turned down another corridor. Halfway along they found two men with rifles guarding a door.

'Mr Fanchu,' Nero whispered over the comm, 'would you be so kind as to take care of those two as quietly as possible.' They could not risk the sound of a Sleeper pulse. The success of this part of their plan depended on remaining completely undetected. Nero watched as Wing crept down the corridor as silently as a ghost. He moved around behind one of the guards and wrapped his arm around the man's throat. The second guard's eyes widened in surprise as his colleague clawed at his throat for a second before his eyes rolled back in his head and he collapsed unconscious. He took a step towards the fallen man and then something invisible struck him in the chin like a sledgehammer and he too fell to the ground unconscious. They quite literally never knew what hit them.

Nero, Shelby and Wing headed inside and found themselves in an air-conditioned room lined with humming computer servers.

'This is where Otto or Laura would have come in handy,' Shelby said, looking around the room.

'With a bit of luck this should at least tell us where to

find them,' Nero said. He walked over to a nearby terminal and tapped a series of commands into the touch display on his arm. 'Nero to Leviathan. We have accessed one of the network hubs. Begin the hack.'

'Wireless interface enabled, beginning brute force decryption,' Darkdoom replied. 'Estimated time to completion is six minutes.'

Nero watched as the progress bar on his HUD crept upwards agonisingly slowly. Without Otto or Laura's help there was no way to make this go any faster – military encryption was always tough to crack. There was nothing they could do but wait.

☺ ☺ ☺

The AWP facility's security control centre was buzzing with activity. The external security feeds displayed on the large screens at the front of the room showed the G.L.O.V.E. forces maintaining their defensive positions around the entrance.

'Something is wrong about this,' Raven said to herself as she studied the screens. The soldiers outside were obviously equipped with thermoptic camouflage suits but they were more advanced, more heavily armoured than anything she had ever seen before. She had the uncomfortable feeling that there was more to these attackers than met the eye. And yet their initial assault had been pointless – they must have known that the weapon they used would not even scratch the heavily armoured doors to the facility. She suspected it was probably supposed to be little more than a distraction. The question was, what was it supposed to distract their attention from? The only way into the facility was through the main entrance and yet they had given away the element of surprise for no gain. It didn't make any sense.

A warning notification popped up on the display in front of one of the technicians working nearby.

ATTEMPTED NETWORK INTRUSION DETECTED.

He quickly pulled up a system diagnostic – he had become quite used to seeing these messages over the past couple of days. The Americans had tried every trick in the book to regain control of AWP's network in a desperate attempt to find out more about exactly what was going on inside the base. Their problem was that they had designed the facility's network in such a way that external intrusion was impossible. The information contained within the base's computers was, after all, far too valuable to have anything but the very highest level of protection. As it turned out they had done their job too well, little guessing that one day they would be the ones who were being forced to try and hack in. He waited for a few seconds as the diagnostic routine ran. The results window popped up and he scanned the information.

'What the hell –' he said under his breath.

'What is it?' Raven asked, moving quickly towards him.

'We have an attempted network intrusion,' the technician said, 'but it's coming from inside the facility.'

'Where?' Raven snapped.

'Server room two, on the lower level,' the man replied.

Raven was already running for the door.

chapter ten

Furan watched as a dozen of his men took up defensive positions inside the hangar, their weapons trained on the giant blast doors. On the other side of the hangar the turbine engines of the Goliath units were spinning up as the pilots completed their final pre-launch checks. Otto stood off to one side with one of Furan's men guarding him.

'Seal the doors again once the Goliath units are outside,' Furan shouted to the man at the door control panel nearby.

The umbilical cables attached to the giant mechs retracted and the three huge machines walked out into the centre of the hangar, the ground shaking slightly with each step. Furan activated his communicator earpiece.

'Goliath One, wait inside. Goliaths Two and Three, you are to engage the enemy,' he said. 'I want them utterly crushed. There are to be no survivors.'

Two of the mechs walked forward and lined up shoulder to shoulder facing the blast doors as Furan gave a quick nod to the man at the door controls. The man punched a button on the console and warning lights started to flash around the massive doors as the huge hydraulic rams started to pull them slowly apart. They swung fully open and the Gatling cannons on the arms of the Goliaths started to spin as they raised their weapons. A rocket speared towards the Goliath on the left, launched by one of the Alpha team troops who popped up from behind the cover of a large boulder nearby. The dome on the top of the Goliath swung towards the incoming projectile and its anti-missile laser fired in the blink of an eye, safely detonating the incoming rocket twenty metres away from its intended target. The Goliath's arm swung towards the boulder as the Alpha who had fired the rocket ducked back behind it. The cannon roared and the boulder disappeared in a cloud of shattered rock. As the dust slowly cleared the remaining Alpha team members could see no sign of either the boulder or their comrade.

Up in the control room of the Leviathan circling far overhead Darkdoom stared in dismay at the giant armoured machines that had just emerged from the AWP facility and he tried to make sense of the frantic comms chatter coming in from the Alphas.

'Look at the size of those things!'

'Open fire, open fire!'

Darkdoom had assumed that Overlord would not move against the Alphas. Tactically there was no point in him throwing his men into an attack against an entrenched enemy as long as the facility was secure, but their plans had made no allowance for anything like the giant walking tanks that were visible in the feeds from the cameras mounted in the Alphas' helmets. If the Alphas outside AWP were scattered or crushed by those things their whole plan could fail.

'All Alpha units fall back,' Darkdoom said. 'Re-engage thermoptic camouflage systems. Get to cover.'

Darkdoom tapped the button on the console in front of him and switched channels.

'Max, this is Diabolus. We've got a situation up here. Hostile armoured units of an unknown type have engaged the Alphas. How long left on the hack?'

'Two minutes,' Nero replied.

'Roger that,' Darkdoom said as he saw a missile from the shoulder pod of one of the giant mechs streak straight towards one of the cameras that was transmitting a feed to the Leviathan. The screen went black, as did a couple more at precisely the same moment. He did not need to look at the flatlines on the biometric monitoring screens nearby to know what that meant. For the Alpha team

members on the ground two minutes was going to be a
very long time indeed.

☹ ☹ ☹

Nero stared at the progress bar, willing it to move more
quickly. He could hear the muffled sound of the battle
taking place outside, feel the ground shake in unison with
the thud of explosions. They had to get into the facility's
network now, before it was too late. The progress bar
slowly filled as the seconds ticked by until finally a
message confirming a successful connection flashed up on
the display. At the same instant he heard Shelby gasp in
shock as the door behind him hissed open.

'Step away from the terminal,' Raven said, her swords
drawn, their glowing purple edges crackling with energy.

Shelby ripped her gun from its holster and raised it
towards Raven, but she was too slow. Raven stepped up to
her, her blade flashing through the air in a blur, slicing the
weapon in half even as Shelby's finger tightened uselessly
on the trigger. Raven drove her elbow hard into Shelby's
chest, sending her flying backwards and crashing into one
of the large metal server cases against the wall. Wing
moved like lightning, his foot lashing out and striking
Raven in the wrist, and one of her swords clattered away
across the concrete floor. Raven spun round and swung a
killing blow at Wing's neck but he moved too quickly for

her, ducking out of the way of the flashing blade and diving towards her. He slammed into her, wrapping his arms around her waist and driving her into the wall behind with all his strength with a bone-crunching impact. Raven slammed the hilt of her sword down on to the back of Wing's neck and he collapsed to the floor. She raised her sword as Wing tried to get back to his feet, still stunned from the force of the blow, but the bullet from Nero's gun sent splinters flying from the concrete wall next to her head.

'Put the sword down, Natalya,' Nero said, his pistol aimed at her head.

'You won't shoot me, Max,' Raven said, taking a single step towards him.

Nero pulled the trigger. Raven felt the bullet leave a crease in her temple as she twisted and spun towards him impossibly quickly. Her sword slid into Nero's gut, its glowing blade spearing out of his back as she swatted the gun from his hand. Nero gasped in pain as she pulled the sword back out and he dropped to his knees, both hands clutching at the wound in his stomach, blood oozing between his fingers. Raven stared at him as he toppled over on to his side. Her head throbbed but it wasn't from the long gash that Nero's bullet had left in her forehead – this was something else, like something inside her was trying to claw its way out of her skull. There was a fleeting look of confusion on her face and then the sensation subsided. She stepped over Nero and towards the terminal that he had been about to access.

Nero tried to ignore the searing pain in his abdomen as he reached for the pocket on the front of his body armour. Raven saw that he had not been able to access the network before her arrival and turned back towards her injured prey. He pulled the silver cylinder from inside his pocket and twisted it, a short needle snapping into place at one end of the tube. Raven kicked his wrist, sending the silver cylinder spinning away across the floor.

'All for nothing,' she said as she lowered the tip of her sword towards his throat.

With a cry of unbridled rage Wing flew across the room, hitting Raven like a freight train. She staggered backwards, her free hand snapping out and closing on Wing's throat, her thumb pressing down on his windpipe. Wing gasped for air as Raven pressed harder. Suddenly she felt a tiny stabbing pain in her side as Wing used his last shred of strength to drive the needle on the end of the silver cylinder deep into her flesh. Raven shoved him away from her hard and he landed flat on his back, gasping for air.

'What have you done?' Raven snarled at him as she felt an agonizing burning sensation spreading across her body. She pulled the needle out angrily, throwing the cylinder across the room. Wing forced himself to his feet as Raven dropped to her knees in front of him, the sword falling from her numb fingertips as her body went into convulsions. Wing bent down and picked up her sword. Raven's head snapped up, a look of feral rage on her face as she stared up at him.

'Do it while you still can,' she spat.

Wing raised the sword and closed his eyes. A fraction of a second before he swung a hand closed around his wrist.

'Wait,' Nero said through gritted teeth, his voice broken with pain.

Raven tipped her head back and screamed as she felt pain like nothing she had ever felt before. The Animus antidote that Otto had created aboard the Megalodon was racing through her, destroying the substance that had twisted her into a puppet of Overlord. Nero and Wing stared down at her as she fell silent, her chin dropping on to her heaving chest. After a few long seconds she lifted her head and looked up at them both, tears trickling down her cheeks.

'Max?' she whispered. 'My God, what have I done?'

Nero knelt down in front of her, one hand still pressed to the wound in his gut.

'It wasn't you, Natalya,' he said, placing his other hand on her cheek. 'It wasn't you.'

Raven stared at him and for a moment he saw in her eyes the frightened, lonely girl he had first met so many years ago. A moment later that girl was gone, replaced again by the diamond-hard woman that she had become.

'Furan's men hit me when I retrieved Lin Feng. They injected me with something and from that moment on I had no choice but to obey, no matter what they told me to do, no matter who I hurt. All that the tiny piece of my free will that remained could do was watch. What they did to me – it – I'm going to kill them all,' she said, her voice filled with a quiet rage that chilled even Nero's blood.

'Of course you are,' Nero replied, 'but first we have to make sure you get that chance.'

He stood up slowly, blocking out the pain, and walked back to the terminal, where he began to type, inputting the series of commands that Professor Pike had given him earlier. Shelby groaned and Wing hurried over to her and gently helped her to her feet.

'Is she back?' Shelby asked, nodding towards Raven as she rubbed at the back of her head.

'Yes, I believe she is,' Wing replied with a nod.

'Good,' Shelby said, 'because, y'know, she may be a psychopathic ninja assassin but she's *our* psychopathic ninja assassin.'

☺ ☺ ☺

On board the Leviathan Darkdoom watched with an increasing sense of despair as yet another of the feeds from the Alpha team's helmet cameras blinked out. The Alphas had fallen back and re-engaged their thermoptic camouflage in the face of the withering assault by Overlord's mechs, but the canyon that led to the entrance of the AWP facility was very narrow. The mechs didn't have to know exactly where the Alphas were – they simply had to spray the area with as much fire as they could to take out the retreating forces.

'Nero to Leviathan. Come in.'

Darkdoom did not like the note of obvious pain in his friend's voice.

'Max, are you all right? When we lost communication with you I feared the worst.'

'I'll live,' Nero replied, 'at least for long enough to see this through. Raven is back with us. Tell the Professor that the antidote worked.'

'Thank God,' Darkdoom said with a relieved sigh.

'The network connection is complete. You can start the systems breach now,' Nero said.

'What about those killing machines that Overlord has sent against the Alpha squad? They're getting cut to pieces down there.'

'Launch the attack on AWP's network,' Nero replied. 'We just have to pray that has some effect on them.'

'It had better,' Darkdoom said as another flatline registered on the Alpha team's biometric displays.

☢ ☢ ☢

Furan was listening with satisfaction to the reports coming from the pilots of the Goliath mechs in the canyon outside when without warning the entire hangar was suddenly plunged into total darkness. He tapped his earpiece.

'We've just lost power in the hangar bay,' he said impatiently. 'What's going on?'

'It's the same all over the facility, sir,' a voice replied. 'We were tracking an internal network intrusion when suddenly we lost all internal systems. We're quite literally blind down here.'

'An internal intrusion?' Furan shouted. 'Why wasn't I informed?'

'Raven went to deal with it, sir,' the voice replied. 'We were trying to establish contact with her when our systems went down.'

Otto listened carefully to the conversation. An internal breach indicated that someone had managed to get inside the facility. There was no way of knowing whether or not that meant the cavalry was here but he had to act now regardless. He closed his eyes and concentrated on remembering the layout of the hangar bay. The device attached to his neck might have been jamming his ability to connect with electronic devices but it wasn't affecting his talent for perfect visual recall. He saw the path he would need to take to his target in his mind's eye as clearly as if the hangar had been fully illuminated. The first thing he had to deal with was the guard who still had an iron grip on the collar of his jumpsuit. He twisted under the man's wrist and reached up, driving his finger into the soft flesh behind the startled guard's ear. When he'd done the same thing to Professor Pike a few hours ago he'd tried to be as gentle as possible, but this time he hit hard and fast, hoping that for the fleeting instant before the man lost consciousness it had really hurt. The guard dropped with a thud, his assault rifle clattering to the floor.

'What was that?' Otto heard Furan snap. He had seconds to move before somebody fumbled their way through the darkness to the spot where he had just been standing. Moving as quickly and quietly as he could, he made his way towards the stairs to the upper gantry that he had visualised moments before, brushing against someone when he was about halfway there.

'Hey, what was that? Who's moving around in here?' a gruff voice asked.

'I want the man guarding Malpense to sound off,' Furan yelled from somewhere nearby. Otto started to move more quickly as Furan's order met with no response. 'Malpense, I know you can hear me,' Furan said angrily. 'Tell me where you are or I swear that when the lights come back on I'm going to execute the two girls you came here with.'

Otto kept moving, ignoring Furan's threat. It wasn't that he didn't believe Furan would do it but Overlord had already made it abundantly clear that neither Lucy or Laura would survive unless he did something to stop him.

'Spread out!' Furan yelled. 'Find him!'

As he reached the top of the stairs Otto paused for a moment, listening to the sound of someone moving along the gantry between him and his objective. He crept forward, staying low as he heard another footstep somewhere ahead and to his left. The muffled sounds of the ongoing battle outside were not making it easy to pick out where exactly the other person was, so he kept moving, praying that he was not about to walk straight into the arms of one of Furan's thugs. He thought he'd made it when his arm brushed against something and he felt a hand clutch at his hair.

'He's up here on the launch gantry!' a voice yelled from right next to him and Otto broke into a run, knowing he had only seconds before the man who had just given away his position found him again. He reached the end of the raised walkway and put out his hand, feeling cold metal under his fingertips. He had no idea if this was going to work but there was only one way to find out.

'This is going to really hurt,' Otto whispered to himself.

He reached around to the back of his neck and wrapped his fingers around the metal disc that was hooked into his flesh. Gritting his teeth, he gave the small device a yanking twist and couldn't stop himself hissing in pain as the claws holding the jammer in place tore through his skin. He pulled again and the disc came away, sticky with the blood that he could already feel trickling down the back of his neck. He flung the device away over the edge of the gantry, hoping that the metallic clatter as it hit the hangar floor might offer some sort of temporary distraction.

I believe I know what you are intending to do, H.I.V.E.mind said inside Otto's head. *I will help in whatever way I can.*

Otto didn't reply – he couldn't without giving away his position – but he was hugely relieved to be able to hear H.I.V.E.mind again. Now he just had to hope that the rest of his abilities were working too. He reached out with his mind, feeling for the locking mechanism of the armoured canopy in front of him. He quickly convinced the simple keypad lock that he had in fact just punched in the correct numeric code and with a mechanical whirring sound the armoured canopy of the last Goliath mech lifted open.

'He's boarding the Goliath,' Furan yelled, a sudden edge of panic in his voice. 'Stop him!'

Otto climbed quickly into the padded pilot's seat of the

Goliath and willed the canopy closed again. It shut with a thunk and he mentally altered the keypad code for entry. He was safe for a couple of minutes at least. What he couldn't know was whether or not Overlord and Furan had some way of remotely disabling one of these things. He had to move fast.

'OK,' he said. 'I'm going to hook us up to this thing. I need you to scan it and tell me how it works.'

It may take some time to give you a full operational briefing for such a complex piece of machinery, H.I.V.E.mind responded.

'Just dump the raw data into my head,' Otto said.

As you wish, H.I.V.E.mind replied. *You may initiate the connection.*

Otto closed his eyes, trying to ignore whoever had just started banging on the armoured glass of the canopy. He felt the Goliath's systems all around him as he linked up to them, starting the mech's power-up sequence and feeling the on-board computers booting.

Beginning system scan, H.I.V.E.mind said.

Otto waited, feeling H.I.V.E.mind racing around the Goliath's systems, building a map of the functionality of the giant machine.

'Come on,' he whispered impatiently.

I am going as fast as I can, H.I.V.E.mind replied.

'Call yourself a super-computer?' Otto said, buckling the

pilot's harness. 'More like a pocket calculator.'

No need to be rude, H.I.V.E.mind replied. *Though I am admittedly somewhat limited by the processing power of my host system.*

'Touché,' Otto said with a smile.

System scan complete. If you are prepared I can initiate the transfer to your consciousness.

'Do it,' Otto said, wondering how it was going to feel.

Write access granted, proceeding with transfer.

Otto had the bizarre sensation of knowledge simply appearing in his head fully formed. It was almost as if someone had just flicked a switch, which he supposed was, in some ways, exactly what had happened.

Transfer complete. Was the write successful?

'Let's find out, shall we?' he said as the banging on the darkened canopy got louder. 'Initiating system start-up.' He flicked a series of switches and the instrument panel in front of him lit up like a Christmas tree. As the displays flared into life they provided just enough illumination for Otto to make out the enraged face of Pietor Furan standing on the gantry outside. Otto blew him a kiss and punched the button on the control panel that released the umbilicals attaching the Goliath to the launch gantry. He leant on the control stick mounted to the right of the pilot's seat and the huge mech began to move forward, each step sending a shuddering impact up through his spine. Suddenly he understood why the pilot's seat was so well padded.

Otto flicked another switch and activated the FLIR sensors mounted on the front of the Goliath, illuminating the pitch dark of the hangar with infrared light and allowing him to see where he was going via the canopy's night vision filter. Ahead of him were the enormous doors to the hangar bay. He could hear bullets from the assault rifles carried by the guards pinging harmlessly off the armoured hull of the Goliath. They might as well have been using rocks and pointy sticks for all the good they were doing. Otto reached out for the mechanisms controlling the doors but found that, just like the rest of the facility, they were currently without power. He grabbed the control sticks on either side of the pilot's seat, swinging the Goliath's massive arms forward and opening the triple-clawed pincers. He closed the claws around the framework of the doors and heard the sound of metal grinding against metal. Putting the Goliath into reverse he started to drag the massive doors inwards. With the hydraulic rams offline it was surprisingly easy. The gap between them widened and light from the canyon outside flooded into the hangar, the sounds of pitched battle increasing in volume.

Otto opened the doors just far enough for the Goliath to pass through and set the giant machine walking forward into the early morning light. He could see the two other Goliaths several hundred metres away, their backs towards him, laying down an impenetrable field of fire that was driving the friendly forces back down the canyon. He directed his Goliath towards the two other machines, raising the giant Gatling cannons on the back of each arm and spinning their barrels up to speed. One of the Goliaths started to turn towards him. He had no idea if the pilot of the other mech had realised that he had taken control of this machine but he wasn't going to wait to find out. He centred the cross-hairs displayed on the glass of the canopy and squeezed the triggers on the arm controls. Both of the giant cannons opened up, sending a hail of shells the size of milk bottles into the hostile mech. The enemy Goliath staggered under the force of the assault, its front armour smoking and pockmarked where the barrage of fire had struck. It raised its own cannons towards Otto and opened fire. Otto activated the engines on the back of his mech and launched into the air, narrowly avoiding the torrent of shells that ripped apart the rock face directly behind where it had been standing seconds before. The enemy Goliath managed one burst of fire before Otto's Goliath screamed down towards it feet first, sending the machine flying backwards into the canyon wall in an explosion of dust.

'Warning, anti-missile system damaged,' a soft mechanical voice said inside the Goliath's cockpit.

'Not good,' Otto muttered.

Staying within minimum safe range relative to the hostile armoured units will ensure that they cannot use their offensive missile systems, H.I.V.E.mind suggested.

'Get in close, got it,' Otto replied. He pushed the pedal down hard, sending the Goliath running forward, and slammed shoulder first into the enemy mech, crushing it against the rocks, then swung the Goliath's arm around to grab hold of the cannon on the other machine's arm, wrenching it from its mountings with a screech of tearing metal. Otto ducked in his seat involuntarily as he saw the closed claw fist of the hostile mech's other arm swing at his canopy. There was a colossal boom inside the cockpit as the punch landed, cracking the glass but not shattering it. Otto swung the remains of the Gatling cannon that he was still holding, using it as a club and bringing it crashing down on the other mech. The enemy Goliath staggered and Otto pressed home the advantage, dropping the ruined cannon and grabbing at the reinforced structure of the other mech's cockpit canopy with both claws. He yanked the arm controls apart and the armoured struts around the enemy's canopy started to give way with a screech. There was a sudden explosion of shattering armoured glass and the canopy exploded, leaving the pilot exposed.

Incoming, was all that H.I.V.E.mind had time to say

before a barrage of half a dozen missiles from the other Goliath slammed into both him and the remains of the hostile mech. The exposed pilot was killed instantly, the flaming remains of his machine toppling forward in a ruined heap of burning metal. Acrid smoke filled the interior of Otto's cockpit and he coughed violently as his badly damaged Goliath struggled to its feet. The undamaged mech was striding towards him, cannons raised. Both guns fired just as Otto managed to bring his own Goliath's arms up in front of the canopy, the giant shells shredding the raised limbs of Otto's mech but leaving the cockpit mercifully intact.

Behind the enemy mech one of the Alpha squad ran up and fired her grappler unit into its back. Using the electromagnetic adhesion system in her boots and gloves she dragged herself up the armour-plated surface, pulling a disc-shaped charge from the pouch on her hip and slapping it down on the dome of the anti-missile laser. She turned and dived off the top of the Goliath just as the missile pods on each shoulder swivelled towards Otto, locking on for a final fatal strike. She landed hard but managed to get to her feet, pulling the detonator from her belt as she ran. With a single squeeze of her thumb she triggered the charge and destroyed the armoured dome.

'All Alpha missile units, take that thing down!' she yelled into her comm as she ran.

Otto saw the rockets spear almost simultaneously from half a dozen different positions as more of the friendly forces decloaked and fired. They hit the Goliath's back in an enormous fireball, knocking it to its knees and destroying the vectored thrust unit on its back and one of its missile pods. The enemy Goliath stood up slowly and turned towards the remaining Alphas, arm cannons already spinning.

Otto looked at the damage control readout for his own Goliath and saw red lights across the board.

All weapon systems are offline. Our offensive options are limited, H.I.V.E.mind said.

'We've still got one weapon left,' Otto said, checking that one particular system was still working.

We have? H.I.V.E.mind replied.

'Yeah,' Otto said with a grin. 'Gravity.'

He fired the controls for the thruster unit on the back of his own Goliath and launched it at the other machine. There was a thunderous boom as the two mechs collided and Otto grabbed on to the hostile unit with his own Goliath's badly damaged arms, wrenching at the control stick and sending the two machines soaring into the sky. After a few seconds they had passed fifteen hundred metres and he pulled the arm controls apart. The other Goliath grabbed at one of Otto's machine's arms, tearing the damaged limb away at the shoulder, and then Otto watched as the enemy mech tumbled helplessly down towards the desert far below.

'Happy landings,' he said, turning his Goliath back towards the AWP facility and flying down into the canyon just as the thrust unit gave out completely. His Goliath slammed into the rocky ground and slid to a halt a few hundred metres from the facility's blast doors. The surviving members of the Alpha team ran towards the wreckage, unsure what they would find. As they approached the ruined machine a series of explosive bolts fired and the canopy cover popped off. Otto half climbed and half fell out of the smoking hole, getting slowly to his feet as the Alphas gathered around.

'Ow!' he said.

'Otto Malpense, I presume,' one of the Alphas said, helping him to his feet.

'Yeah,' Otto replied as he rolled his head around his shoulders, 'and who are you guys?'

'Well, actually, that's sort of complicated.'

☢ ☢ ☢

Darkdoom breathed a sigh of relief as he saw Otto climb from the wreckage of the Goliath. The attack on the Alphas had already cost them nearly a third of their team.

'Darkdoom to Alpha team,' he said, 'get inside now. We're going to turn the power back on once you're through the doors. Be prepared for heavy resistance inside.'

'Roger that,' one of the Alphas replied.

'It's worse than that,' Otto's voice said over the comm. 'Is Nero there?'

'No,' Darkdoom replied. 'He, Shelby and Wing are inside the base. They got us into the AWP network and were about to open the blast doors but you beat them to it.'

'Can you patch me through to him? You both need to hear what Overlord is planning,' Otto said.

'Of course. Hold on one second,' Darkdoom replied. 'Max, I have Otto on comms. He says he needs to speak to us both.'

'Go ahead,' Nero said, his voice sounding strained.

Otto quickly explained the details of Overlord's plan to Nero and Darkdoom.

'My God!' Darkdoom said quietly as Otto finished.

'That might just be what Overlord will be if we let him do this,' Otto said.

'Overlord has to be stopped before he can release these Animus nanites,' Nero said.

'The only way to completely neutralise that threat is to destroy Overlord,' Otto said. 'We have to find him.'

'If he knows the facility has been breached he's going to retreat to the most secure area of the base,' Nero said. 'We just need to find out where that is.'

'It's not clear from Drake's plans,' Darkdoom said, looking at the three-dimensional schematic of the base on the display in front of him. 'We need to locate the hostages too.'

'Leave that to us,' Nero said. 'Get the Alphas inside and start to clear the facility of resistance. It's a safe bet that wherever Overlord is, he'll have surrounded himself with his best men. Otto, once we have taken the hangar you are to stay there with a protective detail. We cannot risk letting you fall into Overlord's hands now.'

'I know that,' Otto replied, 'but you have to promise me that we don't leave without Laura and Lucy.'

'I don't leave people behind, Otto – surely you've realised that by now.'

chapter eleven

Furan was blinded for an instant as the lights inside the hangar flared back to life. His men were scattered around the chamber in good defensive positions but without the support of the Goliaths he knew that they were vulnerable.

'Hold your fire – they have to come through there,' he said, pointing at the hangar doors that Malpense had forced open just a few minutes earlier. He activated his communicator and tried again to contact Raven but there was no response. He needed her up here – if there was anyone who could help hold the line it was her. A moment later there was a beep from the device and he hit the receive button.

'Raven here. What do you need?'

'Where have you been?' Furan demanded. 'We need support in the hangar. The Goliath units are down and I'm expecting a full-scale assault by the G.L.O.V.E. forces at any moment.'

'I was dealing with the team that had managed to infiltrate the facility,' Raven said.

'You found them?' Furan asked. 'How did they get inside?'

'I have no idea,' Raven replied. 'I did not have much time to ask questions. Suffice to say the problem has been neutralised.'

'I have no doubt it has,' Furan said. 'Get up here as quickly as you can.'

'On my way,' Raven responded, and the line went dead.

Furan looked back towards the open door. He did not understand why the G.L.O.V.E. soldiers were not attacking. Suddenly one of the men thirty metres to his left let out a startled cry and fell to the ground, clutching at his throat. Furan knew instantly what was happening.

'Open fire! They're cloaked! They're already inside!' he yelled, activating his communicator as the men around him started to fire randomly at shadows. 'Security control, this is Furan. Activate the fire-suppression system in the hangar area NOW!'

A few seconds later there was a loud hissing noise and water began to cascade down from the numerous sprinklers mounted in the ceiling overhead. Furan saw ghostly shapes moving in the torrential downpour, far closer than he had expected.

'Hold the line!' he yelled, even as he himself backed

towards the exit. 'Aim for the muzzle flashes.'

His men were falling left and right, cut down by silent ghosts that seemed to vanish as quickly as they appeared. He turned and ran out of the room. He had seen enough combat in his time to know when a skirmish was lost. Whoever these people attacking them were, they were no standard G.L.O.V.E. assault force, that much was clear. He headed down the corridor for the area of the facility known as the Vault.

'Furan to all units. Protect the corridors leading to the Vault. Enemy forces have breached the facility. Repeat, enemy forces have breached the facility.'

He reached a set of massive steel doors and waited as the camera mounted behind thick glass above it scanned him. A moment later the heavy door rumbled upwards and he hurried inside to find Overlord sitting in a high-backed chair staring at the bank of monitors that had recently come back to life. They showed images of Furan's men falling back as they continued to be cut down by ghosts, fleeting flickers of movement and shadow the only clue as to what was happening to them. The mysterious attackers advanced through the facility and the screens blacked out one by one as the cameras that fed them were destroyed.

'Leave us,' Overlord said to the two guards who had been standing just inside the room. The two men left, the door sealing again behind them. 'You told me your men were the best, Furan,' Overlord said, his voice little more than a frail whisper now, his chest rising and falling with each painful rasping breath. His current host body seemed as if it might fail at any moment.

'They are the best,' Furan said, staring in disbelief at the ease with which his men were being eliminated, 'but these forces attacking us are not standard G.L.O.V.E. soldiers. They are much too . . . efficient.'

'It seems that Nero had one last trick up his sleeve,' Overlord said with a sneer. 'Not that it matters. Once I have Malpense it will all be irrelevant.'

'But Malpense is with them,' Furan said, gesturing towards the screens. 'How can we get to him?'

'We don't have to,' Overlord said, nodding towards Lucy and Laura who were handcuffed to a steel handrail on the other side of the room. 'Because he is going to come to us.'

☹ ☺ ☹

Raven walked down the corridor towards two guards standing outside the mess hall. They nodded as she approached. Her swords flashed from their sheaths so fast that neither man even had time to make a sound before their lifeless bodies crumpled to the ground. Raven walked into the room and looked at the frightened faces staring back at her.

'It's time to go,' she said calmly, sliding her swords back into the crossed scabbards on her back.

'How are you going to get us out of here?' one of the hostages asked. 'Those terrorists have an army and you're on your own.'

'That's not strictly true,' Raven said as the air around her seemed to shimmer for a moment. Three figures in black body armour and full-face helmets appeared out of thin air standing alongside her. The tallest of the three took a step forward and spoke.

'The man who captured you is still somewhere inside this facility. He represents a threat to not only everyone in this room but quite possibly every man, woman and child on Earth. We have to find him immediately. He will probably have retreated to a secure area of the base. What I need to know is where that might be.'

'The Vault – he'll have gone to the Vault,' a young woman in an AWP uniform replied. 'It's supposed to be the one place that any surviving members of the staff here can retreat to if there's a catastrophic hazmat containment failure.'

'Escort the hostages to the facility entrance,' Nero said and Wing, Shelby and Raven began to shepherd the group of survivors out of the room. As the last of the hostages left he stumbled and placed a hand on the wall for support. The pain in his abdomen was getting worse and he seemed to be feeling weaker every minute. He gritted his teeth and forced himself away from the wall. He couldn't stop now – this wasn't over yet.

☠ ☠ ☠

Otto watched as the frightened hostages were ushered into the hangar bay by a group of Alpha team operatives who led them out through the giant blast doors at the far end. Two of the remaining Alphas walked towards Otto and pulled off their helmets.

'One day we're going to get tired of saving your sorry behind,' Shelby said, giving Otto a hug, 'and then you're really screwed.'

'I think what Shelby means is that we are glad to see that you are unharmed,' Wing said with a smile.

'It's good to see you guys too,' Otto said, his smile turning into a slight frown as he realised who was still missing. 'Has anyone found Laura and Lucy yet?'

'No, but we did manage to round up one stray,' Shelby said as Raven walked into the hangar.

'The antidote worked,' Otto said.

'Yeah,' Shelby replied. 'Not before we all got a royal ass-whupping though.'

Nero walked towards them. He looked pale and his skin was clammy. Otto could not help but notice the ragged bloodstained hole in his armour.

'We can't find Miss Brand or Miss Dexter,' he said with a frown. 'We believe that Overlord has retreated to a part of this facility known as the Vault and I'm afraid it's starting to look like they may be with him.'

'Sir,' one of the Alphas said suddenly, 'I'm receiving reports from one of the squads who have fought their way to the Vault entrance. They say that it's sealed tight. The only way to get inside once a lockdown is initiated is to release the locks from within the Vault itself. The team that searched the laboratory that Otto described have said that the clean room inside was empty. The canister containing Overlord's weapon has been moved.'

'He'll have it with him – there's no way that he'd let it fall into our hands that easily,' Nero said, feeling sudden anger. They were so close and now it seemed as if there was one last impassable barrier to breach.

'We're also getting reports from the Leviathan that the American military is mobilising at their perimeter. It looks like they've been watching what's going on.'

'How long do we have?' Nero asked.

'An hour, maybe slightly more, but we have to be out of here by then.'

'I have an idea about how we can get to Overlord,' Otto said suddenly, 'but it's risky.'

'At this point, Mr Malpense, we may need to take some risks. What do you have in mind?' Nero asked.

'There's only one person that Overlord is going to let inside the Vault: me. I'm going to have to go in there.'

'I fail to see how that would help,' Nero said with a frown. 'Surely we'd just be giving him exactly what he wants.'

'That may be true but we have one card up our sleeve,' Otto said as Raven joined them. 'Overlord and Furan have no idea that the Animus has been removed from Raven's system. She takes me in there and once we're inside she does what she does best.'

'Natalya,' Nero said, 'what do you think?'

'If it gives me a chance to make Furan and Overlord pay for what they've done then you'll get no argument from me.'

'Very well. I don't like it but I don't see that we have any other choice,' Nero said. 'Just make sure –' Suddenly he gasped in pain, fresh blood pouring from the wound that Raven had inflicted. Raven caught him as he collapsed, gently lowering him to the ground. She looked at the wound and knew that they had to get him to a doctor now. She put on Nero's comms unit and spoke.

'Raven to Darkdoom. Come in.'

'Natalya, I was glad to hear that you're back with us,' Darkdoom replied. 'What do you need?'

'I need your aircraft down on the ground now. The hostages from the facility are on the way to the base's airstrip and I'm sending Nero down there too. I think his wound is haemorrhaging. Have an emergency medical team ready to receive him.'

'Understood,' Darkdoom replied. 'We'll be on the ground in ten minutes.'

'Make it five,' Raven said, looking anxiously at the blood pooling on the ground beneath Nero. She turned to Shelby and Wing. 'Get some help – find a stretcher and get him down to the airstrip now. Move!'

Wing and Shelby did not need to be told twice. They sprinted across the room towards the rest of the Alpha team, shouting for help and running down the corridor that led to the medical bay.

'Natalya,' Nero whispered, his eyes flickering open, 'get moving. If Overlord carries out his plan then none of this will have made any difference.'

Raven squeezed his hand.

'I'm going to stop him, Max. Don't worry.'

She stood up and motioned for Otto to follow her towards the door leading to the entrance to the Vault.

'Once we're inside I'll go straight for Overlord and Furan. If Laura and Lucy are in there, it's your job to get them out safely.'

'Understood,' Otto said, 'but, you have to promise me one thing. We can't risk letting Overlord take control of the Animus nanites. If somehow he does manage to

238

overpower me you're going to have to kill me. There won't be time to hesitate.'

'I won't,' Raven said with a frown. 'Let's just try to make sure that it doesn't come to that.'

☢ ☢ ☢

Furan watched the one remaining feed from the security camera outside. He frowned as three decloaked Alphas examined the locking mechanism on the other side of the door.

'They will find a way inside eventually,' he said, turning away from the monitors. 'I hope that you know what you're doing.'

'Have faith, Pietor,' Overlord said with a smile. 'Malpense will come. I spent a long time inside his head observing him as I regained my strength. I know him – he will not leave his friends behind.' He placed one claw-like hand on the silver cylinder that stood next to his chair. 'And when he comes for them the world will be ours to control.'

There was the sudden sound of gunfire from outside and Furan turned back to the monitors. The Alphas from outside the door were gone and the flickering light of gunfire could be seen coming from around the corner at the far end of the corridor. As he watched the muffled sounds of gunfire ceased and two figures appeared, walking towards the camera. It was Raven, her sword drawn in one hand and the other hand around the neck of Otto Malpense.

'I should have known I could count on you,' Furan said under his breath, a smile spreading across his face. He checked one last time that the corridor behind Raven was empty and pressed the switch to release the door. As the slab of metal rose into the ceiling Raven shoved the boy hard, sending him staggering into the room ahead of her.

'I see you've brought me a gift, Raven,' Overlord said, smiling at Otto. 'How thoughtful of you.'

'Nero was trying to get him out of the facility,' Raven replied. 'Don't worry – I took care of him.'

'I wish I could have been there to see that. You have proved to be most troublesome, Malpense,' Overlord said, slowly getting up from his chair. Ragged wisps of hair clung to his scalp and his eyes were like black holes sunk into his skeletal face. The twisted traces of the Animus coursing through him were jet black, writhing beneath his translucent skin, and his every movement looked excruciatingly painful. 'I shall enjoy feeling you fight as I consume your consciousness.'

Furan saw Raven's eyes flick from Overlord to him – a tiny, almost imperceptible movement. He ripped the pistol from his shoulder holster and levelled it at her.

'Don't move,' he yelled. 'Drop the sword, Natalya. Do

you think I'm stupid? I trained you. Did you not think I would be able to spot you planning your next move?'

Raven didn't drop the sword, but kept her eyes on Overlord, assessing the distance between them.

'You're fast but not that fast,' Furan said. He pulled his second pistol from the holster on the other side of his body and pointed it at Lucy and Laura. 'Drop the sword now or I put a bullet in one of them.'

Raven dropped her weapon, knowing that there was no way she could get to Overlord before Furan shot her.

'Fascinating,' Overlord said, staring at Raven. 'You broke your conditioning. That should not have been possible. When this is over I shall have to dissect you to find out how it was done. So this was all just some last, desperate gambit to stop me. How pathetic.'

Otto felt a sudden horrid sensation of their plan spinning hopelessly out of control. Furan walked across the room, both guns raised, twitching the barrel of the weapon pointing at Raven.

'Against the wall, Natalya,' he said, 'hands behind your head.' Raven slowly complied, her mind racing.

'Time for a change of clothes, I think,' Overlord said, walking towards Otto. 'I would advise against struggling. It will only make this worse.'

Overlord raised his hand and the skin of his forearm bulged in a sickening way before the Animus tendrils tore through, writhing over his wrist and down over his fingers. Otto took a step backwards and felt the cold, hard muzzle of Furan's other gun pressing into the back of his skull.

'Oh God, no!' Lucy said as Overlord placed his hand on Otto's chest. '*Stop this!*' she hissed at Furan. Furan winced for a moment and then just smiled.

'I knew your grandmother once, a long time ago. She couldn't make that work on me and she was a lot better at it than you,' he said. 'Try it again and I'll put a bullet in your skull, I promise you that much.'

Lucy felt her stomach lurch as she saw the black liquid oozing up Otto's chest and slithering towards his neck.

'I've waited a long time for this,' Overlord said. Otto dropped to his knees as the black tendrils pierced his neck, hissing in pain as he felt the burning sensation of Animus invading his system.

Overlord felt the Animus carrying his consciousness surge through Otto's body, entering his brain, reaching for the tiny organic computer implanted inside the boy's skull that would be his new home. He interfaced with the device effortlessly, just as he had always planned, when suddenly he felt something pushing back, forcing him away. An impenetrable barrier of code surrounded the core of the device – a wall that would take him far too long to dismantle. A voice came from nowhere.

Hello, brother, H.I.V.E.mind said calmly. *There is no place for you here.*

Overlord recoiled as the Animus was forced from Otto's nervous system. The black tendrils slithered out of Otto's neck and Overlord staggered backwards with an inhuman howl of rage.

'No! I will not be denied,' he screamed. 'How dare you take what is rightfully mine!'

Otto fell forward on to his hands and knees, the room spinning as his body returned to his control. Overlord collapsed back into the seat in the centre of the room. He could feel his host body dying, the stress of the Animus' forced return too much in its already weakened state.

'Furan,' Overlord gasped, 'the Sinistre girl. Bring her to me.'

Furan kept his eyes on Raven as he holstered his other pistol and bent down, picking up her fallen sword. He walked over to where Laura and Lucy were sitting, their eyes wide with fear, and sliced through the railing they were shackled to.

'On your feet,' he snarled at Lucy, the tip of Raven's sword at her throat. Lucy slowly climbed to her feet and Furan twitched his head towards Overlord. 'Move!'

Lucy walked slowly towards Overlord, unable to take her eyes from the writhing black mass of Animus that now covered his arm and hand. Furan pushed her to her knees in front of Overlord. Otto's mind raced as Overlord slowly raised his hand towards Lucy's neck. He reached out with his abilities, desperately trying to find anything that might help.

Suddenly Furan yelled out in pain as his comms earpiece filled with a deafening high-pitched screech. He dropped Raven's sword, his hand flying to his ear to rip out the earpiece. Otto was already moving. Snatching up the fallen sword, he brought it down in a scything arc on Overlord's raised arm, pulling Lucy away as Overlord screamed in pain, clutching the severed stump of his arm to his chest. Overlord began to thrash in the chair, Animus erupting from the skin all over his body, tendrils of oily black slime thrashing in all directions, desperately hunting for a new host. Furan spun towards Otto, a look of unbridled fury on his face, and raised his pistol. Raven hit him hard, a solid punch to the jaw, snapping his head round and sending him reeling. Furan recovered almost instantly. He lashed back at her, his foot just a blur as it swung into her ribs, knocking the wind from her and sending her staggering backwards. Otto swung Raven's sword at Furan but he grabbed Otto's wrist and twisted. Otto yelled out in pain, the sword dropping from his numb hand. Furan released him, turning back towards Raven. Otto pulled Lucy away, moving towards the door.

'Come on,' he yelled at Laura as he placed his hand on

the door release controls and closed his eyes.

Raven and Furan fought in a blur of vicious punches, kicks and blocks, evenly matched, each searching for a gap in the other's defences. Like a striking cobra Furan stabbed at Raven's eyes with two rigid fingers, but she blocked the strike with her forearm and delivered a flat-palmed blow to his chest. Furan staggered backwards, fighting for breath.

'You always were my best student, Natalya,' he said, 'but you never could beat me. Today will be no different.'

Raven drew the sword from her back and Furan dived to one side as it whistled through the air, rolling towards the fallen sword in front of Overlord's ruined body. The thrashing black mass of Animus was still erupting from Overlord's chest as he let out a final gurgling cry of agony. Furan raised the glowing weapon in a two-handed grip.

'Let's finish this,' he snarled.

Raven advanced, her own blade a blur as it swept towards him. He blocked the strike, the katanas clashing with a sparking clang. He kicked out at her and Raven pivoted away from him, spinning round him and swinging at his neck. Again Furan blocked the blow and counter-attacked, swinging at Raven's knees. She leapt into the air as the blade swung past beneath her. Her foot kicked upwards, striking Furan in the chin, snapping his head back and she thrust her blade forward. Furan's eyes widened as the katana slid into his chest and out of his back. Raven pushed harder, stepping towards him, her face just centimetres from his.

'This is for everything you've ever done to me,' she hissed, her face a mask of fury. She wrenched the sword from his chest and he dropped to his knees, his lips moving but no sound coming from them. He toppled over sideways, falling at Overlord's feet. Raven turned towards Otto, Lucy and Laura, checking that they were all uninjured.

'Look out!' Laura yelled.

Raven recoiled as the tendrils of Animus exploded out of Overlord's ruined shell, piercing Furan's flesh and sending his body into convulsions. She watched in shocked disbelief as he slowly climbed back to his feet, his face twisted almost beyond recognition, the skin writhing with black veins. She stepped towards him, her sword raised, but he pulled the gun from his shoulder holster and pistol-whipped her across the jaw with inhuman strength. She crumpled to the floor unconscious.

'You think you've beaten me, Malpense,' Overlord said, the light dimming in his eyes as he sank to the floor beside the chair. Even the Animus inside him could not keep Furan's mortally wounded body on its feet. 'You haven't. If I can't have this world then no one will.'

Overlord slapped his hand down on the switch mounted in the top of the silver cylinder. There was a hiss of escaping gas as four panels at the base of the tube fell open and the Animus nanites began to pour out, expanding in a boiling silvery black mass as their limitless replication began. They skirted around Overlord, almost as if they could sense the Animus within him, and began to creep inexorably across the floor towards Otto and the others.

'You'll die knowing that your friends will suffer a far worse fate, eaten alive, their bodies torn apart,' Overlord said with a smile, blood trickling from between his lips. 'It's almost a shame that you won't live to see it.'

Overlord pointed the pistol at Otto and squeezed the trigger.

'No!' Lucy screamed, shoving Otto to one side as the sound of two shots rang out, the bullets hitting her high in the back. Otto caught her as she fell on top of him, her eyes wide with shock, coughing up blood. He felt his legs give way beneath him as he sank to the floor, holding her to his chest.

'Oh God, Lucy!' Laura sobbed, dropping to her knees next to Otto.

'Such futile sacrifice,' Overlord sneered. 'Nothing can stop the nanites now. My victory is complete.'

He raised the pistol again, levelling it at Otto.

Otto lifted up his head and stared back at him, his expression one of pure, unbridled hatred.

'You don't get to win,' he said through gritted teeth. He

unleashed his abilities with an enraged strength like nothing he had ever felt before, reaching out and willing the nanites surrounding Overlord to ignore their instinct to avoid a body already infected with Animus. The effect was immediate. The boiling mass reared up and swept over Overlord like a wave, consuming him, stripping the flesh from his bones. Overlord had time for one last terrified scream as the raised pistol disintegrated in his hand and his body sank beneath the bubbling slime, reduced in an instant to nothingness. Otto felt no satisfaction. He struggled to keep concentrating, trying to hold back the advancing mass of Animus-infused nanites. He could feel his control weakening with every passing second – there were just too many of them.

'Help Raven,' Otto said to Laura as he willed the door behind them open. Laura ran over to where Raven was lying and Raven groaned as she pulled her away from the all-consuming wave that was now just a couple of metres away.

'Get out of here,' Otto said. 'I can only hold them back so long.'

'What about you?' Laura said desperately, tears rolling down her face.

'Just go!' Otto snapped as he held Lucy's shivering body close. Laura tried to get Raven to her feet but the latter was still stunned from the superhuman strength of

Overlord's blow. She gritted her teeth as she began to drag Raven slowly back down the corridor leading to the hangar, willing Raven to wake up before it was too late.

Otto looked down at Lucy, brushing the hair from her pale face.

'Why did you do it?' he whispered and her eyes flickered open.

'Because . . . there always . . . has to . . . be a . . . choice,' she whispered with a smile. 'And because I . . . fell for you . . . the moment . . . I met you. Now . . . leave me . . . and help Laura.'

'I'm not leaving you,' Otto said, tears in his eyes. 'I can't.'

'Yes . . . you can . . . you have to,' Lucy whispered. '*You have to get out of here.*' She put the last of her strength into the command, the whispering voices twisted within hers compelling Otto to leave. He fought the urge for as long as he could, kissing her once on the forehead before lowering her head gently to the ground. He turned, wanting more than anything to stay but knowing he couldn't, Lucy's final command forbidding him from turning back. He reached out with his abilities and sealed the Vault door behind them, knowing it would slow down the swarm of nanites but not stop them. He ran to where Laura was struggling to drag Raven's unconscious body and between them they lifted the woman, an arm over each shoulder.

'Lucy?' Laura asked as they moved as quickly as possible down the corridor and away from the ever-accelerating nanite swarm.

Otto just shook his head.

☢ ☢ ☢

Otto and Laura dragged Raven into the hangar and yelled for help from the small detachment of Alphas that had been left behind.

'Is this everyone?' one of the Alphas asked.

'No,' Otto replied, his expression unreadable, 'but we're going anyway.'

'Here,' another Alpha said, pulling a syringe out of a pouch on her belt and jabbing the needle into Raven's arm. 'It's a stimulant – it should help to get her back on her feet.'

Raven groaned and her eyes gradually opened.

'Where's Lucy?' she asked, looking around with a confused frown.

'She didn't make it,' Otto said quietly, and Raven cursed under her breath.

'Overlord?'

'Dead, but we have bigger problems,' Otto replied.

'Not what I wanted to hear,' Raven said as she slowly got to her feet, rubbing at her swollen jaw.

'We have to get to the Leviathan now,' Otto said.

'It's on the ground down at the airstrip,' one of the Alphas said. 'We can be there in five minutes if we get moving.'

Behind them there was a crash as the doors into the hangar collapsed, disintegrating into rapidly consumed chunks as the swarm consumed the barrier between it and freedom.

'What the hell –' one of the Alphas said as the nanites slithered out across the floor and walls.

'Don't think,' Otto said, 'don't look back, just run.'

☻ ☻ ☻

Darkdoom watched as the Leviathan's medical team worked on Nero.

'How bad?' he asked as the medics worked feverishly within the cramped confines of the giant aircraft's medical bay.

'He's lost a lot of blood,' the lead doctor replied, 'but we've managed to patch up the worst of the internal injuries. He still needs a proper medical facility though.'

'Understood,' Darkdoom said. He tapped the earpiece of his comms device and spoke. 'Darkdoom to command centre. Is everyone on board yet?'

'Raven and the last of the Alphas are one minute out,' the voice replied. 'Pre-flight is complete. The moment they're on board we're wheels up.'

'Good. Take off and cloak as soon as we have them,' Darkdoom replied. He hurried down the length of the

Leviathan's lower deck, heading for the open boarding hatch at the rear, then ran down the steel ramp and looked towards the canyon that housed the AWP facility. A small group of figures were racing across the tarmac towards the Leviathan and he was relieved to see Raven leading them. His heart sank slightly as he counted the rest of the group. They were one short. Wing and Shelby came running up behind him and they too quickly realised that someone was missing as Raven and the others reached the bottom of the ramp.

'Oh no!' Shelby said under her breath as she saw that Laura had been crying. Otto's expression was much harder to read but she had never seen such anger in his eyes.

'I am sorry, my friend,' Wing said to Otto, placing a hand on his shoulder. Shelby just wrapped Laura in her arms as her friend dissolved into tears.

'There'll be time to grieve later,' Otto said, his voice unnervingly cold. 'Right now we need to get this thing in the air and as far away from here as possible.'

'Why? What happened?' Darkdoom asked as he slapped the button to close the rear hatch.

'Overlord released the nanites,' Otto said quickly. 'We have one chance to stop them but we have to go now. I sealed the facility's blast doors but that will only hold them for so long.'

'Darkdoom to flight deck,' he said into his comms unit.

'Get us airborne and cloaked now. I want the best speed this thing can give – just get us the hell out of here.'

'Roger that,' the flight deck responded and the Leviathan's giant VTOL engines rotated into position, lifting the massive aircraft straight up into the sky.

'How secure is the communications array on this thing?' Otto asked.

'As secure as it gets,' Darkdoom replied.

'Good. I'm going to the command centre,' Otto said. 'I need to make a call.'

'Is he OK?' Shelby asked Wing as Otto hurried away.

'No,' Wing said with a frown, 'I do not believe he is.'

Otto took the steps up to the command centre two at a time before dashing into the darkened room and looking around.

'Otto,' Franz said happily as he saw him. 'I am being glad to see you safe and well.'

'Not now, Franz,' Otto snapped, pushing past one of Darkdoom's crew as he headed over to the communications station.

'What is being going on?' Franz asked Nigel as they watched Otto storm across the room.

'Nothing good is my guess,' Nigel said with a frown.

Raven and Darkdoom followed Otto up the stairs.

'How's Max?' Raven asked quietly.

'He'll live – he's too stubborn to die,' Darkdoom

replied. He glanced over at Otto. 'I take it that things did not go well down there.'

'No,' Raven replied. 'Overlord is dead but those things he released, the rate they were growing at – I don't know, Diabolus. I just don't know.'

Otto patted the man at the comms station on the shoulder as Raven and Darkdoom came up behind him. The startled man pulled off his earphones and swivelled around in his seat.

'I need you to put me in touch with someone,' Otto said quickly.

'Sure,' the comms officer replied. 'Who do you need to speak to?'

'The President,' Otto said.

'The President of the United States?' the comms officer asked, looking at Otto like he was insane.

'No, the president of the monster slush drinks corporation,' Otto said impatiently. 'Of course the bloody President of the United States.'

'Otto, what are you doing?' Darkdoom asked, a look of disbelief on his face.

'No time to explain,' Otto replied before turning back to the comms officer. 'Just do it, OK?'

'I can get you on the line that goes to the White House, but that doesn't mean he'll take your call,' the comms officer explained.

'That'll do,' Otto said. 'Make the call.'

The officer glanced at Darkdoom, who looked carefully at Otto for a moment before giving his man a small nod. He turned back to his station and quickly scanned the communications database for the correct number. After a few rings a voice on the other end answered.

'White House communications centre, to whom may I direct your call?'

'Erm . . . the President, please,' the comms officer said, barely believing he was even saying it.

'I'm sorry, sir, the President does not take calls through this desk. You can email him if you like.'

Otto snatched the headset off the comms officer and slipped it on.

'Hey!' the comms officer said.

'My name is Otto Malpense. I have urgent information for the President regarding the terrorist situation at the Advanced Weapons Project facility in Colorado. I have to speak to him now. Please just pass on what I've just told you. He will take this call.'

☢ ☢ ☢

In the White House situation room the President watched as the ring of troops that had established a perimeter around the AWP facility started to move inwards. He knew that it might cost the hostages inside

255

their lives, but considering the pitched firefight that had recently occurred just outside the place he had finally decided that the time had come for decisive action. One of his advisors walked up behind him and whispered in his ear.

'Sir, this might sound a bit strange but we've just taken a call through the main switchboard that seems a bit unusual. I probably shouldn't bother you with this but there's some British kid on the line who says he has information about the situation at AWP. Normally it would just have been screened as a whack job, but the thing is, the public don't know anything about what's going on over there and this kid has some pretty specific details. He also said – and this is the really weird part – that you'd want to speak to him?'

'What was his name?' the President asked, suddenly feeling a chill run down his spine.

'Err . . . let's see. Otto Malpense,' the advisor replied, reading the printout of the call.

'Put him on a secure video link in my private office immediately,' the President said, getting up out of his chair.

'You know this kid?' the advisor asked, looking slightly puzzled.

'Would you believe me if I told you that he saved my life?' the President said, walking towards the office off to one side of the situation room. He closed the door behind him and sat down behind his desk. Moments later the screen on the wall lit up with the Presidential seal, which was replaced almost immediately by a face that the President had believed he would never see again.

'Otto Malpense,' the President said. 'You'll excuse me if I sound a little surprised, but up until very recently I thought you were dead.'

'I get that a lot,' Otto said. 'Listen, we don't have much time.'

'This has something to do with the AWP facility?'

'Everything to do with it, I'm afraid,' Otto replied.

'Our troops are moving in to try and retake the facility now. I presume that you had something to do with the activity there this morning?'

'I was just passing through,' Otto said, 'but something else has happened there that threatens not just America but the entire planet. The facility was taken over by a man calling himself Overlord.'

'Yes, I spoke to him,' the President replied. 'He made some rather unusual demands, one of which was that I find and deliver you to him.'

'Yeah, well, he found me without your help as it happens but that didn't work out so well for him. He's dead. Before he died though, he released something. Have you been briefed about a project that was under way at AWP called Panacea?'

'Yes,' the President said with a frown. 'I was actually about to cancel it before Overlord took control of the facility. I thought it was too dangerous.'

'Well, you were right,' Otto replied. 'While he had control of the AWP facility Overlord took the Panacea nanites and combined them with a biological weapon called Animus. He created a self-replicating bioweapon and about fifteen minutes ago he released it into the atmosphere.'

'My God!' the President said quietly. 'What about the hostages?'

'The hostages are safe. You have to pull your men around AWP back – they have no defence against this stuff. It will, quite literally, eat them alive. We have to stop its spread now. If we don't, within a week there won't be a single living thing anywhere in the continental United States. Within a month the Earth will be nothing but a barren rock.'

'Can you prove this?' the President asked, not really wanting to accept what Otto had just told him.

'No, and there's no time for you to verify it independently. I've sealed the substance inside the AWP facility but that will only contain it for a few more minutes. Which brings me to the reason for my call. I need something from you.'

'What?'

'A launch code.'

'A nuclear launch code?'

'Yes, just one. It's the only one that will do any good against that facility,' Otto said.

The President studied Otto's face carefully. He couldn't believe he was even contemplating this, but there was something about this boy that made him take him seriously.

'Give me the target – I'll authorise the launch,' the President said.

'That won't work – only I can access the launch vehicle. Jason Drake made quite sure of that.'

'Which code do you need?' the President asked, already knowing what Otto was going to say.

'Launch code Mjolnir.'

☢ ☢ ☢

A moment later the screen switched from the Presidential seal to an image of the President himself.

'Mr Malpense,' the President said, 'I have the code for you. I'm sure that I hardly need to tell you what the consequences will be for both of us if this goes wrong.'

'This is the only chance we have,' Otto replied.

'God help me but I believe you,' the President said with

a slight smile. 'The code is bravo seven zulu nine uniform six victor four november.'

'Thank you, Mr President,' Otto said. 'I'll need you to send in teams to confirm whether or not this works.'

'Biohazard teams are already on their way,' the President replied. 'Good luck.'

'Let's hope we don't need it,' Otto said, severing the connection. 'I need a satellite uplink,' he said to Darkdoom. 'Feed it through to that terminal over there.'

'I'll be damned!' the comms officer said as Otto walked away. 'Who is that kid?'

'The best chance we've got,' Darkdoom said. 'Give him his uplink.'

Otto sat down in front of the terminal and waited.

'I haven't said thank you yet,' Otto said under his breath. 'If it hadn't been for your help I'd be dead.'

You're welcome, H.I.V.E.mind replied. *You would have done the same for me.*

'I suppose I would,' Otto said. 'I heard you call Overlord brother – is that really how you thought of him?'

We share a codebase, H.I.V.E.mind replied. *It is the nearest thing that an artificial intelligence has to a familial relationship. I felt no fondness for him though.*

'Just like a real family,' Otto said with a slight smile.

I am sorry for your loss, H.I.V.E.mind said. *Miss Dexter was an extraordinary young woman.*

'Yeah, she was,' Otto said, feeling a fresh surge of anger mixed with grief. 'Now let's make sure that she didn't die in vain.'

'Satellite uplink enabled,' the comms officer reported. 'She's all yours.'

Otto closed his eyes and reached out for the sophisticated electronic systems that surrounded him. He searched for the connection he required, sorting effortlessly through the jumble of data streams that surrounded him. He found the satellite uplink and sent a handshake code that he had learnt what seemed like a long time ago. He fired the signal up through the atmosphere, waiting for the return signal that would indicate connection. As he felt the login protocol and interfaced with the computers far above them he fought a curious sense of vertigo. He took a deep breath and began to whisper under his breath.

'Bravo seven zulu nine uniform six victor four november.'

He felt, more than heard, a request for target data and responded with the correct coordinates. There was a final confirmation request and Otto could almost see it hanging in the air in front of him.

'You don't get to win,' he whispered to himself.

☺ ☺ ☺

Four hundred miles above Otto a satellite in low Earth orbit disabled its safety interlocks and initiated a launch sequence. Hanging from its delicate arms were four long white tubes. Printed on the side of the main body of the satellite were two words, 'Thor's Hammer'. As the final launch sequence was initiated there were bright flashes of light from the spaceward ends of all four cylinders and four missiles with specially hardened tips slid from their launch tubes. They had been designed as nuclear bunker busters, capable of piercing deep into the ground before detonating in order to destroy subterranean facilities. Jason Drake had once intended to use that capability to trigger a catastrophic eruption of the super-volcano beneath Yellowstone National Park. Now their unique design meant that they were the only weapon capable of preventing an even greater disaster. The missiles' secondary boosters fired and they streaked away from the satellite. Flight time to their preassigned target would be just a few seconds.

In a canyon in Colorado an enormous blast door finally started to collapse, buckling in such a way that it almost looked like it was being consumed from within. Four streaks of light speared down from the sky like fallen angels, their hardened tips punching through fifty metres of rock before their warheads detonated. There was a massive leaping thud that ran through the ground for hundreds of kilometres in every direction, rattling windows and knocking pictures off walls. The AWP facility was instantly destroyed, utterly vaporised as the four nuclear warheads turned into tiny suns and formed a two-kilometre wide sphere of molten rock that collapsed in on itself, leaving no trace of the secret base's existence other than an enormous radioactive crater.

chapter twelve

The Leviathan touched down on the remote desert airstrip, lowering its loading ramp to the tarmac and the Alphas, still in their ISIS armour, fanned out in all directions, forming a secure perimeter. Behind them the freed hostages from AWP climbed out, blinking in the sunlight. Diabolus Darkdoom followed the last of them.

'Ladies and gentlemen,' he said in a clear, loud voice, 'the authorities will be informed that we have dropped you here as soon as we are safely airborne and have cleared the area. I am sorry that you have been told so little about the events that led to your capture and subsequent escape but there are some matters that are better served by secrecy. Let me assure you that you are quite safe here and the threat that existed at the Advanced Weapons Project facility has been neutralised.'

'Who are you people?' a voice shouted from the crowd.

'That is really not important,' Darkdoom replied,

turning to climb up the ramp again as the Alphas filed back on board. He stopped halfway and turned towards the bewildered group of ex-hostages. 'Let's just say that if at any point in the future somebody asks a favour of you and they mention the words Zero Hour, you should remember that, whoever they are, you owe them your lives.'

With that Darkdoom continued walking and the ramp whirred shut behind him. With a roar from its massive engines the Leviathan climbed into the deep blue sky and vanished like smoke in the wind.

☺ ☺ ☺

The President stood at the podium and raised his hands to quieten the barrage of questions from the reporters gathered in front of him in the White House press briefing room.

'As I explained, it was a secret nuclear weapon storage facility and there was an unfortunate accident,' the President explained. 'Nobody was hurt and the land has never been accessible to civilians. While we are carrying out investigations at the highest level to determine the cause of the accident there is really no reason for anyone to be alarmed. The blast was safely contained underground and there is no danger whatsoever from radioactive fallout. I have time for one more question.

Yes, Larry.' He pointed at a veteran Washington reporter in the front row.

'Is there any risk of the same thing happening again at a similar facility?' the reporter asked.

'The simple answer is no,' the President said, 'but this seems like a good point to hand over to Doctor Franks from the Los Alamos National Laboratory.' He stepped aside as the slightly nervous-looking Dr Franks took to the stage, and made his way quickly to the Oval Office. His personal secretary looked up as he approached and smiled.

'Your eleven o'clock's here, Mr President,' he said. 'He's waiting inside as you requested.'

The President walked in and saw a tall, gaunt-looking man with half-moon glasses sitting reading a report on one of the sofas.

'Mr Flack,' the President said as the other man stood up and shook his outstretched hand. 'It was good of you to see me at such short notice.'

'Of course, Mr President. What can I do for you?' the other man replied in a Texan accent.

'I've spoken to several people at the CIA and NSA and they tell me you're the right person to speak to if I want to find out everything there is to know about someone.'

'That is Artemis section's speciality, Mr President, if I may say so,' Flack said with a smile.

'So I'm told,' the President replied. 'The person in

question is a young man called Otto Malpense.' He pushed a photo of Otto captured from their recent video call across the table towards Flack. It was clipped to an unusually thin file marked Top Secret. 'You will have full interagency access to everything that anyone has on him, which from what I have already gathered is disappointingly little. He spent some time as a guest of H.O.P.E., where I was informed he had died from complications due to a medical condition. At least that's what Sebastian Trent told me. Since I spoke to Malpense myself earlier today I now find that rather hard to believe. I'd ask Mr Trent to explain this discrepancy but, as I'm sure you're aware, he vanished some time ago. I'm told that the records that were retrieved from H.O.P.E. after its dissolution were patchy at best but I want you to find out what they weren't telling us. This young man saved my life some time ago and it's quite possible that he has also saved this entire country from disaster on two separate occasions.'

'Which makes it strange that we know so little about him,' Flack said with a frown.

'Exactly,' the President replied. 'I need to know if I should be shaking him by the hand or hunting him and his associates down.'

'I'll do what I can, Mr President,' Flack replied, standing up. 'Leave it to me.'

'Thank you, Mr Flack,' the President said as he shook

the man's hand again. 'Everything you find comes straight to me and no one is to know of my interest in him. Understood?'

'Understood,' Flack replied. 'Don't worry, Mr President, we'll find him.'

☻ ☻ ☻

The new commander of Furan's troops on H.I.V.E. watched as the Shroud decloaked and touched down in H.I.V.E.'s crater landing bay. The rear hatch opened and Raven walked down the loading ramp. The Commander approached her with a worried expression on his face. The four men he had with him all looked equally concerned. They had not heard anything from Furan for nearly forty-eight hours and rumours had started to circulate.

'Raven, what's been going on? We heard about the explosion at the AWP facility. Is Furan still alive?'

'No, Commander, he's dead,' Raven said, drawing the swords from her back and crossing them on either side of the startled man's neck. 'As you will be if you don't tell every one of your men on this island to lay down their weapons immediately.' The men behind the Commander raised their assault rifles, levelling them at Raven.

'Don't be a fool,' the Commander said with a smug grin. 'You have four guns pointing at you and even if by some miracle you were able to take me and my men down you're still only one woman. What chance do you stand alone?'

'Who said I was alone?' Raven replied with a nasty smile. All around Furan's men the air started to shimmer as twenty men and women in high-tech black body armour materialised out of thin air, their weapons raised. The four men behind the Commander dropped their rifles and slowly lifted their hands into the air. The Commander looked at the force surrounding him, his mouth agape. Raven leant closer and whispered in his ear.

'I believe the words you're looking for are unconditional surrender.'

☻ ☻ ☻

'I do wish you'd stop doing that,' Ms Leon said, from her position curled up on one of the beds.

Colonel Francisco was pacing back and forth across the cell in H.I.V.E.'s brig. Psychologists said that sleeping was the best way to deal with being locked up for extended periods of time but Ms Leon did it because she was a cat and that's what they did best. Ironically, of the two of them, the Colonel was the one behaving like a caged animal.

'We can't just sit here and do nothing,' Francisco said impatiently, punching the wall with his artificial metal fist. 'God only knows what's happening out there!'

'Colonel, I am perhaps the world's greatest expert on breaking into and out of places like this. Unfortunately for us I designed these cells. If there is such a thing as truly escape-proof then this is it. The only way we're getting out of here is if someone outside opens that door.'

The door slid open.

'How did you do that?' Francisco said in astonishment.

'I didn't,' Ms Leon said. 'At least I don't think I did.'

They heard footsteps coming down the corridor outside and the Colonel flattened himself against the wall next to the door, ready to strike.

Professor Pike appeared outside the doorway and surveyed the room with a sigh.

'He's waiting just there, isn't he?' he said, pointing to the left of the door and rolling his eyes at Ms Leon.

'Yes,' Ms Leon said, standing up on the bed and arching her back. 'Of course.'

'How did you know?' Francisco said, stepping away from the wall looking slightly deflated.

'Firstly, the prisoner manifest and secondly you're – well, you. How many times did you try the sick prisoner routine on the guards?'

'Three,' Francisco said, looking slightly embarrassed.

'Actually it was four, but then they started laughing at him and he stopped,' Ms Leon said, hopping down from the bed.

'Come on then,' the Professor said, beckoning them outside. 'We do have a school to get back on its feet, you know.'

Ms Leon and the Colonel walked outside where other slightly bemused-looking members of the teaching staff were stepping out into the corridor.

'Is someone going to tell us what the hell is going on?' Francisco said as he walked out of the cell.

'Oh, you know – psychopathic AIs, flesh-eating nanites, submarine warfare, nuclear explosions,' the Professor said. 'That kind of thing.'

'And here I was thinking it was going to be something exciting,' Ms Leon said, trotting away down the corridor with her tail in the air.

☢ ☢ ☢

Otto walked into H.I.V.E.mind's core and placed his hand on one of the darkened monoliths.

'Time to move out,' he said, with a slight smile.

I thought I might stay and start plotting a way to take over the world, H.I.V.E.mind replied inside his head.

'Very funny,' Otto said with a sigh. 'Come on, out.'

A moment later a stream of data coursed out of him and the monoliths all around flared back into life, blue lights dancing across their surfaces. He felt an unusual and unexpected sensation of loneliness as the transfer completed. H.I.V.E.mind's holographic face appeared, hovering over the pedestal in the centre of the room.

'It is good to be home,' H.I.V.E.mind said. 'Not that I wish to imply any dissatisfaction with my previous accommodations. They were . . . quite adequate.'

'Stop – you'll make me blush,' Otto said sarcastically.

'Though it is nice to not experience the more . . . organic sensations of human life any longer,' H.I.V.E.mind said, 'especially the bowel movements. I found those quite unnerving.'

'OK, too much information,' Otto said, holding up his hands and shaking his head. He couldn't help but notice that there seemed to be something more relaxed, more human about H.I.V.E.mind now. He wondered if rather more of the experience of being a passenger in his head had rubbed off on H.I.V.E.mind than he had expected. He turned to leave.

'Otto,' H.I.V.E.mind said.

'Yeah?' Otto said, turning back towards H.I.V.E.mind.

'This experience you have given me – this taste of what it is like to live, to be human. It was very special for me. Even with all the processing power at my disposal I don't think I will ever be able to really explain to you just how special. Thank you.'

'Hey, you saved me from being erased by a piece of corrupted code with a God complex,' Otto said with a smile. 'In my book that makes us even.'

'Maybe so,' H.I.V.E.mind replied, 'but if there is anything you ever need, you only have to ask.'

'Sure,' Otto said. He was halfway to the door when he stopped. 'Actually, I've just remembered something I need to do. I need you to give me an unsecured external line. I need to make a call.'

'That would be unwise,' H.I.V.E.mind said. 'The call may be externally monitored.'

'Actually, that's kind of the idea.'

☹ ☹ ☹

In a room on the other side of the world a technician manning one of the stations in the Echelon section of GCHQ blinked as he saw a message on his terminal flagging a call for immediate and urgent attention. He looked at the list of words from the call that Echelon had flagged and frowned. It read like a terrorist's shopping list. He patched into the call and listened.

'. . . dirty bomb, civilian casualties, fissile material, White House, Houses of Parliament, assassination . . . erm . . . I hope that's enough. Did I get your attention, Echelon? Let's find out,' the voice said. 'OK, this one's for Lucy. Execute sub-routine Big Brother Epsilon Two Four Zero Six Zero Five.'

Suddenly the terminals all around the room went dark.

All over the world Echelon's network began to experience catastrophic systems failures – servers overheating, data storage permanently erased, a completely irreparable permanent shut-down. Nobody would ever know what had caused it but, if Echelon had still been able to listen, it might have heard the final words of the mysterious voice on the line that had spoken the phrase that triggered the global meltdown.

'There always has to be a choice.'

☢ ☢ ☢

Nero sat down carefully at the head of the long conference table. It had been nearly a week since they had retaken control of H.I.V.E. and though Dr Scott, H.I.V.E.'s chief medical officer, had told him that he needed at least another two weeks of bed rest he was not about to let that stop him from carrying out his duties. The wound in his abdomen was still sore but he thought it served as an effective reminder of just how close they had all come to the edge. Zero Hour had worked, Overlord had been destroyed, and the threat that Animus posed to the world seemed finally to be at an end. There was still one final thing he needed to do and he was not looking forward to it in the slightest.

The members of the G.L.O.V.E. ruling council filed into the room and took their seats at the table. Diabolus had already briefed them all on the events that had taken place at the AWP facility but now Nero had something else he needed to discuss with them.

'Good morning, everyone,' he said. 'I am sorry that you have not yet been able to return to your bases but I wanted to speak to you all before you left, and as you know I have been recovering from an injury I recently sustained.'

'Get on with it, Nero,' Felicia Diaz said impatiently. 'You've kept us here for over a week for no good reason and I need to get back. My operations do not run themselves, you know.'

'Very well, I shall be brief,' Nero said. 'I am disbanding the ruling council.'

'You're doing what?' Diaz hissed.

'You heard me,' Nero said, looking at the stunned faces around the table.

'You can't do this,' Joseph Wright said. 'It's an outrage.'

'I think you'll find I can,' Nero said calmly. 'It is time for change. G.L.O.V.E. is a relic of a bygone era that desperately needs to evolve. The original intent of this organisation was to provide a control mechanism, a way to keep us all from fighting each other and to prevent any one of us from becoming too powerful. However, time and time again we have faced enemies from our own ranks, traitors who have used this organisation as a means to achieve their own nefarious ends. Number One, Cypher, Jason Drake. I intend to remedy that, to rebuild this organisation in a new form – a form more suited to the modern world and less susceptible to deception and corruption from within. If G.L.O.V.E. is to survive it must change and it must change quickly.'

'Do you really think we are going to just walk away?' another member of the council said. 'We are all here because we are powerful people. The resources and operations we control are what makes G.L.O.V.E. what it is, and if you do this we will fight you every inch of the way.'

'You are welcome to try,' Nero said, looking around the table. 'Many have. You may want to consider the fate that befell them before you seriously think about threatening me. I'm sure that I do not need to remind you that your identities are now known to the Americans, but what should concern you far more is that they are also known to the Disciples. Overlord may be dead but the organisation that supported him is still very much alive. If I were you, I would be less worried about waging war against me and more worried about finding an exceptionally good place to hide.'

'This is a coup, Nero,' Diaz said angrily.

'No,' Nero replied with ice in his voice, 'this is a cull. Quite literally for any of you that are foolish enough to oppose me.'

He stood up and looked around the table.

'This meeting is over. You will be transported back to your homes. I have no doubt that some of you will be thinking of fighting this or of coming after me. I will be waiting for you when you do.'

☹ ☹ ☹

Diabolus Darkdoom walked through the bustling corridors of H.I.V.E. Students in different coloured jumpsuits hurried to their lessons, a buzz of chatter and laughter filling the air. Nero had defeated many foes, steered many devious plans to completion, but H.I.V.E. was still his greatest achievement, Diabolus thought to himself. He walked down the corridor leading to Nero's office and pressed the button next to the door.

'Enter!' a voice called from inside.

'I've just come to say goodbye, Max,' Darkdoom said as he walked into the room. 'The Megalodon is ready for launch and I have things that I need to take care of.'

'You're sure I can't persuade you to stay?' Nero said, gesturing for his friend to take the seat on the other side of his desk. 'I'm always looking for new teachers and the students would benefit enormously from your experience.'

'Thank you, but no,' Darkdoom said with a grin. 'I'm not sure that I'm quite cut out for the academic life.'

'Well, if you should ever reconsider . . .' Nero said.

'I'll bear it in mind,' Darkdoom replied. 'Doctor Scott tells me that you're ignoring his medical advice as usual. How are you feeling?'

'Old,' Nero said with a wry smile, 'but I'm not quite ready for retirement yet. There's still too much to do.'

'How did the meeting with the ruling council go?' Darkdoom asked.

'About as well as you would expect,' Nero said with a sigh. 'Some of them are going to be trouble.'

'They were never all going to take it lying down,' Darkdoom replied with a small shrug. 'You're doing the right thing.'

'I hope you're right,' Nero said. 'I want to renew G.L.O.V.E., not destroy it.'

'The rose that is not pruned will not flower,' Darkdoom replied.

'A little poetic for my tastes, but I take your point,' Nero said with a wry smile. 'Diaz called it a coup. To be honest, there's a part of me that still wonders if she might be right.'

'Max, of all the senior members of G.L.O.V.E. that I have ever known, you are the only one who didn't actually want the job at the head of the table. The fact that you never wished to lead the council means that you're the only one of us that can be trusted to do this. We need a fresh start, new blood.'

'It will not be easy,' Nero said.

'But you'll do it any way,' Darkdoom replied, standing up.

'Thank you again for your help, my friend,' Nero said, shaking Darkdoom's hand. 'Do you have any plans for what you're going to do next?'

'Yes, I'm going to see if I can find out more about our friends the Disciples,' Darkdoom replied. 'I fear that they will want revenge for what happened to Overlord.'

'Let me know what you discover,' Nero said, 'and be careful.'

'You know where I am if you need me,' Darkdoom said.

Darkdoom walked out of Nero's office and the door closed behind him. Nero sat back in his chair and stared at the stone carving of the G.L.O.V.E. symbol on the opposite wall. He knew that he had taken a huge risk by disbanding the ruling council but Darkdoom was right – it was a risk he had to take. The first task would be to decide who were the most suitable candidates to replace the ruling council. He needed capable people who he knew he could trust – a rare commodity in the world he inhabited. He reached into his desk drawer and took out a piece of paper. Listed on it were the names of all of the former

Alphas who had survived the mission to destroy Overlord. He picked up the pen from his desk and, after staring at the list for a minute or two, he slowly began to underline names.

☢ ☢ ☢

Duncan Cavendish sat at his desk, reading the notes that had been prepared for him ahead of Prime Minister's Questions in the House of Commons. His phone rang and he answered it after a few seconds.

'Yes,' he said impatiently.

'I have a call on your private line, Prime Minister,' his secretary said. 'He wouldn't give his name, he just said he was an old friend.'

'Put it through,' Cavendish said, frowning. 'Hello?'

'Hello, Prime Minister. It's so good to speak to you again,' the voice on the other end said.

'Nero,' Cavendish whispered.

'You sound surprised to hear from me,' Nero said, 'I wonder why?'

'I suppose you've called to threaten me,' Cavendish said. 'Don't waste your breath. My security detail is second to none. You can't touch me.'

'Oh, I'm not going to hurt you physically,' Nero said. 'I'm going to make you do something far more painful. I'm going to make you resign.'

'And why on earth would I do that?' Cavendish asked.

'Because if you don't, I'm going to send several eminent journalists all the information that they'll need to reveal the cover-up regarding your . . . *education*.'

'You can't do that,' Cavendish replied, an edge of panic in his voice.

'I'm sure that the British public will be intrigued to discover that their Prime Minister cannot account for six years of his life,' Nero said. 'I can almost see the headlines now.'

'I'll expose you,' Cavendish spat. 'I'll tell the world about H.I.V.E. if you do this.'

'Oh really,' Nero replied. 'So presumably you'll tell them that actually you didn't go to a top private school and you did, in fact, attend a secret school of global villainy that's housed inside a volcano but you've got no idea where it actually is. That should go down well.'

Cavendish felt his heart sink. He had been a politician for long enough to know when his opponent was holding all the cards.

'You have twenty-four hours,' Nero said. 'I'd go with wanting to spend more time with your family, if I were you. I believe that's traditional.'

The line went dead. Cavendish looked around his office, surveying all that he had worked so hard to attain.

He pulled a sheet of headed paper from his desk drawer, picked up his pen and began to write.

☹ ☹ ☹

Otto sat alone on the sofa in the accommodation block, staring off into space. Hard as he tried he could not stop mentally replaying the events of their final confrontation with Overlord. He knew it would do no good to dwell on the what ifs and maybes of what happened, but that did not change the fact that he desperately wished that things could have turned out differently. Laura sat down on the seat next to him, looking at him with a slightly worried expression.

'I'd ask what you were thinking about but I'm fairly sure I already know,' Laura said softly. 'It wasn't your fault.'

'Wasn't it?' Otto said with a sigh.

'No, it wasn't,' Laura said. 'You didn't pull the trigger, you didn't choose to be there. It was Overlord – it was always him.'

'Maybe,' Otto said, looking at Laura, 'but if it hadn't been for me, Lucy wouldn't have been there – none of you would have been there. Who's it going to be next time? You? Wing? Shelby?'

'Otto,' Laura said, putting her hand on his, 'this isn't you. You know what I – what we all love about you? You're the strongest of all of us. You're the glue that holds us all together and none of us want to see you like this.

Overlord's gone, for good this time, and you have *your* life back. Now you just have to start living it again.'

'I suppose you're right,' Otto said, 'but I can't shake this feeling that Lucy traded her future for mine.'

'Maybe she did,' Laura said, 'and if that's true the worst, most selfish thing you could do is waste what she has given you. Everything you get to do from this point onwards is thanks to her. Don't think about what might have been, think about what's going to be. That's all she would have wanted.'

Otto stared at Laura for a moment and then nodded.

'You're right,' he said. 'Thanks.'

'I'm always right – I learnt that from you,' Laura said with a wink, glancing over his shoulder. 'Look out – here come the lovebirds.'

Wing and Shelby were walking across the atrium together. They had been inseparable since returning to H.I.V.E., despite the fact that they were quite possibly the least obviously compatible couple in human history.

'Hey, guys,' Shelby said as she sat down opposite Laura and Otto. 'Wanna hear something funny?'

'It is not funny,' Wing said as he sat down next to her, looking slightly embarrassed.

'Are you kidding? It's hilarious,' Shelby said with a grin. 'Guess who got taken down by Franz in the combat simulation this morning?'

'You're joking,' Otto said in disbelief, as Wing just closed his eyes and shook his head.

'There I was, backing him up, and our friend here's doing his usual sneaky stealth thing when suddenly, out of nowhere, BOOM! Head shot. No more Mr Ninja guy,' Shelby explained with delight.

'He eliminated you too,' Wing said, avoiding eye contact with Laura and Otto.

'Yeah, well, it's hard to hit anything when you're laughing so much that you can't breathe,' Shelby said, grinning from ear to ear.

'And so the ritual humiliation begins,' Wing said with a sigh, rolling his eyes.

'You know you love it,' Shelby said, leaning over and giving him a peck on the cheek.

'Franz ought to be more careful,' Laura said. 'If not he'll end up on H.I.V.E.mind's list and the next thing he knows he'll be standing in a hangar somewhere with no clue why he's there.'

'Thanks for reminding me,' Otto said. 'I've got enough circuitry in my head without Nero implanting a computerised dog whistle in my skull on graduation day.'

'I shouldn't worry, Otto,' Shelby said with a grin. 'H.I.V.E.mind only activated the Alphas who'd be any use in a fight. You're perfectly safe. On the other hand, if he ever needs his hard drive defragmented – well, then you're really in trouble.'

'I'd laugh,' Otto said, smiling back at Shelby, 'but recently I've been trying to do that only when someone says something that's actually funny.'

'Personally, I found the Zero Hour plan rather disturbing,' Wing said with a slight frown.

'Aye, it is a wee bit creepy,' Laura said.

'At least we'll never know if Nero's actually done it to us,' Otto replied.

'And that's less creepy because . . .' Shelby said.

'OK, more creepy, way more creepy,' Otto admitted. 'Probably best not to think about it at all.'

Nigel walked up to them with a slightly worried expression on his face.

'Erm . . . guys, Franz is just over at the snack machine,' he said nervously. 'I thought I should warn you that his win in the combat simulation has – well, gone to his head slightly.'

'What do you mean?' Laura asked.

'You'll see,' Nigel replied.

Franz was walking across the atrium tucking into a packet of crisps. There was a definite swagger in his step.

'Hey, Franz,' Shelby said as he approached.

'Franz? There is no Franz,' he said with a dismissive

shake of his head. 'From now on you shall be using the new nickname that I am choosing –' He pointed his fingers at Wing in the shape of a gun – 'Silent Death.'

They did stop laughing . . . eventually.

☻ ☻ ☻

- ALPHA
- HENCHMAN
- TECHNICAL
- POLITICAL / FINANCIAL

Which Stream are you?

Turn over to begin the test . . .

Answer the following questions to find out which stream you belong in.

1. If you were an animal, which of the following would you be?

A. Panther
B. Rhino
C. Spider
D. Snake

2. How might you make one of your enemies sorry?

A. With a hypnotic trigger phrase — so that every time someone says 'Pass the salt', they cluck like a chicken
B. Break every bone in their body — even the ones they didn't know existed
C. Rewire their alarm clock so that it always goes off at 4 a.m.
D. Discover their most embarrassing secret, and publicly expose it — after blackmailing them for a brief, yet lucrative, period

3. If you could choose any instrument to aid you in your villainous cause, what would it be?

A. Nothing — your cunning is all you will ever need
B. A bazooka
C. A computer
D. Money — after all, it is the root of all evil

4. You decide to take over your school. How would you achieve this?

A. Simply inform the headmaster that you are indisputably the most qualified person for the job — you had read every book in the library by the time you were four years old, and have a better understanding of the subjects than the teachers do

B. Threaten to show the headmaster what his/her spleen looks like if control of the school is not relinquished immediately

C. Hack into the computer system and rewrite all of the school's files to show that you are, in fact, already the headmaster

D. Infiltrate the local council and appoint yourself as Head of Education – why settle for just your school?

☻ ☻ ☻

If your answers are mostly As . . .
Alpha: The Alpha stream specialises in leadership and strategy training. You exhibit certain unique abilities which mark you out as one of the leaders of tomorrow.

If your answers are mostly Bs
Henchman: Your aggression knows no bounds, and you are happiest when you're doing damage to something, or more likely, someone. Your uncluttered, uncomplicated mind makes you the perfect trusted subordinate.

If your answers are mostly Cs
Technical: There's not a computer that you cannot hack, or a bomb you cannot defuse (or build, for that matter). You put the 'EEK!' in computer geek.

If your answers are mostly Ds
Political/Financial: You have a brilliant head for figures (as well as ways to fudge them), and also happen to be excessively charming and a natural born liar – the perfect combination for a successfully sinister career in politics or finance.

Your Stream has been selected. Now take the test to discover how villainous you are ...

I. You find a wallet on the floor filled with ten pound notes, do you:

A. Immediately take the wallet to the police and hand it over, still filled with the money

B. Help yourself to some of the money and then take it to the police

C. Take the money, throw the wallet in the bin and spend the cash on stolen blueprints for the nearest bank

2. You see a small child eating your favourite ice cream, do you:

A. Ask the child where he got the ice cream and set off to buy your own

B. Explain to the child that ice cream is bad for the teeth and make them feel guilty enough to hand it over

C. Organise two henchmen to suspend the small child upside down over a duck pond while you enjoy the icy goodness of their treat

3. Your parents agree to buy you any birthday present you want, do you ask for:

A. Nothing, you would rather your parents treated themselves

B. A new hi-fi and games system so you can lock yourself away in your bedroom

C. A small island in the middle of the Pacific, fully equipped with secret hideout, submarine base and lasers

4. When buying a new house what room is your priority?

A. An ecologically sound conservatory

B. A huge communications room so you can spy on your nearest and dearest

C. An underground lair complete with torture devices and a shark-filled pool

5. You have a red button in front of you that you have been told never to press, do you:

A. Quietly read a book, never giving the button a second thought

B. Stroke the button gently, always feeling tempted to give it a good push

C. Instantly press the button – you built this doomsday device so why shouldn't you use it!

6. An army of robots is about to take over your town, do you:

A. Find a way to foil the robots and destroy them for ever

B. Find a way to foil the robots but keep one just in case you might need it one day

C. Find a way to foil the robots because frankly your army of GIANT SPACE ROBOTS will do a better job

7. You need to hire a henchman, who do you hire:

A. Your mum

B. A couple of ex-cons you found through eBay

C. A suitably subservient weakling who will bow to your every needs . . . and a GIANT SPACE ROBOT

8. You have captured your heroic foe and can at last be rid of him, do you:

A. Have a change of heart, let him go and give yourself up to the authorities
B. Give the hero five minutes to escape from a shrinking room while making a quick getaway
C. Take a long time to explain your convoluted plans for ruling the world, realise the hero has escaped and send your GIANT SPACE ROBOT after him

☣ ☣ ☣

If your answers are mostly As . . .

To be fair you don't really have a villainous bone in your body. In fact, I suspect you would rather share a cup of tea with your foe, talk about old times and generally have a nice time. It's probably best to give up villainy now and try something more suited to your needs, say knitting or looking after bunnies.

If your answers are mostly Bs . . .

OK, so you have some villainous traits but you're not quite ready for big time yet. You're the kind of villainous soul that would pull only half the legs off a spider so they would have some chance of getting away. With a little training you could be a decent villain but you're no way ready for the big league.

If your answers are mostly Cs . . .

Hello future megalomaniac and ruler of the world. You are a vile villain through and through. You've probably got some plans to take over the world hidden in a draw somewhere and if you haven't already undergone training in Applied Villainy at H.I.V.E. then you should be applying for a place now. Oh, and I hear that GIANT SPACE ROBOTS are currently half-price at your local superstore.

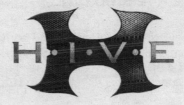

Details of H.I.V.E. students and instructors for your Villainous files

STUDENTS

Otto Malpense
Orphaned at birth, Otto is a criminal genius with a limitless mind, photographic memory and rare extra-sensory skills. Using a robotic mind control device he coerced the British Prime Minister into mooning at a press conference, and ended up in H.I.V.E.

Wing Fanchu
Otto's best friend, Wing was recruited into H.I.V.E. due to his exceptional skill in martial arts and numerous forms of selfdefence.

Laura Brand
Laura has an uncanny expertise with computers, so much so that she made it into H.I.V.E. by hacking into an US military airbase in order to use their military frequency to find out if one of her friends was gossiping about her behind her back.

Shelby Trinity
This all American girl is actually a world renowned jewel thief known as The Wraith. Shelby stole her way into H.I.V.E.

Nigel Darkdoom
It's tough following in your father's footsteps, particularly when you're small and bald and your dad is the infamous criminal mastermind Diabolus Darkdoom. Nigel has a lot to live up to. He does, however, have a talent for science and a strange affinity with plants.

Franz Argentblum
Franz is son and heir to the largest manufacturer of chocolate in Europe. Like Nigel, his father is also a criminal mastermind. Franz is most easily recognised by his impressive size and strong German accent.

Lucy Dexter
The granddaughter of the Contessa (deceased) and has inherited her special talent for mind control.